D0857874

Jules Verne: A Primary
and Secondary Bibliography

Masters of
Science Fiction and Fantasy

Editor
L. W. Currey

Advisory Acquisitions Editor
Marshall B. Tymn

Jules Verne: A Primary and Secondary Bibliography

Edward J. Gallagher
Judith A. Mistichelli
John A. Van Eerde

G.K. HALL & CO.

70 LINCOLN STREET, BOSTON, MASS.

Library of Congress Cataloging in Publication Data

Gallagher, Edward Joseph, 1940-
  Jules Verne : a primary and secondary bibliography.

  Bibliography
  Includes indexes.
  1. Verne, Jules, 1828-1905--Bibliography.
I. Mistichelli, Judith, joint author. II. Van Eerde,
John A., joint author.
  Z8934.G34   [PO2469.Z5]   016.843′8   80-20206
  ISBN 0-8161-8106-3

This publication is printed on permanent/durable acid-free paper
MANUFACTURED IN THE UNITED STATES OF AMERICA

Contents

Preface

Jules Verne: A Primary and Secondary Bibliography is a bibliography of fiction and nonfiction by Jules Verne and of English and French criticism about him. The bibliography is divided into five sections. Parts A, B, and C list published fiction and nonfiction by Verne (novels, short stories, plays, poems, songs, essays, geographical and historical works, letters, introductions, and speeches), while parts D and E provide annotated lists of English language and French language criticism. Parts A, B, and C are arranged chronologically by year as well as within years; parts D and E are arranged alphabetically within years. To facilitate use of the bibliography, there is an index to Verne's works and an author-title-subject index to the criticism.

Part A lists Verne's published novels and short stories and draws upon Piero Gondolo della Riva's Bibliographie analytique de toutes les oeuvres de Jules Verne (E743) for French publication information and chronology. For the novels we have cited the following editions: French serialization; the first French hardback edition; the first English edition and/or the "authorized" Sampson Low, Marston & Co. edition; the first American edition; all translations; editions with important introductions; and special editions such as those produced by the Limited Editions Club and Great Illustrated Classics. After 1960 the Fitzroy edition by I. O. Evans was done by both Arco Publications and Associated Booksellers. When editions by both appeared in the same year, we have listed the Arco one; when editions appear in different years, we chose to include the earlier one. For the short stories, we have cited the French magazine appearance, the first French hardcover collection, and all known appearances in English.

In part A the full publishing history of each work by Verne is provided under date of the first appearance of the work. If the serialization and the first book publication occurred in different years, or if Verne later published the work in another year under another title, then a brief reference under the year of the first book publication or the appearance of the variant title refers the reader back to the first appearance. If only publisher and date of

a work is provided for an entry within a publishing history in this
section, then the title is identical to that of the preceding entry.
"Un Express de l'avenir" (A75) is not listed by Gondolo della Riva;
"Paix sur la planète inconnue" (A106) is not listed by either Gondolo
della Riva or Jean-Michel Margot (E819). Gondolo della Riva lists
"Ascension du Météore" (C8) under fiction, instead of, as we have it,
under nonfiction.

In addition to Gondolo della Riva's work, the best primary bibli-
ography of Verne's fiction to date, we also consulted such reference
works as Catalogue général des livres imprimés de la Bibliothèque
Nationale, the National Union Catalog, the British Museum Catalog, the
American Catalogue, the Library of Congress Catalog of Printed Books,
Books in Print, and the Cumulative Book Index in preparing Part A.
Particularly helpful in listing appearances of the short stories were:
W. R. Cole, A Checklist of Science Fiction Anthologies; William
Contento, Index to Science Fiction Anthologies and Collections; Donald
B. Day, Index to the Science Fiction Magazines, 1926-1950; Norm
Metcalfe, Index of Science Fiction Magazines, 1951-1965; Frederick
Siemon, Science Fiction Story Index; Erwin S. Strauss, Index to the
S-F Magazines, 1951-1965; Donald H. Tuck, The Encyclopedia of Science
Fiction and Fantasy.

Part B lists Verne's published plays, poems, and songs, while Part
C lists his published essays, geographical and historical works,
letters, introductions, and speeches. Part B provides the date and
location of the first play production, and collaborators are cited
both for the plays and songs. In Part C we have provided brief annotations for those essays and letters we were able to see. Items
C1, C2, and C3 are cited as "attributed" to Verne by Margot (E819).
Information is provided on the few English translations of items in
both of these sections. In addition to the works cited above as useful in the compilation of Part A, we also found François Decré's
Catalogue du fond Jules Verne (E801) and Gondolo della Riva's article
on the songs (E438) quite helpful in preparing these sections. It is
important to note here that Gondolo della Riva is preparing another
bibliographical volume on Verne's nonfiction to accompany his volume
on the fiction. We personally verified most, but not all, of the
items in Parts A, B, and C.

Parts D and E contain critical studies on Verne, including books,
scholarly articles, Ph.D. dissertations, book reviews, and even some
newspaper articles and film reviews. The aim here has been to provide
as exhaustive a survey as possible of English and French language
criticism on Verne from his own times through 1978. (Though there
are thirteen 1979 items, no systematic investigation has been done
past 1978.) Almost all of the 455 English language items and the
881 French language items are annotated; those that could not be
located or obtained are preceded by an asterisk and we note our
source of information.

Preface

The indexing/abstracting services consulted for these sections
are: Applied Science and Technology Index, Arts and Humanities
Citation Index, Biography Index, Book Review Digest, Book Review
Index, Book Reviews in the Humanities, British Humanities Index, Dis-
sertation Abstracts International, Essay and General Literature Index,
Humanities Index, Magazine Index, Modern Language Association Bibliography, New York Times Index, Nineteenth Century Readers' Guide, Poole's
Index, Popular Periodical Index, Reader's Guide to Periodical Literature, Science Citation Index, Science Fiction Book Review Index, Social
Science Citation Index, and Social Sciences Index. The collections of
the following libraries in this country were examined: University of
Pennsylvania, Princeton University, Lehigh University, Temple University, and the Library of Congress. In addition, Professor Van Eerde
spent a month in France during the summer of 1978 and worked in the
Bibliothèque Nationale in Paris, the Municipal Library and the Centre
d'Etudes Verniennes in Nantes, and the Société Jules Verne in Paris
and Amiens.

Following the bibliography are two indexes, both compiled in the
letter-to-letter method of alphabetization. The "Index to Verne's
Works" contains an alphabetical list of all the English and French
titles, part titles, and variant titles in Parts A, B, and C, plus
references to the relevant criticism of each work in Parts D and E.
Also included in this index are many English variant titles that did
not meet the selection criteria for Part A. (Mathias Sandorf, for
example, was once reprinted, in an otherwise unimportant edition, as
Dr. Antekirtt, Hypnotist.) Titles we have supplied because a work has
not been translated into English are in brackets. Because of the
great number of English variant titles, all titles refer to the main
French title. For example, readers looking for primary and secondary
information on Twenty Thousand Leagues Under the Sea will be referred
to Vingt Mille Lieues sous les mers. The "Index to Critical Studies"
contains an alphabetical list of authors, titles, and subjects found
in Parts D and E.

We would like to thank the following people for their help: Dr.
Frank S. Hook, Chairman of the English Department, Dean John W. Hunt,
and Provost Albert Zettlemoyer of Lehigh University for granting a
leave to Professor Gallagher during which part of this work was completed; Dr. Steven Louis Goldman, Director of the Science, Technology
and Society program, Dean John W. Hunt, and Vice President Joseph
Libsch of Lehigh University for travel and typing funds; Dr. David
Lewis, Chairman of the Modern Foreign Languages Department, Lehigh
University, for continued encouragement; Luce Courville, Directrice
of the University Center for Vernian Research in Nantes, and Dr.
Olivier Dumas, President of the Jules Verne Society, for invaluable
assistance; the Compère family, Dr. Christian Robin and Ghislain de
Diesbach for giving aid, advice, and courtesies to Professor Van Eerde
while in France; Dorothy Pollet and Catherine Croy, Library of Congress,
for general assistance with the collections and with editions and rare
materials; William Fincke, Nancy Simmers, and Pat Ward of the Lehigh

University Linderman Library Interlibrary Loan Department; Sam
Moskowitz, Ron Miller, Gary Kraidman, and Dr. Francis W. Gravit for
special information; Diane Ferry, Nawal Jabbour, and Betty Jablonski
for typing; Bea Buck and the Lehigh University English Department
secretarial staff for photocopying services; student assistants Dorene
Hari and Karen Talhelm for searching library collections, copying
index entries, and retrieving material; L. W. Currey for help with
primary material; and to the staffs of the following libraries and
organizations: University of Pennsylvania, Temple University (particularly the Contemporary Culture Collection), Library of Congress,
Princeton University, Bibliothèque Nationale, Centre d'Etudes Verniennes in Nantes, Société Jules Verne in Paris and Amiens, the Municipal
Library in Nantes; University of California at Riverside; and Indiana
University.

Finally, we are very much aware that no bibliography, particularly
one on someone with the stature of Jules Verne, can be perfect or
complete. As Sam Moskowitz, the well-known science fiction critic,
wrote to us early on in the project: "I don't envy you the monumental
project of a reference guide to Verne. Any attempt at completeness
staggers the imagination." Thus, Professor Gallagher will keep a
file of additions that he will make available to anyone who inquires.
Send additions and inquiries to him at the Department of English,
Lehigh University, Bethlehem, PA 18015.

Introduction

Jules Verne (1828-1905) is a man who literally needs no introduction. The phrase "like something out of Jules Verne" became part of our cultural vocabulary during his own lifetime, and even today "Vernian" suggests the romantic possibilities of future progress in science and technology. Through sixty-three novels and twenty-one short stories (plus a healthy number of plays, songs, historical works, geographical works, and essays), this prolific Frenchman created the science fiction genre, made science fiction a social influence, "predicted virtually every major technical development of the twentieth century," and "explored every area of the globe not only for its exotic geography but also for its political dynamite."[1]

The familiar outline of Verne's life, moreover, has a similar mythic intensity. After an unsuccessful attempt to escape from his hometown of Nantes as a cabin boy on a ship headed for the West Indies, the eleven-year-old Verne reportedly vowed that thenceforth he would travel only in his imagination. And later, as a young man in Paris studying law, Verne, by his own admission, worked harder at his true love, the theater. Even after a marriage of convenience and a conventional job at the Stock Exchange, Verne worked four to five hours on his writing every day before going to work. At the relatively late age of thirty-five, Verne dramatically climaxed his sputtering writing career by pitching into the fire a manuscript on a balloon flight. His wife saved the manuscript, however, and shortly thereafter Verne met the publisher Hetzel, rewrote the essay as a scientific romance, and signed a lucrative long-term contract that enabled him to quit the Stock Exchange with a flourish. Verne's forty-year association with Hetzel, plus the many translations and dramatic adaptations of his works, brought him fame and riches—"a golden rain" that produced a series of yachts, election to the Town Council at Amiens for almost two decades, the Legion of Honor, and even a Papal blessing from Leo XIII. The surface glitter of his life was significantly marred, however, both by a crippling wound from a pistol fired by a deranged nephew and by an unsuccessful love affair.

Verne's scientific romances were published in a continuing series called the Voyages extraordinaires, and publisher Hetzel's announcement for the series clearly links Verne both to the excitement and enchantment in the nineteenth century popular mind for science and technology, and to the ideological movement called Positivism, which equated material and moral progress:

> The novels of M. Jules Verne have come just at the right time. When an eager public can be seen flocking to attend lectures given at a thousand different places in France, and when our newspapers carry reports of the proceedings of the Academy of Sciences alongside articles dealing with the arts and the theater, it is surely time for us to realize that the idea of art for art's sake no longer meets the needs of the time we live in, and that the day has come when science must take its rightful place in literature. To M. Jules goes the merit of being the first to tread this new ground. . . .
> M. Verne's subsequent books will be added to this series as they appear, a series which will be careful to keep always up to date. The books already printed, together with those still to appear, will cover between them the whole ground the author had in mind when he gave to his work the subtitle of Travels in Known and Unknown Worlds. His plan in fact is to sum up all the information gathered by modern science in the fields of geography, geology, physics and astronomy, and to rewrite. . .the history of the universe.[2]

In his early novels, those best known to us, Verne, stretching the Robinson Crusoe narrative, explores known and unknown worlds on, under, and around this planet. His goal is to fill and enclose the world, to make it entirely part of man's mental terrain. He wants to dominate the world, make it secure, and thus make it better. Such works as Five Weeks in a Balloon (1863), Journey to the Center of the Earth (1864), From the Earth to the Moon (1865), The Adventures of Captain Hatteras (1867), Twenty Thousand Leagues Under the Sea (1869), Around the Moon (1870), Around the World in Eighty Days (1873), The Mysterious Island (1874), and Hector Servadac (1877) are basically adventure narratives that instill a sense of wonder and glorify science and technology. "In these early novels, detailing tremendous voyages to the centre of the Earth, to the bottom of the sea, to the Moon, or off on a comet," says Brian Aldiss, "Verne celebrates man's progress," and "everything works like mad."[3] In these early novels, a basic optimism seems to blend easily with unbounded confidence in progress.

Somewhere around 1880, however, we find a different Verne, one with whom we are not so familiar. Growing awareness of political and social struggles in the world causes Verne to reinterpret the future of the machine age, and his novels move from "shining expositions of the benefits of the machine to darker visions of the dangers of uncontrolled technology."[4] "In Verne's first phase," says Darko Suvin, "the energetic hero always taps a saving electric or volcanic energy; in the second, Prometheus turns into Luciferian blasphemer and energy

into destruction."[5]   Verne, says Jean Chesneaux, "comes face to face
with social realities," and his "scientific forecasts now give place
to the problems of social organization, social conditions, and the
responsibility of scientists toward society."[6]   Since in each case he
reaches a pessimistic conclusion, the later novels are characterized
by "cities of perdition," such graphic symbols of social misorganiza-
tion as Stahlstadt in The Begum's Fortune (1879), Milliard City in
Floating Island (1895), and Blackland in The Barsac Mission (1919),
as well as the mad scientists Thomas Roch of For the Flag (1896) and
Robur of Master of the World (1904).   As Chesneaux points out, the
myth of Atlantis occurs with obsessive regularity in Verne's works,
and in the very late short story, "The Eternal Adam" (1910), Verne
climaxes this pessimistic view of human activity by envisioning a
future civilization looking back at us and through us to an endless
cycle of lost civilizations, an endless series of eternal returns.

    American readers are generally unaware of this second dimension
to Verne and of the range of French scholarship that lies behind it.
Even the recent history of science fiction found in Science Fiction:
History, Science, Vision (1977) by Robert Scholes and Eric S. Rabkin,
for instance, ends its brief discussion of Verne by stating that
surely he "is very much alive in all those literary descendants of
his who delight in the technical side of science fiction and tend to
ignore the problematics of human motivation and the cost of technological progress."[7]   While American readers may not need an introduction to Verne the man or Verne the champion of science and technology,
then, they certainly do need a reference guide such as this one to
engage in significant research and teaching activities on the whole
Verne.

    In a wider sense, however, it is amazing that "The Father of
Science Fiction" has received so little significant bibliographical
attention.   Until now, the only primary bibliography in English that
is more than just a mere list of titles is that prepared by Donald
Tuck (D445), and, except for the more or less brief lists at the end
of several books on Verne, the only bibliography of criticism in
English is Mark R. Hillegas's "Bibliography of Secondary Materials
on Jules Verne" in 1960 (D214).   The French have done better, but not
until quite recently.   Piero Gondolo della Riva's Bibliographie
analytique de toutes les oeuvres de Jules Verne (1977) will no doubt
be the definitive bibliography of primary material.   The first volume
(E743), which was enormously helpful to us, covers Verne's fiction,
while the second volume, shortly to be published, will cover his plays,
nonfiction, and unpublished material.   There have always been limited
French bibliographies of secondary material such as those by Georges
Hermans (E496), Daniel Compère (E690), and by François Raymond, Daniel
Compère, and Peter Hoy (E715, E797).   The major bibliography of criticism, however, is Jean-Michel Margot's recent Bibliographie documentaire
sur Jules Verne (1978), which, unfortunately, was received too late to
be of help in the preparation of our work.   Margot lists 1300 critical
studies, some of which are in English, and he includes an author index

and a key word index, but no title index nor, most importantly, any annotations (E819). The present work, then, is the first to combine a complete primary bibliography that includes significant information about American and English editions, with a comprehensive, annotated collection of both English and French language critical studies.

We hope that this combination of materials will have a catalytic effect on English language scholarship, for English language criticism presents more nodding respect for Verne than actual study of him. This criticism is more hagiographical than analytical, and, consequently, Verne seems more like a giant of the past rather than a man for our day and all time. As Peter Costello has said, Verne is thought of as "merely good fun," or as appealing "only to adolescents, or those with retarded sensibilities."[8] In English language criticism to date, for instance, the same basic four notions seem to be repeated over and over.

First, Verne is thought of as a writer of adventure novels for children. Unlike Gulliver's Travels, "Rip Van Winkle," or Frankenstein, Verne's works do not repay rereading as an adult. This "Homer of the fifteen-year-olds," whose death was lamented like the "passing of Santa Claus," whose fictional world is filled with numbers and machines but is free of women, presents the perfect gospel for the young--work and liberty--and, in particular, the perfect hero for young boys: "tough, sexless, casually brave, resourceful, and making something big."[9] Darko Suvin has stressed that Verne's work is popular with juvenile audiences just approaching science fiction because of the "transient pleasure of adventure," and because it introduces only one easily digestible new technological variable into the old empirical context:

> His "novel of science" can be compared to a pool after a stone has been thrown into it: there is a ripple of excitement on the surface, the waves go to the periphery and back to their point of origin, and everything settles down as it was, with the addition of one discrete fact--the stone at the bottom of the pool. Both the pleasure in adventure as such and the pedagogic addition of one new bit of information at a time are suitable for--and were aimed at--a childish or juvenile audience of pre-teens. As an introduction to SF in an industrial age, Verne's best stories work very well at that boy-scout level of a group of male friends in an exciting mapping venture.[10]

It sounds, then, as though we should put Verne away with our penknives and knapsacks.

Second, Verne is thought of as unreservedly pro-science and pro-technology. This attitude accounts for some of the most obvious stylistic characteristics in, for instance, a novel like Twenty Thousand Leagues Under the Sea. This "literary apostle of popular science" studs his narrative with lectures, mini-scientific essays

that pass important facts on to the reader. His complete, straightforward catalogues of flora, fauna, and mechanica imply a world that
is totally organized, totally comprehensible, supremely classifiable,
and thus logical--while also communicating what might be called the
"poetry of science." His incredible adventures escaping entombment
at the Pole, or fighting the voracious sharks, the macrocephalous
cachalots, and the giant squid involve the reader emotionally with
the facts of nature and science, and show that man virtually always
reigns supreme. Finally, on a metaphysical level, the voyage is a
giant mapping operation, a taking possession of the world from the
Atlantic to the Pacific, from the Pole at the top of the world to the
cellar of the sea 50,000 feet below the surface, from a firm past in
Atlantis to a possible future in nautical towns, from the beginning
of life in coral growth to the end of life in a cold volcano. Neither
the philosophy nor the style of this "Utopianist for Engineers," this
"Evangelist of Utopia," seems palatable to many modern readers. In
a world which has found more relevance in the dystopian vision, Verne
simply seems old-fashioned.

Third, much English language criticism of Verne contrasts him with
the great science fiction writer who preceded him, Edgar Allan Poe,
and the one who followed him, H. G. Wells. On the surface, Poe, "the
doomed poet of the Inward," is a more interesting person than Verne,
"the supreme celebrant of the Outward."[11] And the work of the seem-
ingly satisfied and successful Verne in exploring the physical world
and appropriating already existing space has seemed less of an imaginative achievement than the compulsive twitch of Poe--whose work abounds
in psychology, horror, and metaphysics--in searching for new space in
which to escape the world. Verne took from Poe the nuts-and-bolts,
realistic, plausible dimension that has earned him such titles as
"the poet of hardware," and "the Father of 'Hard' Science Fiction,"
but this quality too has seemed less appealing to modern readers than
Wells's "soft," social science fiction. While Verne was writing
"Facts That Every Boy Should Know" and mechanically writing thrillers
to the end of his life, Wells had a sense of social injustice and thus
performed a social mission.[12] Wells's work reached out to create and
explore profound societal ramifications, an important trait for a
culture suffering future shock and understandably uneasy about the
unforeseen consequences and side effects of scientific and technological advance.

Fourth, Verne, who said, "What one man can imagine, another man
will some day be able to achieve," has been thought of as a prophet
whose careful, scientific presentations have caused imagination to
become reality by inspiring others to great scientific achievements.
This "prophet of our mechanical age," this "novelist and seer," this
"marvelous anticipator," this "Mister Imagination," this "prophet of
the Space Age," this "inventor of the future," then, is credited with
the submarine, the automobile, the helicopter, the telephone, the
Apollo flights, and the like. There is no dearth of evidence for this
kind of judgment. Konstantin Tsiolkovsky, Robert Goddard, Guglielmo

Marconi, Yuri Gagarin, and Frank Borman have all explicitly testified
to Verne's influence. Admiral Byrd said that "Jules Verne leads me
on." Verne sent Santos-Dumont into the air (D42), Simon Lake into the
sea (D65), Norbert Casteret into the bowels of the earth (D97), and
René Dubos into the proper state of mind for the study of science
(D223). And Marshal Louis H. Lyautey proclaimed that "modern science
and technology is nothing else than the gradual realization in practice
of everything that Jules Verne had envisioned in his books." True
as these statements are, prophetic skill is not a good literary
criterion, and Verne's literary currency has faded as the science and
technology he foresaw has advanced.

Thus, English language criticism on Verne has not passed beyond a
sterile and superficial level. There are few provocative overviews,
few close analyses of individual works, and the pessimistic dimension
to his works is virtually unknown. Except for Kenneth Allot's
Jules Verne (D98), I.O. Evans's Jules Verne and His Work (D299),
Peter Costello's Jules Verne: Inventor of Science Fiction (D443),
Ray Bradbury's appreciative article (D148), Marc Angenot's thematic
article (D446), and Darko Suvin's analytical one (D396), the main
insights of English language criticism are relatively undeveloped
and scattered in diverse places. The books by George Waltz (D109),
Catherine Peare (D172), Franz Born (D262), Russell Freedman (D283),
and Beril Becker (D290) should be consulted, but they are of little
value to the serious literary student of Verne. One of the main
reasons for this critical deficiency, of course, as people from Edward
Roth (D8) to Walter James Miller (D420) have pointed out, is the
generally poor quality of Verne translations. Miller, in particular,
has vividly described the emasculation of Verne's work that has resulted from hasty, incomplete, and inaccurate translations in the
nineteenth century. It is precisely these abridged and truncated
versions, contends Miller, that still make Verne "fit merely for boys."
The Miller and the Mendor T. Brunetti translations of Twenty Thousand
Leagues Under the Sea are exemplary examples of new translations of
individual works, but even the most recent new series of Verne's works,
the Fitzroy edition done by I.O. Evans, while valuable for some of its
introductions, still contains abridged texts.

The critical situation is quite different in France, so much so,
in fact, that Miller calls it the phenomenon of "the Two Jules Vernes."
In France, especially since the late 1950s, Verne's work has yielded
itself to several strains of literary criticism, and, according to
Miller, has stood up well against each of them:

> Sociological critics see Verne as one of the first modern
> novelists to promote the anticolonialist and the dropout to
> the rank of Hero. Psychoanalytic critics explain Verne's
> perennial appeal by saying that everyone can identify with
> Verne's basic concerns: the restless search for the perfect
> father, the need of brothers to unite in adversity. Writers

closer to the Jungian school stress Verne's "instinctive"
ability to conjure up archetypes like the vulcanian powers,
the journey of initiation, the blessed city. They judge some
Verne characters, of course, not as personalities expected to
"develop" but as mythic types. Leading structuralists delight
in Verne's "oneiric [dream] mathematics." And Europe's new
psychohistorians seem concerned with how fiercely Verne guarded
the wells of his creative energy from everyone's scrutiny--
including his own.[13]

Marc Angenot supports Miller's view. In a recent two-part survey
of French criticism of Verne, Angenot shows a gradual evolution "winning for Verne a first-rank position in the history of French literature" (D377, D408.1). The first standard biography of Verne was a
pious family biography in 1928 by Marguerite Allotte de la Fuÿe (E47)
which kept silent about many aspects of Verne's life, and which
ratified the view of Verne as a "grand bourgeois" of the provinces"
who published relatively safe material in relatively safe family
periodicals. The 1973 biography by Jean Jules-Verne, however, is
based on family documents and correspondence, and objectively examines
"several previously undocumented aspects of his grandfather's career
and private life" (E575). Jules-Verne's work is a "well-informed
review of public and private events touching on the genesis and
material creation of Verne's work," and thus provides a solid basis
for understanding and judging that work.

Before World War II, continues Agenot, French critics, like those
in America, viewed Verne's work as simple and clear, and tended to
judge its merit in terms of its technical accuracy and prophecy.
During this time Verne was considered a "paraliterary" phenomenon, and
a group of "passionate amateurs" gathered around the Bulletin de la
Société Jules Verne between 1935 and 1938. After World War II, however, Verne's critics became more interested in his "imaginative
gifts, narrative technique, and worldview." Contrast between certain
characteristic situations in Verne's works and recurrent images in
surrealism, for instance, led to Bernard Frank's Jules Verne et ses
voyages (E143), René Escaich's Voyage au monde de Jules Verne (E174),
and Ghislain de Diesbach's Le Tour de Jules Verne en 80 livres (E377).

Critics like Michel Butor and Simone Vierne, according to Angenot,
helped open Verne's novels to the study of myth and psychoanalysis.
Butor's "Le Point suprême" essay (E148) is a landmark in viewing
Verne's novels as "a secret work developing along the ritual steps of
initiation: preliminary purification, perilous travel, ordeal, at-
taining the point suprême, death and transfiguration." Butor, according to Brian Aldiss, sees Verne as "a cryptologist of the universe,"
running variations on the themes of the four elements in which Verne's
characters forever oppose the unruliness of the world with logic.[14]
Simone Vierne's Jules Verne et le roman initiatique (E594) is an extensive study of the "initiatory novel," following in Butor's footsteps,
which is marred, says Angenot, only by Vierne's tendency to carry her
thesis too far.

In Lecture politique de Jules Verne (E486), Jean Chesneaux does not deny the importance of Verne's interests in science and technology, but he, too, sees a secret or second Verne, one whose interests in science and technology are subordinated to a "comprehensive political analysis of man's relation to nature." Chesneaux looks behind the surface bourgeois conservatism and sees that Verne holds startling political views. In particular, Chesneaux finds continual reference to the revolutionary tradition of 1848, utopian socialism, and libertarian individualism. Other major political and social issues evident in Verne's work are the future of the United States, the conflict between nationalism and internationalism, and the role of financial power in human affairs. Angenot further points out that Marie-Hélène Huet's L'Histoire des "Voyages extraordinaires" (E573) follows Chesneaux, but her orientation is aimed more toward specific historical and political contexts than ideological interpretation.

Among other French studies which have helped remove Verne's work from the category of children's literature, Angenot mentions the following: Marcel Moré's Le Très Curieux Jules Verne (E207) and Nouvelles Explorations de Jules Verne (E219), which demonstrate the influence of utopian socialists and English and German romantics on Verne, as well as such psychoanalytic themes as the search for the perfect father; Pierre Macherey's Marxist attempt to show a link between ideology and narrative (E497); Michel Serres's Jouvences sur Jules Verne (E645), which discovers a "mathematical oneiricism," that is, certain laws of mechanics and gravitation in the very form of Verne's works; two earlier essays by Serres (E273, E467); and Roland Barthes's "Par Où Commencer," with its structuralist approach to The Mysterious Island (E421). Any survey of recent French criticism must also call attention to the reappearance of the Bulletin de la Société Jules Verne in 1967, and the work by such people as Daniel Compère, Luce Courville, Olivier Dumas, Yves Olivier-Martin, Robert Pourvoyeur, François Raymond, Christian Robin, Robert Taussat, and Pierre Terrasse. The books by Pierre-André Touttain (E656) and Marc Soriano (E859) also deserve mention.

Fortunately, the English language scholar can sample the different French approaches to Verne. The books by Marguerite Allotte de la Fuÿe (D138), Jean Chesneaux (D366), and Jean Jules-Verne (D417) have been translated, and there are also some translations of Butor (D291, D307), Serres (D395, D408), and Barthes (D363). There is obviously a clear need, however, for a translated volume of selected French criticism to help spread the sociological, psychoanalytic, mythic, structuralist, and psychohistorical insights into Verne.

It is time that "Father Jules," the "prince of the marvelous," the "genial visionary" receives the bibliographical map he deserves, especially so that English language critics can be exposed to the diverse French scholarship. We hope that Jules Verne: A Primary and Secondary Bibliography will aid future teaching and writing on the Father of Science Fiction.

NOTES

1. Walter James Miller, The Annotated Jules Verne: Twenty Thousand Leagues Under the Sea (New York: Thomas Y. Crowell, 1976), p. xv.

2. As quoted in Jean Chesneaux, The Political and Social Ideas of Jules Verne (London: Thames and Hudson, 1972), p. 23.

3. Brian W. Aldiss, Billion Year Spree: The True History of Science Fiction (Garden City, NY: Doubleday & Company, 1973), p. 96.

4. Brian Ash, Faces of the Future (New York: Taplinger Publishing Co., 1975), p. 38.

5. Darko Suvin, "Communication in Quantified Space: The Utopian Liberalism of Jules Verne's Science Fiction," Clio, 4 (1974), 67.

6. Chesneaux, p. 181.

7. Robert Scholes and Eric S. Rabkin, Science Fiction: History, Science, Vision (New York: Oxford University Press, 1977), p. 10.

8. Peter Costello, Jules Verne: Inventor of Science Fiction (London: Hodder and Stoughton, 1978), pp. 16-17.

9. William Golding, "Astronaut by Gaslight," Spectator, 206 (9 June 1961), 841-842.

10. Suvin, p. 59.

11. Aldiss, p. 94.

12. Waldemar Kaempffert, "Evangelist of Utopia," Saturday Review of Literature, 29 (31 August 1946), 8-9.

13. Miller, p. viii. In addition to the Angenot articles cited in the next paragraph, see also François Raymond (E710) for a description of French criticism of Verne.

14. Aldiss, pp. 95-96.

Abbreviations

BSJV *Bulletin de la Société Jules Verne* (The three-volume reprint
edition done by the Société in 1969 was used for the period
1935-1938.) The new series of the *Bulletin* began in 1967 and
continues to the present.

RLM *La Revue des Lettres Modernes*

Part A: Fiction

A1 "Les Premiers Navires de la marine mexicaine," Musée des
     familles, 2nd series, 8 (July).

    In Michel Strogoff, Moscou-Irkoutsk (Part 2); suivi de Un
     Drame au Mexique, 1876 (A40). Rpt. as "Un Drame au
     Mexique."

    "The Mutineers: A Romance of Mexico" in Michael Strogoff,
     The Courier of the Czar. London: Sampson Low, Marston &
     Co., 1877, pp. 343-377 [Tr. W. H. G. Kingston].

    New York: Scribner, Armstrong & Co., 1877, pp. 343-377 [Tr.
     W. H. G. Kingston].

    New York: Fitch [New York News], 1880.

    "The Mutineers, or A Tragedy in Mexico," in Works of Jules
     Verne, ed. Charles F. Horne. Vol. 1. New York: Vincent
     Parke & Co., 1911.

    "A Drama in Mexico," in Dr. Ox, and Other Stories (A34).
     London: Arco Publications, 1964, pp. 29-51 [Tr. I. O.
     Evans].

A2 "Un Voyage en ballon (réponse à l'enigme de juillet)," Musée
     des familles, 2nd series, 8 (August).

    In Le Docteur Ox; Maître Zacharius; Un Hivernage dans les
     glaces; Un Drame dans les airs, 1874 (A34). Rpt. as "Un
     Drame dans les airs."

1

"Drama in the Air," in Dr. Ox's Experiment, and Other Stories.
Boston: J. R. Osgood & Co., 1874, pp. 143-170 [Tr. George
M. Towle]. See A34 for further translations of this volume.

Twenty Complete Novelettes by Popular Authors. New York,
1894, pp. 115-122.

Charles F. Horne, ed. Works of Jules Verne. Vol. 1. New
York: Vincent Parke & Co., 1911.

Amazing Stories, 1 (November 1926), 758-765.

1852

A3   "Martin Paz, Nouvelle historique," Musée des familles, 2nd
series, 9 (July) and 9 (August).

In Le Chancellor: Journal du passager J.-R. Kazallon; Martin
Paz, 1875 (A35, A36).

In The Survivors of the Chancellor. London: Sampson Low,
Marston & Co., 1875 [Tr. Ellen E. Frewer].

In The Wreck of the Chancellor. Boston: J. R. Osgood & Co.,
1875, pp. 219-285 [Tr. George M. Towle].

Martin Paz. London: Sampson Low, Marston & Co., 1876 [Tr.
Ellen E. Frewer].

New York: Fitch [New York News], 1879.

The Pearl of Lima. New York: George Munro, 1879.

Martin Paz. London: John Murray, 1910 [Ed. William M. Poole
and E. A. Lassimonne].

"The Pearl of Lima," in Works of Jules Verne, ed. Charles F.
Horne. Vol. 1. New York: Vincent Parke & Co., 1911.

1854

A4   "Maître Zacharius ou l'horloger qui avait perdu son âme,"
Musée des familles, 21 (April) and 21 (May).

In Le Docteur Ox; Maître Zacharius; Un Hivernage dans les
glaces; Un Drame dans les airs, 1874 (A34).

"Master Zacharius," in <u>Dr. Ox's Experiment, and Other Stories</u>.
    Boston: J. R. Osgood & Co., 1874, pp. 91-142 [Tr. George
    M. Towle]. <u>See</u> A34 for further translations of this volume.

"The Watch's Soul," in <u>Works of Jules Verne</u>, ed. Charles F.
    Horne. Vol. 1. New York: Vincent Parke & Co., 1911.

<u>Amazing Stories</u>, 8 (December 1933), 111-129.

1855

A5 "Un Hivernage dans les glaces," <u>Musée des familles</u>, 22 (March)
       and 22 (April).

    In <u>Le Docteur Ox; Maître Zacharius; Un Hivernage dans les
       glaces; Un Drame dans les airs</u>, 1874 (A34).

    "Winter in the Ice," in <u>Dr. Ox's Experiment, and Other Stories</u>.
       Boston: J. R. Osgood & Co., 1874, pp. 171-263 [Tr. George
       M. Towle]. <u>See</u> A34 for further translations of this volume.

    Charles F. Horne, ed. <u>Works of Jules Verne</u>. Vol. 1. New
       York: Vincent Parke & Co., 1911.

    "Winter Amid the Ice," <u>Amazing Stories Quarterly</u>, 7 (Winter
       1933), 74-90.

1863

A6 <u>Cinq Semaines en ballon: Voyages de découvertes en Afrique</u>.
       Paris: J. Hetzel.

    <u>Five Weeks in a Balloon</u>. New York: D. Appleton & Co., 1869
       [Tr. William Lackland].

    London: Chapman & Hall, 1870.

    London: Sampson Low, Marston & Co., 1874.

    London: Ward, Lock, & Tyler, 1875 [Tr. Frederick Amadeus
       Malleson].

    London: J. M. Dent & Sons, New York: E. P. Dutton & Co.,
       1926 [Tr. Arthur Chambers, introduction by K. B. Meiklem
       and A. Chancellor, with <u>Around the World in Eighty Days</u>].

    London: Bernard Hanison, Ltd., 1958 [Tr. I. O. Evans].

1864

A7 "Les Anglais au Pole Nord: Aventures du Capitaine Hatteras,"
Magasin d'éducation et de récréation, from 1 (20 March
1864) to 2 (20 February 1865). See entries A10, A14,
A15, A16.

Les Anglais au Pole Nord: Aventures du Capitaine Hatteras
(Part 1). Paris: J. Hetzel, 1866.

At the North Pole. Philadelphia: Porter & Coates, 1874
[Copyright by J. R. Osgood & Co.].

The English at the North Pole. London and New York: G.
Routledge & Sons, 1875. Also published as A Journey to
the North Pole [American Catalogue lists Routledge 1874
edition].

A8 "Le Comte de Chanteleine: Episode de la révolution" ["The
Count of Chantelaine: Episode of the Revolution"], Musée
des familles, 32 (October), 32 (November), and 32 (December).

Charles Noël-Martin, ed. Les Oeuvres de Jules Verne. Vol.
49. Lausanne: Editions Rencontre, 1971.

A9 Voyage au centre de la terre. Paris: J. Hetzel.

A Journey to the Centre of the Earth. London: Griffith and
Farran, 1872.

New York: Scribner, Armstrong & Co., [1874].

Boston: H. L. Shepard & Co., [1874].

A Journey to the Interior of the Earth. London: Ward, Lock,
& Tyler, [1876] [Tr. Frederick Amadeus Malleson].

Journey to the Center of the Earth. New York: Ace Books,
1956 [Tr. Willis T. Bradley].

New York: Dodd, Mead & Co., 1959 [Introduction by Arthur C.
Clarke].

London: Arco Publications, 1961 [Tr. I. O. Evans].

Harmondsworth, England: Penguin Books, 1965 [Tr. Robert
Baldick].

New York: Printed for Members of the Limited Editions Club,
   1966 [Introduction by Isaac Asimov].

1865

A10   "Le Désert de glace: Aventures du Capitaine Hatteras,"
   Magasin d'éducation et de récréation, from 2 (5 March) to
   4 (5 December).   See entries A7, A14, A15, A16.

   Le Désert de glace: Aventures du Capitaine Hatteras (Part
   2).   Paris: J. Hetzel, 1866.

   The Desert of Ice.   Philadelphia: Porter & Coates, 1874
   [Copyright by J. R. Osgood & Co.].

   The Field of Ice.   London and New York: G. Routledge and
   Sons, 1875.

A11   "De La Terre à la lune: Trajet direct en 97 heures,"
   Journal des débats politiques et littéraires, from 14
   September to 14 October.   See also entry A21 for sequel.

   De La Terre à la lune: Trajet direct en 97 heures.   Paris:
   J. Hetzel, 1865.

   From the Earth to the Moon: Passage Direct in 97 Hours and
   20 Minutes.   Newark, New Jersey: Newark Printing and
   Publishing Co., 1869   [Tr. J. K Hoyt].

   From the Earth to the Moon Direct in 97 Hours 20 Minutes;
   and A Trip Around It.   London: Sampson Low, Marston &
   Co., 1873   [Tr. Lewis Mercier and Eleanor E. King].

   The Baltimore Gun Club.   Philadelphia: King and Baird,
   [1874]   [Tr. Edward Roth].

   From the Earth to the Moon Direct in Ninety-Seven Hours and
   Twenty Minutes, and A Trip Around It.   New York: Scribner,
   Armstrong & Co., 1874   [Tr. Lewis Mercier and Eleanor E.
   King].

   The American Gun Club.   New York: Scribner, Armstrong & Co.,
   1874.

   From the Earth to the Moon Direct and Round the Moon.
   London: G. Routledge & Sons, 1877   [Tr. T. H. Linklater].

   From Earth to Moon.   London: J. M. Dent & Sons, 1930   [Tr.
   P. F. R. Bashford].

5

From the Earth to the Moon. Westport, Conn.: Associated
   Booksellers, 1959 [Tr. I. O. Evans].

From the Earth to the Moon and Round the Moon. New York:
   Dodd, Mead & Co., 1962 [Introduction by Arthur C. Clarke].

From the Earth to the Moon. New York: Bantam Books, 1967
   [Tr. Lowell Bair].

From the Earth to the Moon, and Around the Moon. New York:
   Printed for the Members of the Limited Editions Club,
   1970 [Introduction by Jean Jules-Verne]. 2 vols.

From the Earth to the Moon. London: J. M. Dent & Sons,
   New York: E. P. Dutton & Co., 1970 [Tr. Jacqueline and
   Robert Baldick, introduction by Roger Lancelyn Green].

The Annotated Jules Verne: From the Earth to the Moon. New
   York: T. Y. Crowell, 1978 [Introduction, translation,
   and annotation by Walter James Miller].

A12 "Les Forceurs de blocus," Musée des familles, 33 (October)
   and 33 (November).

In Une Ville flottante suivi Les Forceurs de blocus, 1871
   (A24, A25).

"The Blockade Runners," in A Floating City, and the Blockade
   Runners. London: Sampson Low, Marston & Co., 1874.

New York: Scribner, Armstrong & Co., 1875 [with A Floating
   City].

London and New York: G. Routledge & Sons, 1876 [Tr.
   Henry Frith, with A Floating City].

London: Sampson Low, Marston & Co., 1876.

The Fireside Library. Chicago, 1876.

New York: Fitch [New York News], 1879.

Charles F. Horne, ed. Works of Jules Verne. Vol. 7. New
   York: Vincent Parke & Co., 1911.

H. C. Harwood, ed. The Novels of Jules Verne. London:
   Gollancz, 1929.

The Omnibus Jules Verne. Philadelphia: J. B. Lippincott
   Co., 1931.

Twenty Thousand Leagues Under the Sea, and The Blockade
    Runners. Reading, Pennsylvania: Spencer Press, 1937.

Twenty Thousand Leagues Under the Sea, and the Blockade
    Runners. Chicago: Fountain Press, 1950.

The Green Ray, Including Also The Blockade Runners (A53).
    London: Arco Publications, 1965 [Tr. I. O. Evans].

A13 "Les Enfants du Capitaine Grant," Magasin d'éducation et de
    récréation, from 4 (20 December 1865) to 8 (5 December
    1867).

Les Enfants du Capitaine Grant: Amérique du Sud (Part 1).
    Paris: J. Hetzel, 1867.

Les Enfants du Capitaine Grant: Australie (Part 2). Paris:
    J. Hetzel, 1867.

Les Enfants du Capitaine Grant: Océan Pacifique (Part 3).
    Paris: J. Hetzel, 1868.

In Search of the Castaways. Philadelphia: J. B. Lippincott
    & Co., 1873.

A Voyage Round the World. London and New York: G. Routledge
    & Sons, 1876–1877: South America (Part 1), Australia
    (Part 2), New Zealand (Part 3). 3 vols.

Captain Grant's Children. London: Arco Publications, 1964
    [Tr. I. O. Evans]: The Mysterious Document (Part 1),
    On the Track (Part 2), Among the Cannibals (Part 3).
    2 vols.

1866

A14 Les Anglais au Pole Nord: Aventures du Capitaine Hatteras
    (Part 1). See entries A7, A10, A15, A16.

A15 Le Désert de glace: Aventures du Capitaine Hatteras (Part
    2). See entries A7, A10, A14, A16.

1867

A16 Voyages et aventures du Capitaine Hatteras. Paris: J. Hetzel:
    Les Anglais au Pole Nord (Part 1), Le Désert de glace
    (Part 2). See entries A7, A10, A14, A15.

The Voyages and Adventures of Captain Hatteras. Boston:
J. R. Osgood & Co., 1875: The English at the North Pole
(Part 1), The Desert of Ice (Part 2).

The Adventures of Captain Hatteras. London and New York:
G. Routledge & Sons, 1876 [American Catalogue lists
Routledge 1875 edition]: The English at the North Pole
(Part 1), The Field of Ice (Part 2).

London: Arco Publications, 1961 [Tr. I. O. Evans]: At the
North Pole (Part 1), The Wilderness of Ice (Part 2).
2 vols.

A17 Les Enfants du Capitaine Grant: Amérique du Sud (Part 1).
See entry A13.

A18 Les Enfants du Capitaine Grant: Australie (Part 2). See
entry A13.

1868

A19 Les Enfants du Capitaine Grant: Océan Pacifique (Part 3).
See entry A13.

1869

A20 "Vingt Mille Lieues sous les mers: Tour du monde sous-marin,"
Magasin d'éducation et de récréation, from 11 (20 March
1869) to 13 (20 June 1870).

Vingt Mille Lieues sous les mers (Part 1). Paris: J.
Hetzel, 1869.

Vingt Mille Lieues sous les mers (Part 2). Paris: J.
Hetzel, 1870.

Twenty Thousand Leagues Under the Seas. London: Sampson
Low, Marston & Co., 1873.

Twenty Thousand Leagues Under the Sea. Boston: George M.
Smith & Co., 1873 [Edition of J. R. Osgood & Co.].

London: G. Routledge & Sons, 1876 [Tr. Henry Frith].
2 vols.

New York: Grosset & Dunlap, 1917 [Introduction by Stanley H. Twist, illustrated with scenes from the photoplay produced by Universal Film Co.].

Chicago and New York: Rand, McNally & Co., 1922 [Tr. Philip Schuyler Allen].

New York: Dodd, Mead & Co., 1952 [Introduction by Allen Klots, Jr.].

London and Glasgow: Collins, 1954 [Introduction by Geoffrey Castle].

Los Angeles: Printed for Members of the Limited Editions Club at The Plantin Press, 1956 [Introduction by Fletcher Pratt].

New York: Fine Editions Press, 1957 [Introduction by Charles Angoff].

London: Arco Publications, 1960 [Tr. I. O. Evans].

New York: Bantam Books, 1964 [Tr. Anthony Bonner, introduction by Ray Bradbury].

New York: Platt and Munk Co., 1965 [Introduction by Isaac Asimov, with Around the Moon].

New York: Washington Square Press, 1965 [Tr. Walter James Miller, afterword by Damon Knight].

New York: Signet New American Library, 1969 [Tr. Mendor T. Brunetti].

London: Heron Books, 1969 [Introduction and appreciation by Douglas Hill].

New York: T. Y. Crowell, 1976 [Introduction, translation, annotation by Walter James Miller].

A21 "Autour De La Lune," Journal des débats politiques et littéraires, from 4 November to 8 December. See also entry A11 for editions with De La Terre à la lune

Autour De La Lune (sequel to De La Terre à la lune). Paris J. Hetzel, 1870.

Round the Moon. London: Sampson Low, Marston & Co., 1876 [Tr. Lewis Mercier and Eleanor E. King].

All Around the Moon. New York: The Catholic Publication
Society, 1876 [Tr. Edward Roth].

Round the Moon. Westport, CT: Associated Booksellers,
1959 [Tr. I. O. Evans].

Around the Moon. New York: Platt and Munk Co., 1965
[Introduction by Isaac Asimov, with Twenty Thousand
Leagues Under the Sea].

London: J. M. Dent & Sons, New York: E. P. Dutton & Co.,
1970 [Tr. Jacqueline and Robert Baldick, introduction
by Roger Lancelyn Green].

1870

A22   Autour De La Lune (sequel to De La Terre à la lune). See
entry A21.

A23   Vingt Mille Lieues sous les mers (Part 2). See entry A20.

A24   "Une Ville flottante," Journal des débats politiques et
littéraires, from 9 August to 6 September.

Une Ville flottante suivi des Forceurs de blocus. Paris:
J. Hetzel, 1871.

A Floating City, and The Blockade Runners. London: Sampson
Low, Marston & Co., 1874.

New York: Scribner, Armstrong & Co., 1874.

London and New York: G. Routledge & Sons, 1876 [Tr. Henry
Frith].

A Floating City. London: Bernard Hanison Ltd., 1958 [Tr.
I. O. Evans].

1871

A25   Une Ville flottante suivi des Forceurs de blocus. See
entries A12 and A24.

A26 "Aventures de trois Russes et de trois Anglais dans
L'Afrique australe," <u>Magasin d'éducation et de récréation</u>,
from 14 (20 November 1871), to 16 (5 September 1872).

<u>Aventures de trois Russes et de trois Anglais</u>. Paris: J.
Hetzel, 1872.

<u>Meridiana</u>. London: Sampson Low, Marston & Co., 1873.

New York: Scribner, Welford, & Armstrong, 1873.

<u>Adventures of Three Englishmen and Three Russians in Southern
Africa</u>. London and New York: G. Routledge & Sons, 187-
[Tr. Henry Frith].

<u>Adventures of Three Englishmen and Three Russians in South
Africa</u>. London: Sampson Low, Marston & Co., 1876 [Tr.
Ellen E. Frewer].

<u>Measuring a Meridian</u>. London: Arco Publications, 1964
[Tr. I. O. Evans].

<u>1872</u>

A27 "Une Fantaisie du Docteur Ox," <u>Musée des familles</u>, 39
(March), 39 (April), and 39 (May).

In <u>Le Docteur Ox; Maître Zacharius; Un Hivernage dans les
glaces; Un Drame dans les airs</u>, 1874 (A34).

"Dr. Ox's Experiment," in <u>Dr. Ox's Experiment, and Other
Stories</u>. Boston: J. R. Osgood & Co., 1874, pp. 1-89
[Tr. George M. Towle]. <u>See</u> A34 for further translations
of this volume.

Charles F. Horne, ed. <u>Works of Jules Verne</u>. Vol. 7. New
York: Vincent Parke & Co., 1911.

<u>Amazing Stories</u>, 1 (August 1926), 420-439, 477.

August Derleth, ed. <u>Beyond Time and Space</u>. New York:
Pellegrini and Cudahy, 1950, pp. 166-204.

<u>Dr. Ox's Experiment</u>. New York: Macmillan, 1963 [Introduc-
tion by Willy Ley, epilogue by Hubertus Strughold].

A28 <u>Aventures de trois Russes et de trois Anglais</u>. <u>See</u> entry
A26.

11

A29   "Le Pays des fourrures," Magasin d'éducation et de récréation,
      from 16 (20 September 1872) to 18 (15 December 1873).

      Le Pays des fourrures (2 Parts). Paris: J. Hetzel, 1873.

      The Fur Country. London: Sampson Low, Marston & Co.,
         1874 [Tr. N. D'Anvers, pseud. of Mrs. Arthur Bell].

      Boston: J. R. Osgood & Co., 1874 [Tr. N. D'Anvers, pseud.
         of Mrs. Arthur Bell].

      London and New York: G. Routledge & Sons, 1875 [Tr. Henry
         Frith]. 2 vols.

      London: Arco Publications, 1966 [Tr. I. O. Evans]: Sun
         in Eclipse (Part 1), Through the Behring Strait (Part 2).
         2 vols.

A30   "Le Tour du monde en quatre-vingts jours," Le Temps, from
      No. 4225 (6 November) to No. 4271 (22 December).

      Le Tour du monde en quatre-vingts jours. Paris: J. Hetzel,
         1873.

      The Tour of the World in Eighty Days. Boston: J. R. Osgood
         & Co., 1873 [Tr. George M. Towle, introduction by Adrien
         Marx].

      Around the World in Eighty Days. London: Sampson Low,
         Marston & Co., [1873] [Tr. George M. Towle, introduction
         by Adrien Marx].

      Round the World in Eighty Days. London and New York: G.
         Routledge & Sons, 1885 [Tr. Henry Frith].

      Around the World in Eighty Days. London: J. M. Dent &
         Sons, New York: E. P. Dutton & Co., 1926 [Tr. P. Desages,
         introduction by K. B. Meiklem and A. Chancellor, with
         Five Weeks in a Balloon].

      New York: Dodd, Mead & Co., 1956 [Introduction by Anthony
         Boucher].

      Los Angeles: Printed at the Plantin Press for the Members
         of the Limited Editions Club, 1962 [Introduction by Ray
         Bradbury].

      New York: Collier Books, 1962 [Tr. Lewis Mercier].

London: Paul Hamlyn, 1965 [Tr. K. E. Lichtenecker].

Round the World in Eighty Days. London and Glasgow: Blackie,
  1965 [Tr. Irene R. Gibbons].

Around the World in Eighty Days. London: Arco Publications,
  1967 [Tr. I. O. Evans].

London: J. M. Dent & Sons, New York: E. P. Dutton & Co.,
  1968 [Tr. Jacqueline and Robert Baldick].

1873

A31 Le Tour du monde en quatre-vingts jours. See entry A30.

A32 Le Pays des fourrures (2 Parts). See entry A29.

1874

A33 "L'Ile mystérieuse," Magasin d'éducation et de récréation,
  from 19 (1 January 1874) to 22 (15 December 1875).

L'Ile mystérieuse: Les Naufragés de l'air (Part 1). Paris:
  J. Hetzel, 1874.

L'Ile mystérieuse: L'Abandonné (Part 2). Paris: J. Hetzel,
  1875.

L'Ile mystérieuse: Le Secret de l'ile (Part 3). Paris:
  J. Hetzel, 1875.

Shipwrecked in the Air (Part 1). Boston: Henry L. Shepard,
  1874.

The Mysterious Island: Dropped From the Clouds (Part 1).
  London: Sampson Low, Marston & Co., 1875 [Tr. W. H. G.
  Kingston].

The Mysterious Island: Abandoned (Part 2). London: Sampson
  Low, Marston & Co., 1875 [Tr. W. H. G. Kingston].

The Mysterious Island: The Secret of the Island (Part 3).
  London: Sampson Low, Marston & Co., 1875 [Tr. W. H. G.
  Kingston].

The Mysterious Island: Dropped From the Clouds (Part 1).
New York: Scribner, Armstrong & Co., 1875 [Tr. W. H. G.
Kingston].

The Mysterious Island: Abandoned (Part 2). New York:
Scribner, Armstrong & Co., 1875 [Tr. W. H. G. Kingston].

The Mysterious Island: The Secret of the Island (Part 3).
New York: Scribner, Armstrong, & Co., 1876 [Tr. W. H. G.
Kingston].

The Mysterious Island. New York: Charles Scribner's Sons,
1918 [Illustrated by N. C. Wyeth].

New York: Dodd, Mead & Co., 1958 [Introduction by Anthony
Boucher].

Baltimore: Printed for the Members of the Limited Editions
Club at the Garamond Press, 1959 [Introduction by Ray
Bradbury].

London: Bernard Hanison Ltd. 1959 [Tr. I. O. Evans]:
Dropped From the Clouds (Part 1), Marooned (Part 2),
Secret of the Island (Part 3). 2 vols.

New York: Bantam Books, 1970 [Tr. Lowell Bair].

A34 Le Docteur Ox; Maître Zacharius; Un Hivernage dans les glaces;
Un Drame dans les airs. Paris: J. Hetzel [Contains also
Paul Verne's "Quarantième ascension française au mont
Blanc"]. See entries A2, A4, A5, A27.

Dr. Ox's Experiment, and Other Stories. London: Sampson
Low, Marston & Co., 1874.

Dr. Ox, and Other Stories. Boston: J. R. Osgood & Co.,
1874 [Tr. George M. Towle].

From the Clouds to the Mountains. Boston: William F. Gill
& Co., 1874 [Tr. A. L. Alger].

Dr. Ox, and Other Stories. London: Arco Publications,
1964 [Tr. I. O. Evans, contains "A Drama in Mexico"
instead of the Paul Verne story].

A35 "Le Chancellor," Le Temps, from No. 4993 (17 December 1874)
to No. 5030 (24 January 1875).

Le Chancellor: Journal du Passager J.-R. Kazallon; Martin
   Paz. Paris: J. Hetzel, 1875.

The Survivors of the Chancellor. London: Sampson Low,
   Marston & Co., 1875 [Tr. Ellen E. Frewer].

The Wreck of the Chancellor. Boston: J. R. Osgood & Co.,
   1875 [Tr. George M. Towle].

The Chancellor. London: Arco Publications, 1965 [Tr. I. O.
   Evans].

1875

A36   Le Chancellor: Journal du Passager J.-R. Kazallon; Martin
      Paz. See entries A3 and A35.

A37   L'Ile mystérieuse: L'Abandonné (Part 2). See entry A33.

A38   L'Ile mystérieuse: Le Secret de l'île (Part 3). See entry
      A33.

A39   "Une Ville idéale," Mémoires de l'Académie des sciences,
      des lettres et des arts d'Amiens, 3rd series, 2 (1875).
      Also known as "Amiens en l'an 2000."

      Académie d'Amiens: Une Ville idéal. Amiens: T. Jeunet,
         1875.

      "An Ideal City," in Yesterday and Tomorrow (A103). London:
         Arco Publications, 1965, pp. 47-65. [Tr. I. O. Evans].

1876

A40   "Michel Strogoff de Moscou à Irkoutsk," Magasin d'éducation
      et de récréation, from 23 (1 January) to 24 (15 December).

      Michel Strogoff, Moscou-Irkoutsk (2 Parts). Paris: J.
         Hetzel, 1876.

      Michel Strogoff, The Courier of the Czar. London: Sampson
         Low, Marston & Co., 1877 [Tr. W. H. G. Kingston].

New York: Scribner, Armstrong & Co., 1877 [Tr. W. H. G. Kingston].

New York: George Munro, 1877.

New York: F. Leslie, [1877] [Tr. E. G. Walraven].

New York: Charles Scribner's Sons, 1927 [Illustrated by N. C. Wyeth].

Westport, CT: Associated Booksellers, 1959 [Tr. I. O. Evans].

A41 "Un Drame au Mexique," in Michel Strogoff, Moscou-Irkoutsk (Part 2); suivi de Un Drame au Mexique. See "Les Premiers Navires de la marine mexicaine," 1851 (A1).

1877

A42 "Hector Servadac: Voyages et aventures à travers le monde solaire," Magasin d'éducation et de récréation, from 25 (1 January) to 26 (15 December).

Hector Servadac: Voyages et aventures à travers le monde solaire (2 Parts). Paris: J. Hetzel, 1877.

Hector Servadac: Travels and Adventures Through the Solar System. New York: George Munro, 1877.

Hector Servadac. London: Sampson Low, Marston & Co., 1878 [Tr. Ellen E. Frewer].

New York: Scribner, Armstrong & Co., 1878 [Tr. Ellen E. Frewer].

To the Sun? (Part 1) Philadelphia: Claxton, Remsen & Haffelfinger, 1878 [Tr. Edward Roth].

Off on a Comet! (Part 2) Philadelphia: Claxton, Remsen & Haffelfinger, 1878 [Tr. Edward Roth].

Hector Servadac. London: Arco Publications, 1965 [Tr. I. O. Evans]: Anomalous Phenomena (Part 1), Homeward Bound (Part 2). 2 vols.

A43   "Les Indes noires," <u>Le Temps</u>, from No. 5823 (28 March) to
      No. 5848 (22 April).

<u>Les Indes-noires</u>. Paris: J. Hetzel, 1877.

<u>The Child of the Cavern</u>. London: Sampson Low, Marston &
      Co., 1877 [Tr. W. H. G. Kingston].

<u>The Black Indies</u>. New York: George Munro, 1878?

<u>Underground City</u>. Philadelphia: Porter & Coates, 1883
      [Tr. W. H. G. Kingston].

<u>Black Diamonds</u>. London: Arco Publications, 1961 [Tr. I. O.
      Evans].

1878

A44   "Un Capitaine de quinze ans," <u>Magasin d'éducation et de
      récréation</u>, from 27 (1 January) to 28 (15 December).

<u>Un Capitaine de quinze ans</u> (2 Parts). Paris: J. Hetzel,
      1878.

<u>Dick Sand; or A Captain at Fifteen</u>. New York: George
      Munro, 1878.

<u>Dick Sands, The Boy Captain</u>. London: Sampson Low, Marston
      & Co., 1879 [Tr. Ellen E. Frewer].

New York: Scribner's Sons, 1879 [Tr. Ellen E. Frewer].

1879

A45   "Les 500 Millions de la Bégum," <u>Magasin d'éducation et de
      récréation</u>, from 29 (1 January) to 30 (15 September).

<u>Les Cinq Cents Millions de la Bégum suivi de Les Révoltés
      de la "Bounty."</u> Paris: J. Hetzel, 1879.

<u>The 500 Millions of the Begum</u>. New York: George Munro,
      1879.

<u>The Begum's Fortune</u>. Philadelphia: J. B. Lippincott & Co.,
      [1879] [Tr. W. H. G. Kingston].

London: Sampson, Low, Marston & Co., 1880 [Tr. W. H. G. Kingston].

London: Bernard Hanison, Ltd., 1958 [Tr. I. O. Evans].

A46   "Les Tribulations d'un Chinois en Chine," Le Temps, from No. 6646 (2 July) to No. 6682 (7 August).

Les Tribulations d'un Chinois en Chine. Paris: J. Hetzel, 1879.

The Tribulations of a Chinaman in China. New York: George Munro, 1879.

London: Sampson Low, Marston & Co., 1880. [Tr. Ellen E. Frewer].

Boston: Lee and Shepard, 1880 [Tr. Virginia Champlin, pseud. of Grace Virginia Lord].

The Tribulations of a Chinese Gentleman. London: Arco Publications, 1963 [Tr. I. O. Evans].

A47   "Les Révoltés de la 'Bounty'," in Les Cinq Cents Millions de la Begum suivi de Les Révoltés de la Bounty. Paris: J. Hetzel, 1879 (A45).

"The Mutineers of the Bounty," in The Begum's Fortune. London: Sampson Low, Marston & Co., 1880 [Tr. W. H. G. Kingston].

A48   "La Maison à vapeur: Voyage à travers l'Inde septentrionale," Magasin d'education et de recreation, from 30 (1 December 1879) to 32 (15 December 1880).

La Maison à vapeur: Voyage à travers l'Inde septentrionale (2 Parts). Paris: J. Hetzel, 1880. 2 vols.

The Steam House: or a Trip Across Northern India. New York: George Munro, 1880-81. 2 vols.

The Steam House. London: Sampson Low, Marston & Co., 1881 [Tr. Agnes D. Kingston]. 2 vols.

New York: Scribner, 1881 [Tr. Agnes D. Kingston]: The Demon of Cawnpore (Part 1), Tigers and Traitors (Part 2). 2 vols.

Westport, CT: Associated Booksellers, 1959 [Tr. I. O.
Evans]: The Demon of Cawnpore (Part 1), Tigers and
Traitors (Part 2). 2 vols.

<u>1880</u>

A49   La Maison à vapeur: Voyage à travers 1'Inde septentrionale
(2 Parts). See entry A48.

<u>1881</u>

A50   "La Jangada: Huit Cents Lieues sur 1'Amazone," Magasin
d'éducation et de récréation, from 33 (1 January) to 34
(1 December).

      La Jangada: Huit Cents Lieues sur 1'Amazone (2 Parts).
Paris: J. Hetzel, 1881.

      The Giant Raft. London: Sampson Low, Marston & Co., 1881
[Tr. W. J. Gordon]: Eight Hundred Leagues on the Amazon
(Part 1), The Cryptogram (Part 2). 2 vols.

      The Jangada. New York: George Munro, 1881-82 [Tr. James
Cotterell]. 2 vols.

      The Giant Raft. New York: Scribner, 1881-82: Eight Hundred
Leagues on the Amazon (Part 1), The Cryptogram (Part 2).
2 vols.

      London: Arco Publications, 1967 [Tr. I. O. Evans]: Down
the Amazon (Part 1), The Cryptogram (Part 2). 2 vols.

A51   "Dix Heures en chasse, simple boutade," Mémoires de 1'Académie
des sciences, des lettres et des arts d'Amiens, 3rd series,
8 (1881).

      In Le Rayon-vert suivi de Dix Heures en chasse, 1882 (A53).

      "Ten Hours Hunting," in Yesterday and Tomorrow (A103).
London: Arco Publications, 1965, pp. 67-86 [Tr. I. O.
Evans].

1882

A52 "L'École des Robinsons," Magasin d'éducation et de récréation,
from 35 (1 January) to 36 (1 December).

L'École des Robinsons. Paris: J. Hetzel, 1882.

Robinsons' School. New York: George Munro, 1883.

Godfrey Morgan: A California Mystery. London: Sampson
Low, Marston & Co., 1883 [Tr. W. J. Gordon].

New York: Charles Scribner's Sons, 1883 [Tr. W. J. Gordon].

The School for Crusoes. London: Arco Publications, 1966
[Tr. I. O. Evans].

A53 "Le Rayon vert," Le Temps, from No. 7003 (17 May) to No.
7730 (23 June).

Le Rayon-vert suivi de Dix Heures en chasse. Paris: J.
Hetzel, 1882.

The Green Ray. London: Sampson Low, Marston & Co., 1883
[Tr. Mary de Hauteville].

New York: George Munro, 1883 [Tr. James Cotterell].

London: Arco Publications, 1965 [Tr. I. O. Evans].

1883

A54 "Kéraban-le-Têtu," Magasin d'éducation et de récréation, from
37 (1 January) to 38 (15 October).

Kéraban-le-Têtu (2 Parts). Paris: J. Hetzel, 1883.

The Headstrong Turk. New York: George Munro, 1883-84
[Tr. J. Cotterell]. 2 vols.

Kéraban the Inflexible. London: Sampson Low, Marston & Co.,
1884-85: The Captain of the Guidara (Part 1), Scarpante
the Spy (Part 2). 2 vols.

1884

A55 "L'Étoile du sud: Le Pays des diamants," Magasin d'éducation et de récréation, from 39 (1 January) to 40 (15 December).

L'Étoile du sud: Le Pays des diamants. Paris: J. Hetzel, 1884.

The Vanished Diamond: A Tale of South Africa. London: Sampson Low, Marston & Co., 1885.

The Southern Star. New York: George Munro, [1885].

The Southern Star Mystery. London: Arco Publications, 1966 [Tr. I. O. Evans].

A56 "L'Archipel en feu," Le Temps, from No. 8463 (29 June) to No. 8497 (3 August).

L'Archipel en feu. Paris: J. Hetzel, 1884.

The Archipelago on Fire. New York: George Munro, 1885.

London: Sampson Low, Marston & Co., 1886.

A57 "Fritt-Flacc," Le Figaro illustré, December.

In Un Billet de loterie (Le Numéro 9672) suivi de Fritt-Flacc, 1886 (A60).

"Dr. Trifulgas: A Fantastic Tale," Strand Magazine, 4 (July-December 1892), 53-57.

Fritt-Flacc. New York: Futuria House, 1947.

"The Ordeal of Dr. Trifulgas," Saturn, 1 (July 1957), 25-31 [Tr. Willis T. Bradley].

"Fritt-Flacc," Magazine of Fantasy and Science Fiction, 17 (November 1959), 40-45 [Tr. I. O. Evans].

In Yesterday and Tomorrow (A103). London: Arco Publications, 1965, pp. 87-96 [Tr. I. O. Evans].

"Dr. Trifulgas," in Before Armageddon, ed. Michael Moorcock. London: W. H. Allen Co., 1975.

1885

A58 "L'Épave du Cynthia," Magasin d'éducation et de récréation,
      from 41 (1 January) to 42 (15 November). With André
      Laurie.

      L'Épave du Cynthia. Paris: J. Hetzel, 1885.

      The Waif of the "Cynthia." New York: George Munro, [1886].

      Salvage From the Cynthia. London: Arco Publications, 1964
      [Tr. I. O. Evans].

A59 "Mathias Sandorf," Le Temps, from No. 8813 (16 June) to No.
      8908 (20 September).

      Mathias Sandorf (3 Parts). Paris: J. Hetzel, 1885.

      New York: George Munro, [1885]. 2 vols.

      London: Sampson Low, Marston & Co., 1886.

1886

A60 "Un Billet de loterie: Le Numéro 9672," Magasin d'éducation
      et de récréation, from 43 (1 January) to 44 (1 November).

      Un Billet de loterie (Le Numéro 9672) suivi de Fritt-Flacc.
      Paris: J. Hetzel, 1886.

      Ticket No. "9672." New York: George Munro, 1886. [Tr.
      Laura E. Kendall].

      The Lottery Ticket: A Tale of Tellemarken. London: Sampson
      Low, Marston & Co., 1887.

A61 "Robur le conquérant," Journal des débats politiques et
      littéraires, from 29 June to 18 August.

      Robur-le-conquérant. Paris: J. Hetzel, 1886.

      The Clipper of the Clouds. London: Sampson Low, Marston &
      Co., 1887.

      Robur the Conqueror. New York: George Munro, [1887].

The Clipper of the Clouds. London: Arco Publications, 1962 [Tr. I. O. Evans].

1887

A62 "Nord contre sud," Magasin d'éducation et de récréation, from 45 (1 January) to 46 (1 December).

Nord contre sud (2 Parts). Paris: J. Hetzel, 1887.

Texar's Vengeance; or, North Versus South. New York: George Munro, [1887] [Tr. Laura E. Kendall].

North Against South: A Tale of the American Civil War. London: Sampson Low, Marston & Co., 1888.

London: Arco Publications, 1963 [Tr. I. O. Evans]: Burbank the Northerner (Part 1), Texar the Southerner (Part 2). 2 vols.

A63 "Le Chemin de France," Le Temps, from No. 9613 (31 August) to No. 9652 (30 September).

Le Chemin de France suivi de Gil Braltar. Paris: J. Hetzel, 1887.

The Flight to France; or, The Memoirs of a Dragoon. London: Sampson Low, Marston & Co., 1888.

New York: F. F. Lovell, [1888].

New York: George Munro, [1889].

London: Arco Publications, 1966 [Tr. I. O. Evans].

A64 "Gil Braltar," in Le Chemin de France suivi de Gil Braltar. Paris: J. Hetzel, 1887 (A63).

Magazine of Fantasy and Science Fiction, 15 (July 1958), 48-53 [Tr. I. O. Evans].

Anthony Boucher, ed. The Best from Fantasy and Science Fiction, 8th series. Garden City, NY: Doubleday & Co., 1959, pp. 116-123 [Tr. I. O. Evans].

In Yesterday and Tomorrow (A103). London: Arco Publications, 1965, pp. 97-105 [Tr. I. O. Evans].

1888

A65 "Deux Ans de vacances," Magasin d'éducation et de récréation, from 47 (1 January) to 48 (15 December).

Deux Ans de vacances (2 Parts). Paris: J. Hetzel, 1888.

Adrift in the Pacific. London: Sampson Low, Marston & Co., 1889.

A Two Years' Vacation. New York: George Munro, [1889].

Two Years' Holiday. London: Arco Publications, 1964 [Tr. I. O. Evans]: Adrift in the Pacific (Part 1), Second Year Ashore (Part 2). 2 vols.

A Long Vacation. New York: Holt, Rinehart and Winston; London: Oxford University Press, 1967 [Tr. Olga Marx].

1889

A66 "Famille-sans-nom," Magasin d'éducation et de récréation, from 49 (1 January) to 50 (1 December).

Famille-sans-nom (2 Parts). Paris: J. Hetzel, 1889.

A Family Without a Name. New York: J. W. Lovell, [1889].

New York: F. F. Lovell, [1889].

New York: George Munro, [1889].

London: Sampson Low, Marston & Co., 1891.

London: Arco Publications, 1963 [Tr. I. O. Evans]: Leader of the Resistance (Part 1), Into the Abyss (Part 2). 2 vols.

A67 "In the Year 2889," The Forum, 6 (February), 662-677. Probably with Michel Verne.

In Hier et demain, 1910 (A103). Rpt. as "Au XXIXe Siècle: La Journée d'un journaliste américain en 2889."

"In the Year 2889," in Forum Papers, second series, ed. B. A. Heydrick and C. R. Gaston. New York: Duffield & Co., 1924-25, pp. 33-53.

Arkham Sampler, Summer 1949.

Groff Conklin, ed. Big Book of Science Fiction. New York:
Crown Publishers, 1950.

"In the Twenty-ninth Century: The Day of an American Journalist in 2889," in Yesterday and Tomorrow (A103). London:
Arco Publications, 1965, pp. 107-124 [Tr. I. O. Evans].

A68 Sans Dessus Dessous. Paris: J. Hetzel.

Topsy-Turvy. New York: J. S. Ogilvie & Co., [1890].

New York: International Book Co., 1890.

The Purchase of the North Pole. London: Sampson Low,
Marston & Co., 1891.

London: Arco Publications, 1966 [Tr. I. O. Evans].

1890

A69 "César Cascabel," Magasin d'éducation et de récréation, from
51 (1 January) to 52 (15 December).

César Cascabel (2 Parts). Paris: J. Hetzel, 1890.

New York: Cassell Publishing Co., [1890] [Tr. A. Estoclet].

London: Sampson Low, Marston & Co., 1891.

London: Arco Publications, 1966 [Tr. I. O. Evans]: The
Travelling Circus (Part 1), The Show on Ice (Part 2).
2 vols.

1891

A70 "Mistress Branican," Magasin d'éducation et de récréation,
from 53 (1 January) to 54 (15 December).

Mistress Branican (2 Parts). Paris: J. Hetzel, 1891.

New York: Cassell Publishing Co., [1891] [Tr. A. Estoclet].

London: Sampson Low, Marston & Co., 1892.

A71 "Aventures de la Famille Raton, conte de fées," <u>Figaro illustré</u>, 2nd series, No. 10 (January).

In <u>Hier et demain</u>, 1910 (A103). Rpt. as "La Famille Raton."

1892

A72 "Le Château des Carpathes," <u>Magasin d'éducation et de récréation</u>, from 55 (1 January) to 56 (15 December).

<u>Le Château des Carpathes</u>. Paris: J. Hetzel, 1892.

<u>The Castle of the Carpathians</u>. London: Sampson Low, Marston & Co., 1893.

New York: Merriam, 1894.

<u>Carpathian Castle</u>. London: Arco Publications, 1963 [Tr. I. O. Evans].

A73 "Claudius Bombarnac," <u>Le Soleil</u>, from No. 284 (10 October) to No. 342 (7 December).

<u>Claudius Bombarnac</u>. Paris: J. Hetzel, 1892.

London: Sampson Low, Marston & Co., 1894.

<u>The Special Correspondent</u>. New York: Lovell, Coryell & Co., 1894.

New York: George Munro, [1894].

<u>Claudius Bombarnac</u>. New York: Hurst & Co., 1894(?).

Chicago: E. A. Weeks & Co., [1894].

1893

A74 "P'tit-Bonhomme," <u>Magasin d'éducation et de récréation</u>, from 57 (1 January) to 58 (15 December).

<u>P'tit-Bonhomme</u> (2 Parts). Paris: J. Hetzel, 1893.

<u>Foundling Mick</u>. London: Sampson Low, Marston & Co., 1895.

A75 "Un Express de l'avenir," <u>Les Annales politiques et lit-</u>
     <u>téraires</u>, 27 August. See <u>RLM</u>, No. 456-461 (1976), p.
     131 for discussion of authenticity and an earlier edition.

     "An Express of the Future," <u>Strand Magazine</u>, 10 (July-
     December 1895), 638-640.

     Sam Moskowitz, ed. <u>Science Fiction by Gaslight</u>. Cleveland,
     Ohio: World Publishing Co., 1968, pp. 115-119. Rpt.
     Westport, CT: Hyperion Press, 1974.

A76 "M. Ré-Dièze et Mlle Mi-Bémol, "<u>Figaro illustré</u>, 2nd series,
     No. 45 (Christmas).

     In <u>Hier et demain</u>, 1910 (A103).

     "Mr. Ray Sharp and Miss Me Flat," in <u>Yesterday and Tomorrow</u>
     (A103). London: Arco Publications, 1965, pp. 125-153
     [Tr. I. O. Evans].

1894

A77 "Mirifiques Aventures de Maître Antifer," <u>Magasin d'éducation</u>
     <u>et de récréation</u>, from 59 (1 January) to 60 (15 December).

     <u>Mirifiques Aventures de Maître Antifer</u> (2 Parts). Paris:
     J. Hetzel, 1894.

     <u>Captain Antifer</u>. London: Sampson Low, Marston & Co., 1895.

     New York: R. F. Fenno & Co., [1895].

1895

A78 "L'Ile à hélice," <u>Magasin d'éducation et de récréation</u>, from
     2nd series, 1 (1 January) to 2 (15 December).

     <u>L'Ile à hélice</u> (2 Parts). Paris: J. Hetzel, 1895.

     <u>Floating Island</u>. London: Sampson Low, Marston & Co.,
     [1896] [Tr. W. J. Gordon].

     New York: W. L. Allison Co., 1900(?).

     <u>Propeller Island</u>. London: Arco Publications, 1961 [Tr.
     I. O. Evans].

1896

A79 "Face au drapeau," Magasin d'éducation et de récréation,
from 2nd series, 3 (1 January) to 3 (15 June).

Face au drapeau. Paris: J. Hetzel, 1896.

For the Flag. London: Sampson Low, Marston & Co., [1897]
[Tr. Mrs. Cashel Hoey].

Facing the Flag. New York: F. T. Neely, [1897].

For the Flag. London: Arco Publications, 1961 [Tr. I. O.
Evans].

A80 "Clovis Dardentor," Magasin d'éducation et de récréation,
from 2nd series, 4 (1 July) to 4 (15 December).

Clovis Dardentor. Paris: J. Hetzel, 1896.

London: Sampson Low, Marston & Co., 1897.

1897

A81 "Le Sphinx des glaces," Magasin d'éducation et de récréation,
from 2nd series, 5 (1 January) to 6 (15 December).

Le Sphinx des glaces (2 Parts). Paris: J. Hetzel 1897.

An Antarctic Mystery. London: Sampson Low, & Co., 1898
[Tr. Mrs. Cashel Hoey].

Philadelphia: J. B. Lippincott Co., 1899 [Tr. Mrs. Cashel
Hoey].

The Mystery of Arthur Gordon Pym by Edgar Allan Poe and
Jules Verne. London: Arco Publications, 1961 [Tr.
I. O. Evans, edited by Basil Ashmore].

An Antarctic Mystery. Boston: Gregg Press, 1975 [Intro-
duction by David G. Hartwell].

The Narrative of Arthur Gordon Pym and Le Sphinx des glaces.
Harmondsworth, England: Penguin, 1975 [Edited by Harold
Beaver].

1898

A82 "Le Superbe Orénoque" ["The Superb Orinoco"], <u>Magasin d'éducation et de récréation</u>, from 2nd series, 7 (1 January) to 8 (15 December).

Le Superbe Orénoque (2 Parts). Paris: J. Hetzel, 1898.

1899

A83 "Le Testament d'un excentrique," <u>Magasin d'éducation et de récréation</u>, from 2nd series, 9 (1 January) to 10 (15 December).

Le Testament d'un excentrique (2 Parts). Paris: J. Hetzel, 1899.

The Will of an Eccentric. London: Sampson Low, Marston & Co., 1900.

1900

A84 "Seconde Patrie," <u>Magasin d'éducation et de récréation</u>, from 2nd series, 11 (1 January) to 12 (15 December).

Seconde Patrie (2 Parts). Paris: J. Hetzel, 1900.

Their Island Home (Part 1). London: Sampson Low, Marston & Co., 1923.

The Castaways of the Flag (Part 2). London: Sampson Low, Marston & Co., 1923.

Their Island Home (Part 1). New York: G. H. Watt, 1924 [Tr. Cranstoun Metcalfe].

The Castaways of the Flag (Part 2). New York: G. H. Watt, 1924 [Tr. Cranstoun Metcalfe].

1901

A85 "La Grande Forêt," <u>Magasin d'éducation et de récréation</u>, from 2nd series, 13 (1 January) to 13 (15 June).

29

Rpt. as Le Village aérien. Paris: J. Hetzel, 1901.

The Village in the Treetops. London: Arco Publications,
    1964 [Tr. I. O. Evans].

A86 "Les Histoires de Cabidoulin," Magasin d'éducation et de
    récréation, from 2nd series, 14 (1 July) to 14 (15
    December). After the second issue the title changed to
    "Les Histoires de Jean-Marie Cabidoulin."

Les Histoires de Jean-Marie Cabidoulin. Paris: J. Hetzel,
    1901.

The Sea Serpent: The Yards of Jean Marie Cabidoulin.
    London: Arco Publications, 1967 [Tr. I. O. Evans].

A87 Le Village aérien. See "La Grande Forêt," 1901 (A85).

1902

A88 "Les Frères Kip" ["The Kip Brothers"], Magasin d'éducation
    et de récréation, from 2nd series, 15 (1 January) to 16
    (15 December).

Les Frères Kip (2 Parts). Paris: J. Hetzel, 1902.

1903

A89 "Bourses de voyage" ["Traveling Scholarships"], Magasin
    d'éducation et de récréation, from 2nd series, 17 (1
    January) to 18 (15 December).

Bourses de voyage (2 Parts). Paris: J. Hetzel, 1903.

1904

A90 "Un Drame en Livonie," Magasin d'éducation et de récréation,
    from 2nd series, 19 (1 January) to 19 (15 June).

Un Drame en Livonie. Paris: J. Hetzel, 1904.

A Drama in Livonia. London: Arco Publications, 1967 [Tr.
    I. O. Evans].

A91   "Maître du monde," Magasin d'éducation et de récréation, from 2nd series, 20 (1 July) to 20 (15 December).

Maître du monde. Paris: Collection Hetzel, 1904.

The Master of the World. London: Sampson Low, Marston & Co., 1914.

Philadelphia: J. B. Lippincott Co., 1915.

London: Arco Publications, 1962 [Tr. I. O. Evans].

1905

A92   "L'Invasion de la mer" ["Invasion of the Sea"], Magasin d'éducation et de récréation, from 2nd series, 21 (1 January) to 22 (1 August).

L'Invasion de la mer. Paris: Collection Hetzel, 1905.

A93   "Le Phare du bout du monde," Magasin d'éducation et de récréation, from 2nd series, 22 (15 August) to 24 (15 December).

Le Phare du bout du monde. Paris: Collection Hetzel, 1905.

The Lighthouse at the End of the World. London: Sampson Low, Marston & Co., 1923.

New York: G. H. Watt, 1924 [Tr. Cranstoun Metcalfe].

1906

A94   "Le Volcan d'or," Magasin d'éducation et de récréation, from 2nd series, 23 (1 January) to 24 (15 December).

Le Volcan d'or (2 Parts). Paris: Collection Hetzel, 1906.

The Golden Volcano. London: Arco Publications, 1962 [Tr. I. O. Evans]: The Claim on Forty Mile Creek (Part 1), Flood and Flame (Part 2). 2 vols.

<u>1907</u>

A95 "L'Agence Thompson and Co.," <u>Le Journal</u>, from No. 5495 (17 October) to No. 5564 (25 December).

<u>L'Agence Thompson and Co.</u> (2 Parts). Paris: Collection Hetzel, 1907.

<u>The Thompson Travel Agency</u>. London: Arco Publications, 1965 [Tr. I. O. Evans]: <u>Package Holiday</u> (Part 1), <u>End of the Journey</u> (Part 2). 2 vols.

<u>1908</u>

A96 "La Chasse au météore," <u>Le Journal</u>, from No. 5635 (5 March) to No. 5671 (10 April).

<u>La Chasse au météore</u>. Paris: Collection Hetzel, 1908.

<u>The Chase of the Golden Meteor</u>. London: Grant Richards, [1909] [Tr. Frederick Lawton].

<u>The Hunt for the Meteor</u>. London: Arco Publications, 1965 [Tr. I. O. Evans].

A97 "Le Pilote du Danube," <u>Le Journal</u>, from No. 5838 (24 September) to No. 5877 (2 November).

<u>Le Pilote du Danube</u>. Paris: Collection Hetzel, 1908.

<u>The Danube Pilot</u>. London: Arco Publications, 1967 [Tr. I. O. Evans].

<u>1909</u>

A98 "Les Naufragés du 'Jonathan,'" <u>Le Journal</u>, from No. 6147 (26 July) to No. 6230 (17 October).

<u>Les Naufragés du Jonathan</u> (2 Parts). Paris: Collection Hetzel, 1909.

<u>The Survivors of the Jonathan</u>. London: Arco Publications, 1962 [Tr. I. O. Evans]: <u>The Masterless Man</u> (Part 1), <u>The Unwilling Dictator</u> (Part 2). 2 vols.

Part A: Fiction

1910

A99 "Le Secret de Wilhelm Storitz," Le Journal, from No. 6471
     (15 June) to No. 6499 (13 July).

     Le Secret de Wilhelm Storitz. Paris: Collection Hetzel,
       1910.

     The Secret of Wilhelm Storitz. Westport, CT: Associated
       Booksellers, 1963 [Tr. I. O. Evans].

A100 "L'Eternel Adam dans quelques vingt mille ans," La Revue
     de Paris, No. 19 (1 October).

     In Hier et demain, 1910 (A103).

     "The Eternal Adam," Saturn, 1 (March 1957), 76-112 [Tr.
       Willis T. Bradley].

     In Yesterday and Tomorrow (A103). London: Arco Publica-
       tions, 1965, pp. 155-188 [Tr. I. O. Evans].

     Sam Moskowitz, ed. Masterpieces of Science Fiction.
       Cleveland, Ohio: World Publishing Co., 1966, pp.
       168-206 [Tr. Willis T. Bradley]. Rpt. Westport, CT:
       Hyperion Press, 1974.

A101 "La Destinée de Jean Morénas," in Hier et demain. Paris:
     Collection Hetzel, 1910 (A103).

     "The Fate of Jean Morenas," in Yesterday and Tomorrow
       (A103). London: Arco Publications, 1965, pp. 13-45
       [Tr. I. O. Evans].

A102 "Le Humbug," in Hier et demain. Paris: Collection Hetzel,
     1910 (A103).

A103 Hier et demain. Paris: Collection Hetzel ["La Famille
     Raton," "M. Ré-Dièze et Mlle Mi-Bémol," "La Destinée de
     Jean Morénas," "Le Humbug," "Au XXIXe Siècle: La Journée
     d'un journaliste americain en 2889," "L'Éternel Adam"].
     See entries A71, A76, A101, A102, A67, A100.

     Yesterday and Tomorrow. London: Arco Publications, 1965
       [Tr. I. O. Evans: "The Fate of Jean Morenas," "An Ideal
       City," "Ten Hours Hunting," "Fritt-Flacc," "Gil Braltar,"

"In the Twenty-ninth Century: The Day of an American
Journalist in 2889," "Mr. Ray Sharp and Miss Me Flat,"
"The Eternal Adam"]. See entries A101, A39, A51, A57,
A64, A67, A76, A100.

1914

A104 "Étonnante Aventure de la mission Barsac," Le Matin, from
      No. 11008 (18 April) to No. 11087 (6 July).

L'Étonnante Aventure de la mission Barsac. Paris: Librarie
      Hachette, 1919.

The Barsac Mission. Westport, CT: Associated Booksellers,
      1960 [Tr. I. O. Evans]: Into the Niger Bend (Part 1),
      The City in the Sahara (Part 2). 2 vols.

1919

A105 L'Étonnante Aventure de la mission Barsac. See entry A104.

1970

A106 "Paix sur la planète inconnue" ["Peace on the Unknown
      Planet"], Le Courrier rationnaliste, January, pp. 9-11
      [Published by Louis Tregaro in an article entitled "Un
      Inédit de Jules Verne"].

Part B: Miscellaneous Media

<u>1850</u>

B1 <u>Les Pailles rompues</u> [Play: <u>Broken Straws</u>]. Paris: Beck. Théâtre historique, 12 June, 1850.

<u>1851</u>

B2 <u>Les Gabiers: chanson maritime</u> [Song: "Seamen: Maritime Song"]. Paris: J. Meissonier Fils. With Aristide Hignard.

<u>1852</u>

B3 <u>Les Châteaux en Californie, ou Pierre qui roule n'amasse pas mousse</u> [Play: <u>Castles in California, or the rolling stone gathers no moss</u>]. <u>Musée des familles</u>, 2nd series, 9 (June). With Pitre-Chevalier.

<u>1853</u>

B4 <u>Le Colin-Maillard</u> [Play: <u>Blindman's Buff</u>]. Paris: Michel Lévy frères. Théâtre lyrique, 28 April, 1853. With Michel Carré and Aristide Hignard.

<u>1855</u>

B5 <u>Les Compagnons de la Marjolaine</u> [Play: <u>The Companions of the Marjolaine</u>]. Paris: Michel Lévy frères. Théâtre lyrique, 6 June, 1855. With Michel Carré and Aristide Hignard.

B6 <u>En avant les Zouaves! Chanson guerrière</u> [Song: "Forward Zouaves! War Song"]. Paris: Ledeulu. With Alfred Dufresne and Jules Lefort.

<u>1857</u>

B7 <u>Daphne: Mélodie</u> [Song: "Daphne: Melody"]. Paris: E. Heu. With Aristide Hignard.

1860

B8 L'Auberge des Ardennes [Play: The Inn of the Ardennes].
    Paris: Michel Lévy frères. Théâtre lyrique, 1 September
    1860. With Michel Carré and Aristide Hignard.

1861

B9 Onze jours de siège [Play: Eleven Days' Seige]. Paris:
    Michel Lévy frères. Vaudeville, 1 June, 1861. With
    Charles Wallut.

1863

B10 Rimes et mélodies: 12 morceaux de chant par Aristide Hignard
    [Songs]. Paris: E. Heu: "Au printemps" ["In Spring"],
    pp. 4-7; "Souvenirs d'Ecosse" ["Memories of Scotland"],
    pp. 8-10; "La Tankadère: chanson chinoise" ["The Tankadere:
    Chinese Song"], pp. 41-43. With Hignard. See B17.

1870

B11 Les Clairons de l'armée [Song: "Army Clarions"]. Paris:
    Léon Gras. With Aristide Hignard.

1873

B12 Un neveu d'Amérique, ou les Deux Frontignac [Play: A Nephew
    from America, or the Two Frontignacs]. Paris: J. Hetzel.
    Théâtre Cluny, 17 April, 1873. With Edouard Cadoul and
    Charles Wallut.

1875

B13 Le Tour du monde en quatre-vingt jours [Play: Around the
    World in Eighty Days]. Paris: F. Debons. Théâtre de la
    Porte Saint-Martin, 7 November, 1874. With Adolphe
    d'Ennery.

    Around the World in Eighty Days. London: S. French, 1875
    [Tr. C. Clark].

1879

B14 Les Enfants du Capitaine Grant [Play: Captain Grant's
    Children]. Paris: Mesnil. Théâtre de la Porte Saint-
    Martin, 26 December, 1878. With Adolphe d'Ennery.

1880

B15 Michel Strogoff [Play]. Paris: Mesnil. Théâtre du Châtelet,
    17 November, 1880. With Adolphe d'Ennery

Michael Strogoff. London: S. French, 1881.

1881

B16   Les Voyages au théâtre [Plays: Voyages in the Theater].
Paris: J. Hetzel [Le Tour du monde en quatre-vingt jours,
Les Enfants du Capitaine Grant, Michel Strogoff]. With
Adolphe d'Ennery. See B13, B14, B15.

1897

B17   Rimes et mélodies, 12 morceaux de chant par Aristide Hignard
[Songs]. Paris: E. Heu: "Au bord du Lac: Sérénade"
["By the Lake: Serenade"], p. 1; "Tout simplement"
["Quite Simply"], pp. 5-8; "Berceuse" ["Cradle-Rocker"],
pp. 9-11; "Les Deux troupeaux: Eglogue" ["The Two Flocks:
Eclogue"], pp. 14-17; "La Douce attente: Villanelle"
["Sweet Waiting: Villanelle"], pp. 20-24; "Notre étoile"
["Our Star"], pp. 30-31; "Chanson scandinave" ["Scandinavian
Song"], pp. 35-37; "Chanson turque" ["Turkish Song"], pp.
38-39. "Au bord du lac" is not attributed to Verne by
Gondolo della Riva (E438) or Margot (E819). With Hignard.
See B10.

1905

B18   Chanson gröenlandaise [Song: "Greenland Song"]. Paris:
Durdilly. With Georges Alary.

1974

B19   Monna Lisa [Play]. In Jules Verne, ed. P.-A. Touttain.
Paris: Editions de L'Herne, pp. 23-56.

1978

B20   "Sonnet sur la morphine" [Poem: "Sonnet on Morphine"],
In'hui, No. 3 (Spring).

No Date

B21   Les Bras d'une mère [Song: "Arms of a Mother"]. Paris:
Michelet. With Aristide Hignard. Same as "Berceuse"
(B17).

Part C: Nonfiction

1852

C1 "Encore un navire aérien" ["Still Another Aircraft"], <u>Musée des familles</u>, 19 (June).

C2 "Machine à labourer" ["A Plowing Machine"], <u>Musée des familles</u>, 19 (June).

C3 "Tissus incombustibles" ["Fireproof Cloth"], <u>Musée des familles</u>, 19 (June).

1863

C4 "A Propos du 'Géant'" ["About the 'Giant'"], <u>Musée des familles</u>, 31 (December), 92-93. About Nadar, the history of the balloon, the development of aviation, and the advent of the helicopter.

1864

C5 "Edgar Poe et ses oeuvres" ["Edgar Poe and His Works"], <u>Musée des familles</u>, 31 (April), 193-208. Credits Poe with creating a unique literary genre. <u>See</u> D448.1.

1867

C6 <u>Géographie illustrée de la France et de ses colonies</u> [Illustrated Geography of France and of the Colonies]. Paris: J. Hetzel.

1870

C7 <u>Découverte de la terre: Histoire des grands voyages et des grands voyageurs</u> [Exploration of the World: History of the Famous Travels and Travellers]. Paris: J. Hetzel. <u>See</u> C11.

1873

C8 "Ascension du Météore" ["The Ascent of the Meteor"], Journal
    d'Amiens, No. 5109 (29–30 September), pp. 1–2. Account
    of his flight in a balloon, September 28, 1873.

   Vingt-quatre minutes en ballon [Twenty-Four Minutes in a
   Balloon]. Amiens: T. Jeunet, 1873.

C9 "Les Méridiens et le calendrier" ["The Meridians and the
    Calendar"], Bulletin de la Société de Géographie, 6th series,
    6 (July–December).

1877

C10 "Lettre à Stahl" ["Letter to Stahl"], Magasin d'éducation
    et de récréation, December, n.p. Letter to Hetzel about
    Dick Sands, the Boy Captain.

1878–1880

C11 Histoire des grands voyages et des grands voyageurs: Découverte
    de la terre (Part 1, 1878), Les Grands Navigateurs du
    XVIIIe siècle (Part 2, 1879), Les Voyageurs du XIXe siècle
    (Part 3, 1880). Paris: J. Hetzel.

   Famous Travels and Travellers. New York: Charles Scribner's
   Sons, 1879 [Tr. Dora Leigh]: Exploration of the World.

   Celebrated Travels and Travellers. London: Sampson Low,
   Marston & Co., 1879–81 [Tr. Dora Leigh and N. D'Anvers,
   pseud. of Mrs. Arthur Bell]: Exploration of the World,
   The Great Navigators of the Eighteenth Century, The Great
   Explorers of the Nineteenth Century. 3 vols.

   Great Voyages and Great Navigators. New York: George Munro,
   1880 [Tr. J. Cotterell].

1881

C12 "Réponse au discours de réception de M. Pacaut" ["Reply to
    the Reception Speech of Mr. Pacaut"], Mémoirs de l'Académie
    des sciences, des lettres et des arts d'Amiens, 3rd series,
    8 (1881).

1889

C13 "Discours d'inauguration du cirque municipal d'Amiens"
    ["Inauguration Speech of the Circus of Amiens"], Journal
    d'Amiens, 24 June. Rpt. César Cascabel, by Jules Verne.
    Paris: Union Générale d'éditions, 1978, pp. 421–431.

1891

C14 "To My English Readers." In A Plunge into Space, by Robert
Cromie. London: F. Warne. Very brief introduction.
Rpt. Westport, CT: Hyperion Press, 1976.

C15 "Trop de fleurs!" ["Too Many Flowers!"], Bulletin de la
Société d'Horticulture de Picardie, 13 (February).

1892

C16 "Réponse au discours de M. Ricquier" ["Reply to the Speech
of Mr. Ricquier"], Mémoires de l'Académie des sciences,
des lettres et des arts d'Amiens, 39 (1892).

1894

C17 "Discours. . .Assemblée générale publique" ["Speech. . .Public
General Assembly"], Bulletin de la Société d'Horticulture
de Picardie, 14 (1894).

1936

C18 Turiello, Mario. "Lettres de Jules Verne à un jeune Italien"
["Jules Verne's Letters to a Young Italian"]. BSJV, 1,
No. 4 (August), 158-161. Thirty-three letters written to
Turiello between 1894 and 1904.

1938

C19 "Soixante-Trois Lettres" ["Sixty-Three Letters"], BSJV, 3,
No. 11-12-13 (June, September, December), 47-129. Written
to his parents between 1848 and 1871.

1949

C20 Parménie, A. "Huit Lettres de Jules Verne à son éditeur
P.-J. Hetzel" ["Eight Letters of Jules Verne to His
Publisher P. J. Hetzel"]. Arts et lettres, No. 15 (1949),
pp. 102-107. Written in 1863, 1876, 1879, 1883, 1884.

1955

C21 "Quelques Lettres" ["A Few Letters"], Livres de France, 6,
No. 5 (May-June), 13-15. Eleven letters written to his
parents between 1849 and 1894.

1966

C22 "Lettre à Nadar" ["Letter to Nadar"], L'Arc, No. 29 (1966),
p. 83. Written August 22, 1903.

1968

C23 Laissus, J. A. "A Propos de L'Albatros" ["Concerning the
Albatross"]. BSJV, NS No. 7-8 (3rd & 4th Trimesters),
pp. 18-21. Letter to the illustrator, Benett, 1886.

1971

C24 Bottin, André. "Lettres inédites de Jules Verne au lieutenant-
colonel Hennebert" ["Unpublished Letters from Jules Verne
To Lieutenant Colonel Hennebert"]. BSJV, NS No. 17 (2nd
Trimester), pp. 36-44. Twelve letters written between
July and September, 1896.

1974

C25 "Deux lettres à Louis-Jules Hetzel" ["Two Letters to Louis-
Jules Hetzel"], in Jules Verne, ed. P.-A. Touttain. Paris:
Editions de L'Herne, pp. 73-74. Written in 1896 and 1897.

C26 "Lettre à Paul Verne, à propos de Turpin" ["Letter to Paul
Verne about Turpin"], in Jules Verne, ed. P.-A. Touttain.
Paris: Editions de L'Herne, pp. 81-82. Written in 1894.

C27 "Lettres à Nadar" ["Letters to Nadar"], in Jules Verne, ed,
P.-A. Touttain. Paris: Editions de L'Herne, pp. 76-80.
Eight letters written between 1864 and 1903.

C28 "Sept Lettres à sa famille et à divers correspondants"
["Seven Letters to His Family and to Other Correspondents"],
in Jules Verne, ed. P.-A. Touttain. Paris: Editions de
L'Herne, pp. 63-70. Written between 1851 and 1895.

C29 "Souvenirs d'enfance et de jeunesse" ["Memories of Childhood
and Youth"], in Jules Verne, ed. P.-A. Touttain. Paris:
Editions de L'Herne, pp. 57-62. Watching ships put out
to sea as a child fueled his desire to travel; recalls
some maritime experiences.

1977

C30 Raeders, Georges. "Une Lettre inédite de Jules Verne sur
La Jangada" ["An Unpublished Letter of Jules Verne on
The Giant Raft"]. In La Bretagne, Le Portugal, Le Brésil:
Echanges et Rapports. Nantes: Université de Nantes, p.
431. Written in 1882.

1978

C31   "Deux Lettres inédites" ["Two Unpublished Letters"]. <u>BSJV</u>, NS No. 48 (4th Trimester), pp. 253-254. One written to Hetzel in 1869, the other to an unknown correspondent 1871 or later.

1979

C32   "Correspondance," <u>BSJV</u>, NS No. 49 (1st Trimester), pp. 31-34. Five letters written between 1876 and 1878 to Ritt, Larochelle, and d'Ennery.

Part D: Critical Studies in English

1872

D1   Anon. Review of Journey to the Center of the Earth. Il-
     lustrated Review, 16 December, pp. 373-374.
        The travelers in this cleverly written and ingeniously
     worked out narrative, apparently suggested by Poe, "are
     in almost as much danger as if they were travelling by our
     underground railway." Verne makes geological records live
     before our eyes. "In reading we at times forget the utter
     impossibility of the adventure of the travellers, and fancy
     ourselves reading merely the account of ordinary travellers."

1873

D2   Anon. "Jules Verne's From the Earth to the Moon." Book
     Buyer, 7 (15 November), 33.
        In regards to wildness of imagination and the skillful
     combination of the possible with the impossible, this may
     be Verne's best novel. The "Prince of the marvellous in
     literature" draws on facts in such a way to render the
     story "instructive as well as amusing."

D3   Marx, Adrien. "Introduction." In The Tour of the World in
     Eighty Days, by Jules Verne. Boston: James R. Osgood,
     pp. 1-13.
        The frontispiece of this edition is a sketch drawn by
     Verne of the skiff Le Saint Michel. The novelist writes
     from 5 A.M. to 1 P.M., then visits factories where he
     studies the machinery. His evenings are devoted to reading
     scientific journals. (Also in London: Sampson Low, 1874
     edition).

1874

D4   Anon. "Jules Verne." Book Buyer, 7 (16 March), 122-123.
        The dash and recklessness of Verne's style appeals to
     the most demure and scholarly American and is winning him
     a big audience here.

D5   Anon. "Jules Verne's New Story." Scribner's Monthly, 7
        (April), 755.
           Short notice marking the serialization of The Mysterious
        Island. Robinson Crusoe and Swiss Family Robinson were
        sufficient for unscientific times, "but now it is necessary
        to show how scientific castaways can manage to live, with-
        out a vessel to break up, and convenient domestic animals
        at hand."

D6   Anon. "Parisian Gossip: An Incident of the Early Career of
        a Popular Writer." New York Times, 27 November, p. 1.
           Verne was introduced to Dumas by an eccentric character
        who claims to have invented a new science called Chirognomy.
        Since then Verne "has devoted himself to these imaginary
        voyages in which a traveler mounts his horse and starts off
        for the moon or elsewhere."

D7   Eggleston, George Cary. Review of The Mysterious Island.
        American Homes, 7 (December), n.p.
           Science destroyed classic wonder stories "by creating in
        us mental habits fatal to their enjoyment," but Verne's
        "congenial marriage" of science and fancy shows that science
        itself can fill the void. By using scientific facts and by
        keeping his imagination in line with science, Verne "has
        succeeded in creating stories more marvellous than any of
        Scheherazade's," but which everyone can believe.

D8   Roth, Edward. "Preface." In The Baltimore Gun Club, by
        Jules Verne. Philadelphia: King and Baird, pp. 3-6.
           Although Verne's works seem to be just the thing for
        "clear-brained, quick witted, inquisitive, restless, reality
        loving" young Americans, publishers in the United States
        have produced hasty, inaccurate translations by British
        hands. Roth attempted to remedy the situation with "careful"
        translations of the novels of the "Daniel Defoe of the Nine-
        teenth Century." He states, however, that he too tinkered
        with Verne's prose. He aimed to "make the most of his strong
        points, throw the weak ones into shade, soften off extrava-
        gance, give the names a familiar sound, correct palpable
        errors. . .simplify crabbed science, explain difficulties,
        amplify local coloring, clear up unknown illusions, put a
        little more blood and heart into the human beings. . . ."

D9   Taylor, Charles H. "A Journey to the Moon." American Homes,
        5 (February), 181.
           If Verne's object was to impart scientific knowledge in
        popular form, he has succeeded. "But in these days of
        Peculiar People, Christadelphians, Little Children Baptists,
        Spiritrappers, and other oddities, it is much to be feared
        that M. Verne will have to be responsible for further ad-
        ditions to our already crowded lunatic asylums." There are
        too many problems on this globe to encourage more curious
        enthusiasts.

1875

D10 Eggleston, George Cary. "Jules Verne and His Work." American
     Homes, 8 (May), 34-35.
     Only a Frenchman "could possibly take liberties with
     the best known facts with as calm an assurance as he,"
     but Verne is a mere dabbler in rather than a diligent
     student of science. Greed has caused him to swell his
     tales outrageously. He writes wonder stories, not novels
     which possess human interest. The reader's curiosity, not
     his heart, is enlisted; he cares only for the mechanism of
     the tale, not for the "absurd automata which stand for
     people."

1877

D11 Anon. "Is Jules Verne a Literary Pirate?" New York Times,
     29 January, p. 3.
     Brief note about a suit brought against Verne by a man
     who wrote a book quite similar to Journey to the Center
     of the Earth, and which seems to have flared because
     Verne overlooked or ignored the man's request for free
     theater tickets.

D12 Cooper, Thompson. Men of Mark: A Gallery of Contemporary
     Portraits of Men Distinguished in the Senate, the Church,
     in Science, Literature and Art, the Army, Navy, Law,
     Medicine, etc. London: Sampson Low, Marston, Searle, and
     Rivington, pp. 23-24.
     Very brief early notice of Verne and a catalogue of
     his works in this prestige volume.

1878

D13 Anon. "Jules Verne." Nature, 17 (10 January), 197-199.
     Verne is a science teacher of a new kind; grant the
     possibility of his chief incident and everything else
     follows quite logically. Because Verne combines amusement
     and instruction, his books are especially recommended for
     young people. Hector Servadac provides fascinating and
     concrete explanations of gravity and the metric system.

1879

D14 Anon. "A Bogus Jules Verne in Massachusetts." New York
     Times, 19 January, p. 9.
     A man, "evidently a New-Englander who had undertaken
     to play a part for which he was not qualified," unsuc-
     cessfully tried to pass himself off as Verne.

1883

D15 Anon. "How Jules Verne Writes His Books." Frank Leslie's
     Illustrated Newspaper, 67 (27 October), 155.
          To see something of the "vigorous vitality" which is
     the chief trait of all of his works, to see the man rather
     than the author, it is necessary to visit him on his
     yacht rather than at Amiens.

D16 Anon. "Ignis." Saturday Review (London), 55 (7 April),
     439-440.
          The unnamed author of the novel Ignis (Paris: Berger,
     Levrault et Cie) succeeded remarkably well in imitating
     the style of Verne. Ignis relates the trials of a group
     attempting to derive light and heat from the center of
     the Earth. Deep wells are dug and a city, Industria, is
     built. A race of metal creatures, called Enginemen or
     Atmophytes, are designed to do all the manual labor in
     the city. Eventually the Atmophytes rebel and all is
     destroyed in the ensuing conflagration.

D17 Anon. "Jules Verne's New Play." New York Times, 24 Septem-
     ber, p. 2.
          Unfavorable review of Kéraban the Inflexible. Verne
     misses the collaboration of dramatist d'Ennery badly in
     this play. His prose is turgid, a long ballet scene is
     an imitation of "Excelsior," and there is only one novel
     effect in the entire play.

D18 Hazeltine, Mayo Williamson. "Jules Verne's Didactic Fiction."
     In Chats About Books, Poets and Novelists. New York:
     Charles Scribner's Sons, pp. 337-346.
          Verne compares unfavorably with Swift, Defoe, and Poe
     in his use of scientific fact. "A notable contribution
     to the crudities and figments afloat in current conversa-
     tion may be traced to the writings of Jules Verne. Every
     young woman in society has read them, every vivacious
     young man can quote them, and impart to his discourse a
     scientific glimmer which resembles knowledge as the
     phosphorescence of decayed bones resembles a calcium
     light." Verne has "chronic unveracity"; he can rarely go
     a dozen pages without some perversion of fact.

1885

D19 Kennedy, William Sloane. "Edward Everett Hale." Century
     Magazine, 29 (January), 338-343, esp. 340-341.
          Hale reminds one of Verne instead of Poe, but when Hale
     began to write "in this vein the Frenchman had produced
     only one or two books, which were untranslated and scarcely
     heard of outside of France." Downplays Verne's influence
     in America.

Part D: Critical Studies in English

1886

D20 Anon. "The Attempt to Kill Jules Verne." New York Times,
22 March, p. 2.
Reprints the London Times story of March 11 on the
shooting of Verne by his nephew from which he never quite
recovered. A later article on April 5 (p. 4) indicates
that the wound is more serious than first expected.

1889

D21 Anon. "Around the World." New York World, 14 November,
p. 1.
"Can Jules Verne's great dream be reduced to actual
fact?" An account of the trip around the world planned
by Nellie Bly, "a female Phineas (sic) Fogg."

D22 Anon. "Jules Verne's Home Life." New York Times, 22
December, p. 16.
Appears to be an excerpt from a Pall Mall Gazette
article on a visit to Verne in Amiens.

1890

D23 Anon. "Jules Verne." Book News, 8 (July), 380.
Very brief notice of Verne's life and work. "The
author attempts in his stories to inculcate scientific
truths, and though in many cases there has not been
sufficient knowledge on his part to connect his catastrophe
either with any law or the breaking of one, one seldom
catches him tripping. Once granted the possibility of
his chief incident and all the surroundings are secundem
artem."

D24 Anon. "Jules Verne." Book Buyer, 7 (August), 281-282.
Brief sketch that seems to be drawn from previously
published interviews and reviews. Verne "combines imagin-
ativeness with a sanity and clarity of vision that are
essentially Gallic."

1892

D25 Anon. "Belles Lettres." Westminster Review, 137 (January),
108-109.
A short, derogatory review of the original French
edition of Mistress Branican that labels the work "long-
winded." The lack of "marvellous" impossibilities and
defects in character delineation are also noted.

Jules Verne

1893

D26 Anon. "Human Documents." McClure's Magazine, 1 (August),
213, 218.
Four portraits of Verne, at ages twenty, thirty, forty,
and fifty-eight, are accompanied by a brief biographical
statement.

D27 Anon. "Literary Notes and News." The Dial, 14 (1 May), 289.
"Jules Verne" is a pen name. By birth a native of
Warsaw, the novelist's real name is Olchewitz. When he
began to write, he translated the initial syllables of
his family patronymic (which is "beech" in English) into
the French equivalent, the result being "Verne." He is
the youngest of three brothers. The eldest died a few
years ago at the age of 110.

1894

D28 Anon. "How Jules Verne Lives and Works." The Review of
Reviews, 9 (February), 217-218.
Quotes from the Sherard article (D29), particularly
about Verne's appearance, his home, and his work habits.

D29 Sherard, R. H. "Jules Verne at Home. His Own Account of His
Life and Work." McClure's Magazine, 2 (January), 115-124.
An interview with Verne prefaced by his sad remark,
"the great regret of my life is that I have never taken
any place in French literature." Verne's appearance and
house are described, and he talks of such things as his
youth, his literary influences, his education, and his
work habits. Verne, for instance, states that he never
studied science, but that he is a great reader and note
taker -- like a character in Dickens.

1895

D30 Belloc, Marie A. "Jules Verne at Home." Strand Magazine,
9 (February), 206-213.
Account of an interview with Verne at Amiens. Verne
says that it was his interest in geography that gave him
the idea of writing scientific romances. He writes
several hours per day on a regular, heavy schedule, and
his wide reading and precise note taking stand behind
the accuracy of his work. Scott, Cooper, and Dickens are
among his favorite writers, and women characters are indeed in his fiction. Some emphasis is placed on the
kindly Mrs. Verne, who is always in the background. See
E782.

50

1897

D31   Anon. "Two Stories by Jules Verne." Spectator, 79 (6
      November), 624-625.
           The only interest in Clovis Dardentor is the humor of
      the young Parisians and the contrast between the impulsive
      Dardentor and his reserved servant. For the Flag, however,
      is Verne in the domain of scientific fiction where he
      excels, telling a fascinating story of great inventions.

D32   De Amicis, Edmondo. "A Visit to Jules Verne and Victorien
      Sardou." The Chautauquan, 24 (March), 701-705.
           A visit with Verne at Amiens elicits information about
      his life style and working habits, but the strongest
      impression is the difference between the man and his works.
      He looks like anything but an artist. "My first sensation,
      after the pleasure of seeing him, was one of stupefaction.
      Apart from the friendly look and affable demeanor, I could
      recognize nothing in common with the Verne who stood before
      me and the one that had a place in my imagination." How
      could all this adventure come out of so quiet and simple
      a man?

1898

D33   Bates, Katherine Lee. American Literature. New York:
      Macmillan Company, p. 295.
           The narratives of Verne and Frank L. Stockton mirror
      those of Edgar Poe who constructs "accurately calculated
      probabilities" on a base of impossibility. All three
      writers have "patient respect for the minutiae of truth"
      and, if Poe is the model, "restless craving for super-
      human knowledge."

D34   [Williams, Basil]. Review of The War of The Worlds, by H. G.
      Wells. Athenaeum, 5 February, p. 178. Rpt. H. G. Wells:
      The Critical Heritage, ed. Patrick Parrinder. London:
      Routledge and Kegan Paul, 1972, p. 67.
           In The War of The Worlds, Wells imitates Verne's method
      of creating plausibility with exactness of detail.

1899

*D35 Bassett, Rosa. Helps for the Study of Jules Verne's Voyage
      au Centre de la Terre. London: Edwin Arnold.
           Not seen (listed in British Museum General Catalogue
      of Printed Books (1965), Vol. 12, p. 529).

1901

D36   Anon. "A Dreamer of Things Impossible." The Academy, 61
      (28 September), 263-264.
         The effect of the stories in Edgar Poe's Ms. Found in
      a Bottle is achieved through the gradual accumulation of
      "matter-of-fact details." This technique anticipates
      Verne.

D37   Ghéon, Henri. Review of The First Men in the Moon, by H. G.
      Wells. L'Ermitage, 23 (December), 471-472. Rpt. H. G.
      Wells: The Critical Heritage, ed. Patrick Parrinder.
      London: Routledge and Kegan Paul, 1972, pp. 99-100.
         Wells and Verne begin with the same point of view --
      science and imagination. But Verne is too "infantile."
      Wells, the philosopher and psychologist, possesses the
      greater inventive gifts.

1902

D38   Bennett, E. A. [Arnold]. "Herbert George Wells and His Works."
      Cosmopolitan, 33 (August), 465-471. Rpt. Arnold Bennett
      and H. G. Wells, ed. Harris Wilson. Urbana: University
      of Illinois Press, 1960, pp. 260-276.
         Wells does not belong to the "vast Jules Verne school."
      Bennett contrasts Verne's From the Earth to the Moon and
      Around the Moon with Wells's First Men in the Moon.
      Verne's works are farcical, and he troubles little with
      science. His "entirely delicious" style diverts but does
      not convince. Wells's scientific education is apparent
      in his works as well as his "deeply satiric" voice.

1903

D39   Sherard, Robert H. "Jules Verne Re-Visited." T.P.'s Weekly,
      9 October, p. 589.
         An interview with Verne in which he claims to be years
      ahead of his publishing schedule, disclaims the notion
      that his fictional inventions became factual inventions,
      and remarks on the importance of names in his fiction.
      Most important, though, is the oft-quoted comparison with
      Wells: "It occurs to me that his stories do not repose
      on very scientific bases. No, there is no rapport between
      his work and mine. I make use of physics. He invents."

1904

D40   Anon. "Jules Verne on Himself and Others." The American
      Monthly Review of Reviews, 30 (July), 112.
         Short summary of the Gordon Jones article (D41), quoting
      Verne on the beginning of his career and his work habits.

D41 Jones, Gordon. "Jules Verne at Home." <u>Temple Bar</u>, 129
(June), 664-671.
Recounting an interview with the aging Verne, Jones
quotes Verne as stating that his literary career was
brought about by the sudden impulse to blend his scientific
education with romance. All of his inventions, Verne
continues, rest on "a practical basis" with imaginative
elaboration. Asked to name his favorite author among
the dead and among the living, Verne replies Charles
Dickens and H. G. Wells. Dickens is admired for his
characterization and Wells for his purely imaginative
constructions.

D42 Santos-Dumont, A. <u>My Air-Ships</u>. New York: Century Company,
pp. 29-30.
This famous aviator recounts that as a child Verne was
his favorite author. "The wholesome imagination of this
truly great writer, working magically with the immutable
laws of matter, fascinated me from childhood." Verne
helped him to see that with mechanics and science Man would
become a demigod.

<u>1905</u>

D43 Anon. [H. Lamont?]. "Jules Verne." <u>Nation</u>, 80 (30 March),
pp. 242-243.
Verne's characterizations are feeble. Lacking vitality,
his "creatures" are knowledgeable but "hollow inside."
Jean Passepartout described Phileas Fogg as "'a genuine
automaton.'" Despite this limitation, the novels have
the appeal of mystery. The lineal descendants of genii
and sorcerers are Verne's "'wizards of science.'"

D44 Anon. "Jules Verne." <u>Spectator</u>, 94 (1 April), 470-471. Rpt.
<u>Living Age</u>, 245 (6 May), 377-379.
Verne's death brings a sense of loss to all those who
read the journeys when schoolboys. The importance of
Verne's writing lies in its courage. Although the author
lacked a deep knowledge of applied science, no situation
was beyond his scope. He marched into "difficulties and
obscurities" despite his not always being able to work out
his plot. This slight limitation does not detract from
his genius. While <u>From the Earth to the Moon</u> may be an
"absurdity," many of Verne's predictions have been
realized: he "built better than he knew."

D45 Lowndes, Marie Belloc. "Jules Verne: A Reminiscence." <u>The
Academy</u>, 68 (1 April), 363-364.
In the last thirty-five years of his life, Verne did
all of his writing from five to eight A.M. He wrote with
half-page margins to accommodate detailed revisions.
Madame Verne and her husband were totally complementary
to each other.

D46   Anon. "Jules Verne Dead." New York Times, 25 March. p. 9.
      This brief note suggests Verne may have been trapped
      financially by a long term contract made before he became
      famous. "In Jules Verne there passes away one who is
      still the idol of boys, who is still the idol of many who
      were boys fifty years ago."

D47   Anon. "Jules Verne, Novelist and Seer." The American Monthly
      Review of Reviews, 31 (May), 579.
      Very short death notice. "His was an imagination that
      predicted the semi-miraculous without jarring too severely
      the reader's sense of the probable."

D48   Anon. "Jules Verne: True Friend of Every Boy." Current
      Literature, 38 (May), 395-396.
      "Wherever love of adventure, coupled with curiosity as
      to the mechanism of the universe, exists, there Jules
      Verne finds his disciples." His books are the Arabian
      Nights fitted with all modern improvements. Though
      schoolboys will shed his facts, a book like Twenty Thousand
      Leagues Under The Sea will give them a vivid conception of
      the immensity and mystery of the ocean.

D49   Anon. "The Late Jules Verne." Bookman, 21 (May), 230-234.
      Verne was an inveterate homebody; "the slightest
      variation from the even tenor of his existence he regarded
      with horror." Most of his "extravagant dreams" have been
      realized; there is not one of his books that has not been
      seriously discussed.

D50   Anon. "Science In Romance." Saturday Review (London), 99
      (1 April), 414-415.
      Verne is the best known and "most superficial" exponent
      of the "pseudo scientific novel." He deals with physical
      and mechanical facts but ignores human, moral, political,
      religious, and social questions. His fiction is for
      children. It is better to have science appear as science
      and not to divert readers from fiction by scientific
      elements. Scientific romance is "crude," and thus does
      not have much of a future.

D51   R., W. "Jules Verne." Athenaeum, 1 April, p. 400.
      In Verne's fiction the "grotesque bordered so closely
      on the impossible, and even the ridiculous." His success
      lies in the verisimilitude of the stories and his versa-
      tility. Dickens and Cooper were among the French novelist's
      favorite authors.

D52 W., W. L. "Jules Verne." The Academy, 68 (1 April), 363.
      The contrast between the municipal councilor of Amiens
      and the "adventurous creator of Captain Nemo" is the
      likely cause of the diverse opinions of Verne that have
      been expressed on the occasion of his death. They vary
      from enthusiasm to a "placid irony" that defends the
      novelist against the charge of the perversion of youth
      by blending "falsehood and science." H. G. Wells is
      obliged to Verne as Doyle is to Poe or Kipling to
      Swinburne.

D53 [Warren, Thomas Herbert]. Review of A Modern Utopia, by
      H. G. Wells. Spectator, 95 (21 October), 610-611. Rpt.
      H. G. Wells: The Critical Heritage, ed. Patrick Parrinder.
      London: Routledge and Kegan Paul, 1972, pp. 117-121.
      Verne wrote "'fairytales of science'" for children.
      He amused his audience by suggesting the "marvellous and
      delightful possibilities" of science.

1909

D54 Anon. "Chronicle and Comment." Bookman, 29 (July), 467.
      In an article published in La Revue in Paris, Henri
      Potez discusses the influence of Edgar Allan Poe on Verne.
      See E33. Verne created his winning formula by lessening
      the horrible element in Poe and retaining the mysterious
      and exotic. Potez provides detailed tracings of Verne's
      more important books back to works by Poe. This article
      lists title relationships for nine novels.

1910

D55 Sanborn, Alvan F. "Latest Gossip of Paris." New York Times,
      22 January, section 2, p. 43.
      The Survivors of the Jonathan is wearisome, but no
      doubt it would have been better if Verne had lived to
      finish it.

1911

D56 Anon. "The Original Phileas Fogg." Bookman, 34 (December),
      337-339.
      Relates an unsubstantiated account of an eccentric,
      mentally disturbed American doctor living near Amiens who
      believed eternal youth could be achieved by constantly
      moving as fast as possible toward the rising sun, thus
      gaining a day each time the globe is circled. Verne may
      have known or heard tales of this person.

D57   Horne, Charles F.   "Jules Verne."   In <u>Works of Jules Verne</u>,
       ed. Charles F. Horne.   Vol. 1.   New York: Vincent Parke
       and Company, pp. vii-xviii.
              French critics expressed varied opinions of Verne:
       some considered him to be a leading educator and the most
       popular author of the twentieth century, yet others "made
       a mock of his work."   Not an "intricate analyst," Verne
       spoke for the masses.   He created a literature that ap-
       pealed to the businessman by establishing a new form in
       which scientific wonders were interwoven with the simplest
       facts of human life.   As the "prophet of our mechanical
       age," Verne foresaw such inventions as the submarine,
       automobile, airplane, telephone, moving pavements, com-
       pressed air, and compressed food.

<u>1915</u>

D58   Brooks, Van Wyck.   <u>The World of H. G. Wells</u>.   New York:
       Mitchell Kennerley, pp. 19-20.
              Verne's marvels are "delightful, irresponsible plunder-
       ings from a helpless universe."   They have a quality of
       "pathetic futility" because they are brought together
       without any principle of selection.   In contrast, H. G.
       Wells, in his tales, demonstrates "an inevitable attitude
       toward life and the world."

D59   Moffett, Cleveland.   "Motion Pictures Under the Sea."
       <u>American Magazine</u>, 79 (January), 11-15, 74.
              Detailed description of the diving tube used by the
       Williamsons to film <u>Twenty Thousand Leagues Under the Sea</u>,
       and detailed descriptions of the men involved and their
       experiences.   Ernest Williamson, for instance, volunteered
       to kill a shark himself in order to get the necessary
       footage.

<u>1916</u>

D60   Anon.   "Method of Taking Cinematograph Films Under the Sea."
       <u>Current Opinion</u>, 60 (April), 262.
              Brief essay on the realism of the undersea portions of
       <u>Twenty Thousand Leagues Under the Sea</u>.

D61   Brent, Loring.   "A Motion Picture Drama from the Ocean
       Bottom."   <u>Scientific American</u>, 115 (22 July), 78-79.
              Description of the apparatus used by Williamson to film
       the 1916 version of <u>Twenty Thousand Leagues Under the Sea</u>.

D62   Worts, George F.   "Twenty Thousand Leagues Under the Sea."
       <u>Illustrated World</u>, 26 (16 September), 33-35.
              Brief account of the movie of the Verne novel done by
       the Williamson brothers.

1917

D63 Twist, Stanley H. "Forward." In <u>Twenty Thousand Leagues</u>
<u>Under the Sea</u>, by Jules Verne. New York: Grosset and
Dunlap, pp. vii-xi.
The Williamson brothers invented the deep sea photogra-
phic chamber, then made the first film version of <u>Twenty</u>
<u>Thousand Leagues Under the Sea</u>. Their exploits in filming
the submarine sections of the film are related.

1918

D64 Anon. "Most Wonderful of All Vindications of the True
Scientific Imagination." <u>Current Opinion</u>, 64 (February),
110-111.
Verne's <u>Twenty Thousand Leagues Under the Sea</u> vindicates
the use of imagination in science. He did not deal in
pseudoscience, nor did he convey false ideas. He erred
only on points of detail in the application of principle.
His novel "is a substantial contribution to our knowledge
of the value of the poetical in science, a proof of the
contention that the imagination of the French is essentially
scientific as distinguished from the imagination of the
English which is in the main poetical." It also proves
that the imagination is a more reliable faculty than the
intelligence.

D65 Lake, Simon. <u>The Submarine In War and Peace</u>. Philadelphia:
J. B. Lippincott, p. 119.
This submarine pioneer recalls that he "had become
interested in the submarine by reading Jules Verne's
<u>Twenty Thousand Leagues Under the Sea</u>."

1920

D66 Williamson, Claude C. H. "The Religion of Mr. H. G. Wells."
In <u>Writers of Three Centuries, 1789-1914</u>. Philadelphia:
George W. Jacobs and Company, pp. 452-453.
Wells's <u>The Food of the Gods</u> is, to a certain extent,
a "plagiarism" of Verne. But whereas the Frenchman
represented men of science inventing things that were
possible in reality, Wells's science was a "hybrid thing"
with no scientific value and no bearing on the future of
scientific discovery.

1922

D67 Allen, Philip Schuyler. "Preface." In <u>Twenty Thousand</u>
<u>Leagues Under the Sea</u>, by Jules Verne. Chicago and New
York: Rand, McNally and Company, pp. ix-x.

If there had been no Verne, the tales of H. Rider
Haggard, Rudyard Kipling, Conan Doyle, and H. G. Wells
probably would not have been written. Three features of
Twenty Thousand Leagues Under the Sea make it one of the
finest books for children: Captain Nemo, the Nautilus,
and minute analysis of the submarine world. Verne acknowledged the influence of Poe's stories of "scientific
investigation into untrodden realms."

D68   Anon. "Going Jules Verne One Better." New York Times, 12
         November, section 8, p. 9.
            Compares the speed in Around the World in Eighty Days
         with present-day fact. The trip can now be made in
         seventy days.

D69   Gernsback, H. "Verne Inspires Katonah." New York Times, 27
         July, p. 16.
            In this letter to the editor, Gernsback calls attention
         to the prophetic relationship between Verne's Five Weeks
         in a Balloon and the gold seekers of Katonah in the Belgian
         Congo.

1923

D70   Levy, Georges. "An Ideal City as Described by Jules Verne."
         House Beautiful, 53 (February), 160, 208.
            Description of the city of France-Ville that Verne
         created in The Begum's Fortune.

1924

D71   Metcalfe, Cranstoun. "Translator's Note." In The Lighthouse
         at the End of the World, by Jules Verne. New York: G.
         Howard Watt, n.p.
            Verne will be remembered as a prophet rather than as a
         writer of romances. The "supreme merit" of his books is
         the plausibility of the mechanical inventions. However,
         The Lighthouse at the End of the World demonstrates that
         Verne was also master of the adventure story. The pure
         action, excitement, plus an element of dread create the
         novel's success.

1925

D72   Bond, F. Fraser. "Jules Verne, Master of the Improbable."
         New York Times, 4 January, section 3, p. 21.
            Review of Their Island Home, Castaways of the Flag,
         Lighthouse at the End of the World. Verne still appeals
         to the boy of today because of the "velocity and the
         variety of his narrative." "The boy reader, with his

superabundant bodily energy, craves mental playing fields
as well as material ones in which to work off his excess
animal spirits," and Verne saw to it that something was
always happening.

1926

D73 Gernsback, Hugo. "A New Sort of Magazine." Amazing Stories,
1 (April), 3.
Gernsback used Verne's tombstone as his logo, published
Verne in the early issues of Amazing Stories, and in this
prefatory piece includes Verne in a well-known definition
of the kind of fiction he was trying to promulgate in his
magazine: "By 'scientifiction' I mean the Jules Verne,
H. G. Wells, and Edgar Allan Poe type of story -- a
charming romance intermingled with scientific fact and
prophetic vision."

D74 Green, Alexander. "Introduction." In Le Tour du Monde en
Quatre-Vingts Jours, by Jules Verne. Boston: D. C. Heath
and Company, pp. xi-xviii.
By blending travel and romance with clever scientific
and geographic details, Verne became the "literary apostle
of popular science." His success is due largely to his
gift for "scientific divination." Delineation of character
is his major fault: his personages are either "caricatures
or automatons."

1927

D75 Cambiare, Celestin Pierre. "Poe and Jules Verne." In The
Influence of Edgar Allan Poe In France. New York: G. E.
Stechert and Company, pp. 241-253. Rpt. New York:
Haskell House, 1970; St. Clair Shores, Michigan: Scholarly
Press, 1971.
Verne is, "undoubtedly, the best representative of the
pseudo-scientific novel in France." Although he decided
that Poe's horrors must be lessened, Verne realized that
a combination of "Poe's rendering of mystery and strange-
ness, Dumas' humor and love of adventure," and various
qualities of his own genius would create masterpieces.
Plot elements borrowed from Poe are evident in semi-
fantastic sections of Verne's novels. An Antarctic
Mystery continues The Narrative of Arthur Gordon Pym, and
parts of "Ms Found in a Bottle" and "A Descent Into the
Maelstrom" appear in Twenty Thousand Leagues Under the Sea.
Also, "Doctor Ox's Experiment" has "many analogies" to
Poe's "The Devil in the Belfry." In this instance, Verne
substitutes gas for the devil.

D76　Knowlton, Don. "His Strange World Came True." <u>Popular Science Monthly</u>, 111 (July), 37-38, 110.
　　　　Verne's mechanical prophecies were not taken seriously by his contemporaries, perhaps because his books were "nightmares of adventure." His predictions were shrewd and errors were largely related to the nature of power utilized to run his machines. Electricity and water were chosen instead of petroleum. But was this a mistake, or is Verne ahead of our time too?

D77　Schwartz, William Leonard. <u>The Imaginative Interpretation of the Far East in Modern French Literature, 1800-1925</u>. Paris: Librarie Ancienne Honoré Champion, pp. 121-123.
　　　　Published only three years after the opening of the Suez Canal, <u>Around the World in Eighty Days</u> made "'girding the globe' fashionable." It was an indirect influence on the travels of such men as Cernuschi, Duret, and Guimet. <u>The Tribulations of a Chinaman in China</u> contains inaccuracies and "references to fictitious books." Verne pictures the Chinese as extremely progressive and "magnifies their good qualities."

1928

D78　Anon. "Lost Jules Verne Script Discovered." <u>New York World</u>, 18 September, p. 16.
　　　　In this 1903 manuscript, Verne "reveals that he spent weeks in research to make his fictitious inventions scientifically plausible," but he disclaims credit for inspiring many of the inventions that have revolutionized the world.

D79　Dean, Richard. "One Hundred Years of Jules Verne." <u>Mentor</u>, 16 (June), 18-19.
　　　　Brief notice focusing on Verne's commitment to a life of fantasy. He was the same as all boys till age twelve, but "for him the fantasies lived on. He definitely resisted disillusionment. To the end of his days he resisted it. . . . All along his life journey scientific achievement tempted him on one side, adventure lured on the other. He chose to keep a path between, a path leading nowhere, yet everywhere."

D80　Kaempffert, Waldemar. "Science Now Wears Jules Verne's Halo." <u>New York Times</u>, 5 February, section 5, pp. 4-5, 20.
　　　　Verne is more ingenious than imaginative, and he did not pretend to an extraordinary imagination or a profound knowledge of science. He wrote books of wonder in which whole pages are popular articles on science. His success lay in the piling up of exciting incidents. He was a master sensationalist and architect who knew how to attain Himalayan heights by pyramiding episodes.

D81   Lockhart, R. N. B.   "Jules Verne as Prophet."   The New
        Statesman, 30 (11 February), 560-561.
            Short account marking the hundredth anniversary of
        Verne's birth.   Verne appeals to all peoples because of
        the universal desire to see the future.   His genius lies
        in the extraordinary accuracy of his prophecies; practical-
        ly everything he predicted is now commonplace.   As science
        reduces the wild improbabilities of his imagination to
        realities, however, his books will lose their main
        attraction.

D82   Slagle, E. Harvey.   "The Father of Science Fiction Has a
        Centenary."   New York Times Book Review, 5 February, p. 5.
            Focuses on the scientific and realistic aspects of
        Verne's work, and his appeal to the young.   "His dreams
        of yesterday have become the realities of today."

D83   Souday, Paul.   "A Rush of Anniversaries in Paris."   New York
        Times Book Review, 4 March, p. 34.
            Brief notice of the hundredth anniversary of Verne's
        birth.   He cannot properly be called a great author for
        he has "no more style than Dumas Père."   But he told
        stories well, had a good imagination and scientific in-
        tuition, and was a "marvelous anticipator."

1929

D84   Martyn, T. J. C.   "Jules Verne: The Prophet of Aviation."
        New York Times Magazine, 27 October, pp. 13, 22.
            Uses the occasion of the French Geographical Society's
        acclaim of Verne's contribution to modern aeronautics to
        look carefully at Verne's airship in Robur the Conqueror
        (Clipper of the Clouds).   Verne had an amazing knowledge
        of aeronautics for his time, was extraordinarily logical,
        and had great powers of observation and deduction, but
        what he did most of all was "to sow the seed of airminded-
        ness."

1930

D85   Maurois, André.   "Jules Verne Sets the Pace for Modern
        Adventure."   New York Times Magazine, 23 March, pp. 6, 22.
            Concentrating on Verne's prophetic vision, Maurois
        relates a conversation between several contemporary French
        scientists who agree that all modern life is "like a story
        from Jules Verne."   Verne anticipated the automobile in
        The Steam House, wrote of talking film in The Castle of the
        Carpathians, suggested the possibility of submarines,
        dirigibles, hydroplanes, bombs carrying poisonous gases,
        and television.   Also mentioned is Verne's admiration for
        Edgar Poe, especially the American author's studies of
        hallucination and his inventive genius.   Poe may have
        inspired "Martin Paz" and "Master Zacharias."

D86 Peet, Creighton. "The Mysterious Island." <u>Outlook and
Independent</u>, 154 (1 January), 33.

    Short, unfavorable review of the movie. "Jules Verne
may not have been accurate in every detail, but he always
built up his stories so that they sounded possible. <u>The
Mysterious Island</u> is even less possible than Little Nemo
used to be."

D87 Thomson, Valentine. <u>Briand: Man of Peace</u>. New York:
Covici-Friede, pp. 22-29.

    A friend of Aristide Briand was fortunate enough to
have Verne as his guardian, and thus Briand became very
well acquainted with Verne and had access to his house.
Verne made Briand a character in <u>Two Years' Holiday</u>. This
leader of the French Labor Party saw that Verne "knew what
it was to work and to be satisfied."

1931

D88 Anon. "Jules Verne's Novels Form a Shelf of Staples."
<u>Publishers' Weekly</u>, 119 (11 April), 1914-1915.

    Sales of the Everyman and Burt reprints of Verne's
novels indicate that the most popular titles are <u>Twenty
Thousand Leagues Under the Sea</u>, <u>Five Weeks in a Balloon</u>,
<u>The Mysterious Island</u>.

D89 Owen, Russell. "Phileas Fogg Does It Again -- In 37 Days."
<u>New York Times</u>, 15 March, section 5, pp. 4-5, 16.

    Fogg and Passepartout are revived again for a brief
fictional account of the modern trip around the world.

1932

D90 Weisinger, Mortimer. "The History of Science Fiction -- Part
VII." <u>The Time Traveller</u> (fanzine), 1 (August), 12; 1
(September), 2.

    "Jules Verne was the world's greatest scientific
prophet." Verne's real service was that he illumined the
path, inspiring hordes to build as he urged. We have the
submarine as in <u>Twenty Thousand Leagues Under the Sea</u>, the
automobile as in <u>The Steam House</u>, and the airplane as in
<u>Clipper of the Clouds</u>, as well as electricity, the phono-
graph, the value of oxygen as a stimulant, concentrated
foods, and marvelous weapons.

1933

D91 Parsons, Coleman O. "Lunar Craters in Science and Fiction:
Kepler, Verne, and Wells." <u>Notes and Queries</u>, 164 (20
May), 346-348.

    Comments on the appearance of Kepler's theory in Verne
and Wells. Wells was familiar with Verne, but he must
have known about Kepler's theory from other sources.

1934

D92 Morley, Christopher. "The Bowling Green." Saturday Review
of Literature, 10 (7 April), 609.
The best parts of A Floating City are in the illustrations of the Great Eastern and her passengers.

D93 Walbridge, Earle F. "Jules Verne Over Here." Saturday
Review of Literature, 10 (14 April), 631.
Short letter-to-the-editor type article in "The Bowling
Green" section mentions Verne's visit to America.
Probably a followup to the Morley article (D92).

D94 Wells, H. G. "Preface." In Seven Famous Novels by H. G.
Wells. New York: Alfred A. Knopf, p. vii.
Rather than being an "English Jules Verne," Wells
contends that there is "no literary resemblance" between
the Frenchman's "anticipatory inventions" and his
"fantasies." Verne deals with possible inventions,
discoveries, and forecasts while Wells's stories are
"exercises of the imagination" that explore impossibilities.

1935

D95 Maurois, André. Prophets and Poets. Tr. Hamish Miles. New
York: Harper and Brothers, p. 81.
Wells's use of symbolism distinguishes him from Verne.
Whereas Verne "sought to prove nothing," the marvelous
for Wells is "always utopian and satiric in essence."

1936

D96 Williamson, J. E. Twenty Years Under the Sea. Boston: Hale,
Cushman and Flint, pp. 118-223.
The production of the first undersea film, a version of
Twenty Thousand Leagues Under the Sea, is chronicled by
the innovator of underwater photography and motion pictures.
The creation of the "unique and extraordinary props" as
well as changes in Verne's story necessitated by a technical
inability, in 1915, to reproduce the novelist's imagination
are detailed. The sequel, a lavish million-dollar production of The Mysterious Island, became merely a "silent
spectre" as talkies beat it to the box office.

1938

D97 Casteret, Norbert. Ten Years Under the Earth. Tr. Barrows
Mussey. New York: Greystone Press, p. xiv.
In the preface to this book, the famous underground
explorer indicates that his "passion for caverns is a
vague and infinitely distant nostalgia for vanished aeons

when men lived in caves," but he also adds: "almost as
influential as my natural penchant was a marvelous book,
which impressed and fascinated me more than any other --
Jules Verne's Journey to the Center of the Earth. I have
re-read it many times, and I confess I sometimes re-read
it still, each time finding anew the joys and enthusiasm
of my childhood."

1940

D98 Allott, Kenneth. Jules Verne. London: Crescent Press. Rpt.
Port Washington, NY: Kennikat Press, 1970.
The first English critical biography. Verne's life and
works are discussed in four periods (1828-1863, 1863-1870,
1870-1886, 1886-1905), and in the context of the crucial
clash in the nineteenth century between positivism and
romanticism. The books written by 1870 set the key patterns
for the Voyages extraordinaires, and are his best works.
After the fall of the Empire, the death of his father, and
his move to Amiens, he wrote "tirelessly, like a mongoose
running backwards and forwards along the wirenetting in
front of its cage." Verne was a Peter Pan creating a
childlike world in which there were action, adventure,
curiosity, mystery, and practical jokes without real evil
or real women. He was popular because people sought escape
from contemporary ugliness. "Verne stimulated beliefs in
progress, science and industrialism, while he provided an
escape from the impersonality and squalor" of the early
industrial age.

D99 Anon. "Hitler Prototype Found in Old Jules Verne Novel."
New York Times, 5 May, p. 43.
Refers to Herr Schulze in The Begum's Fortune, who
develops a racial theory and scourges the world.

D100 Anon. "Jules Verne Society Formed." New York Times, 22 May,
p. 21.
Very brief notice of the founding and aims of this
American society.

D101 Anon. "The Visions of Jules Verne, Romance of Man's
Mechanical Progress, A Myth Maker of Modern Science."
Times Literary Supplement (London), No. 2027 (7 December),
p. 616.
Review of Kenneth Allott's Jules Verne. Discusses the
romantic aspects of Verne's life and work and regrets the
loss of the potential for a "romance of the machine."
Rather than machines, it is the rare man of imagination,
Verne being one of the greatest, who inspires the romantic
sensibility. See D98.

1941

D102 Orwell, George. "Two Glimpses of the Moon." New Statesman
      and Nation, new series, 21 (18 January), 64.
            Review of Allott's biography (D98). "Like most
      writers, Verne was one of those people to whom nothing
      ever happens. . . . It seems strange that so unliterary
      a writer. . .should have behind him the familiar history
      of a nineteenth century Frenchman of letters." Verne
      belongs to the "Command Over Nature" early scientific
      period, but one result of his later disillusionment is
      the disappearance of sympathetic Englishmen.

D103 Pryce-Jones, Alan. Review of Jules Verne, by Kenneth Allott.
      Horizon, 3 (January), 76, 78.
            Verne's literature is strangely English: "middle-class,
      imaginative, unfashionable, permanent best-seller."
      Allott (D98) avoids the actual Verne and substitutes a
      "model of a nineteenth-century thinker and writer."
      Verne should be studied by a "connoisseur of the fantas-
      tic." The novelist was a "wonderfully competent writing-
      machine with a splendid fecundity of imagination."

1942

D104 Lafleur, Laurence J. "Marvelous Voyages -- I, III, IV."
      Popular Astronomy, 50 (January), 16-21; (April), 196-198;
      (June), 315-317; (August), 377-379; (October), 431-433.
            A series of articles that briefly describes and lists
      "errors" in the physics, chemistry, biology, and astronomy
      in Verne's Journey to the Center of the Earth, From the
      Earth to the Moon, and Around the Moon. Readers are
      challenged to find and submit additional instances of
      scientific misconceptions or faulty calculations. No
      responses were subsequently published.

D105 West, Jack. "A Jules Verne Fantasy." Fantastic Adventures,
      4 (August), 222-226.
            Uses Verne as a springboard for discussion of submarines
      in warfare. "Jules Verne never intended that the submarine
      become a tool of war. He had always thought of it as an
      efficient means of ocean transportation."

1943

D106 Anon. Review of Jules Verne: The Biography of an Imagina-
      tion, by George H. Waltz. New Yorker, 18 (13 February),
      70-71.
            This short review comments that Waltz's biography
      (D109) is "fascinating" in its account of Verne's influence
      on later writers.

D107   Anon.   "Topics of the Times." New York Times, 5 May, p.
       26.
           Comparison of Around the World in Eighty Days with a
       man who actually made the trip in 160 hours flying time.

D108   Berger, Meyer. "To the Moon Via Pen and Paper." New York
       Times Book Review, 21 February, p. 9.
           Almost all the "engines and vessels" Verne conjured
       up with his "crystal-ball brain" a hundred years ago are
       now part of the general scheme: heavier-than-air ships,
       the submarine, radio, television. George Waltz's Jules
       Verne: The Biography of an Imagination (D109) does
       little justice to the man, much less his imagination.
       Verne is depicted as a "disembodied thing, . . .a creature
       done in onion-skin paper."

D109   Waltz, George H., Jr. Jules Verne: The Biography of an
       Imagination. New York: Henry Holt and Company.
           This fictionalized biography attempts to trace the
       effects of Verne's adventures and prophecies on later
       scientists, writers, and the general public. Constant
       attention to insignificant details, such as street and
       theater names, results in an ineffective biography and a
       less than convincing account of Verne's influence.

D110   _____. "Jules Verne's Dreams Come True." Science Digest,
       13 (June), 26-30.
           Description of Verne's influence on such people as
       Admiral Byrd, William Beebe, Simon Lake, and Norbert
       Casteret. Condensed from Waltz's biography (D109).

1944

D111   Gould, Rupert T. "Jules Verne." In The Stargazer Talks.
       London: Geoffrey Bles, pp. 114-120.
           This talk for "The Children's Hour" B.B.C. radio
       show summarizes several of Verne's novels and draws
       biographical material from Kenneth Allott's book.

1946

D112   Anon. "Topics of the Times." New York Times, 13 June. p.
       26.
           A high naval officer commenting on the atom bomb at
       retirement hints at the possibility of "things that until
       recently appeared to be Jules Verne fantasies." His
       reference to Verne instead of Wells shows he is a member
       of the older generation and indicates that Verne's vision
       hovered closer to the earth than Wells's.

D113 Babits, Seth. "The Wonderful Dream Submarine." <u>Scholastic</u>,
      49 (23 September), 227.
          A brief comparison of the <u>Nautilus</u> with actual
      submarines. The real submarines have been developed as
      instruments of war, whereas Verne's submarine was a
      refuge from human bickering and injustice, a source of
      tranquillity.

D114 Borges, Jorge Luis. "El Primer Wells." Collected in his
      <u>Otras inquisiciones</u>. Buenos Aires: Emece, 1960, pp.
      125-128. Rpt. <u>Other Inquisitions</u>. University of Texas,
      1964. Rpt. <u>H. G. Wells: The Critical Heritage</u>, ed.
      Patrick Parrinder. London: Routledge and Kegan Paul,
      1972, pp. 330-332.
          Wells and Verne are "incompatible." Verne is a
      "journeyman" whose stories for adolescents deal with
      things that are possible. Occupied with the improbable
      or the impossible, Wells's more substantial work is
      capable of ambiguity. Written on the occasion of Wells's
      death.

D115 Kaempffert, Waldemar. "Evangelist of Utopia." <u>Saturday
      Review of Literature</u>, 29 (31 August), 8-9.
          Both Verne and Wells are descendants of Poe, and both
      make the most of the romantic wonder surrounding science
      in the late nineteenth century. But Verne was practical,
      writing "Facts That Every Boy Should Know," and Wells had
      more imagination and was inclined to sociology. While
      Verne wrote thrillers mechanically to the end of his life,
      Wells dropped them because he had a social mission to
      perform. Verne had little social sense, but Wells had a
      sense of social injustice and was imbued with the idea
      of Progress and social change brought about by science.

D116 Montgomery, Elizabeth. "Fiction That Became Fact." In <u>The
      Story Behind Great Books</u>. New York: Dodd, Mead and
      Company, pp. 108-112.
          A short sketch of Verne's preparation for <u>Twenty
      Thousand Leagues Under the Sea</u>, written for children.

<u>1947</u>

D117 Anon. "Introduction." In <u>Frritt-Flacc</u>, by Jules Verne.
      New York: Futuria House, pp. i-ii.
          It is his short stories, which are unknown to most
      readers, that contain many of Verne's most remarkable
      prophecies including "television, experimental music,
      electronic street-illumination, monopoly capitalism,
      moving sidewalks." A fantasy, "Frritt-Flacc" is,
      perhaps, "the weirdest tale Verne ever penned."

D118 Bailey, J. O. <u>Pilgrims Through Space and Time: Trends</u>
<u>and Patterns in Scientific and Utopian Fiction</u>. New
York: Argus Books, passim. Rpt. Westport, CT:
Greenwood Press, 1972.

Many of Verne's works are mentioned in relatively
brief fashion in various parts of this book, which
provides a history of science fiction through 1946 with
consideration of story content, style, conventions, and
ideology. Verne and the effort to prepare for the Machine
Age in light of evolutionary theory are seen as the two
main influences in the period from 1871-94. Verne's
importance is due "to the use he made of invention as a
means to a new kind of geographic story, voyage of
wonders, and exuberant adventure."

D119 Fisher, Clyde. "Introduction." In <u>From the Earth to the</u>
<u>Moon Including the Sequel, Round the Moon</u>, by Jules
Verne. New York: Didier, pp. v-vi.

Fisher, honorary curator of Astronomy and of the
Hayden Planetarium, American Museum of Natural History,
believes Verne had an "active imagination that antici-
pates scientific research." Verne was a pioneer in
creating "genre word-paintings of imaginary voyages."
His "selenography," or geography, is largely accurate,
and the novelist foresaw "the achievements of scientific
and mechanical invention."

1948

D120 Nicolson, Marjorie Hope. <u>Voyages to the Moon</u>. New York:
Macmillan Company, pp. 161, 243-247.

<u>From the Earth to the Moon</u> is seen in the context of
the many other world journeys which preceded it. Verne's
contribution to nineteenth-century fiction is the exact-
ness of his science; his stories are less flights of
fancy than straightforward reporting. There is a direct
connection between Michel Ardan and Cyrano de Bergerac,
and the philosophy of the novel includes the familiar
microcosm-macrocosm emphasis. Verne's description of
the moon is more Kepler than Poe, but he even goes beyond
Kepler in describing the dark side.

1949

D121 Eagan, Edward P. F. "Introduction." In <u>Round the World</u>
<u>in Eighty Days</u>, by Jules Verne. New York: Didier,
pp. 7-9.

Eagan, president of the Circumnavigators Club, made an
around the world trip in 147 hours, 15 minutes. He
explains that Verne's novel inspired many people to try
to break Phileas Fogg's record. The fad was started by
George Francis Train. His time was beaten by Nellie Bly.

D122 Hillyer, Robert. <u>The Death of Captain Nemo: A Narrative
      Poem</u>. New York: Alfred A. Knopf.
           Captain Nemo's demise, as dramatized by Verne in <u>The
      Mysterious Island</u>, serves as the inspiration of this
      poem. Two American sailors stop off at the volcanic
      island just in time for Nemo's death. The captain's
      life, from fatherless boyhood, is traced from the journal
      he leaves. The sailors discover that Nemo was guided by
      love for a lady referred to only as the "Princess";
      however, he was, for some years, under the "malign in-
      fluence of a woman of occult powers," called the "Witch."
      The sailors sink the <u>Nautilus</u> with Nemo's body lying in
      state in the main cabin. Nemo's spirit rises to guide
      the sailors' ship.

D123 Holcomb, Claire. "The S-F Phenomenon in Literature."
      <u>Saturday Review of Literature</u>, 32 (28 May), 9-10.
           Verne kept a sharp eye on laboratories and journals,
      so his fiction was always just a few years ahead of
      reality.

D124 McKeithan, D. M. "Mark Twain's <u>Tom Sawyer Abroad</u> and Jules
      Verne's <u>Five Weeks in a Balloon</u>." <u>University of Texas
      Studies in English</u>, 28 (1949), 256-270.
           Catalogs the similarities between these two journeys
      by balloon over the Sahara Desert. Details that Twain
      may have borrowed and adapted include: attacks by wild
      animals, the witnessing of a caravan buried alive in a
      sandstorm, illness from extreme heat alleviated by
      ascension to a cooler atmosphere, splendid rescues,
      navigation in a dense fog, and ridicule of the balloon's
      inventor.

D125 Streeter, Harold Wade. "Introduction." In <u>Vingt Mille
      Lieues Sous Les Mers</u>, by Jules Verne. Boston: D. C.
      Heath, pp. ix-xv.
           As a result of his interest in scientific matters,
      Verne gave new direction to the imaginary voyage. The
      works of Poe, Cooper, Scott, and Dumas helped shape
      Verne's style. All of these writers created "impossibly
      dauntless heroes." Captain Nemo has the attributes of
      a Romantic hero: love of nature and liberty, wanderlust,
      misanthropy, egocentricity.

<u>1950</u>

D126 Carlisle, Norman and Madelyn Carlisle. "Jules Verne Un-
      canny Prophet." In <u>Five Weeks in a Balloon</u>, by Jules
      Verne. New York: Didier, pp. 3-6.
           Among the technological wonders predicted by Verne
      more than half a century before their existence are

television, radio, the telephone, atomic power, the
helicopter, and high-speed air liners. His prophecies
have a "contemporary ring" and incredible accuracy. The
most amazing anticipations were in the areas of transportation and communications. Marconi, Simon Lake,
William Beebe, Auguste Piccard, and Admiral Byrd acknowledge Verne as a source for their ideas.

D127 Derleth, August. "Introduction." In Beyond Time and Space.
New York: Pellegrini and Cudahy, p. ix.
Derleth credits Verne with producing the "most
prophetic fiction" in the genre of science fiction.
This collection includes a "slightly edited" text of
"Dr. Ox's Experiment" on pages 166-204.

D128 Tompkins, Harry G. "Jules Verne: Uncanny Prophet."
Coronet, 27 (January), 152-155.
Verne anticipated scientific headlines by half a
century. The phrase "like something out of Jules Verne"
is now fixed in our language. Deals briefly with the
giant telescope, helicopter, paper, electricity, submarine, radio, and atomic power.

1951

D129 Ley, Willy. Rockets, Missiles, and Space Travel. New
York: Viking Press, pp. 40-42, 262-264.
Verne's moon novels acquainted the public "with the
fact that a trip to the moon is a question of velocity."
The gun is merely a literary device, but it teaches a
lot about the actual problem. "If the experiment had
actually been made, the experimenters would have found
to their great surprise, that their ball would have
landed 100 feet from the muzzle," and the passengers
would have been spread into a thin film. Verne's ideas
are subjected to scientific scrutiny.

D130 Ronne, Finn. "Introduction." In The Adventures of Captain
Hatteras, by Jules Verne. New York: Didier, pp. v-vi.
Ronne, a noted Antarctic explorer, finds Verne's
"thrilling, graphic imaginary voyage into the Arctic
extremely accurate." Verne must have thoroughly studied
the geography and conditions experienced in polar explorations. His realistic descriptions of topographic
features are as convincing as those in contemporary
accounts. The areas reached by Verne's ship The Forward
were actually discovered in 1909.

1952

D131   Klots, Allen, Jr. "Introduction." In Twenty Thousand
       Leagues Under the Sea, by Jules Verne. New York: Dodd,
       Mead [unpaged, 8 pp.].
            The increasing preoccupation with science in the
       nineteenth century contributed to the popularity of this
       novel. More than any other individual, balloonist Felix
       Nadar influenced Verne's career. Verne obtained much of
       his knowledge of the ocean depths from Cyrus Field and
       others aboard the Great Eastern. Captain Nemo's world
       of the Nautilus is a utopia where he is master of his
       machines. However, Nemo ultimately must answer to the
       forces of Nature.

D132   Perelman, S. J. "Cloudland Revisited; Roll On, Thou Deep
       and Dark Scenario, Roll." New Yorker, 28 (16 August),
       24-27.
            The 1916 film version of Twenty Thousand Leagues Under
       the Sea, available in the film library of the Museum of
       Modern Art, is a bizarre hodgepodge of "subaqueous
       marvels," "hallucinatory plot and characters." The film
       combines three additional Verne novels: The Mysterious
       Island, Five Weeks in a Balloon, and The Steam House.
       Stuart Paton, its director, deserves homage from "votaries
       of Surrealistic film." Captain Nemo is Melville's Ahab
       "with French dressing," and the interior of the Nautilus
       is "pure early Matisse." The group that ends up on the
       Mysterious Island is the best "convocation of loonies
       anywhere."

1953

D133   Clarke, Arthur C. "Science Fiction: Preparation for the
       Age of Space." In Modern Science Fiction: Its Meaning
       and Its Future, ed. Reginald Bretnor. New York: Coward-
       McCann, pp. 207-209.
            The idea of the space gun did not originate with Verne,
       but his "projectile must be considered as the first really
       scientifically conceived space vessel." Though Verne
       writes facetiously about his mammoth cannon, others have
       actually attempted to see if there are any conditions
       under which a space gun could operate.

D134   De Camp, L. Sprague. "Imaginative Fiction and Creative
       Imagination." In Modern Science Fiction: Its Meaning
       and Its Future, ed. Reginald Bretnor. New York: Coward-
       McCann, pp. 139-140.
            The science fiction writer is often trying to convey
       an idea to the reader, and during the last century the
       straight information element predominated. "Jules Verne

71

provides his stories with an indefatigable lecturer and
an inexhaustible listener so that the former could ex-
pound the science of the time to the latter a whole
chapter at a stretch." Nowadays, one must be more subtle.

D135　　　　. Science Fiction Handbook. New York: Hermitage
House, pp. 14-15. Rpt. Philadelphia: Owlswick Press,
1975, pp. 14-15.
Verne is often cited as a prophet of scientific
advances, but he was a cautious prophet who read the
technical literature of his time and applied his readings
to his stories. "His stories have little characterization
or plot but much lively action, Gallic wit, and good-
natured satire on the supposed characteristics of various
nationalities."

D136　DeSchweinitz, Karl, Jr. "The Price System." In Man and
Modern Society, eds. Karl DeSchweinitz, Jr. and Kenneth
W. Thompson. New York: Henry Holt and Company, pp.
175-225, esp. pp. 182-186.
In a discussion of the economic problems of primitive
areas, DeSchweinitz analyzes Jules Verne's The Mysterious
Island. Engineer Cyrus Harding devises a division of
labor among the castaways. Their process of discovery on
the island leads to expanded wants and needs, so Harding
organizes them for productive activity. However, each
new project, such as brick building, demands time and
energy formerly spent on other tasks like food gathering.
The cost of the bricks, then, is food not procured.
DeSchweinitz explains that engineering skills could not
solve the economic problems of the community; they could
only facilitate construction of things valued by individuals. A balancing of values is as necessary as technical
expertise.

D137　Luce, Stanford L. Jr. "Jules Verne Moralist, Writer,
Scientist." Ph.D. dissertation, Yale University.
Following a summation of published criticism on Verne,
Luce considers Verne as Christian moralist; as a skillful
writer of "tireless imagination"; and as a scientist who,
while enthused with progress, yet feared the possibility
of man exceeding his bounds. Verne's success was due to
his sympathy with and appeal to the bourgeois middle
class. He explored new literary fields of science and
travel at an opportune time -- the height of the Industrial
Revolution. Among the few who saw society whirled along
by technological inventions, Verne recognized the coming
sacrifice of "mind and individuality. . .to the omnivorous
machine." In appendices, Luce includes plot summaries of
the novels and stories, and Verne's sources for many of
his works.

1954

D138 Allotte de la Fuÿe, Marguerite. Jules Verne. Tr. Erik de
Mauny. London: Staples Press Limited.
Biography. See E47.

D139 Anon. "Jules Verne Still Has a Tomorrow." Life, 36 (22
February), 28.
Short editorial compares Walt Disney's science in his
Twenty Thousand Leagues Under the Sea film with the novel.
"Real life is only beginning to overtake Jules Verne.
We had better complete the job before we start calling him
old-fashioned."

D140 Castle, Geoffrey. "Introduction." In Twenty Thousand
Leagues Under the Sea, by Jules Verne. London: Collins,
pp. 11-15.
Twenty Thousand Leagues Under the Sea was written in
the years 1867-70 when Verne and his public were aware
of their ambiguous feelings toward technology. Dreams
of unlimited power and speed seduced imagination, but
awareness of the implications of power "wielded by
limited intelligence" created apprehension. Verne
expressed his inner conflict in the characters Captain
Nemo and Professor Aronnax. Since his personal friends
included many scientists, Verne was equipped to make his
tales plausible, but each of his Voyages depends on a
"prime mover which could not be justified by any known
scientific fact." His audience accepted his assumptions
because they knew just enough to realize their world
contained "undisclosed marvels." Today, science fiction
writers must abandon plausibility and make "extravagant
assumptions" because the audience is technically so well
educated that it does not marvel at anything.

D141 De Camp, L. Sprague. Lost Continents: The Atlantis Theme
in History, Science, and Literature. New York: Gnome
Press, p. 256 ff. Rpt. New York: Dover Press, 1970.
In a survey of literary references, Twenty Thousand
Leagues Under the Sea is seen as responsible for the
fictional revival of Atlantis, which has made it a
standard setting in science fiction.

D142 Everson, William K. "Horror Films; Though Their Ingredients
Vary They All Depend Upon the Manipulation of Fear."
Films In Review, 5 (January), 12-23, esp. 20.
Everson notes that one of the first uses of sound "to
increase the melodramatic thrills" occurred in MGM's The
Mysterious Island, made in 1929. French "specialist of
the macabre," Maurice Tourneur, was responsible for the

production, which utilized "weirdly whirring machines, screams of terror, howling wolves, wind, thunderstorms, crashing orchestrations."

D143 Gibbs-Smith, C. H. A History of Flying. New York: Frederick A. Praeger, pp. 146-148.
      Verne was a member, along with George Sand, Nadar, Dumas, Pline, and others, of a "syndicate" to promote aviation in France. One of "the most powerful aerial propagandists," Verne created the helicopter ship, or "aeronef," named "Albatross," in Clipper of the Clouds. Its equipment included navigational instruments, dynamite, a library, printing press, an india-rubber boat, but no parachutes because Robur, the captain, did not believe in such accidents. Includes an illustration of "Albatross."

D144 Kent, George. "Mister Imagination." Saturday Review, 37 (5 June), 9-10, 39-40. Rpt. Great Adventures In Science, by Helen and Samuel Rappaport. New York: Harper and Brothers, 1956, pp. 303-310.
      Few twentieth-century wonders were not foreseen by Verne. Admiral Byrd, Simon Lake, Auguste Piccard, and Marconi acknowledged his work as a source of inspiration. Kent provides anecdotes from Verne's life including his friendship with Alexander Dumas and the worldwide excitement generated by the exploits of Phileas Fogg. A Paris newspaper eulogized Verne with brevity: "The old story teller is dead. It is like the passing of Santa Claus."

1955

D145 Anon. "A Plush Parlor For Captain Nemo." Life, 38 (10 January), 42-43.
      Picture spread on the lavish interior of the Nautilus designed for the Disney movie.

D146 Anon. "What Verne Conceived." New York Times, 7 June, p. 32.
      Brief notice marking the fiftieth anniversary of Verne's death. Many of his inventions have become reality, almost as many have become obsolete, but the trip to the moon is still to come.

D147 Bishop, Claire Huchet. "Children and Science Fiction." Commonweal, 63 (18 November), 172-174.
      Verne's work retains appeal for both children and adults because his stories deal with "essential human problems," specifically, freedom -- freedom from war, colonization, tyranny, slavery, and from the "technocrat

totalitarian city." Among those who have acknowledged a
debt to Verne are Savorgnan de Brazza, Lyautey, Tolstoy,
Gorki, and Byrd.

D148 Bradbury, Ray. "Marvels and Miracles -- Pass It On!" New
York Times Magazine, 20 March, pp. 26-27, 56, 58.
Imaginary conversation with Verne on the fiftieth
anniversary of his death. "To clear the wilderness for
Man" is the single motive of all his "Geographical
Romances." Man travels to know and to know is to survive,
but society needs the teller of tales to run ahead and
beckon it on. The search for meaning and survival should
now move to space; the only obstacle is the wilderness in
man himself that causes him to dream of mushroom clouds.
See E602.

D149 Genet. "Letter From Paris." New Yorker, 31 (9 April),
112-113.
A brief account of the celebration in Paris that
honored Verne on the fiftieth anniversary of his death.
Participating scientists consider Verne's genius to be
his "idea that science would dominate modern society."

D150 Liberatore, E. K. "Verne's Helicopter." New York Times,
10 April, section 6, p. 19.
Reply to Bradbury's article (D148) that calls attention to the men from whom Verne got his ideas about the
helicopter.

D151 Willams, Beryl and Samuel Epstein. "Jules Verne, Spur of
the Space Ship Builders." In The Rocket Pioneers: On
the Road to Space. New York: Julian Messner, Inc., pp.
31-51.
Brief description of space travel before Verne, and a
description of his life with emphasis on From the Earth
to the Moon. In this novel Verne stated the basic problem
in space travel -- obtaining the sufficiently high rate
of speed -- and hinted at the use of rockets. "The
rocket pioneers of the twentieth century have admitted,
almost to a man, that their reading of Verne's book fired
their own minds with dreams of space travel, and directed
their energies and imaginations toward studies that might
someday make voyages in space a real possibility."

1956

D152 Anon. "The Absolute Utmost." Nation, 183 (1 December),
470.
Around the World in Eighty Days has been praised in
ultimate terms. The New York Times declares bluntly

that "Michael Todd's show makes this a better world."
The <u>Christian Science Monitor</u> summed it up with "magna-
gorgeous," while the World-Telegram and Sun leveled a
stunned "WHEE-EEEE." Max Leibman judged it "the miracle
of miracles."

D153   Anon.   "The Camera on Wings." <u>Newsweek</u>, 48 (29 October),
       98–99.
           Brief review of the <u>Around the World in Eighty Days</u>
       film. To Verne's adventure story, producer Mike Todd
       adds the values of a travelogue, a circus, a costume
       piece, a revue, a two-reel comedy, and an all-star
       revival.

D154   Anon.   "Introduction." In <u>Around the World in Eighty Days</u>,
       by Jules Verne. New York: Grosset and Dunlap, pp.
       v–viii.
           More than merely founding the genre of science fiction,
       Verne's novels have "action, suspense, ingenious plot
       turns, fabulous characters," and also an understanding
       of human nature and a comic appreciation of human foibles.
       Like Alexandre Dumas, his writing exhibits "romantic
       excess," and "picturesque verve." One of the best
       features is the relationship between Phileas Fogg, the
       methodical Englishman, and Passepartout, Verne's alter
       ego.

D155   Anon.   "The New Pictures; 'Around the World in Eighty Days.'"
       <u>Time</u>, 68 (29 October), 72, 74.
           Todd's "slice" of Jules Verne's nineteenth-century
       "globaloney" is a mighty spectacle with a cast of 68,804
       people and 7,959 animals. S. J. Perelman's script is a
       spoof of Verne's book, which was a spoof of the English.
       Scriptwriter James Poe is contesting in court the credit
       for the screenplay.

D156   Anon.   "When the World Was Wider." <u>Life</u>, 41 (22 October),
       81–85.
           A photographic essay on Mike Todd's movie, <u>Around the
       World in Eighty Days</u>.

D157   Boucher, Anthony. "Introduction." In <u>Around the World in
       Eighty Days</u>, by Jules Verne. New York: Dodd, Mead, and
       Company, pp. v–viii.
           Although Verne is lauded as the "Father of Science
       Fiction," most of his tales are "voyages." <u>Around the
       World in Eighty Days</u> occurs in the past and depends upon
       technologies already achieved. Verne became wealthy from
       the dramatic version of this novel written by Verne and
       Adolphe d'Ennery. The character of Phileas Fogg, the

machine-like "precise, imperturbable, self-assured"
essential Englishman, is the reason for the vitality of
the story. The interactions between Fogg, Passepartout,
and Fix create "comic interplay of character."

D158   Clareson, Thomas D. "The Emergence of American Science
       Fiction, 1880-1915." Ph.D. dissertation, University of
       Pennsylvania, pp. 120-122, 225, 332.
           Verne and H. Rider Haggard influenced the transforma-
       tion of the "imaginary voyage" into the American "lost
       race" novel. Elements from Verne in the latter fiction
       include "lengthy descriptions of natural phenomena and,
       only occasionally, mechanical devices; a hero who dis-
       cussed accurately the latest scientific theories and
       speculations." Verne also inspired the "boy-inventor"
       stories typified by Lu Senarens's Frank Reade Jr. tales.
       Haggard and Verne are the "most pervasive influences"
       in the science of science fiction.

D159   Cohen, Victor. "Jules Verne." Contemporary Review, 190
       (October), 220-224.
           A compact overview of Verne's life. He "novelized"
       faith in science, stood at the crossroads between
       Romanticism and Realism, saw no conflict with religion,
       and exalted courage and nobility. "He remains the Homer
       of youth, placing before their vision vistas of chal-
       lenging wonder."

D160   Dugan, James. Man Explores the Sea. London: Hamish
       Hamilton, pp. 150-158.
           Information on John Williamson, who filmed Twenty
       Thousand Leagues Under the Sea with special underwater
       equipment despite a series of incredible accidents.

D161   Evans, I. O. Jules Verne: Master of Science Fiction.
       London: Sidgwick and Jackson.
           A twenty-five page introduction precedes selections
       from fifteen Verne works. The introduction discusses
       such matters as Verne's relations with Poe, Wells, Scott,
       Cooper, and Defoe; his fallacies and tendency to "date";
       his satiric humor, idealism, reluctance to dwell on sex
       and violence, surprise endings, and religious conviction.
       Verne's "besetting sin" is overloading, physically and
       mentally, and his great strengths are austerity and
       religious faith. See D182.

D162   Goodman, Ezra. "Rounding Up Stars in 80 Ways." Life, 41
       (22 October), 87-88, 91-92.
           Tells how producer Mike Todd got such stars as
       Fernandel, Noel Coward, John Gielgud, Marlene Dietrich,
       Frank Sinatra, and Red Skelton to play in Around the
       World in Eighty Days.

D163 Hartung, Philip T. "The Screen; Beaver!" <u>Commonweal</u>, 65 (9
November), 151-152.
In the prologue to the film <u>Around the World in Eighty
Days</u>, Edward R. Murrow comments on Jules Verne and the
changing times. Clips from Georges Méliès's fantastic
silent film, <u>A Trip to the Moon</u>, and 1956 shots of a
rocket launching at White Sands, New Mexico follow.
Verne would have been surprised at S. J. Perelman's
amusing script, Victor Young's delightful score, and
Todd's technical production methods. The movie is a
travelogue, an adventure thriller, a satiric spoof on
nationalities, and a game for viewers.

D164 Hatch, Robert. "Films." <u>Nation</u>, 183 (10 November), 417-418.
The mammoth size and scope of Mike Todd's <u>Around the
World in Eighty Days</u> drives the viewer to look for something man-size. This is found in David Niven's portrayal
of Phileas Fogg. His ability to make a "global race
against time as unremarkable as a trip to the barber" is
part of the jest, but the monotony is "dramatically
catastrophic." The highlight of the film is the performance of Cantinflas with his "small, athletic body
and an original turn of irony."

D165 Holmes, H. H. Review of <u>Jules Verne: His Life</u>, by Catherine
O. Peare. <u>New York Herald Tribune Book Review</u>, 13 May,
p. 36.
Many imaginary conversations with Verne are included
in this biography for young teens. Attention is given
to Verne's planning for his famous books and the influence
of Scott, Poe, and Cooper. <u>See</u> D172.

D166 Knight, Damon. Review of <u>Journey to the Center of the Earth</u>.
<u>Infinity Science Fiction</u>, 1 (October), 69.
Those for whom Verne is associated with Méliès's
primitive movies will find that the Willis F. Bradley
translation is not creaky or awkward in the slightest.
The work has no conventional plot, but it is filled
adroitly with spectacle.

D167 Kurnitz, Harry. "The Antic Arts: Movies; 'Around the World'
With Mike Todd." <u>Holiday</u>, 20 (October), 77, 112.
<u>Around the World in Eighty Days</u> is produced on a
"scale reminiscent of Cecil B. DeMille and the Emperor
Nero." Todd built his spectacle "onto the slender Jules
Verne plot." S. J. Perelman's screenplay arranges the
story so that plot and characters play second and third
fiddle to extravaganza.

D168 MacKenzie, Norman. "Four Million Words Without a Ghost."
      New Statesman and Nation, 52 (15 September), 320-321.
          I. O. Evans's argument in Jules Verne: Master of
      Science Fiction (D161) that Verne is a "literary curio-
      sity" is a limited view of the novelist. While Verne
      merged the adventure stories of Scott and Cooper with the
      "neo-necromancy" of Poe to accomplish "the transition
      from magic-fiction to science-fiction," his reflection
      of nineteenth-century France is more fascinating. In-
      fluenced by Saint-Simon and the views of the bourgeois
      industrialists and technologists serving under Napoleon
      III, Verne depicts their rebellion and drive for power
      just as H. G. Wells reflects the "social tensions of the
      lower middle class" in England. Verne is a "satirist and
      a utopian" in the sense that he rejects the values of his
      society but feels powerless to change its course.

D169 McCarten, John. "The World as Todd's Oyster." New Yorker,
      32 (27 October), 158-159.
          Mike Todd's movie is an "improvisation loosely adapted"
      from Verne's novel. He employed almost seventy thousand
      people and shot footage in thirteen countries. The movie
      begins with a solemn prologue delivered by Edward R.
      Murrow and clips from Méliès's 1902 French film, A Trip
      to the Moon.

D170 Meyer, Sheldon. "Introduction." In The Mysterious Island,
      by Jules Verne. New York: Grosset and Dunlap, pp. v-vi.
          A product of the "new world of industrialism," Verne
      projected extravagant inventions into the future. "No
      one has utilized scientific advancement more skillfully
      in fiction." In The Mysterious Island, Verne's most
      interesting novel, Cyrus Harding and companions transform
      a primeval island into an "industrial beehive." None of
      the inventions seem contrived, since Verne carefully
      explains how everything is built from raw materials.

D171 Morehouse, Ward. "Mike Todd: Broadway's Man in Motion."
      Theatre Arts, 40 (October), 17-19.
          Todd's film of Around the World in Eighty Days is "not
      just a picture; it's show business. . . . There's flesh
      and blood theatre in it, and that's what I love." Todd
      goes on to say that it's "a show on film. . .designed for
      theatre audiences. . .to capture the spirit and feel of
      the theatre."

D172 Peare, Catherine O. Jules Verne: His Life. New York:
      Henry Holt and Company.
          Drawing material from the studies of Allott, Allotte
      de la Fuÿe, and Waltz, Peare creates a fictionalized

biography of Verne for children aged nine to twelve.
While no new factual material is presented, the account
reflects the dedication and diligent work through which
Verne achieved fame.

D173   Pratt, Fletcher. "Introduction." In Twenty Thousand
       Leagues Under the Sea, by Jules Verne. Los Angeles:
       Plantin Press for Members of the Limited Editions Club,
       pp. vii-xi.
           The process of writing science fiction is not very
       different from that of historical fiction; however, the
       results are distinct. The science fiction story concerns
       the future, where each step is into the unknown. Twenty
       Thousand Leagues Under the Sea has defects as a novel;
       plot elements are left unresolved and characters are not
       delineated. But Verne's imagined devices are "propheti-
       cally accurate." He was "far better at scientific anti-
       cipation than H. G. Wells."

D174   Speicher, Charlotte Bilkey. "New Films From Books; 'Twenty
       Thousand Leagues Under the Sea.'" Library Journal, 80
       (22 October), 555, 578.
           Verne's contrived plausibility, which permits suspen-
       sion of disbelief, is lost in the Buena Vista/Walt Disney
       movie. This film is a stock sea adventure yarn with
       "suggestions of atomic energy" and its use in a "brave
       new world." Ned Land (Kirk Douglas) is directed solely
       for laughs; he shares the camera with a trained seal.

D175   _____. "New Films From Books; 'Around the World in Eighty
       Days.'" Library Journal, 81 (15 November), 2676.
           Verne must be sending "celestial applause" to Todd, a
       "20th century imagination of like proportions." Superb
       aspects of the film include S. J. Perelman's "satirical
       script," Cantinflas's miming, Victor Young's "magnificently
       melodic and impishly mischievous" musical score, and the
       "bits" played by fifty famous stars.

D176   Walsh, Moira. "Films; 'Around the World in Eighty Days.'"
       America, 96 (3 November), 140.
           The United Artists/Mike Todd film will be recorded in
       film history as the longest (2 hours, 58 minutes) and
       most expensive ($7 million) movie ever made with tongue
       in cheek. Todd, who transformed Verne's novel into a
       "combination travelog, period piece, comic adventure
       story and five-ring circus," never previously produced
       a film. The presence of distinguished extras adds "just
       the right note of extravagance and calculated lunacy."
       Scriptwriter S. J. Perelman's single alteration in Phileas
       Fogg's itinerary is a jaunt by balloon.

D177 Weinbaum, Martha. "Around the World in Eighty Days."
      Collier's, 17 February, pp. 63–66.
            Verne's novel is tailor-made for the grandiose treat-
      ment given by producer Mike Todd in the film version.
      The journey is a perfect vehicle for the appearance of
      fifty top stars in cameo roles.

1957

D178 Angoff, Charles. "Introduction." In Twenty Thousand
      Leagues Under the Sea, by Jules Verne. New York: Fine
      Editions Press, pp. v–vii.
            Twenty Thousand Leagues Under the Sea is the first
      major successful science fiction novel, and it is still
      the best due to its tight organization, swift movement,
      and daring imaginary leaps into the unknown. Romance
      between man and woman is ignored in lieu of romance
      "between the human mind and the glorious world without."

D179 Anon. "Rifts in the Moonscapes." Time, 70 (5 August),
      78–79.
            A review of I. O. Evans's Jules Verne: Master of
      Science Fiction (D161) that takes issue with Evans's
      pronouncement that Verne is now "humdrum." Verne's
      classics are sustained by the "Homeric nature of his
      heroes, villains, and imagined perils," while readers
      are awed by the "precision and brilliance of his descrip-
      tions."

D180 Becker, May Lamberton. "Introduction, How This Book Came to
      be Written." In The Mysterious Island, by Jules Verne.
      Cleveland: World Publishing Company, pp. 7–10.
            Verne's "adventure literature" may include the fantas-
      tic, but his starting point is always scientific fact.
      The Mysterious Island, one of literature's best "island"
      stories, presents a group of men who must use their
      knowledge and courage to utilize the abundant raw mate-
      rials available to them.

D181 Boucher, Anthony. Review of Off On a Comet. Magazine of
      Fantasy and Science Fiction, 13 (December), 95.
            This is "Verne's only novel to voyage farther into
      space than the moon; and one hates to confess that its
      science is wholly preposterous and its fiction so thin
      in character and plot that one can hardly believe that
      the same man wrote Around the World in Eighty Days four
      years earlier."

D182 Cotts, S. Review of Jules Verne, Master of Science Fiction,
      by I. O. Evans. Amazing Stories, 31 (November), 121.

Very brief notice. "Those who have been bottle fed
on the slick writing in some of our present-day magazines
may be a bit annoyed" at Verne's style, but they should
remember that he was setting precedent rather than
following it. See D161.

D183 Evans, Ernestine. "Dreamer." Saturday Review, 40 (9
February), 14.
Very brief notice of Marguerite Allotte de la Fuÿe's
biography (D138, E47). "Verne was a humanist, not a
scientist but a respecter of science. He can still
lift readers by his imagination out of fear into freedom."

D184 Holmes, H. H. Review of Jules Verne, Master of Science
Fiction, by I. O. Evans. New York Herald Tribune Book
Review, 18 August, p. 9.
In this collection Evans's selection of excerpts from
Verne's Voyages extraordinaires emphasizes the science,
now dated, and neglects the fiction, which retains its
"incomparable zest." Evans uses the "wretched" original
translations. See D161, D182.

D185 Miller, P. Schuyler. Review of Journey to the Center of
the Earth. Analog, 58 (January), 158.
Verne does not fall into the trap that Edgar Rice
Burroughs did, as many people believe, of putting his
subterranean world on the inner surface of a hollow
sphere.

D186 Moore, Patrick. "The Genius of Verne." In Science and
Fiction. London: George G. Harrap and Company, Ltd.,
pp. 43-62.
It was Verne's critical attitude that made him great.
"Even with the most light-hearted of his Voyages he
always tried to keep his facts within the bounds of
reason." Journey to the Center of the Earth, From the
Earth to the Moon, and Around the Moon are discussed in
relation to contemporary scientific knowledge and theory.

D187 Partuondo, José Antonio. "Jules Verne's America." Américas,
9 (October), 30-35.
Calls attention to those stories set in North and
South America. South America "is as a rule merely a
frame for adventure and a pretext for ample geographical
description and more or less exact ethnographic references." Verne's attitude toward the United States "is
one of somewhat ironical admiration for the practical
and enterprising spirit." "Those who wish to overcome
the anguish of this hour should turn their eyes occasionally to the clear and rationalist universe of Jules Verne,
to recover their faith in the future of man."

1958

D188   Anon. "Jules Verne's Amazing Vision: Life in America in
        2890." This Week, 28 December, pp. 8-13.
             Contains a portion of Verne's "Day of an American
        Journalist in 2889 A.D."

D189   Boucher, Anthony. "Introduction." In The Mysterious Island,
        by Jules Verne. New York: Dodd, Mead and Company, [un-
        paged, 4pp.].
             In their robinsonades, Defoe and Wyss "pampered"
        their characters with provisions of supplies. "Vexed"
        by these comfortable circumstances, Verne chose to
        abandon his heroes with no equipment except the "contents
        of their pockets." The novel's success is due to three
        factors: plausible factuality, classic toughness of the
        problem, a wealth of stories interwoven in the tale of
        Man versus Island.

D190   Bracker, Milton. "Jules Verne's Fictional Nautilus Sailed
        Under Antarctic Icecap." New York Times, 9 August, p. 7.
             The feat of the real submarine Nautilus occasioned
        this article comparing it to Verne's voyage in Twenty
        Thousand Leagues Under the Sea.

D191   Brady, Charles A. "Lunatics and Selenophiles." America,
        26 July, pp. 448-449.
             Mention of From the Earth to the Moon and Around the
        Moon in a survey of personal, psychological, and literary
        interest in the moon.

D192   Evans, I. O. "Introduction." In Five Weeks in a Balloon,
        by Jules Verne. London: Associated Booksellers, pp.
        7-9.
             The "art-form of the Machine Age, science fiction"
        was inaugurated with Five Weeks in a Balloon. The novel
        decided its author's masculine style. As in many of
        Verne's novels, the satiric opening fades as the theme
        gripped the author. The conclusion is typical of the
        surprise ending based on an "unexpected technical point."
        Verne's constant striving for "matter-of-fact realism"
        is also evident.

D193   Gale, Floyd C. Review of From the Earth to the Moon and A
        Trip Around It. Galaxy, 17 (December), 102.
             "Although Verne never laid hand to experimental object,
        no single person can claim as much credit for man's
        present efforts to escape the confines of Earth."

194   Green, Roger Lancelyn. <u>Into Other Worlds: Space-Flight in
        Fiction, from Lucian to C. S. Lewis</u>. New York and
        London: Abelard Schuman, pp. 93-104. Rpt. New York:
        Arno Press, 1975.
            A summary of <u>From the Earth to the Moon</u> and <u>A Trip
        Around the Moon</u>. Verne's most glaring absurdity is the
        assumption that his space travelers could survive the
        initial shock of the discharge, but he shows he is aware
        of the problem. Fearing, perhaps, that his reputation
        for scientific accuracy was at stake, Verne does not
        describe the dark side of the moon.

D195   Stevenson, K. "Jules Verne in Victoria." <u>Southerly</u>, 19
        (No. 1), 23-25.
            Summarizes for an Australian audience Verne's novel
        about Australia, <u>A Voyage Round the World -- Australia</u>,
        originally called <u>Captain Grant's Children</u>. "What a
        rich textbook this particular volume would make for
        secondary schools here -- a thrilling adventure story,
        crammed with useful information and offering boys and
        girls of this generation a vivid picture of the Victoria
        of ninety years ago!"

D196   Walsh, Moira. "Films, 'From the Earth to the Moon.'"
        <u>America</u>, 100 (6 December), 327-328.
            The Warner Brothers film adds a pair of young lovers
        to Verne's "novelized imaginings" about the first trip
        to the moon. While uneven, the film is beautifully
        photographed in technicolor. Verne was wrong when he
        supposed munitions makers would provide the "impetus for
        interplanetary research," yet his tale holds up well as
        science fiction.

<u>1959</u>

D197   Anon. "New Films: Anything Down There?" <u>Newsweek</u>, 54
        (28 December), 65.
            The characters in the Twentieth Century-Fox production
        of <u>Journey to the Center of the Earth</u> are "pleasant, even
        tempered, colorful but not <u>too</u>." Professor Lindenbrook
        (James Mason) is "blunt" but "clearly a friend to man."

D198   Anon. "Wonders Down at the Earth's Core." <u>Life</u>, 47 (21
        December), 59.
            Twentieth Century-Fox's "glittering" <u>Journey to the
        Center of the Earth</u> is "all scientific fantasy and fun."
        The film "never lets scientific verisimilitude get in the
        way of telling a good adventure tale."

D199   Bradbury, Ray. "Introduction." In <u>The Mysterious Island</u>,
        by Jules Verne. Baltimore: Garamond Press for members
        of the Limited Editions Club, pp. v-x. Rpt. New York:
        Heritage Press, 1959.

Walt Disney and Mike Todd are greatly responsible for Verne's reputation in the United States, but the Voyages extraordinaires are still read because "we cry against a reality become too real, against art forms that have lost all sense of magic and exhilaration." Verne is "sublimely cinematic" with real ability to create narrative suspense. "Above all, Verne was out to help man clear the wilderness, conquer Time which gobbles us, and to keep the Desert from swallowing the Town." Self-preservation is evident in all the novels.

D200   Clarke, Arthur C. "Introduction." In A Journey to the Center of the Earth, by Jules Verne. New York: Dodd, Mead and Company, pp. v–viii.
The idea for this novel came from a conversation with a scientist who had explored the volcanic island Stromboli. Professor Hardwigg is a typical Vernian hero: determined, ambitious, and lacking a sense of humor. Verne achieves "absolute plausibility" through strict attention to detail. Norbert Casteret, the French cave explorer, admits that Journey to the Center of the Earth was the original source of his interest in subterranean exploration.

D201   Evans, I. O. "Introduction." In Dropped From the Clouds; including Part One of Marooned, by Jules Verne. Westport, CT: Associated Booksellers, 1959, pp. 7–8.
The trilogy The Mysterious Island, the first half of which is contained in this volume, was influenced by such works as Robinson Crusoe, The Swiss Family Robinson, and the desert island stories of James Fenimore Cooper. Verne's story of castaways on an uninhabited island is more ambitious, however, since his heroes adapt with more initiative and resourcefulness. Dropped from a balloon, they develop a "highly mechanized civilization" with nothing more than a watch, compass, and the raw materials of the island. The work illustrates Verne's strengths: inventiveness, character development, excitement, description, love of freedom.

D202   _____. "Introduction." In Michael Strogoff, Courier of the Czar, by Jules Verne. Westport, CT: Associated Booksellers, pp. 7–8.
The invasion methods Verne devised for the defeat of Foefar-Khan proved to be prophetic. They are similar to the "scorched earth policy" and the "general winter" effective against Napoleon and Hitler. The dramatic effects of Michael Strogoff led to its successful adaptation to the stage and films.

85

D203 _____. "Introduction." In <u>The Demon of Cawnpore</u>; Part One
of <u>The Steam House</u>, by Jules Verne. Westport, CT:
Associated Booksellers, pp. 7-8.

    The aftermath of the horrible and efficient British
suppression of the Indian mutiny is Verne's subject.
His character, Nana Sahib, was the actual leader of the
mutiny who probably perished after escaping in the
Himalayas. Since Sahib's fate was uncertain, it was
plausible for Verne to recreate him for further vengeance.
The success of the elephant in the theatrical production
of <u>Around the World in Eighty Days</u> may have influenced
Verne's creation of "Behemoth," the mechanical elephant
that is the central figure in this novel.

D204 Forman, Harrison. "Verne -- His Visions and Voyages."
<u>Saturday Review</u>, 42 (14 March), 36-37.

    "The Father of Science Fiction" did not consciously
write science fiction; he wrote about travel. Verne
was more concerned with the wonders and miracles to be
seen than with the means of transport. <u>Around the World
in Eighty Days</u> was his greatest success. It was im-
mediately turned into a play, and it inspired several
actual attempts to beat the fictional record. "The
Father of Accelerated Travel" himself, however, traveled
very little.

D205 Hartung, Philip T. "There's Still Time, Brother."
<u>Commonweal</u>, 71 (25 December), 374-375.

    The explorers in the film <u>A Journey to the Center of
the Earth</u> demonstrate that despite all hardships and
trials Man's spirit "can not be quenched."

D206 Knight, Arthur. "The Wonderful Wide-Screen World of Mike
Todd." <u>Saturday Review</u>, 42 (14 March), 41-44.

    Todd did not live to see the worldwide success of
<u>Around the World in Eighty Days</u>. The total gross to
date is $65 million from 4000 theatres in fifty-three
countries. Michael Todd Productions has assisted with
special lenses, projection, and box office procedures
for theatres in many countries. In Stockholm the film
has been seen by more people than the total population
of the city. Its success is based on the curiosity of
people everywhere about their neighbors in other parts
of the world -- the same feeling that contributed to
Verne's success.

D207 Miller, P. Schuyler. Review of <u>Five Weeks in a Balloon</u>,
<u>The Begum's Fortune</u>, and <u>A Floating City</u>. <u>Analog</u>, 63
(July), 153-155.

    These works illustrate three facets of Verne's career:
an extraordinary voyage, a utopia, and a travel book.

1960

D208 Amis, Kingsley. <u>New Maps of Hell: A Survey of Science</u>
      <u>Fiction</u>. New York: Harcourt, Brace and Company, pp.
      34-39. Rpt. <u>Science Fiction: The Future</u>, ed. Dick
      Allen. New York: Harcourt, Brace, Jovanovich, 1971,
      pp. 245-262. Rpt. <u>Science Fiction: A Collection of</u>
      <u>Critical Essays</u>, ed. Mark Rose. Englewood Cliffs, NJ:
      Prentice-Hall, 1976, pp. 9-29.
          "Verne's importance is that, while usually wrong or
      implausible or simply boring in detail, his themes fore-
      shadow a great deal of contemporary thinking, both inside
      and outside science fiction." He developed the tradition
      of the technological utopia and satire that is also a
      warning. Most valuable is his progressive political tone
      and his fascinated yet skeptical attitude toward tech-
      nology.

D209 Anon. "The New Pictures: 'A Journey to the Center of the
      Earth.'" <u>Time</u>, 85 (15 February), 85.
          Producer Charles Brackett smiles at some of Verne's
      "most preposterous pseudoscientific poppycock." Thus
      the Twentieth Century-Fox film is a spoof of the "boy's
      book." Few of the situations in the film can be found
      in the book. The movie enhances Verne's reputation as
      "the best dead writer Hollywood ever had." In the last
      five years, three films made from his novels (<u>Twenty</u>
      <u>Thousand Leagues Under the Sea</u>, <u>Around the World in</u>
      <u>Eighty Days</u>, <u>From the Earth to the Moon</u>) have grossed
      $45 million.

D210 Evans, I. O. "Introduction." In <u>The Begum's Fortune</u>, by
      Jules Verne. London: Arco Publications, pp. 7-9.
          The Franco-Prussian War revealed to Verne the menace
      of militarism and mechanized war. This novel reflects
      these fears as well as the "potentialities for good of
      science and invention." Verne's interest in town planning
      is also evident in the idea of two rival cities, and
      Dickens's <u>Bleak House</u> suggested a plausible device for
      bringing them into being. The character study of Otto
      that Verne attempts herein is "deplorable." However,
      some of Verne's most striking forecasts are contained
      in <u>The Begum's Fortune</u>, including the artificial satel-
      lite, long-range bombardment with incendiary bombs, mass
      evacuation. The illustrations of Herr Schultz in the
      original French edition "resemble a portrait of Bismarck
      deprived of his mustache."

D211 _____. "Introduction." In The City in the Sahara; Part
Two of The Barsac Mission, by Jules Verne. Westport,
CT: Associated Booksellers, pp. 7-9.

This book shows that Verne was able to incorporate
inventions made toward the end of his life, especially
wireless telegraphy, and that he shared the contemporary
belief that liquid air was the power of the future.
Blackland typifies the material advance and moral decay
associated with technology, but Verne's strong religious
faith forbade despair. Out of the destruction of the
stronghold of human progress come decent people, preserved by their idealism, sense of duty, moral integrity,
and faith.

D212 _____. "Introduction." In Into the Niger Bend; Part One
of The Barsac Mission, by Jules Verne. Westport, CT:
Associated Booksellers, pp. 7-9.

In the first book of this novel Verne's style is
related to Conan Doyle, Edgar Wallace, H. Rider Haggard
and other Romantic novelists, and the narrative of the
first book and several chapters of the second has a
light-heartedness reminiscent of the early Verne. Much
of the book was probably written early in his career,
then revised as Verne's outlook darkened, till he decided
to make it his swan song.

D213 _____. "Introduction." In The Mystery of Arthur Gordon
Pym by Edgar Allan Poe and Jules Verne, ed. Basil
Ashmore. Westport, CT: Associated Booksellers, pp.
79-81.

Verne derived his worst fault from Poe -- interruption
of the narrative with long passages of factual detail.
However, it was from Poe that he acquired an enthusiasm
for science fiction, credibility through description,
and surprise endings. Verne deplored Poe's "materialism";
in contrast, his sequel to Poe's tale exhibits "an overriding Providence."

D214 Hillegas, Mark R. "A Bibliography of Secondary Materials
on Jules Verne." Extrapolation, 2 (December), 5-16.

Sixty-nine items, with annotations, under the headings
of books, periodicals, and articles. Contains some
German, French, Spanish, and Italian items.

D215 Leighton, Peter. "By Rocket to the Moon." In Moon Travellers: A Dream That is Becoming a Reality. London:
Oldbourne, pp. 209-228.

Long excerpts from From the Earth to the Moon and
Around the Moon dominate this chapter in a book about
imaginary moon voyages from Lucian to Wells. "Verne's
account of a missile launched from Florida ninety-four
years ago reads uncannily like a newspaper report of
1960."

D216 Miller, P. Schuyler. Review of <u>Purchase of the North Pole</u>.
      <u>Analog</u>, 66 (October), 163-165.
           "Read for its fun-poking, the book is still entertain-
      ing. Today's theories are not those of Verne's day, and
      some time with a pad of paper would probably blast a hole
      in his math, especially the part which would shoot sea-
      level cities five miles into the air. The plot gimmick
      that saves everybody is still being used, and is no more
      convincing now than it was in 1889, but Verne was one of
      the first in line."

D217 Pohl, Frederik. Review of <u>Journey to the Center of the
      Earth</u>. <u>Worlds of If</u>, 10 (March), 104.
           "Verne's talents were not literary; his characters
      are knotty pine; his touches of background description
      float immiscibly on the stream of the story, like the
      grenadine in a pousse-cafe." But Verne got things
      started, and his special merit is not that he wrote well,
      but that he wrote at all.

D218 Walsh, Moira. "'Journey to the Center of the Earth.'"
      <u>America</u>, 102 (9 January), 429-430.
           Although the Twentieth Century-Fox movie contains
      much that is not in the Verne classic, including a duck
      named Gertrude, portions of Verne's plot that do make it
      to the screen are less than credible, for example, "the
      homicidal stratagems of a mad scientist," or the ejection
      of the adventure party back to the surface via a volcano.

D219 Wilson, Harris, ed. <u>Arnold Bennett and H. G. Wells; A Record
      of a Personal and a Literary Friendship</u>. Urbana: Uni-
      versity of Illinois Press, pp. 73-74, 260-276.
           Correspondence between Wells and Bennett is contained
      herein. In a letter dated February 8, 1902, Wells states
      that there is an element in his work that differentiates
      it from that of Verne just as "Swift is differentiated
      from Fantasia." The volume also reprints Bennett's
      article on Wells from <u>Cosmopolitan Magazine</u>, August
      1902 (D38). Bennett emphatically states that Wells is
      "not the English Jules Verne" and compares <u>From the
      Earth to the Moon</u> and <u>First Men in the Moon</u>.

<u>1961</u>

D220 Anon. "Verne Incognito." <u>Times Literary Supplement</u>, 27
      January, p. 54.
           Marcel Moré, is his psychological study (E207)
      speculates freely, takes quotations out of context, and
      extrapolates from fact to "improbable supposition."
      Readers are assured that Verne buried cryptograms in most
      of his novels. It is assumed that Verne's desire for a

father figure is responsible for the "mysterious beauty" of the novels in which Captain Nemo appears; however, Moré is unaware of the influence of Romanticism on the development of Nemo.

D221 Bergonzi, Bernard. The Early H. G. Wells: A Study of the Scientific Romances. Manchester: Manchester University Press, pp. 17-18, 157-158.
   The scientific element is essential to the conception of Verne's stories; however, for Wells it is "merely present rhetorically." Reprints Wells's discussion, from the introduction to his Seven Famous Novels, of the distinction between his work and that of Verne, and Verne's remarks on Wells's The First Men in the Moon from the 1903 interview in T. P.'s Weekly. See D39.

D222 Downs, Robert B. Molders of the Modern Mind: 111 Books That Shaped Western Civilization. New York: Barnes and Noble, pp. 295-297.
   Of particular interest in our era of Sputniks and space satellites is Verne's From the Earth to the Moon and Around the Moon. The technical details are carefully plotted, and, to give the stories the appearance of truth, Verne overloads the narrative with discourses on physics, mathematics, and astronomy. Inventors such as Simon Lake and La Cierva have acknowledged his influence.

D223 Dubos, René. The Dreams of Reason: Science and Utopias. New York: Columbia University Press, pp. 6-7.
   Contains the following interesting statement on Verne's influence: "As probably is true of many boys all over the world, my first contact with science was made through Jules Verne. I am sure that his stories could not instill valid knowledge or critical judgment or scientific spirit in anyone, but they can certainly foster a taste for the unknown and a desire for adventure. This is not without importance, because the longing for the uncommon and for the unexpected is a powerful motivating force in many scientists -- indeed perhaps the only one in some of them."

D224 Esslin, Martin. The Theatre of the Absurd. New York: Anchor Books, p. 89.
   Reference is made to the staging of The Bald Soprano in which was utilized "the conception of the English character conveyed by the novels of Jules Verne, whose English people have a peculiar decorum and 'sang-froid,' which has been brilliantly captured by the original illustrators in the stiff, bewhiskered figures of the Editions Hetzel."

D225 Evans, I. O. "Introduction." In <u>At the North Pole</u>; Part
One of <u>The Adventures of Captain Hatteras</u>, by Jules
Verne. Westport, CT: Associated Booksellers, pp. 7-8.
      Verne was well acquainted with the literature of
Arctic exploration. He integrated accounts of actual
expeditions by such explorers as Sir John Franklin,
Elisha Kane, and the French lieutenant Bellot into this
narrative. <u>At the North Pole</u> is the second of the
<u>Extraordinary Voyages</u> to be written. The extract from
the works of Sir Edward Belcher, which appears in the
novel, was probably taken by Verne from a French translation rather than the English original.

D226 _____. "Introduction." In <u>Black Diamonds</u>, by Jules Verne.
Westport, CT: Associated <u>Booksellers</u>, pp. 9-10.
      Originally titled <u>Les Indes noires</u>, Verne's story of
the Scottish Caledonian coal mining industry has been
translated as <u>Child of the Cavern</u>, <u>Strange Doings Under-
ground</u>, <u>The Underground City</u>, and <u>The Black Indies</u>.
Verne was impressed and saddened by sights of wrecked and
abandoned machinery indicative of an industry in decay.
His heroes in this tale are Nature, and the miners and
engineers who brought the "black diamonds" to the sun-
light.

D227 _____. "Introduction" and "Editorial Postscript." In <u>For
the Flag</u>, by Jules Verne. Westport, CT: Associated
Booksellers, pp. 7-9, 191-192.
      Verne never described a war of the future between the
Great Powers, but he did, as in this novel, describe
appalling weapons in the hands of private individuals.
Verne may have derived his theme from the experience of
real life chemist, Eugène Turpin, who sued him for
defamation of character. The Roch Fulgurator is described
in detail in the postscript.

D228 _____. "Introduction." In <u>Journey to the Center of the
Earth</u>, by Jules Verne. Westport, CT: Associated Booksellers, pp. 7-9.
      Interest in the Earth's geological past was aroused
by this novel. Perhaps due to the fact that <u>Journey to
the Center of the Earth</u> appeared before the Franco-Prussian War, the character Professor Leidenbrock is cranky
but good-hearted and very distinct from the sinister Herr
Schultz of <u>The Begum's Fortune</u>. The name of the character
Arne Saknussemm may have been inspired by that of Icelandic
scholar, Arni Magnusson. A French translation of Baron
Holberg's <u>Nicholas Klim</u> (1741), about a descent through
an abyss to a central core, may have been read by Verne.
The description of the underworld is based on information
provided to Verne by seismologist Charles Sainte-Claire

Deville. Journey to the Center of the Earth is the first "wonder story to be neither a utopia, satire, or fantasy."

D229 _____. "Introduction." In Propeller Island, by Jules Verne. Westport, CT: Associated Booksellers, pp. 7-9.
Verne's interest in town planning is expressed in this novel in his creation of Milliard City, a materialist utopia where each citizen has an annuity of one hundred thousand dollars. The city is destroyed not by technical defects or attack but by the conflicting ambitions of its people. Satire on human vanity is joined with science fiction. Inventions first appearing in the novel include the escalator and the "telautograph."

D230 _____. "Introduction." In Twenty Thousand Leagues Under the Sea, by Jules Verne. Westport, CT: Associated Booksellers, pp. 7-8.
Freedom, music, and the sea, Verne's three passions, are primary elements in the thematic structure of Twenty Thousand Leagues Under the Sea. Captain Nemo, the character Verne drew most deliberately, personifies one aspect of his creator: "the misanthrope who chafed at the claims of society and hated publicity." Evans states that he omitted "long passages of factual description" in this translation.

D231 Golding, William. "Astronaut by Gaslight." Spectator, 206 (9 June), 841-842. Rpt. The Hot Gates and Other Occasional Pieces. New York: Harcourt, 1966, pp. 111-115.
When we revisit Verne as an adult, unlike Gulliver's Travels for instance, we find that we missed little, except perhaps the heavy-handed satire aimed at the Gun Club of Boston. His gusto and enthusiasm carry us forward, but it is the charm of his nineteenth-century interiors, the clubs, and the charm of such traits as his enchantment for manmade light that attracts us today. There is a total lack of women in his work; he is spurred by the love of technology rather than science; and his heroes are just right for twelve-year-old boys: "tough, sexless, casually brave, resourceful, and making something big."

D232 Miller, P. Schuyler. "Verne on Wide Screen." Astounding, 68 (November), 160-164.
There are three ways in which film has used Verne's books: in a straight translation like Twenty Thousand Leagues Under the Sea, a delightful frolic hung on his plot like Around the World in Eighty Days (which is probably how he wrote his own play adaptions), and an abortion such as From the Earth to the Moon. Richard Matheson does a

good job translating the two Robur books into the film
Master of the World. The Czech Fabulous World of Jules
Verne starts as a gentle pastiche on Verne and his
clichés, and by the end it is parodying Verne and itself.

D233 Thomas, Theodore L. "The Watery Wonders of Captain Nemo."
Galaxy, 20 (December), 168-177.
Very strong attack against Verne's scientific accuracy
with reference to Twenty Thousand Leagues Under the Sea.
Verne continuously shows evidence of a lack of information that was easily available, and he doesn't deserve
a reputation for scientific prediction. "There is not a
single bit of valid speculation in it; none of its predictions have come true. The purported science in it is not
semi-science or even pseudo-science. It is non-science."

1962

D234 Auden, W. H. The Dyer's Hand and Other Essays. New York:
Random House, pp. 139-143.
A discussion of Around the World in Eighty Days illustrates the use of the master-servant relationship as
a parable of agape. Fogg, like an ancient stoic, has
disciplined his passions and trained himself to be
superior to circumstance; the last thing he wants is a
personal friend. Passepartout wants his master to be
formal, impersonal, an unfeeling automaton. The moral
choice that Fogg makes because of Aouda changes the
situation; thereafter, each sacrifices his life for the
other.

D235 Bandy, William T. The Influence and Reputation of Edgar
Allan Poe in Europe. Lecture at the 37th Annual Commemoration of the Edgar Allan Poe Society, October, 1959;
the Edgar Allan Poe Society of Baltimore, Inc., p. 11.
"The breadth of Poe's genius was such that he was
able to win the admiration of both the highly intellectual
Valéry and the popular and unpretentious Jules Verne."
Before he published any of his famous novels, Verne
published an essay pointing out the weaknesses in Poe,
which he then proved right by putting his theory into
practice. Around the World in Eighty Days was inspired
by Poe's "Three Sundays in a Week."

D236 Bradbury, Ray. "The Ardent Blasphemers." In Twenty Thousand
Leagues Under the Sea, by Jules Verne. New York: Bantam
Pathfinder Editions, pp. 1-12.
Verne's Captain Nemo and Melville's Ahab represent
positive and negative aspects of the American attitude
toward Nature. As our machines cut across the wilderness,
we are "ardent in our blasphemy." The characteristic

American boy mechanic has always resembled Nemo -- "Tom
Swift and his Flying Machine plus his AC-DC IBM Power-
Circuited Grandmother." But in this age of electronics,
we are emerging from an era inclined toward Ahab's
madness, hopelessness, and terror. Ahab is driven to
kill the white whale that resents inquiry, but Nemo
builds the Nautilus, a machine of curiosity. Verne's
acceptance of Nature is clear as Nemo asks Man to
reform; however, Melville rages against natural forces
and Ahab demands that God change.

D237 _____. "Introduction." In Around the World in Eighty
Days, by Jules Verne. Los Angeles: Plantin Press for
Members of the Limited Editions Club, pp. vii-xii. Rpt.
New York: Heritage Press, 1962.

  The characters Phileas Fogg and Passepartout objectify
the two halves of man -- the thinking and the doing,
master and servant. Fogg is the eccentric genius, man
of taste and imagination, but also the impetuous man of
action. Passepartout is "the rest of us," that is, those
who long to be creators but must be content to be "the
imp in a great man's shadow." The novel appeals to us
today because we do not test ourselves in our comfortable
world of speed. Verne slows the pace and brings back
"texture, sights, sounds and smells."

D238 Clarke, Arthur C. "Introduction." In From the Earth to the
Moon and Round the Moon, by Jules Verne. New York:
Dodd, Mead and Company, pp. v-viii.

  The "realization that the actualities of science
could be as exciting and romantic as the magic of Sinbad
or the Arabian Nights" was Verne's contribution to
literature. The calculations for the trip to the moon
were made by a professional astronomer for Verne. While
he made errors, Verne's concepts of weightlessness and
rocket thrust in a vacuum were examples of exceptional
scientific foresight. His description of the moon "can
stand almost unchanged today."

D239 Evans, I. O. "Introduction." In Clipper of the Clouds,
by Jules Verne. Westport, CT: Associated Booksellers,
pp. 7, 9-10.

  The invention rather than the inventor is the focus
of this narrative. Verne wrote the story around the
helicopter and had little interest in other aspects of
the novel. The work is reminiscent of the dispute during
Verne's lifetime between advocates of the aerostat
(dirigible) and the aeronef (flying machine). In his
acknowledgements on page 7, Evans declares his debt to
Dr. R. C. Pankhurst of the National Physical Laboratory

and includes the scientist's comments on Verne's helicopter. Pankhurst notes that Verne's arrangement of a large number of rotors arranged longitudinally anticipated a principal feature of the propulsion system of the supersonic airliner in which a large number of jet engines are arranged in rows.

D240 _____. "Introduction." In Master of the World, by Jules Verne. Westport, CT: Associated Booksellers, pp. 7-9.

A distrust of science is evident in this tale of a dictator who achieves control of the world with one technical invention. Verne's ambivalent attitude saw science and technology as able to liberate man, but also capable of imprisoning and bullying him. The inventor in this tale combines technical skill with courage and arrogance.

D241 _____. "Introduction." In The Masterless Man; Part One of The Survivors of the Jonathan, by Jules Verne. Westport, CT: Associated Booksellers, pp. 7-8.

Verne's political philosophy is displayed in this novel, which was published posthumously. His tenure on the Amiens town council obviously influenced this work. He reveals distrust of socialism and detestation of communism but a fascination with anarchism. His politics consisted of the advocacy of order and reason, proportion, and respect for justice and culture. If Verne had lived during World War II, he probably would have found himself in a concentration camp.

D242 _____. "Introduction." In The Unwilling Dictator; Part Two of The Survivors of the Jonathan, by Jules Verne. Westport, CT: Associated Booksellers, pp. 7-8.

In The Survivors of the Jonathan, Verne creates a situation in which colonists develop an ideal island community where there is no government or law. The settlement is threatened from within by a socialist, a communist, and by personal conflicts.

D243 Fadiman, Clifton. "Afterword." In Twenty Thousand Leagues Under the Sea, by Jules Verne. New York: Macmillan Company, pp. 371-372.

Verne and Wells together created modern science fiction. Less fantastic than Wells, Verne projected known scientific fact into the future. Among his anticipations are electric guns and speedometers, and food derived from ocean vegetation. The style and characterization of this novel are not noteworthy except that Captain Nemo has a "sinister fascination."

D244 Hillegas, Mark R. "An Annotated Biography [sic] of Jules
 Verne's Voyages extraordinaires." Extrapolation, 3
 (May), 32–47.
 An annotated bibliography of sixty-five novels or
 short story collections by Verne first published in
 French by Hetzel under the title Voyages extraordinaires.
 The annotations deal mainly with content, but sometimes
 there are references to biography, technique, and history.

D245 Maurois, André. "A Note on Jorge Luis Borges." Paris
 Review, 7 (No. 28), 118–119.
 Borges creates "imaginary and symbolic worlds" but is
 "indignant" that Oscar Wilde defined him as "'a scientific Jules Verne.'" Verne speculates on "probability,"
 Wells on "possibility" or "impossibility," but neither
 deals with ambiguity.

D246 Miller, P. Schuyler. Review of For the Flag and Black
 Diamonds. Analog, 70 (October), 165–166.
 Although the plot is mild, Black Diamonds is one of
 Verne's best novels because it contains fascinating
 details about mining technology.

D247 Raknem, Ingvald. "The First Men in the Moon and Other
 Stories à la Jules Verne." In H. G. Wells and His
 Critics. Universitetsforlaget, Norway: George Allen
 and Unwin Ltd., pp. 405–415.
 Discussion of Wells's When the Sleeper Wakes, Food
 of the Gods, and The First Men in the Moon in the context of early criticism linking Wells to Verne. Although
 Wells was labelled "the English Jules Verne," such critics
 overlooked the fact that his stories had a moral implication and that Wells was always interested in the plight
 of humanity. Because the sociological import is absent
 in Verne's stories, their likeness to Wells is only
 superficial. The difference between the two can best
 be illustrated by comparing "Dr. Ox's Experiment" with
 Food of the Gods. Dr. Ox's experiment is only one
 episode, after which life returns to normal; the gas has
 no lasting effect on the townspeople. Verne's gas is
 only a discovery, whereas Wells's food is a symbol of
 man's upward struggle.

*D248 Redman, Harry, Jr. and Bernard Clarke Weber. "Jules Verne's
 Visit to Malta in 1884." Scientia, 28 (1962), 7–12.
 Not seen (cited in 1963 Modern Language Association
 International Bibliography, p. 142, #7714).

D249 Valéry, Paul. "Our Destiny and Literature." In History
 and Politics. New York: Pantheon Books, pp. 181–182.

Though Verne invented imaginary worlds, he did not attempt anything on the intellectual side, such as imagining the arts of the future. He "did not foresee our electronic music, nor did he think up new combinations or compositions, nor some yet unknown kind of aesthetics." What he did foresee required only an elementary imagination.

D250 Wells, Lester G. <u>Fictional Accounts of Trips to the Moon</u>. Syracuse, New York: Syracuse University Library, pp. 17-20.

This booklet for an exhibition contains brief accounts of moon trips from Lucian to Wells. The summary of Verne's <u>From the Earth to the Moon</u> focuses on its "remarkably sound scientific background."

<u>1963</u>

D251 Evans, I. O. "Introduction" and "Editorial Postscript." In <u>Burbank the Northerner</u>; Part One of <u>North Against South</u>, by Jules Verne. Westport, CT: Associated Booksellers, pp. 7-8, 186-189.

Verne's historical stories, which are not so well known as they deserve, always have the same general theme of the struggle against imposed authority. Inspired by a passionate love of freedom, Verne was always on the side of the underdog. The postscript details the Battle of Hampton Roads, which is not so clear in Verne's novel as it should be.

D252 _____. "Introduction." In <u>Carpathian Castle</u>, by Jules Verne. Westport, CT: Associated Booksellers, pp. 5-6.

Marguerite Allote de la Fuÿe has implied that this novel was written in a mood of deep sadness, possibly as a result of an unhappy platonic love affair. Verne was influenced by Poe, and the supernatural surely had an appeal to him. But "how in Verne's hands the Gothic story is blended into science-fiction is left for the reader to discover."

D253 _____. "Introduction." In <u>The Claim on Forty Mile Creek</u>; Part One of <u>The Golden Volcano</u>, by Jules Verne. Westport, CT: Associated Booksellers, pp. 7-8.

The effects produced by gold fever is the theme of this narrative based on the Klondike gold rush. Evans admits that in his translation he did not attempt to reproduce the characteristic modes of speech of French and English Canadians, "Hispano-American half-breeds, taciturn Amerindians, or semi-inarticulate Irishmen."

D254 _____. "Introduction." In <u>Into The Abyss</u>; Part Two of
<u>Family Without a Name</u>, by Jules Verne. Westport, CT:
Associated Booksellers, pp. 7-10.
   Verne based this story on the 1837 revolt of the
Quebec French-Canadians against British rule. Following
a synopsis of Part One, <u>Leader of the Resistance</u>, Evans
explains that if Verne exaggerated the ferocity of
British forces dealing with the insurrection, it was
probably because of the inaccuracy of the accounts he
read.

D255 _____. "Introduction." In <u>Leader of the Resistance</u>; Part
One of <u>Family Without a Name</u>, by Jules Verne. Westport,
CT: Associated Booksellers, pp. 7-10.
   Verne's narrative is based on the 1837 French uprising
against British rule in Canada, and this introduction
gives some background on the separatist movement.

D256 _____. "Introduction." In <u>The Secret of Wilhelm Storitz</u>,
by Jules Verne. Westport, CT: Associated Booksellers,
pp. 7-8.
   Verne derived his theme from the old stories of wonder-
working magicians, from a Wells story, and from the unexpected death of his brother Paul, to whom he was deeply
attached.

D257 _____. "Introduction." In <u>The Tribulations of a Chinese
Gentleman</u>, by Jules Verne. Westport, CT: Associated
Booksellers, pp. 7-8.
   The jocular good humor with an undercurrent of respect
and sympathy reflects the attitude of tolerant amusement
and admiration with which many Westerners regard the
Celestial Empire, but the macabre theme shows the in-
fluence of Poe.

D258 Ley, Willy. "Introduction: Jules Verne, The Man and his
Works." In <u>Dr. Ox's Experiment</u>, by Jules Verne. New
York: Macmillan Company, pp. 1-10.
   A brief biographical sketch notes fantastic tales
circulated about Verne and describes the novelist's
limited travels. It is suggested that Verne must have
joined Tournachon in a balloon voyage since the fine
details of <u>A Drama in the Air</u> could not have been totally
invented. Turning to a discussion of the genre of Verne's
works, Ley discards "science fiction" for an unnamed
literary group with three subdivisions: imaginary
voyages, utopias, and robinsonades.

D259 Moskowitz, Sam. "Around the Worlds with Jules Verne." In
<u>Explorers of the Infinite: Shapers of Science Fiction</u>.
Cleveland: World Publishing Company, pp. 73-87. Rpt.
Westport, CT: Hyperion Press, 1974, pp. 73-87.

Verne's writing, like Wells's, moves from science
fiction in his youth, to general fiction in middle age,
and then back to science fiction to express his disil-
lusion and near despair in the failure of science to
bring a better world. Verne was influenced by Poe, and
his formula for success was the combination of scientific
adventure with a strong stress on credibility. Twenty
Thousand Leagues Under the Sea is his best novel, Nemo
and Robur his best characters. Ends with a survey of
his imitators and disciples, especially in France.

D260 Strughold, Hubertus. "Epilogue: Jules Verne, Physiologist."
In Dr. Ox's Experiment, by Jules Verne. New York:
Macmillan Company, pp. 81-87.
Strughold, a professor of space medicine, explains
why, contrary to Verne's depiction in "Dr. Ox's Experiment," an enriched oxygen level will not cause "emotional
excitement and raucous behavior." Verne may have been
influenced by the combustion theories of Lavoisier and
Paul Bert's experiments with animals in which exposure
to pure oxygen led to convulsions and death. However,
the ability of the blood to regulate absorption of
oxygen was unknown to Verne. Despite the error in
physiological effect, the story helped popularize
scientific knowledge about oxygen.

1964

D261 Anon. "A Portrait of Genius: Ray Bradbury." Show, 4
(December), 53-55, 102-104.
In this interview, Bradbury says that Verne is his
favorite science fiction writer. Verne "makes one proud
to be a human being." He sets tests for mankind, dares
to lift himself by his bootstraps, honors work and the
searching mind. "In an age which has often bankrupted
its fund of ideals," Verne "calls out to better goals
and warns man, not to worry so much about his relationship with God, but rather to see his kinship with other
men."

D262 Born, Franz. Jules Verne: The Man Who Invented the Future.
Tr. Juliana Biro. Englewood Cliffs, NJ: Prentice-Hall.
Overview sketch of Verne's life that marks his change
to pessimism with Clipper of the Clouds, and which
contains longish summaries of his main works as well as
facts that relate them to the real life exploits of such
men as Simon Lake, Norbert Casteret, and Admiral Byrd.
Verne's work made his readers realize they were in the
midst of a new era, and presented them with a new hero
-- "a man of iron energy who could systematically carry
out his plans and was never at a loss for a solution to
his problems." See D272.

D263 Cooke, Richard P. "Return of Phileas Fogg." <u>Wall Street</u>
<u>Journal</u>, 30 June, p. 16.
Brief review of a dramatic version of <u>Around the World</u>
<u>in Eighty Days</u>.

D264 Dalgliesh, Alice. Review of <u>Jules Verne: The Man Who</u>
<u>Invented the Future</u>, by Franz Born. <u>Saturday Review</u>, 47
(16 May), 58.
This reviewer finds "pathos" in the fact that
Alexandre Dumas tutored Verne to write at a set time
every day. However, this did not work for the novelist
of "extraordinary imagination." Born's statement that
Verne was first to envision the helicopter is in error
-- this was done by Leonardo da Vinci (D262).

D265 Davidson, Avram. Review of <u>Dr. Ox's Experiment</u>. <u>Magazine</u>
<u>of Fantasy and Science Fiction</u>, 26 (January), 42–43.
Very brief review. Not many people think of Verne
with a sense of humor, but this volume shows he had one.

D266 Evans, I. O. "Introduction." In <u>Adrift in the Pacific</u>;
Part One of <u>Two Years' Holiday</u>, by Jules Verne. Westport,
CT: Associated Booksellers, pp. 7–9.
The present narrative is the only work Verne wrote
expressly for young readers. In it he takes particular
care with characterization. The lad Briant is based on
the schoolboy friend of Verne's son, Aristide Briand.
(<u>See</u> D305.) Verne's works were intended for adults; his
interests were geography and science. He created two new
art forms: science fiction and the story in which the
chief interest is in technical matters. A few of the tales
are marred by national or racial prejudice.

D267 _____. "Introduction." In <u>A Floating City</u>, by Jules Verne.
London: Arco Publications, pp. 7–9.
A passage on the <u>Great Eastern</u> provided the material
for this novel. Perhaps Verne may have been lured to
the huge vessel by its evil reputation: "dogged by mis-
fortune," the ship "ruined her promoters, broke the
heart of her designer," killed several of the crew. The
added romantic interest in this tale is far from successful. His ineptitude at describing romantic scenes and
the female character is obvious. However, the work
does reveal Verne as an acute observer of contemporary
life. But the manners of his Englishmen are decidedly
French, indicating that Verne's travels were mostly in
an armchair.

D268 _____. "Introduction." In Measuring a Meridian, by Jules Verne. Westport, CT: Associated Booksellers, p. 9.
Verne saw the adventurous possibilities in his subject by coupling it with "Darkest Africa."

D269 _____. "Introduction." In The Mysterious Document; Part One of Captain Grant's Children, by Jules Verne. Westport, CT: Associated Booksellers, pp. 7-8.
The original subtitle of the three volumes of Captain Grant's Children, Voyage autour du monde (Voyage Around the World), became the English title when the work was first translated. While the idea of the cryptogram with ambiguous significance came from Poe, several characters in this novel, such as Lord and Lady Glenarvan, Major MacNabbs, and Captain Grant, may have been inspired by the works of Sir Walter Scott. Rousseau's concept of the "noble savage" may have suggested the Indian Thalcave.

D270 _____. "Introduction." In Salvage From the Cynthia, by Jules Verne and André Laurie. Westport, CT: Associated Booksellers, pp. 7-8.
Possibly because it was written in collaboration, this work has not been previously translated. The factual basis is the discovery of the Northeast Passage by Nordenskiold in 1878-79. A brief biographical sketch of Paschal Grousset, who used the Laurie pseudonym, is provided.

D270.1 _____. "Introduction." In The Village in the Treetops, by Jules Verne. Westport, CT: Associated Booksellers, p. 9.
Since Verne was "a sincerely religious man" and a Roman Catholic, he regarded the proponents of the Darwinian theory with skepticism. The evolutionary controversy raging during Verne's lifetime centered, at one point, on the possibility of a "missing link" creature between man and ape. This novel can be viewed as a "suggestion of the manner in which the problem might be solved."

D271 Fritz, Sigmund. "Pictures From Meteorological Satellites and Their Interpretation." Space Science Reviews, 3 (November), 541-580, esp. 541.
The accuracy of Verne's depiction of the Earth's cloud cover when viewed from space is briefly noted. Although about one hundred years elapsed before real successors to Verne's "Lunarnauts" of From the Earth to the Moon and Around the Moon actually saw the cloudscape, the novelist's description of "rings of clouds placed concentrically round the terrestrial globe" and "parts brilliantly lighted" as indicative of high mountains have counterparts in meteorological photographs taken by satellites.

D272 May, Charles Paul. Review of <u>Jules Verne: The Man Who
      Invented the Future</u>, by Franz Born. <u>New York Times
      Book Review</u>, 22 March, p. 22.
        Born relates modern scientific developments to Verne's
      imaginings in the novels. There are many exaggerations
      and errors in the study. <u>See</u> D262.

1965

D273 Amis, Kingsley. "Science Fiction: A Practical Nightmare."
        <u>Holiday</u>, 37 (February), 8, 11, 13-15.
        The innovation in science fiction attributed to Verne
      is the substitution of technology for gadgetry in utopian
      adventure. Mistakes in physics do not reduce the power
      of his symbols which serve as "archetypal myths."

D274 Anon. "About Jules Verne." In <u>Twenty Thousand Leagues
      Under the Sea and Around the Moon</u>, by Jules Verne. New
      York: Platt and Munk, Publishers, pp. 553-558.
        The intellectual and the adventurous, both strong in
      Verne's nature as a boy, were reflected in his novels.
      His <u>Voyages extraordinaires</u> dramatized the meaning of
      scientific discoveries to the masses. This brief biogra-
      phical sketch notes the events which inspired the most
      popular novels. Gradually, concern for tyranny usurped
      his interest in scientific inventions.

D275 Asimov, Isaac. "Father Jules." In <u>Twenty Thousand Leagues
      Under the Sea and Around the Moon</u>, by Jules Verne. New
      York: Platt and Munk, Publishers, pp. 9-13.
        The "literary father of all modern science fiction,"
      Verne looked beyond the mechanical inventions of his day
      to the "untried reaches of scientific exploration." He
      studied the scientific publications of his day and con-
      structed his imaginings according to the rules of science.
      He is most popular in the United States and Russia, the
      two pioneers in the space travel he foretold.

D276 Evans, I. O. "Introduction." In <u>Anomalous Phenomena</u>; Part
      One of <u>Hector Servadac</u>, by Jules Verne. Westport, CT:
      Associated Booksellers, pp. 7-9.
        This is the strangest of Verne's extraordinary journeys,
      and sinister too, as can be seen by spelling Servadac
      backwards. The story is marred by the malicious character
      study of the Jewish peddler, who may be the result of the
      trouble caused when a stranger accused Verne of actually
      being a Polish Jew who renounced his religion in an at-
      tempt to marry a wealthy lady. There is no other evidence
      of deliberate anti-Semitism in Verne's work, and there is
      a sympathetic Jew in <u>The Castle of the Carpathians</u>.

D277 _____. "Introduction." In The Chancellor, by Jules Verne. Westport, CT: Associated Booksellers, p. 5.

The most grim of Verne's tales details the continuous disasters besetting the unfortunate vessel, The Chancellor. The story was derived from three sources: the voyage of the vessel Sarah Sands in 1857; Captain Bligh's open-boat voyage following the mutiny on the Bounty; the painting, "The Wreck of the Medusa," by French artist J. L. A. Theodore Géricault.

D278 _____. "Introduction." In The Green Ray; Including also The Blockade Runners, by Jules Verne. London: Arco Publications, pp. 7-8.

The influence of two English authors is evident in this novel. The Scottish setting was derived from the works of Sir Walter Scott. Several characters are reminiscent of personages in Charles Dickens's Nicholas Nickleby. The "green ray" is a genuine nautical pheno-menon which has been described by scientists. It is seen by sailors as the sun sets.

D279 _____. "Editorial Postscript." In Homeward Bound; Part Two of Hector Servadac, by Jules Verne. Westport, CT: Associated Booksellers, pp. 191-192.

Why did Verne end this novel with the ambiguous notion that it could be either dream or reality? Sully André Peyre has suggested that Verne had an inkling of the Theory of Relativity, and Charles Ravel theorized that Verne created an eternal instantaneousness during which his travelers dropped out of time and space. More likely, Verne, who often hurried over endings, simply did not think out his conclusion.

D280 _____. "Introduction" and "Editorial Appendix." In The Hunt for the Meteor, by Jules Verne. Westport, CT: Associated Booksellers, pp. 7, 191.

Use of the theory of the electrical nature of matter, and hints of the theory of "continuous creation," later put forward by Fred Hoyle, demonstrate that near the end of his life Verne was still in touch with contemporary developments in science. A French commentator has called the portrait of the eccentric scientist in this novel a mirror image of Verne. The erratic character of the scientist, however, is totally unlike Verne. It is used for light relief as are the malapropisms of the house-keeper, Mitz. Evans admits not being able to translate this humor. Verne's idea of using the disintegration of matter to produce attractive or repulsive rays has been used by later writers who probably developed it independently. His conception of the rays is scientifically inaccurate.

D281 _____. "Introduction." In <u>Package Holiday</u>; Part One of
    <u>The Thompson Travel Agency</u>, by Jules Verne. Westport,
    CT: Associated Booksellers, p. 7.
        Package vacations were already in vogue at the turn
    of the century. Verne's English characters make a bad
    showing compared with the charming American heroines and
    the gallant, debonair Frenchmen. Verne had contempt for
    the English establishment, but great admiration for the
    adventurous English "men of action."

D282 _____. "Introduction." In <u>Yesterday And Tomorrow</u>, by
    Jules Verne. London: Arco Publications, p. 11.
        Some of Verne's shorter works were first published
    in a volume five years after his death. Contents are:
    "The Fate of Jean Morénas," "An Ideal City," "Ten Hours
    Hunting," "Frritt-Flacc," "Gil Braltar," "In the Twenty-
    ninth Century: The Day of an American Journalist in
    2889," "Mr. Ray Sharp and Miss Me Flat," and "The Eternal
    Adam." Editor of the collection probably was Michel
    Jules Verne.

D283 Freedman, Russell. <u>Jules Verne, Portrait of a Prophet</u>.
    New York: Holiday House.
        Verne's novels and the forecasts therein are considered
    in relation to the social, economic, scientific, and
    political climates of the nineteenth century. Written
    for readers aged twelve and older, this biography empha-
    sizes that Verne's reputation as a prophet was achieved
    by his ability to see the future with amazing accuracy.
    Among his predictions were motion pictures, the recorded
    book, air conditioner, synthetic materials, prefabricated
    mass housing, air pollution control, satellites, super
    weapons, lethal fallout.

D284 Knight, Damon. "Afterword." In <u>Twenty Thousand Leagues</u>
    <u>Under the Sea</u>, by Jules Verne. New York: Washington
    Square Press, pp. 383-386.
        Provides a biographical sketch and considers the
    turning point in Verne's life to be his friendship with
    the balloonist Félix Nadar. Verne's talents for character-
    ization and narrative were small and "he never produced
    anything resembling literature." Success came from
    enthusiasm for science and a plot formula that joined
    travelogue, melodrama, and prophecy.

D285 Lowndes, Robert A. W. "Introduction." In <u>Master of the</u>
    <u>World</u>, by Jules Verne. New York: Airmont Publishing
    Company, pp. 3-9.
        Baudelaire's translations of Edgar Allan Poe's works
    began to appear in 1852. Verne was greatly influenced
    by the American poet's use of precision of detail. <u>The</u>

<u>Master of the World</u> concerns an inventor who builds a superb machine with which he can control the world. Hugo Gernsback's type of fiction was originated by Verne: "precision of detail, scientific fact and reasonable theory, concentration upon story and prophecy."

D286 Miller, Walter James. "Jules Verne in America: A Translator's Preface." In <u>Twenty Thousand Leagues Under the Sea</u>, by Jules Verne. New York: Washington Square Press, pp. vii–xxii.

English translators, through omissions, inaccuracies, and alterations, have damaged the reputation of Verne in America to the extent that readers are unable to judge the nature and range of his talents. The predominantly used translation of <u>Twenty Thousand Leagues Under the Sea</u>, that of Lewis Page Mercier, eliminates subtleties of characterization, omits extensive portions of the text, dulls the humor, and carelessly converts technical terms and measurements. The purpose of the present edition is to restore the integrity of the work as Verne conceived it.

D287 Stirling, Nora. "Jules Verne." In <u>Who Wrote the Classics</u>. New York: John Day Company, pp. 145–166.

Verne was born into a world that was experiencing rapid change due to the Industrial Revolution and Darwin's theories. Science became the new god, but people yearned for simplicity and romance. Verne was influenced by Walter Scott and Fenimore Cooper. His "demonic imagination" enslaved him to constant writing. A resulting disinterest in people accounts for the "woodenness" of his characters. The stories followed a formula that required three males -- one for intellect, one for physical action, one for comic relief.

D288 Vedro, Alfred S. "Shades of Jules Verne and H. G. Wells." <u>School Paperback Journal</u>, 1 (February), 18–19.

The best contemporary science fiction offers three major values for teaching: the study of science is rendered dramatic, science fiction introduces social problems, and it can be studied as a literary genre in itself. Man's relationship to society and the impact of technologies on morality, cultural traditions, and politics is effectively presented by writers such as Clarke, Asimov, Pohl, Van Vogt, and Bradbury. Despite the title, Verne is not stressed.

<u>1966</u>

D289 Asimov, Isaac. "An Introduction to this Edition." In <u>A</u>
<u>Journey to the Center of the Earth</u>, by Jules Verne.
New York: Limited Editions Club, pp. vii–xiv. Rpt.
New York: Heritage Press, 1966.
Fictional trips to the underground are a feature of
all mythologies, but the best of the nineteenth-century
tales is that of Verne. Conservative in his attitude
toward science, Verne was not interested in pseudoscienti-
fic notions of hollows in the Earth. His stories are
based as closely as possible on scientific fact. Although the tales do include elements of fantasy, Verne
is more enthusiastic about descriptions of his explorers'
instruments. Use of accepted "scientific jargon" helped
Verne deal with difficulties of heat and darkness in the
interior of the earth. "Electricity" in the air served
as a source of light.

D290 Becker, Beril. <u>Jules Verne</u>. New York: G. P. Putnam's
Sons.
A writer of science books for teenagers, Becker's
biography of Verne is aimed at adolescents. He centers
on the <u>Voyages extraordinaires</u> and the novelist's technological inventions. The treatment reveals the power of
Verne's gift to make the wildly improbable scientifically
believable. But Becker is also careful to record his
subject's realization that the power of machines can be
corrupted by egocentric individuals. The moral lesson
to be gleaned from the novels is an understanding of
"the ugliness of self-interest."

D291 Butor, Michel. "Homage to Jules Verne." Tr. John Coleman.
<u>New Statesman</u>, 72 (15 July), 94.
When he decided to write for the <u>Magasin d'éducation</u>
<u>et de récréation</u>, Verne, with encyclopedic diligence,
described true worlds known only to a few adults "in
order to create for children a world outside that of
their parents," a world that adults cannot challenge or
deny.

D292 Clarke, I. F. <u>Voices Prophesying War, 1763-1984</u>. London:
Oxford University Press, pp. 70-73.
Whitman's verse is a program for Verne's work. Verne's
heroes are not real, but manifestations of tremendous
energy. <u>The Begum's Fortune</u> is the nearest Verne came
to contemplating the type of war made possible by technology. Verne "stands half-way between the earlier occasional and incidental treatment of future warfare in
fiction and the full development of that theme in the
last fifteen years of the nineteenth century."

D293 Clements, Robert J. "The European Literary Scene." Saturday
      Review, 49 (4 June), 41.
            In 1966 French publishers produced a million copies
      of Verne's works. His success may be explained by Michel
      Butor's claim that "Verne's fantasies are the subterranean
      source for all modern science fiction." Two comments
      about Verne are noted. Apollinaire exclaimed, "What a
      style Verne has! Nothing but nouns." Jean Cocteau
      attributed one of his anxieties to Verne: "The moon
      gives me anguish, a fear coming from a Jules Verne il-
      lustration I saw as a child."

D294 Evans, I. O. "Introduction." In The Flight to France, by
      Jules Verne. London: Arco Publications, pp. 5-7.
            Set during the French Revolution, the novel concerns
      the defense by Republicans against the pro-Royalist
      invasion by forces from beyond the Rhine. Evans relates
      that one French critic (unnamed) has suggested that the
      narrative exhibits the influence of two French historical
      writers who collaborated under the signature Erckmann-
      Chatrian.

D295 ____. "Introduction." In The Purchase of the North Pole,
      by Jules Verne. London: Arco Publications, pp. 7-10.
            Written as a sequel to From the Earth to the Moon and
      Around the Moon much later in Verne's life, The Purchase
      of the North Pole heaps ridicule on Barbicane, Nicholl,
      and Maston, characters Verne once loved. A distrust of
      science is evident here, for the three "scientists"
      work with disregard for human welfare.

D296 ____. "Introduction." In The Southern Star Mystery, by
      Jules Verne. London: Arco Publications, pp. 7-8.
            The attitudes of whites toward African natives and
      of the British toward the Dutch, which led to apartheid
      and the Boer War, are depicted by Verne in this novel.
      John Watkins, Verne's rough British farmer, is "a type
      of the overbearing and unscrupulous British colonist in
      South Africa." He is balanced, however, by a hardworking,
      British man of action, Lancashire miner Thomas Steel.
      This detective story "abounds in melodramatic excitement."

D297 ____. "Introduction." In Sun in Eclipse; Part One of The
      Fur Country, by Jules Verne. London: Arco Publications,
      pp. 7-8.
            All of Verne's Arctic stories have an incident in
      common -- "an attack on a group of adventurers by hunger-
      maddened bears." Written as a thriller and a detective
      story, the narrative contains clues which lead to the
      "surprise ending."

D298 _____. "Introduction." In <u>The Travelling Circus</u>; Part
One of <u>César Cascabel</u>, by Jules Verne. London: Arco
Publications, pp. 7-9.
    While a member of the Amiens town council, Verne
supervised the finances of the local theatre and also
looked after the welfare of vagrant entertainers. In
his reports, he urged the establishment of a permanent
circus. The local color of <u>César Cascabel</u> resulted from
Verne's contact with the circus and its people.

D299 _____. <u>Jules Verne and His Work</u>. New York: Twayne
Publishers.
    Focusing on Verne's work rather than his life, Evans's
study attempts to provide a "comprehensive account" of
the writer's literary powers: unflagging industry,
versatility, description, imagination, and moral idealism.
Also considers Verne as founder of science fiction, in
other literature, his contributions to town planning, and
translations of his work.

D300 Fuller, Edmund. "A Refurbished 'Nautilus.'" <u>Wall Street
Journal</u>, 22 March, p. 18.
    Verne's <u>Nautilus</u> and its skipper, Captain Nemo, have
"passed into the folklore of the Modern World." Walter
James Miller's accurate translation of <u>Twenty Thousand
Leagues Under the Sea</u> (D286) gives the novel fresh interest and charm. Most disappointing is the "shallow"
afterword by Damon Knight. Verne writes with "esprit,"
his characters are striking types even if "flat," and he
stirs the imagination with "adroit extrapolations from
the state of applied science in his time." Captain Nemo's
"manic-depressive majesty" is still haunting.

D301 Gauthier, Guy. "Musee imaginaire de la science fiction."
<u>Image et son</u>, 194 (May), 40-44. Rpt. <u>Focus on the Science
Fiction Film</u>, ed. William Johnson. Englewood Cliffs, New
Jersey: Prentice-Hall, 1972, pp. 97-103.
    A writer can only give a marvelous invention a "poetic"
existence; the film-maker is less fortunate, since he must
show the invention. Verne's <u>Nautilus</u> is the ancestor of
today's submarines, but it looks to the past, more an
extension of the sea serpent than a foreshadowing of
scientific progress, and thus we accept the disparity of
Nemo's salon and the vessel that contains it. In the
1955 film, however, the full detail of the interior is
realistic and thus clashes with the salon. Karel Zeman's
<u>The Wonderful Invention</u> is affected by the illustrations
in the old Hetzel editions.

D302 Lennon, Peter. "Yesterday's Future." <u>The Guardian</u>, 31
March, p. 10.

After one hundred and one years the landing on the moon has caught up with Jules Verne's imagination. In March 1966 a Paris pocketbook firm brought out ten volumes of Verne's works in editions totaling one million copies. Verne worked out the "logical projection of scientific knowledge of his time," but he was pessimistic about man's use of power. The Begum's Fortune concerns a German leader who is obsessed with destruction and racial extermination. In For the Flag atomic warfare is foreseen.

D303 Nicoletti, Manfredi. "Flash Gordon and the Twentieth Century Utopia." Architectural Review, 140 (August), 87-91.

Cartoonist Alex Raymond's scheme of conflict between his hero Flash Gordon and evil utilization of technological power follows the pattern devised by Jules Verne. However, the moral conclusions are distinct. For Verne, the triumph of good characters is unavoidable, while the bad are destroyed by the technology they have misused. Thus, the Nautilus eventually gets even with Captain Nemo. "Verne's technology has an inner sense of ethical principles." For Raymond, however, technology is everyone's ally, and since power is limitless, no one prevails.

D304 Slonim, Marc. "Revival of Jules Verne." New York Times Book Review, 22 May, p. 42.

Reports that "a wave of wholly adult admirers has appeared in France, seeing in Verne not only the prophet of many technical discoveries of the 20th century. . .but also a writer of genius, a visionary, a literary figure of the first magnitude."

1967

D305 Bergh, Sven-Erik. "Introduction." In A Long Vacation, by Jules Verne. New York: Holt. Rinehart and Winston, pp. 5-6. Rpt. London: Oxford University Press, 1967.

Besides mechanical inventions, Verne anticipated "more intangible aspects of modern life," such as the social and psychological approach to literature. A Long Vacation (Adrift in the Pacific) demonstrates the sociological developments that would occur in a colony of boys of various nationalities. The character Briant is based on Aristide Briand, a classmate of Verne's son who later became Prime Minister.

D306 Bessy, Maurice. Méliès. Paris: L'Avant-Scene/C.I.B. Section rpt. Focus on the Science Fiction Film, ed. William Johnson. Englewood Cliffs, NJ: Prentice-Hall, 1972, pp. 26-30.

Méliès's film, A Trip to the Moon, was inspired by
Verne's From the Earth to the Moon. He uses the space
gun, but then departs from Verne by landing his people
on the moon. Méliès's Twenty Thousand Leagues Under the
Sea (1907) has little to do with Verne's novel, since
it takes the form of a dream. The Queen of the Ocean
appears and turns a fisherman into a naval captain in
command of a submarine.

D307 Butor, Michel. "Science Fiction: The Crisis of its Growth."
Tr. Robert Howard. Partisan Review, 34 (Fall), 595-602.
Rpt. SF: The Other Side of Realism, ed. Thomas Clareson.
Bowling Green, OH: Bowling Green University Popular Press,
1971, pp. 157-165.
Science fiction is distinguished from other genres of
the fantastic by its plausibility, but most authors today
are unable to master the range of contemporary science.
The work of Verne is first degree science fiction, "but
the day is almost past when a Verne could easily handle
the notions implied in all the technological applications
achieved in his age, and anticipate other applications
while remaining perfectly clear to the high school
students who formed his public." See E163.

D308 Costa, Richard Hauer. H. G. Wells. New York: Twayne
Publishers, pp. 32, 46-49.
Although Wells acknowledged more of a debt to Verne's
From the Earth to the Moon than to any other tale of a
cosmic voyage, the distinctions in The First Men in the
Moon are more significant. Verne was preoccupied with
machines and ignored characterization and description
of the lunar surface. Wells began where Verne left off
with richly developed characters and elaborate details
of the moon's landscape, but he never worried about
mechanical technicalities.

*D309 Dakkar (fanzine), 1 (no date, late 1967), 25 pp. + ix.
Not seen. Published by Ron Miller and Laurence Knight.
Contents: Ron Miller, "The Life and Times of Jules
Verne"; L. Knight, "The Mightiest Motion Picture of Them
All" (Disney's Twenty Thousand Leagues Under the Sea);
"Chronology of the Life of Prince Dakkar"; L. Knight,
"George Méliès"; "Shadow of Scartaris"; Ron Miller,
"Magnificent Jules and His Flying Machine"; Ron Miller,
"The Man of the Seas" (Nemo); "The Green Ray"; "The
Cryptographers"; Tom Miller, "From Mars to Earth" (War
of the Worlds and From the Earth to the Moon): artwork by
Ron Miller, L. Knight, Tom Miller, and Doug Byrum. Infor-
mation provided by Ron Miller.

D310   Evans. I. O.   "Introduction."   In <u>Around the World in Eighty Days</u>, by Jules Verne.   London: Arco Publications, pp. 7–9.

Verne's idea for a "beat the clock" tour of the world came from an article in <u>Le Magasin pittoresque</u> that discussed how the construction of the Suez Canal would expedite world travel and also suggested an itinerary. The novel was a spectacular bestseller and was dramatized by Adolphe d'Ennery.   Among the many people who set out to duplicate Phileas Fogg's journey was American journalist Nellie Bly.   She picked up a rich husband on the way.

D311   _____.   "Introduction."   In <u>The Danube Pilot</u>, by Jules Verne.   London: Arco Publications, pp. 7–8.

An historical novel, the narrative is set in the period about thirty years before it was written.   It concerns a "grim dictatorship confronted by a heroic resistance movement."   Written in the form of a <u>roman policier</u>, it fails as a detective story, but it is a "thriller." This edition is the first appearance of the novel in England.

D312   _____.   "Introduction."   In <u>Down the Amazon</u>; Part One of <u>The Giant Raft</u>, by Jules Verne.   London: Arco Publications, pp. 7–9.

The narrative exhibits Verne's enthusiasm for cryptography, an interest he derived from Poe.   Verne's use of the skill is, however, "rather elementary."   Evans explains that in his translation he rendered the original French message into English, then reenciphered it using the same method as did Verne.

D313   _____.   "Introduction."   In <u>A Drama in Livonia</u>, by Jules Verne.   London: Arco Publications, pp. 7–8.

Interests in the detective story and foreign affairs are joined by Verne in this novel about the clash of Teuton and Slav nationalities in the Baltic States.   As a patriotic Frenchman, Verne's sympathies were with the Russians.

D314   _____.   "Introduction."   In <u>The Sea Serpent; The Yarns of Jean Marie Cabidoulin</u>, by Jules Verne.   London: Arco Publications, pp. 7–9.

Intrigued by the possibility of huge sea monsters, Verne studied evidence for and against their existence, then wrote this tale of a serpent.   Evans, as translator, apologizes for his lack of knowledge of nautical matters.

D315 Hillegas, Mark R. The Future as Nightmare; H. G. Wells and
the Anti-Utopians. New York: Oxford University Press,
pp. 10-11.
　　　　Although most of Verne's science fiction was written
early in his career, he established the genre as a
"distinct mode of writing" and prepared the way for Wells
and others. He appealed to the "romantic interests of
the nineteenth century" despite limitations of characterization and style.

D316 Honan, William H. "They Live in the Year 2000: The Futurists
Take Over the Jules Verne Business." New York Times
Magazine, 9 April, pp. 56-57, 59-60, 62, 64, 66, 68, 72,
74.
　　　　Businessmen are retaining science fiction writers like
Frederik Pohl to describe the future. Our "future orientation" has spawned a new field of professionals called
"futurists." Because they are unnerved by the accelerated
rate of technological change, businessmen turn to science
fiction writers who are used to coping with the problem.
While writers such as Verne, Wells, Anatole France, and
Swift have succeeded as prophets of the future, technological sociological forecasting is full of famous
blunders. Verne is one of the few who guessed right
consistently.

D317 Jacobs, Will. Review of A Long Vacation. New York Times
Book Review, 26 November, p. 62.
　　　　While similar to adventure tales like Robinson Crusoe
and Swiss Family Robinson, Verne adds a unique element
in A Long Vacation. There is a "delicate interplay of
social and psychological relationships" in the colony
of English, French, and American schoolboys. They
consciously reproduce "a model Anglo-Saxon society."

*D318 Miller, Ron. "The Fantastic World of Jules Verne." Cosign
(fanzine), 10 (May).
　　　　Not seen. Listed in the collection on Verne at
Spaced Out Library of the Toronto Public Library, 40
St. George St., Toronto, Ontario M5S2E4.

D319 Sprout, Monique. "The Influence of Poe on Jules Verne."
Revue de littérature comparée, 41 (January-March), 37-53.
　　　　A brief account of the publishing of translations of
Poe's works in mid-nineteenth-century France is followed
by a review of critical studies that consider Verne's
indebtedness to the American. Sprout then presents her
findings, which detail similarities in character development, situations, and the device of utilizing concrete
facts and encyclopedic lists to add realism to fantasy.
Poe's influence on Strange Doings Underground (Child of
the Cavern) is analyzed at length.

D320 Toffler, Alvin. Review of <u>Future Perfect: American Science Fiction of the Nineteenth Century</u>, by H. Bruce Franklin. <u>Technology and Culture</u>, 8 (January), 151-153.

In preface to his discussion of this collection, Toffler notes the success of an exhibition in Paris that celebrated the sale of the millionth copy of a paperback edition of Verne's novels. Seven to ten thousand people a day came to honor the man who prophesied the helicopter in 1889, the automobile in 1869, and suggested a manned moon venture in 1865. In his greeting, Yuri Gagarin wrote, "reading Jules Verne made me devote my life to space."

<u>1968</u>

D321 Armytage, W. H. G. <u>Yesterday's Tomorrows: A Historical Survey of Future Societies</u>. London: Routledge and Kegan Paul, pp. 39-40.

Brief discussion of "The Eternal Adam" and "Day of an American Journalist in 2889 A.D." French speculation about the future was almost exclusively associated with Verne. The dual vision of catastrophe succeeding catastrophe over the ages in the "Eternal Adam" gives the work "a sense of gloom quite absent from the earlier work."

D322 Clarke, Arthur C. <u>The Promise of Space</u>. New York: Harper and Row, pp. 7-11.

Although much of it is written facetiously, <u>From the Earth to the Moon</u> is important because it is the first moon voyage to be based on sound scientific principles. In <u>The Begum's Fortune</u> he also made passing reference to artificial satellites.

D323 Clarens, Carlos. <u>An Illustrated History of the Horror Film</u>. New York: Capricorn Books, pp. 4-6.

Méliès's <u>A Trip to the Moon</u>, derived from Verne, is the movies' first venture into science fiction and interplanetary travel. It is a "mixture of surrealism, humor, stage pantomime, and one amazing instant of pure cinema thinking"; as the rocket leaves, the audience becomes part of the adventure rather than simply a spectator.

*D324 <u>Dakkar</u> (fanzine), 2 (July), 57 pp. + xii.

Not seen. Published by Ron Miller and Laurence Knight. Contents: I. O. Evans, "H. G. Wells War in the Air"; L. Knight, "The Invisible People of Wells and Verne"; I. O. Evans, "Jules Verne Iceland"; James C. Iraldi, "Visit to a Shrine -- part one of A Day in Amiens"; Sam Moskowitz, "The Influence of the American Boys' Weeklies on Jules Verne"; Ron Miller, "Who Invented the Albatross"; reviews of several books and movies; artwork by Ron Miller, Tom Miller, L. Knight, Beverly Neill, Mike Wendelken, David Lorek. Information provided by Ron Miller.

D325 Doyle, Brian. Who's Who in Children's Literature. New
York: Schocken, pp. 278-281.
Short, factual biography with a selected list of
Verne's works. "Unusual explorations, shipwrecks, inventions, discoveries, space-voyages, secret codes,
floating islands, giant ocean liners, airships, balloons
and adventures by the thousand -- Jules Verne had them
all at his finger-tips and enthralled readers of all
ages (but especially boys) throughout the world."

D326 Geduld, Harry M. "Return to Méliès: Reflections on the
Science Fiction Film." Humanist, 28 (November/December),
23-28. Rpt. Focus on the Science Fiction Film, ed.
William Johnson. Englewood Cliffs, NJ: Prentice-Hall,
1972, pp. 142-147.
Méliès originated the science fiction film genre with
such films as A Trip to the Moon, which was inspired by
Verne. Aside from remarkable technical innovations,
Méliès's films are characterized by the satirizing of
pomposity, erudition, and technology, and by a view of
the universe as a place of inexplicable wonder and magic.
Science might enable man to voyage through space, but
it would be unable to explain the wonders he would see.

D327 Moskowitz, Sam. Science Fiction by Gaslight: A History
and Anthology of Science Fiction in the Popular Magazines,
1891-1911. Cleveland: World Publishing Company, p. 115.
Rpt. Westport, CT: Hyperion Press, 1974.
Short introduction to the little known "An Express of
the Future," which deals with pneumatic tubes that will
propel a vehicle under the Atlantic from America to
France at record speeds. The story was inspired by a
novel by André Laurie.

1969

D328 Appel, Benjamin. "The Father of Science Fiction." In The
Fantastic Mirror: Science Fiction Across the Ages.
New York: Pantheon Books, pp. 82-100.
Brief mention of a few works which may have influenced
Verne precedes lengthy excerpts from Twenty Thousand
Leagues Under the Sea, Journey to the Center of the Earth,
and From the Earth to the Moon. Some illustrations from
editions of Verne's works are included.

D329 Birnie, William A. H. "Jules Verne's Trip to the Moon."
Readers Digest, 95 (October), 112-114.
Notes several remarkable similarities between From
the Earth to the Moon and Around the Moon and the Apollo
11 flight.

D330 Brunetti, Mendor T. "Foreword." In Twenty Thousand Leagues
      Under the Sea, by Jules Verne. New York: New American
      Library, pp. vii-x.
          Brief biography and comments on this one novel.
      Twenty Thousand Leagues Under the Sea exhibits Verne's
      great passions for freedom, music, and the sea. Verne
      creates his most memorable character in this story, and
      lavishes as much care on description of nature as most
      authors do on the psychological details of their
      characters.

D331 Chesneaux, Jean. "Jules Verne's Image of the United States."
      Tr. Frances Chew. Yale French Studies, 43 (November),
      111-127.
          Verne saw America as the frontier linking the known
      and the unknown worlds, as the closest thing to the model
      of progress he envisioned for humanity. America is the
      land where everything seems possible, the land of
      mechanics and engineers, where scientific problems are
      the concern of the man on the street, where the confronta-
      tion of man and nature takes place on a vast scale, where
      men of action breed an atmosphere of progress and success,
      and where the repressive machinery of the State is least
      felt. From 1890 onwards, however, Verne's view becomes
      quite pessimistic.

D332 Hill, Douglas. "Introduction" and "Appreciation." In
      Twenty Thousand Leagues Under the Sea, by Jules Verne.
      London: Heron Books, pp. xiii-xvi and pp. 281-309.
          Verne is far from an artist of genius. Kingsley Amis
      bluntly labeled him a "stylistic barbarian." However,
      his works are mind-expanding because he made the machine
      age accessible by popularizing science. Believing in the
      perfectibility of man, Verne is a romantic whose modern
      progeny wear the costumes of engineer, technician,
      inventor, researcher. At the same time, he recognized
      that technological advances could not, by themselves,
      bring Heaven on Earth. Along with technology, the two
      other forces dominating his thoughts were religious faith
      and wanderlust. Journey to the Center of the Earth
      deserves recognition as the first work of science fiction.
      Twenty Thousand Leagues Under the Sea provides "intel-
      lectual reassurance" in a world dominated by science.
      "If the technological age has a mythology, then Captain
      Nemo is one of its greatest mythic figures." He is
      "private Verne wish-fulfillment." This edition includes
      reproductions of diagrams of primitive submarines, il-
      lustrations from the original edition, and other Verniana.

D333 Jan, Isabelle. "Children's Literature and Bourgeois Society in France Since 1860." Tr. Wyley L. Powell. Yale French Studies, 43 (November), 69-71.

At the base of the Verne-Hetzel relationship was a misunderstanding. Hetzel expected to use Verne for didactic purposes, to bring modern knowledge to the young, pointing everywhere to the supremacy of the white man's intelligence, knowledge, and energy. But, in writing for children, Verne became a literary innovator; the didactic intention takes a backseat. Verne abandoned the idea that the novel is primarily a piece of psychological analysis, and attempted to make science itself the object of literature.

D334 Kontaratos, A. N. "The Amazing 1865 Moon Shot of Jules Verne." Look, 33 (27 May), 74-78.

With From the Earth to the Moon and Around the Moon Verne created "a prescient burlesque of American technocracy." Illustrations and excerpts from the text of the novels reveal the resemblances between Verne's vision and the reality of the Apollo 9 moon shot. Similarities include location of launch site, the Gun Club's telescope and NASA's telescopic cameras, shape and composition of projectile, the effect of zero gravity, splashdown.

D335 Sweeney, Thomas. "If Verne Could Look at NASA." National Review, 21 (20 May), 489-490.

Verne's "uncanny" predictive accuracy hit upon the country, state, latitude, splashdown area, and many other facts of the Apollo 8 moon flight. Despite choosing Tampa as the blastoff site, he even mentioned Cape Canaveral as one of only two alternate places. Predicting our future with "a Verne's chance of success," Sweeney sees the colonization of space with selectively bred superbrains.

D336 Warner, Harry, Jr. All Our Yesterdays: An Informed History of Science Fiction Fandom in the Forties. Chicago: Advent, pp. 4-5.

"The only specific Verne element in general fandom until the 1960's was a kind of early groping toward Hugo awards. This was the Jules Verne Prize Club that had a frail and temporary life around 1933. Raymond A. Palmer was its chairman. It cost two bits to join. The purpose was to sponsor voting for the best science fiction stories of the year, and provide cups for the authors. It seems never to have accomplished its purpose even once." See D394.

D337 Winandy, André. "The Twilight Zone: Imagination and Reality
in Jules Verne's Strange Journeys." Tr. Rita Winandy.
Yale French Studies, 43 (November), 97-110.
"Verne's fiction creates the realm of the twilight
zone, a fusion of the imaginary and the real." His plots
always present variations on the one basic structure of
the journey, through which the familiar themes of children's literature are expounded. The "mark of the other"
is present in the journeys in plot devices, in references
to other novels and characters, and in the presence of
the Divine. The purpose of the journey into the unknown
is to make it serve man better. Verne's graphic language
is a fusion of representation and invention, a combination
of scientific documentation and powerful imagination, and
he always places the unknown in conjunction with the known.
Also discusses Verne's use of the narrator.

1970

D338 Baxter, John. Science Fiction in the Cinema. New York:
A. S. Barnes and Company, p. 15.
Méliès' A Trip to the Moon, derived from Verne, is
probably the first example of a science fiction film,
and it differs little from the polished products of today.
It is basically a theatrical performance, with the Folies
Bergère chorus line serving the same function as the
sexy heroines of Fifties' space opera.

D339 Brautigan, Richard. "Jules Verne Zucchini." In Rommel
Drives Deep into Egypt. New York: Delacorte Press,
p. 22.
The five-line poem bemoans man's adventuresomeness
which drives him to the dead moon while millions of
people starve on the fertile world.

D340 Corliss, William R. Mysteries Beneath the Sea. New York:
Thomas Y. Crowell Company, pp. 138-143.
Verne converted the story about the ship Alecton
being attacked by a twenty-four foot squid, a story
discredited by the French Academy, into the kracken
attack in Twenty Thousand Leagues Under the Sea.

D341 Evans, I. O. "Introduction" and "Editorial Postscript."
In The Cryptogram; Part Two of The Giant Raft, by Jules
Verne. Bridgeport, CT: Associated Booksellers, pp. 7-8,
151-152.
The concluding document from Torres is obviously a
cipher, and Verne, who gained an interest in cryptography
from Poe, thought he made it completely insoluble. The
postscript suggests a method by which a French student
may have solved it.

D342 Green, Roger Lancelyn. "Introduction." In <u>Around the Moon</u>,
by Jules Verne. New York: E. P. Dutton and Company,
pp. ix-xiii.
   Verne's astronauts only orbited the moon because he
was aware that gravity made it impossible for a spaceship
to land then blastoff again from the surface of the moon.
For a century after Verne, fictional travelers in space
were propelled by purely imaginary means such as H. G.
Wells's "Cavorite" and Hugh MacCool's "Apergy." Verne
preferred to base his fantasy on known science. Barbicane
and Company created a log quite similar to those of Apollo
8 and Apollo 10. The <u>Voyages extraordinaire</u> contain
"some of the most amazingly accurate prophecies in
literature."

D343 Green. Roger Lancelyn. "Introduction." In <u>From the Earth
to the Moon</u>, by Jules Verne. New York: E. P. Dutton
and Company, pp. viii-xii.
   The history of fictional lunar voyages is outlined.
<u>The Man in the Moone</u>, by Francis Goodwin, 1638, "was as
accurate science fiction as anything by Bradbury or
Aldiss." Verne's account was the first to be based on
scientific fact. Green then compares Verne's trip to
that of Apollo 8.

D344 Hengen, Nona. "The Perception of Danger in Action Illustrations." <u>AV Communication Review</u>, 18 (Fall), 250-262.
   An illustration by N. C. Wyeth for an edition of
<u>Michael Strogoff</u> (New York: Charles Scribner's Sons,
1927) is used in an investigation of the properties of
pictures that evoke certain emotions in the observer.

D345 Jules-Verne, Jean. "Introduction." In <u>From the Earth to
the Moon and Around the Moon</u>, by Jules Verne. New York:
Limited Editions Club, pp. v-xiv. Rpt. New York:
Heritage Press, 1970.
   Verne claimed he chose a cannon as means of propulsion
for the moon shot in order to satirize "those cannon-
crazy specialists." He considered scientific progress
to be a new theme for a novelist. Able to "bring dreams
alive by making them seem possible," Verne was an extraordinary prophet. He believed that "anything one man is
able to imagine, some other man is able to accomplish."

D346 Philmus, Robert M. <u>Into the Unknown: The Evolution of
Science Fiction from Francis Godwin to H. G. Wells</u>.
Berkeley and Los Angeles: University of California
Press, pp. 25, 31-36.
   George Griffith borrows from Verne for his <u>Outlaws of
Air</u>. It is common to classify science fiction into the
line of Verne, realizable technological advances, and the
line of Wells, satiric mythifications of reality, but

this generalization admits of too many exceptions.
Verne often devotes only the most cursory attention to
plausibility. Their real difference lies in the distinction between public myth and private myth. Wells's
science fiction always relates outward to the public
world, but "Verne's private myth is an introverted
vision of man seeking self-enclosure," which explains
his mania for factual detail and the tendency of the
stories to refer to one another.

D347 Raines, Charles A. Jules Verne's Twenty Thousand Leagues
Under the Sea and Around the World in Eighty Days, Journey
to the Center of the Earth, The Mysterious Island, Michael
Strogoff. New York: Monarch Press.
The study guide contains a brief biography of Verne
along with summaries and critical commentaries on the
novels listed in the title. Typical essay questions and
suggested answers are provided. Short excerpts from
published criticism and a brief annotated bibliography
complete the volume.

D348 Roberts, Walter Orr. "After the Moon, the Earth." Science,
167 (2 January), 11-16, esp. 11.
From the Earth to the Moon had significant impact on
"world expectations for space travel."

D349 Weber, Eugen. "Pierre de Coubertin and the Introduction of
Organized Sport in France." Journal of Contemporary
History, 5 (No. 2), 3-26, esp. 11.
Paschal Grousset, founder of the Ligne Nationale de
l'Education Physique and an advocate, along with Coubertin,
of the revival of sports in school curricula, may have
collaborated with Verne on The Salvage of the Cynthia.

1971

D350 Amis, Kingsley. "Founding Father." In his What Became of
Jane Austen? And Other Questions. New York: Harcourt
Brace Jovanovich, pp. 33-37.
Verne, like Dickens, improves in retrospect; he has
the curious property of making his effect after the book
is shut. Five Weeks in a Balloon shows his usual trio of
character types: the eccentric but resourceful scientist,
the hot-tempered but honorable man of action, the faithful
but comic servant. The book rouses expectations that are
never properly fulfilled. Adventures are never brought
to a fever-pitch, and the most obvious chances for drama
are missed. Some irresponsible sensationalism would have
counteracted his deadening concern for probability and
facts.

D351 Blume, Mary. "In the Footsteps of Phileas Fogg." <u>Interna-</u>
<u>tional Herald Tribune</u>, 30-31 January, p. 14.
    An account of S. J. Perelman's plans to duplicate the
eighty-day tour around the world.

D352 Brunner, John. "The Educational Relevance of Science
Fiction." <u>Physics Education</u>, 6 (November), 389-391.
    Like all science fiction writers, Verne was influenced
by the climate of opinion surrounding him. His work
reflects "the naive Victorian belief in man's ability to
conquer the universe by the power of steam." Verne
examined the economic and political changes resulting
from improvements in transportation. Questions he considered include whether frontiers would disappear, and
if increased trade would eliminate financial barriers
between rich and poor.

D353 Connelly, Wayne C. Review of <u>The Space Novels of Jules</u>
<u>Verne</u>. <u>Science Fiction Review</u>, 43 (March), 32-33.
    The Dover editions with the translation of Edward Roth
and the original illustrations is superior to the I. O.
Evans editions. They are not abridged, they retain the
humor of the original French, and the scientific explanations are intact.

D354 de Chirico, Giorgio. "On Metaphysical Art." In <u>Metaphysical</u>
<u>Art</u>, by Massimo Carrà. New York: Praeger Publishers,
p. 87.
    Mentions Verne as an influence on his work. "But who
was more gifted than he in capturing the metaphysical
element of a city like London, with its houses, streets,
clubs, squares, and open spaces; the ghostliness of a
Sunday afternoon in London, the melancholy of a man, a
real walking phantom, as Phileas Fogg appears in <u>Around</u>
<u>the World in Eighty Days</u>?"

D355 Field, James A., Jr. "Transnationalism and the New Tribe."
<u>International Organization</u>, 25 (Summer), 353-372.
    Although he was not an Anglo-Saxon sympathizer, Verne
recognized the potential of English to become the world
language. As early as 1869, his character Pierre
Aronnax, in <u>Twenty Thousand Leagues Under the Sea</u>, states
that English is "à peu près universelle."

D356 Gay, William T. "Jules Verne: The Prophet of the Space Age."
<u>The Futurist</u>, 5 (April), 76-78.
    Since Verne started with known facts and then developed
his futuristic inventions, he foresaw the Apollo flights
in <u>From the Earth to the Moon</u> and <u>Around the Moon</u>. "His
success as a forecaster appears to be due in no small

measure to the fact that many of his readers were inspired
to realize the inventions and feats he dreamed about."
Such people as Konstantin Tsiolkovsky, Robert Goddard,
Guglielmo Marconi, and Yuri Gagarin have acknowledged
his influence.

D357 Kagarlitski, Julius. "Realism and Fantasy." In SF: The
Other Side of Realism, ed. Thomas D. Clareson. Bowling
Green, OH: Bowling Green University Popular Press, pp.
29-52.
Realistic fantasy such as written by Verne developed
not by assimilating but by rejecting romantic fantasy.
Verne, a positivist who saw no distinction between moral
progress and material progress, is inflexible, non-dia-
lectical, and ill-adept at analysis of complex social
contradictions. The fantasy of Verne is a "fantasy of
objects"; Wells, on the other hand, has roots in romanticism. The spirit of science has changed in this century,
rendering the realism of Verne now unacceptable.

D358 Lewis, Anthony. "Perelman Plans Trip, Verne-Style, Around
World in 80 Days." New York Times, 7 January, p. 2.
S. J. Perelman discusses his plans to follow Verne's
tracks in Around the World in Eighty Days and test his
reliability. An article on May 25 (p. 5) notes his less
than triumphant return.

D359 Lundwall, Sam J. Science Fiction: What It's All About.
New York: Ace Books, pp. 34-36.
Brief overview of Verne's works that indicates the
move from optimism in the early works to pessimism in
The Begum's Fortune, Floating Island, and For the Flag.
"By reading up intelligently on the technical developments of his time, he was able to speculate on possible
future developments. . . . A somewhat more nearsighted
form of this speculation is now done under the name of
'future research' in private and military research
centers."

D360 Schmidtchen, Paul W. "The Father of Science Fiction."
Hobbies, 76 (December), 135-136, 145.
Enthusiastic discussion of Verne as prophet. Verne
did not come up with his "fantastic kernels" out of a
vacuum, but we must still pay homage to the "sober and
industrious Frenchman prescient enough to make fact dance
harmoniously to the tune" of his fiction.

D361 Wollheim, Donald A. "Verne or Wells?" In The Universe
Makers: Science Fiction Today. New York: Harper and
Row, pp. 16-23.

The dialogue and characterizations label Verne's work
as "primarily for juvenile readers." His tales of
imaginary voyages and remarkable inventions never
ventured into social satire. He "remained to the end a
typical small-minded French bourgeois nationalist."

1972

D362   Anon. "The Bourgeois Facade." Times Literary Supplement,
       17 November, p. 1391.
           Jean Chesneaux's study, The Political and Social Ideas
       of Jules Verne (D366, E486), is "enthusiastic, informa-
       tive but somewhat blinkered" because what he considers
       political commitment is more probably "acceptance of a
       Romantic literary tradition." The anarchist Captain
       Nemo would be less a paradox in the light of Verne's
       bourgeois conservatism if the hero is seen as a "Byronic
       outlaw." In his last chapter, Chesneaux becomes less
       sure of the political and social context of the Voyages
       extraordinaires.

D363   Barthes, Roland. "The Nautilus and the Drunken Boat." In
       Mythologies. Tr. Annette Lavers. New York: Hill and
       Wang, pp. 65-67.
           The basic activity in Verne is appropriation. He
       constantly sought to shrink the world to a known and
       enclosed space, and the apt image for this in his writing
       is the ship, an emblem of closure and cherished seclusion.
       The Nautilus is the most desirable of all caves, and the
       enjoyment of being enclosed reaches its height when the
       vagueness of the outside can be contemplated through its
       large window. See E195.

D364   Berger, Albert I. "The Magic That Works: John W. Campbell
       and the American Response to Technology." Journal of
       Popular Culture, 5 (Spring), 867-943, esp. 871-873.
           In a study that looks at science fiction as a mode of
       understanding the average man's reaction to the techno-
       logical society, Verne is considered to be the first
       "fantast" to relate visions to "the realities of engineer-
       ing practice in the industrial states." While none of
       the science of Twenty Thousand Leagues Under the Sea is
       especially advanced, the potentials of new "curiosities,"
       such as electricity and the submarine, are channeled into
       weapons with which to fight tyranny.

D365   Cap, Biruta. "A French Observer of the Baltic." Journal
       of Baltic Studies, 3 (Summer), 133-137.
           A Livonian Tragedy (Drama in Livonia) was the result
       of a voyage through the Baltic in 1881. It contains a

wealth of accurate data because Verne knew the area was
unknown to Western Europeans. The novel shows that he
was clairvoyant in human affairs as well as scientific
matters, for its thesis is that the area was passing
from German influence to Slavic. It is a mystery story,
but based on physical, political, and social realities,
not clichés.

D366 Chesneaux, Jean. The Political and Social Ideas of Jules
 Verne. London: Thames and Hudson.
 See E486, D389.

D367 Johnson, William. "Further Comment." In his Focus on the
 Science Fiction Film. Englewood Cliffs, NJ: Prentice-
 Hall, pp. 158-160.
 Contains very brief comments by Richard Fleischer,
 director of the film version of Twenty Thousand Leagues
 Under the Sea (1955), comparing it with his work on
 Fantastic Voyage. Ray Harryhausen cites Mysterious
 Island as a good example of how a story is changed to
 embrace the entertaining visuals that can be produced
 by special effects. Verne's story was changed for
 audience acceptance and cinematic needs.

D368 Jonas, Gerald. "Onward and Upward With the Arts: S.F."
 New Yorker, 48 (29 July), 33-36, 38, 43-44, 46, 48-52.
 In this discussion of the emergence of science fiction
 into academic respectability, two types of literature in
 the genre are recognized by Robert Silverberg: "high"
 SF written by authors like Verne, Wells, Orwell, and
 Huxley, and the commerical kind, which has been treated
 until recently as a "literary ghetto." Lately the two
 are converging. The actualization of technologies, such
 as the moon landing, has liberated science fiction writers
 from the "delusion" that their business is technological/
 scientific prophecy. The reader "left behind" with Verne
 will have difficulty making "satiric sense" of the
 gadgets in modern science fiction.

D369 Perelman, S. J. "Around the Bend in Eighty Days." New
 Yorker, 47 (1 January), 22-24. Rpt. in his Vinegar Puss.
 New York: Simon and Schuster, 1974, pp. 31-75.
 With pungent humor, Perelman recounts his association
 with Mike Todd in the filming of Around the World in
 Eighty Days, and then, fifteen years later, his redis-
 covery of the novel and consequent desire to test Verne's
 accuracy.

D370 Richardson, Joanna. "Jules Verne: A Portrait." History
 Today, 22 (December), 886-887, 889.

An overview of Verne's life and work which briefly
mentions his friendship with the balloonist Nadar after
whom Verne modeled several characters, and notes the
geographical and historical studies as well as the
Voyages extraordinaires.

D371　Steinbrunner, Chris and Burt Goldblatt.　Cinema of the
　　　Fantastic.　New York:　Galahad Books, pp. 3-14, 235-254.
　　　　　Long summaries of Méliès's A Trip to the Moon and the
　　　Disney Twenty Thousand Leagues Under the Sea, with copious
　　　illustrations.

D372　Suvin, Darko.　"On the Poetics of the Science Fiction Genre."
　　　College English, 34 (December), 372-383.　Rpt.　Science
　　　Fiction:　A Collection of Critical Essays, ed. Mark Rose.
　　　Englewood Cliffs, NJ:　Prentice-Hall, 1976, pp. 57-71.
　　　　　Brief mention of Verne in this essay defining science
　　　fiction.　Verne's scientific novel is a legitimate form
　　　of science fiction, but is a lower stage in its develop-
　　　ment.　It is popular with audiences just approaching
　　　science fiction "because it introduces into the old
　　　empirical context only one easily digestible new techno-
　　　logical variable."　Verne's novels are like a pond after
　　　a stone has been thrown in:　momentary commotion, waves,
　　　then a settling down as before.

D373　Veszy-Wagner, L.　"The Corpse in the Car:　A Minor Myth
　　　Creation."　American Imago, 29 (Spring), 53-69, esp. 67.
　　　　　A psychological situation so common to be termed a
　　　"modern myth" occurs to one who feels exploited or
　　　dependent upon another, and he creates a fantasy where
　　　both victim and victimizer (sometimes as corpse) are
　　　trapped in a car.　Verne's novel, Around the World in
　　　Eighty Days, is a literary interpretation of a dream
　　　state in which the hero is persecuted but always manages
　　　to escape.　The time element accentuates the dream
　　　quality.

D374　Willis, Donald C.　Horror and Science Fiction Films:　A
　　　Checklist.　Metuchen, NJ:　Scarecrow Press.
　　　　　Contains factual information about the various Verne
　　　films, with an occasional, brief comment.

1973

D375　Aldiss, Brian W.　Billion Year Spree:　The History of
　　　Science Fiction.　Garden City, NY:　Doubleday and
　　　Company, pp. 94-99.
　　　　　Verne follows Poe in his use of scientific detail and
　　　the way in which his protagonist stands outside society,
　　　but "where Poe is the doomed poet of the Inward, Verne

is the supreme celebrant of the Outward." His early
work celebrates progress -- "everything works like mad"
-- but the "later novels clog with satanic cities instead
of super-subs." The negative features of his writing are
a flat tone, thin characters, lectures, and a nonsensual
world. The positive features are a fascination with
scientific possibility, a passion for geography, affection
for liberty and the underdog, political awareness, and
relish for a good story.

D376 Allen, L. David. Science Fiction: An Introduction.
      Lincoln, NB: Cliffs Notes, pp. 12-13, 15-23.
          Analysis of Twenty Thousand Leagues Under the Sea.
      Verne is the archetypal practitioner of "Extrapolative
      Hard Science Fiction," and Hal Clement is his best
      descendent. Everything that Verne included in Twenty
      Thousand Leagues Under the Sea was valid according to
      the scientific knowledge and theory of 1870. The voyage
      has several purposes: to exhibit the Nautilus, to portray
      the wonders of the undersea world, and to convince people
      that much can be learned from the sea. Verne's major
      theme is the joy of discovering the many wonders revealed
      by science, but lesser themes include the nature of free-
      dom and happiness and ecological damage.

D377 Angenot, Marc. "Jules Verne and French Literary Criticism."
      Science-Fiction Studies, 1 (Spring), 33-37.
          A bibliographic essay that surveys recent publications
      on Verne. Contemporary critics are concerned with Verne's
      "imaginative gifts, narrative techniques, and world view."
      The novels are studied in terms of myth and psychoanalysis.
      See D408.1.

D378 C., D. G. Review of The Political and Social Ideas of Jules
      Verne, by Jean Chesneaux. Journal of European Studies,
      3 (March), 89.
          In contrast to Verne the man, a conservative bourgeois,
      the novelist is a supporter of utopianism, individualism,
      and is opposed to oppression and capital exploitation.
      Chesneaux, in his study (D366, E486), stresses Verne's
      "evolution from Saint-Simonian confidence towards pessi-
      mism." Beginning with The Begum's Fortune, the "steel
      city of Stahlstadt" overshadows the "'radiant city'" of
      Franceville, while science fiction gives way to political
      fiction with a Wellsian tone.

*D379 Clough, Raymond Joseph. "The Metal Gods: A Study of the
      Historic and Mythic Aspects of the Machine Image in
      French Prose from 1750 and 1940." Ph.D. dissertation,
      State University of New York at Buffalo.

Verne is discussed in Chapter 2, which treats the
period from 1860 to 1890. During this time the dangers
of technology became evident and the machine image blends
with the myths of Prometheus, Pygmalion, and Galatea.
Not seen (information taken from Dissertation Abstracts
International, 34 (1974), 5959 A).

D380 Emme, Eugene M. "Space and the Historian." Spaceflight,
15 (November), 411-417.
In a footnote, Emme considers Verne's From the Earth
to the Moon along with the works of H. G. Wells and Kurd
Lasswitz, to have been "inspirational" to astronautical
scientists Tsiolokovsky, Goddard, and Oberth.

D381 Farmer, Philip José. The Other Log of Phileas Fogg. New
York: Daw Books, Inc.
Verne did not know of or tell the whole story of
Phileas Fogg. About 200 years ago Earth was visited by
Capelleans and Eridaneans who lived forty-five light
years away. They fought here, and survivors on both
sides went underground, passing as humans, and enlisted
humans as allies. Fogg is an Eridanean, and his trip
around the world is part of the continuing warfare
between the two races. Nemo appears as a Capellean.
Included as an appendix is "a Submersible Subterfuge or
Proof Impositive" by H. W. Starr, in which evidence is
included to show that Nemo is related to Professor James
Moriarity of the Sherlock Holmes stories.

D382 Jan, Isabelle. On Children's Literature. London: Allen
Lane, pp. 134-140.
Discussion of Verne under "Adventure" stories. Verne's
"absolute forest of numbers" affects the reader hypnot-
ically and satisfies a childish liking for precision and
competition. It keeps the narrative's boundless extrav-
agance within reasonable limits. "Ultimate discovery,
power or happiness cannot be experienced on earth; the
only hope is to get as far from earth and as near to the
unattainable as possible -- and then, like Robinson
Crusoe, recreate a familiar, practical, sheltered world."
Except for those adventures that are social instead of
individual, Verne's works are definitely for the fifteen-
year-old. See E390.

D382.1 Lowndes, Robert A. W. "Three Oldtimers." In Three Faces
of Science Fiction. Boston: NEFSA Press, pp. 55-65.
Compares Verne, Wells, and Edgar Rice Burroughs on
the basis of invention, suspense, characterization,
surprise, richness, and demand.

D383 MacKenzie, Norman and Jeanne MacKenzie. H. G. Wells: A
      Biography. New York: Simon and Schuster, pp. 117-118.
      The distinction between Wells the pessimist and
      Verne the positivist is obscured by the similarity of
      their subject matter. While Wells was concerned with
      the social implications of man's mastery of nature,
      Verne did not question progress and attempted to predict
      the scientific marvels of the future.

D384 Moskowitz, Sam. "Lost Giant of American Science Fiction
      -- A Biographical Perspective." In The Crystal Man, by
      Edward Page Mitchell. Garden City, New York: Doubleday
      and Company, pp. ix-lxxii, esp. pp. xix-xliii.
      Contains information on early American reprintings
      of Verne works and excerpts of early reviews. Verne
      was not really popular in America until 1873, so it is
      truer to say that the American dime novel influenced
      Verne, rather than vice versa. Edward S. Ellis, Harry
      Enton, and Luis P. Senarens had created successful
      "invention story" formulas before translations of Verne
      appeared.

D385 Pereira, Arty. "Jules Verne; He Started a New Era." In
      They Won Fame and Fortune. Delhi: Hind Pocket Books,
      pp. 11-18.
      Technical prophecies are accentuated in this brief
      biographical sketch. Verne wrote science articles for
      a children's magazine, and the inventions created in his
      novels include television, helicopter, neon lights, air
      conditioning, guided missiles, and the submarine. A
      comparison of Verne's trip in From the Earth to the Moon
      and the actual journey in 1969 reveals extraordinary
      similarities in locale, and the projectile's size, shape,
      and crew.

D386 Stover, Leon E. "Anthropology and Science Fiction." Current
      Anthropology, 14 (October), 471-474, esp. 472.
      Because he "antedates the research revolution," Verne
      is not a science fiction writer. His heroes are indivi-
      duals, skilled mechanics and craftsmen of the industrial
      revolution. Nemo and Robur are today viewed as madmen
      because "they are not team members of some research and
      development enterprise." But Verne did inaugurate the
      subgenre of science fiction that speculates about pre-
      historic man with his novel The Village in the Treetops.

D387 Williamson, Jack. H. G. Wells: Critic of Progress.
      Baltimore: Mirage Press, pp. 4, 9, 85, 112.
      Wells termed his novels "scientific romances" to
      distinguish them from Verne's "anticipatory inventions."

While Verne dealt with the "actual possibilities of
progress," Wells created fantasy that humanized a fantastic notion by "translation into commonplace terms."
Verne could never understand Wells's acceptance of the
purely fantastic. Wells did utilize material from Verne,
however. The moon ship in The First Men in the Moon is
similar in shape and equipment to Verne's projectile in
From the Earth to the Moon.

1974

D388 Bester, Alfred. The Computer Connection. New York:
      Berkley Publishing Corporation, esp. pp. 29-35.
         Captain Nemo appears as a character in this science
      fiction novel about a future world where everything and
      everyone is monitored and largely controlled by super-
      computer, Extro. Nemo is a lesser member of a group,
      called "Molemen," all of whom have achieved eternal life
      through a biochemical accident that results from devasta-
      ting physical injury. Among the Molemen, all epileptics
      incidentally, are Jesus, Edison, Lucretia Borgia, H. G.
      Wells, Samuel Pepys, and Oliver Cromwell. The waterlogged
      Captain arrives with a huge, affectionate octopus named
      Laura in tow. Nemo has created her with transplants,
      including a mouth that produces a Japanese accent.

D389 Cahm, Eric. Review of The Political and Social Ideas of
      Jules Verne, by Jean Chesneaux. History, 59 (February),
      136-137.
         The infrequency of personal comments and the vastness
      of Verne's literary output make conclusions about his
      political and social views difficult to ascertain.
      While a more elaborate and systematic sampling than
      that produced by Chesneaux is necessary, humanitarian
      and progressive notions he attributes to Verne do reflect
      the novelist's "encyclopaedic knowledge of his period."
      See D366, E486.

D390 Cohen, William B. "Literature and Race: Nineteenth Century
      French Fiction, Blacks and Africa 1800-1880." Race, 16
      (July), 181-205.
         Fiction echoes the attitudes of Frenchmen of this
      period toward the black race. Verne was certain of the
      white man's mission and confident of the efficacy of the
      spread of Western science, technology, and power. In
      Five Weeks in a Balloon and Southern Star Verne sees "no
      moral dilemma in colonization." While he acknowledges
      the clash of two cultures, Verne assumes that the natives
      want knowledge. The relations between the races in The
      Mysterious Island are at best of the master-servant type,
      but the black servant Neb and the beast are very similar.

D391 Frewin, Anthony. <u>One Hundred Years of Science Fiction Il</u>-<u>lustration, 1840-1940</u>. New York: Pyramid Books, pp. 42-45.

Illustrations from the original editions of <u>From the</u> <u>Earth to the Moon</u> and <u>Clipper of the Clouds</u> are reproduced. The engraving by Hildebrand depicting the effects of weightlessness upon the pioneer astronauts is labeled one of science fiction's most famous illustrations. Frewin states that Verne's technology existed in a vacuum, with few social consequences.

D392 Friend, Beverly. <u>Science Fiction: The Classroom in Orbit</u>. Glassboro, NJ: Educational Impact, Inc., pp. 11-13.

In this guide for a high school-level course, Verne and Wells are considered the two fathers of science fiction. While Verne wrote "Gadget-adventure," Wells produced "Social SF." Verne imagined invention grounded in scientific possibility. Since his mechanisms change neither their creators nor users, "his characters remain caricatures."

D393 Ketterer, David. <u>New Worlds for Old: The Apocalyptic</u> <u>Imagination, Science Fiction, and American Literature</u>. Garden City, NY: Anchor Books, pp. 50-52, 57.

Because of the direct line between Poe and Verne, some recent critics see Poe as contributing to the "nuts and bolts" kind of science fiction, but Poe's contribution to science fiction has been blurred by Verne's selective use of his themes. Poe's use of pseudoscience within the context of a hoax is severely different from Verne's. "In providing a visionary reality out of space and time with a science fiction rationale, Poe inaugurated that visionary tradition of science fiction that owes nothing to Jules Verne but that includes many of the masterpieces of the genre."

D394 Moskowitz, Sam. <u>The Immortal Storm: A History of Science</u> <u>Fiction Fandom</u>. Westport, CT: Hyperion Press, pp. 16-17.

Brief mention of the Jules Verne Prize Club, formed by science fiction fans in 1933 to select the best science fiction stories of the year. The club was to carry "forward the torch ignited by the immortal Jules Verne" and to "help make the world science fiction conscious." <u>See</u> D336.

D395 Serres, Michel. "India (The Black and the Archipelago) on Fire." <u>Sub-Stance</u>, 8 (Winter), 49-60.

<u>The Steam House</u>, a novel that breaks down into annexed short tales, gains coherence and continuity through fire.

With the power generated by the Industrial Revolution,
the West attempts to master the world. Verne depicts
this energy and force in the mobile steam engine built
in the shape of an elephant within which Colonel Munro
and his compatriots try to overrun Indian rebels. But
the Steel Giant explodes, ripping men into tiny fragments
of flesh. The elephant is a symbol of the triumph of
fetishism. In this novel, science and technology have
traveled from west to east, back to Nature and man's
origins. Natural fires, the sun, lightning, and summer
are shown to be fecund and artistic; but science's fire
is evil, produces madness, works in the interest of
death and exploitation. It kills in a white flash.
India, the "backward" nation triumphs -- science has a
culture on its back.

D396　Suvin, Darko. "Communication in Quantified Space: the
　　　　Utopian Liberalism of Jules Verne's Science Fiction."
　　　　Clio, 4 (October), 51-71.
　　　　　　Influenced by Saint-Simon, Verne's innovative machines
　　　　are vehicles that communicate industrial liberalism. The
　　　　"clean technology" and fellowxhip that foster scientific
　　　　advances result in a utopian vision interpolated into
　　　　rather than extrapolated from the present. But after
　　　　1875 Verne's outlook becomes gloomy and his explorers
　　　　turn into "power-mad inventors." The later works pre-
　　　　figure the dark forces in the energy man has mastered
　　　　from nature.

D397　Wright, Pearce. "Turning to Verne in Fuel Crisis." Times
　　　　(London), 18 March, p. 7.
　　　　　　In The Mysterious Island, Verne said man will burn
　　　　water when there is no more coal, and now scientists are
　　　　attempting to produce hydrogen from water on a massive
　　　　scale as an alternative energy source.

1975

D398　Ash, Brian. Faces of the Future -- The Lessons of Science
　　　　Fiction. New York: Taplinger Publishing Company, pp.
　　　　37-41.
　　　　　　The first speculative writer to fully exploit the
　　　　potential of the machine, Verne's early work reflects a
　　　　consideration of technology as a vehicle of freedom from
　　　　a bourgeois society. Gradually, however, his interpreta-
　　　　tions picture the machine as out of control, corrupting,
　　　　and leading to the "dehumanization of man."

130

D399   Clareson, Thomas D. "Lost Lands, Lost Races: A Pagan
       Princess of Their Very Own." Journal of Popular Culture,
       8 (Spring), 714-723, esp. p. 717. Rpt. Many Futures,
       Many Worlds: Theme and Form in Science Fiction, ed.
       Thomas D. Clareson. Kent State University Press, 1977,
       pp. 117-140.
            Between 1870 and 1930 the most popular kind of imagin-
       ary voyage was the "lost race" novel, a new primitivism
       that rejected the increasingly complex urban-technological
       society. Heralded by Verne's Five Weeks in a Balloon,
       the essay-like topical debates gave way to increased
       emphasis on story as the period progressed. Verne pro-
       vided the basic formula for the juvenile audience.

D400   Gunn, James. "A Victorian Engineer: 1828-1905." In his
       Alternate Worlds: The Illustrated History of Science
       Fiction. Englewood Cliffs, NJ: Prentice-Hall, pp. 63-76.
            An overview of Verne's life with pointed comments about
       his important works. Verne was a man of his times, ac-
       cepting and glorying in science and invention, and he
       wrote two types of science fiction: the wonderful journey
       and the wonderful invention. Verne was no visionary. He
       would take something reasonably possible and then through
       research, invention, scientific explanation, and emphasis
       on entertainment, he would convince his readers it was
       about to happen. Poe was a literary influence, but Verne
       was a social one. "His direct influence on future writers
       and their work would not be great; but because of him
       there was an audience for what they wrote -- and a market."

D401   Hammond, Paul. Marvellous Méliès. New York: St. Martin's
       Press, pp. 119-120 and passim.
            Méliès is closer to the Carroll of The Hunting of the
       Snark than to Verne. His films are parodies of Verne's
       sober romances. "Verne's Voyages extraordinaires became
       Méliès ludicrous expeditions."

D402   Hartwell, David G. "Introduction." In An Antarctic Mystery,
       by Jules Verne. Boston: Gregg Press, pp. v-ix.
            The major distinction between Verne's novel and Poe's
       The Narrative of Arthur Gordon Pym lies in the authors'
       attitudes toward the supernatural. For Verne the super-
       natural is limited to the human soul; whereas for Poe it
       is externalized as mystery in the natural world. Verne
       substitutes a marvelous scientific fact for the enigmatic
       finale left by Poe. While Poe's works influence the
       fantasy of Lovecraft and Bradbury, Verne's reliance on
       science leads the way to Gernsback's modern science
       fiction.

D403 Hillegas, Mark. "Victorian 'Extraterrestrials.'" In The
      Worlds of Victorian Fiction, ed. Jerome H. Buckley.
      Cambridge: Harvard University Press, pp. 391-414.
          Nineteenth-century scientific and technical advances
      led novelists to strive for plausibility in fictional
      journeys into space. Verisimilitude became firmly
      established with Verne's From the Earth to the Moon and
      Around the Moon. Three stories serve as forerunners to
      Verne's lunar tales: George Tucker's A Voyage to the
      Moon (1827); Edgar Poe's "Hans Pfaall" (1835); and the
      moon hoax perpetrated by the New York Sun in a series of
      articles by Richard Adams Locke titled, "Great Astronom-
      ical Discoveries Lately Made By Sir John Herschel at the
      Cape of Good Hope." Verne's two novels influenced other
      tales for fifty years. Hillegas details Verne's indebt-
      edness to works in descriptive and sidereal astronomy,
      and notes that Paschal Grousset's bizarre novel, The
      Conquest of the Moon (English trans. 1889), is derived
      from Verne's stories.

D404 Menville, Douglas. A Historical and Critical Survey of the
      Science-Fiction Film. New York: Arno Press, passim.
          Brief mention of the Verne films in this survey of
      science fiction films through 1957.

D405 Miller, James G. "Living Systems: The Society." Behavioral
      Science, 20 (November), 366-535, esp. 461.
          The technology needed for the use of hydrogen as fuel,
      produced by electrolysis of sea water, has been developed
      for use in spaceships. Distributed through existing gas
      lines, the process would not pollute. Verne foresaw this
      as early as 1874. In The Mysterious Island his engineer
      states that when coal and other fuels are exhausted, the
      hydrogen and oxygen in water, used singly or together,
      will be an inexhaustible source of energy.

D406 Rottensteiner, Franz. The Science Fiction Book: An Il-
      lustrated History. New York: Seabury Press, pp. 66-77.
          Discussion of Verne in such short chapters as "The
      French Father of Science Fiction," "The Mysterious
      Captain Nemo," "A World in the Moon," "Two Moon Journeys:
      Verne and Wells," and "Into the Hollow Earth." But this
      book is most valuable for its illustrations and movie
      stills. See E680.

D407 Salkeld, Robert. "Space Colonization Now?" Astronautics
      and Aeronautics, 13 (September), 30-34.
          Among the earliest expressions of the notion of "small
      self-contained worlds in space" is Verne's Off On a Comet
      (Hector Servadac).

D408   Serres, Michel. "Jules Verne's Strange Journeys." Tr.
Maria Malanchuck. Yale French Studies, 52 (September),
174-188.
By relating Verne's work to Homeric epic and Greek
mythology, Serres demonstrates that the Voyages extraordinaires constitute circles upon circles of knowledge
delineating both spatial and temporal "maps." It is
through imagination that man can travel beyond the
circles within which he is limited by his knowledge and
which determine his identity. Someone who calls himself
"I," that is, an "ego," must remain "immobile" within
the familiar. The hero ventures beyond the known and
discovers that he is "nobody." "The more I know, the
less I am; the more I know, the more I move." Nemo and
Ulysses mean "No one."

1976

D408.1   Angenot, Marc. "Jules Verne and French Literary Criticism
(II)." Science-Fiction Studies, 3 (March), 46-49.
Since the first part of this study (D377), "six
significant studies have conclusively placed Jules Verne
among those writers whose works mark a turn not only in
the history of utopian and technologico-adventurous SF
but also from the 19th to 20th century." Summarizes
works by Jean Jules-Verne, Marie-Hélène Huet, Simone
Vierne, Michel Serres, and P.-A. Touttain.

D409   Anon. "Le Grand Jules." Economist, 260 (18 September),
124-125.
Verne's kind of story was a "documentary," the product
of "magpie-like research," "scientific information, moral
exegesis and the minimum of character development." Jean
Jules-Verne's "uninformative" biography (D417) only hints
at the pessimism and anarchy felt by the novelist after
he lost his "faith in science as a moral agent in the
improvement of mankind." Also of influence in this regard
were Poe, a frustrating domestic life, and critics who
misinterpreted his work. Verne lamented in 1905: "What
could I do without my work? What would become of me?"
He deserves better than this "appetiser of a biography."

D410   Ash, Brian. Who's Who in Science Fiction. New York:
Taplinger Publishing Company, pp. 197-198.
Short survey of Verne's writing career. Verne's
forte in the early period was a sense of wonder coupled
with glorification of the machine, but the character of
Robur in Master of the World (1904) indicates his feeling
that technology was being misused. These darker visions
are also present in The Begum's Fortune, Floating Island,
and For the Flag.

D411 Atkins, Thomas R. <u>Science Fiction Films</u>. New York:
    Monarch Press, a division of Simon and Schuster, pp.
    6-8.
        Borrowing ideas from Verne, Georges Méliès's <u>A Trip</u>
    <u>to the Moon</u> contains many of the basic ingredients of
    the science fiction genre: egotistical scientists,
    space travel, alien creatures, bizarre plantlife, lobster-
    clawed monsters, and even attractive females. This 1902
    film convinced everyone of the creative potential in
    movies, and the entire science fiction genre derives
    from it. Like <u>2001</u>, this film is a conjurer's show,
    appealing predominantly to the senses, offering magical
    and mystical views, and full of humor and awe.

D412 Benthall, Jonathan. <u>The Body Electric: Patterns of Western</u>
    <u>Industrial Culture</u>. London: Thames and Hudson, pp.
    38-46.
        Although influenced by Saint-Simon's emphasis on the
    political power of technical specialists, Verne does not
    create scientists who are pioneering heroes of an indus-
    trial culture. Instead, they are "figures of fun, mis-
    anthropes, even madmen." Many of the novels set in
    America reflect a disillusionment with large-scale
    industry and the power of money. <u>The Begum's Fortune</u>
    presents the threat of the "total perversion of science."

D413 _____. "The Great Technologist." <u>Spectator</u>, 237 (21
    August), 20.
        Jean Jules-Verne's biography (D417) is written in a
    dry, understated, commonsense way, and owes much of its
    structure to skirmishes with other biographers. Verne's
    most striking importance is "in the history of commercial
    publishing," and the book is "like the leisurely history
    of a family firm by the founder's heir." Verne can be
    read today for his passion for sonorous dictionary words
    and for his mannerist flourishing of narrative devices.
    <u>Castle of the Carpathians</u>, with its conflict between
    rustic superstition and objective technology, is an
    underrated novel.

D414 Clareson, Thomas D. "The Emergence of the Scientific
    Romance, 1870-1926." In <u>Anatomy of Wonder: Science</u>
    <u>Fiction</u>, ed. Neil Barron. New York: R. R. Bowker
    Company, pp. 38-40, 75-76.
        The basic ingredients of a Verne story are "a man of
    reason (a scientist) who will both invent the necessary
    gadgetry and provide factual information; a journey to
    some exotic destination, generally somewhere on earth;
    and a series of largely disconnected adventures, most
    often involving the threat of pursuit and capture."
    Verne adopted the traditional imaginary voyage by making

the voyage itself rather than the unknown society the raison d'etre of his narrative. Emphasis on new technology, particularly the hardware of transportation, and encyclopedic inclusion of facts are his main contributions to science fiction.

D415 Edelson, Edward. <u>Great Science Fiction From the Movies</u> (originally titled <u>Visions of Tomorrow: Great Science Fictions From the Movies</u>). New York: Pocket Books, pp. 20-27.

By the time filmmakers became interested in Verne, events had moved too far ahead. "By playing it deadpan -- in effect, by imagining that the twentieth century has never happened -- filmmakers have been able to turn out some versions of the Verne novels that are entertaining, if nothing else." In order to film Verne they must turn their backs on the idea that science fiction is a vision of the future.

D416 Holt, Cherryl. Review of <u>Jules Verne</u>, by Jean Jules-Verne. <u>Smithsonian</u>, 7 (November), 178-179.

So far ahead of his time, Verne is thought of as a twentieth-century man traveling on a "time warp." In 1889 he foresaw the invention of "television, electronic calculators, and picture telephones." His concern for mankind tempers his advocacy of technology with a fear of its misuse. His novels show the benefits of knowledge and the consequences of its abuse. <u>See</u> D417.

D417 Jules-Verne, Jean. <u>Jules Verne: A Biography</u>. Tr. Roger Greaves. New York: Taplinger. Also London: MacDonald and Jane's, 1976.

In this factual account by Verne's grandson, interpretation and speculation are limited. The author does contend with some material presented by other biographers, such as the psychoanalytic interpretations of Marcel Moré, and Marguerite Allotte de la Fuÿe's somewhat romanticized depiction. The focus of the biography is on Verne's publications. Originally published by Librarie Hachette in 1973 (<u>see</u> E575), additional materials in this edition include a bibliography that lists first editions and first English translations of Verne's works, details about Paul Verne and Verne's friend Herminie, and certain photographs. <u>See</u> D409, D413, D416, D418, D421.1, D424, D425, D434.

D418 Korn, Eric. "Extrapolating Hopefully." <u>Times Literary Supplement</u>, 17 December, p. 1576.

His "energetic optimism," "remorseless pedagoguery and his dreadful jokes" put us out of sympathy with Jules Verne. Jean Jules-Verne's biography (D417) is eccentric,

old-fashioned, defensive, and unexciting. Verne despised
tyranny and colonialism, was skeptical of public opinion,
and enjoyed "autocratic heroes -- a little like Wells in
his New Machiavelli phase." More than a "utopianist for
engineers," Verne's characters frequent the abyss as
regularly as they reach for the stars. His final weak-
ness is that he "extrapolated rather than speculated."

D419 Kyle, David. A Pictorial History of Science Fiction.
London: Hamlyn Publishing Group, pp. 23-27.
Brief overview of Verne's work, embellished with
illustrations, which notes the influence of Poe, the
move away from science fiction in mid-career, and the
loss of idealism at the end of his career.

D420 Miller, Walter James, ed. and tr. The Annotated Jules
Verne: Twenty Thousand Leagues Under the Sea. New
York: Thomas Y. Crowell Company.
A "reconstructed" edition that exposes the large-scale
omissions and alterations existing in most earlier English
translations of Verne's work. Miller strives to substan-
tiate Verne's respected European reputation by restoring
abridged text, and by providing generous, detailed annotations that supply information on natural and scientific
phenomena as well as evaluate "literary maneuvers." The
"Foreword" and "Afterword" discuss Verne's life, the
"crimes" of translators, and analyze the literary merit
of the novel. Reproductions of engravings from the
original French edition accompany illustrations from
scientific treatises, periodicals, textbooks, and an
1873 encyclopedia. See D431.

D421 Moskowitz, Sam. Strange Horizons: The Spectrum of Science
Fiction. New York: Charles Scribner's Sons, pp. 25-27,
55-56.
In discussing the attitudes of early science fiction
writers toward Jews and Blacks, Moskowitz finds Verne
quite disappointing. Anti-Semitism is evident from the
very beginning of his career, and the Jew-baiting in
Hector Servadac becomes embarrassing. Robur the Conqueror
(Clipper of the Clouds) was inspired by a Frank Reade
story, but Verne makes his black character a contemptible
coward.

D421.1 Nicol, Charles. "Jules Verne by His Grandson." Science-
Fiction Studies, 3 (November), 311.
Review of the biography by Jean Jules-Verne (D417,
E575). Jules-Verne's observations about Nemo are a good
example of the way in which his close attention to Verne's
life make his book superior to the biographies by Allote
de la Fuÿe and Allott.

D422 Strick, Philip. <u>Science Fiction Movies</u>. London: Octopus
      Books, pp. 37–39, 118–123.
        Consideration of many of the films made from Verne
novels. The cinema has treated this "most prolific
writer about social immaturity" very well "by maintaining
the 19th-century background to his stories and emphasizing
at a safe distance of one hundred years, that he wasn't
far from the mark here and there."

D423 Turner, E. S. "No Love For Nemo." <u>The Listener</u>, 26 August,
      p. 254.
        Verne, who worried "mightily about the insolence of
science," was influenced by ancient religious epics,
"'the chthonian powers' and other mystical forces."
The emphasis on plot summaries in Jean Jules-Verne's
biography (D417) makes the novelist's penchant for
explosions evident. Scientific extravaganzas, horrors,
adventures, masses of ideals and prejudices are all
there. What is lacking is the love element.

<u>1977</u>

D424 Brooks, Idamae. Review of <u>Jules Verne</u>, by Jean Jules-Verne.
      <u>Psychology Today</u>, 11 (June), 117.
        Verne's "villains with redeeming virtues" and "heroes
with weaknesses" all have a streak of naiveté. Jean
Jules-Verne's biography (D417) is "a bit dry of blood,"
keeping the reader distant from Verne the man. The
silent films based on Verne's works, with their "fantastic
yet practical" "wonderful mechanisms," are memorable.

D425 Budrys, Algis. "Books." <u>Magazine of Fantasy and Science
      Fiction</u>, 52 (June), 13–16.
        Review of the biography by Jean Jules-Verne (D417).
Verne is one of those writers like Michael Crichton or
Martin Caidin after him for whom there is no such thing
as dialogue or narrative. They give bills of lading
rather than description, media rather than language.
They are not people who discover and highlight the world,
but who arrange props and spotlight them.

D426 Chernysheva, Tatyana. "The Folktale, Wells, and Modern
      Science Fiction." In <u>H. G. Wells and Modern Science
      Fiction</u>, eds. Darko Suvin and Robert M. Philmus.
      Lewisburg, PA: Bucknell University Press, pp. 35–47.
        Since his concern was machines, not human societies,
it is not surprising that Verne exiled the folktale from
his scientific novels. Like Verne, Russian science
fiction writer Alexsandr Belyaev has a sensitivity to
scientific novelties and a capability to envision their
further prospects.

D427 Coste, Didièr. "Politextual Economy: In Defence of an
      Unborn Science." In The Radical Reader, ed. Stephen
      Knight and Michael Wilding. Sydney, Australia: Wild
      and Woolley, pp. 37-53.
         Using the model of "textual economy," discusses Five
      Weeks in a Balloon and The Mysterious Island to see if
      the Voyages extraordinaires are reactionary or progres-
      sive. The answer is reactionary: "While Jules Verne's
      work announces itself as directed to the invention of
      the future (knowing the unknown, that is producing it),
      to its own expansion as a world, it is a 'closed' work
      built on the principle of mission accomplished, and so
      doing it only reproduces its own conditions of production,
      the execution of an order."

D428 Garfield, Eugene. "Negative Science and 'The Outlook for
      the Flying Machine.'" Current Contents, Physical and
      Chemical Sciences, 17 (27 June), 5-16.
         The history of heavier-than-air flying, even after
      the Wright Brothers' feat, is full of pessimistic prognoses
      and even "proofs," such as Simon Newcomb's famous argument
      and a New York Times editorial. After airplanes achieved
      commercial success, ridicule was directed at rocketry.
      However, Verne's fictional forecast of a flight to the
      Moon had prophetic accuracy. Most of his astronauts
      were American, they blasted off from Florida, encountered
      weightlessness, and landed their capsule in the Pacific.
      Because technological forecasting is professionally
      "risky," some of the most accurate predictions are made
      by science fiction writers rather than scientists.

D429 Gunn, James. "The Indispensable Frenchman." In The Road
      to Science Fiction: From Gilgamesh to Wells. New York:
      New American Library, pp. 253-255.
         Brief introduction to excerpts from Twenty Thousand
      Leagues Under the Sea and Around the Moon. "Verne wrote
      simple stories about uncomplicated people. His ideas
      were not particularly original; most of them he got from
      authors he admired. His plots consisted of abductions,
      searches, mysteries, and ambitious undertakings; the
      events of the stories were often marked by accident and
      coincidence."

D430 Komatsu, Sakyo. "H. G. Wells and Japanese Science Fiction."
      In H. G. Wells and Modern Science Fiction, eds. Darko
      Suvin and Robert M. Philmus. Lewisburg, PA: Bucknell
      University Press, pp. 179-190, esp. pp. 181-182, 184,
      188-189.
         Because of the technical inventions Verne foresaw,
      Komatsu states that "World War II could be called the
      War of Verne." Verne's works began appearing in Japanese

around 1880. A publishing boom resulted, largely attributed to the enthusiasm of people cut off geographically and culturally from communications. Prose literature was considered "vulgar," thus the novels of Verne and Wells were classed in the lowest order. However, Verne "unlocked a door to the future and the international world outside the claustrophobic islands." Many native imitations followed.

D431 Mitgang, Herbert. "Publishing: Volga Spacemen." New York Times, 4 February, p. C 20.
     In an article discussing recent publication of Soviet science fiction, Mitgang also mentions Walter Miller's definitive edition of Twenty Thousand Leagues Under the Sea (D420). The text is twenty-three percent longer than familiar translations; illustrations, text, and special materials were provided by the New York Public Library, Library of Congress, and the New York Times. Some of Verne's prophecies, mentioned by Miller, are noted: the ecology crisis, "renascence of African peoples," industrialization of China, French separatism in Canada, "prostitution of science by power elites."

D432 Osborn, Michael. "The Evolution of the Archetypal Sea in Rhetoric and Poetic." Quarterly Journal of Speech, 63 (December), 347-363.
     Change in the metaphoric use of the sea is traced from classical disorder, to medieval individualism and alienation from society, on to the Renaissance concept of suffering and redemption at sea, finally to Romantic freedom from social responsibilities and harmony with the self. The alienated Romantic identified with an outlaw, thus Captain Nemo, in Twenty Thousand Leagues Under the Sea, can exclaim his independence from all masters while in the "bosom of the waters."

D433 Parish, James Robert and Michael R. Pitts. The Great Science Fiction Pictures. Metuchen, NJ: Scarecrow Press.
     Provides factual information about the Verne films, and also succinct critical commentary that frequently refers to other reviewers.

D434 Richardson, Joanna. "The Foresight of Verne." History Today, 27 (January), 56-57.
     Verne's scientific predictions, especially his anticipation of the Apollo 9 mission, and the "pathetic" aspects of his life are emphasized in this review of Jean Jules-Verne's biography (D417).

D435 Rovin, Jeff. <u>The Fabulous Fantasy Films</u>. South Brunswick,
NJ, and New York: A. S. Barnes and Company, pp. 172-176.
Verne's novels were the basic material for several
films that highlighted special effects. Rovin discusses
Disney productions <u>Twenty Thousand Leagues Under the Sea</u>
(1954) and <u>Journey to the Center of the Earth</u> (1959).
In these films characterization loses the spotlight to
fantastic monsters. "The players are less animated than
the giant squid." Other films discussed are <u>Mysterious
Island</u> (1961), <u>Captain Nemo and The Underwater City</u>
(1965), <u>Master of the World</u> (1961), and <u>The Fabulous
World of Jules Verne</u> (1961).

D436 _____. <u>From Jules Verne to Star Trek: The Best of Science
Fiction Movies and Television</u>. New York: Drake Publishers.
Among the one hundred films considered in this compilation are three movies derived from Verne novels: Disney's
<u>Twenty Thousand Leagues Under the Sea</u>, the 1959 Twentieth
Century-Fox production of <u>Journey to the Center of the
Earth</u>, and Columbia Pictures' 1961 rendition of <u>Mysterious
Island</u>. Rovin provides synopsis of plot, comments on
strengths and weaknesses as well as the place of the
film in science fiction film history. Data on studio,
cast, director, year of release, and running time are
also included. In regard to the film <u>Twenty Thousand
Leagues Under the Sea</u>, Rovin notes that the Verne novel
is a "complex saga of men, machines and morality," but
in the film version, everything is a "caricature."

D437 Scholes, Robert and Eric S. Rabkin. <u>Science Fiction:
History, Science, Vision</u>. New York: Oxford University
Press, pp. 9-10, 196-200.
Verne is quite different from Poe. As Poe descends
from Swift and Blake, Verne descends from Defoe and Comte.
He is the poet of hardware, his technology is closely
limited by the science of his time, and he is resolutely
unspeculative. Whereas Shelley was ambivalent toward
science, Verne embraced it. <u>Twenty Thousand Leagues
Under the Sea</u> is scientific adventure with obsessive
enthusiasm; the overall story intended to tie the episodes together is really not memorable at all.

D438 Shrum, Edison. "Jules Verne, Father of Science Fiction."
<u>Hobbies</u>, 82 (September), 152.
Brief overview of Verne's major works focusing on his
"remarkable foresight."

D439   Suvin, Darko.   "Introduction." In <u>H. G. Wells and Modern Science Fiction</u>, eds. Darko Suvin and Robert M, Philmus. Lewisburg, PA: Bucknell University Press, pp. 9-32, esp. pp. 20-21.

For Verne, science was the "bright noonday certainty of Newtonian physics." H. G. Wells continued the development of science fiction by going beyond Verne with an "ambiguously disquieting strangeness."

1978

D440   Angenot, Marc.   "Science Fiction in France Before Verne." <u>Science-Fiction Studies</u>, 5 (March), 58-66.

Verne's ideological niche as "the father of SF" and his status as a writer for the young are not fortuitous, but "rather the product of institutional movements and specific ideological occultations." French science fiction before Verne is surveyed, and the social constraints within which he worked are indicated. Verne brought to science fiction "a benign social justification: the promotion of a literature for young people, progressivist and 'virile,' with no exaggerated display of moralism and with good literary value."

D441   Binyon, T. J.   "Triumphantly Romantic." <u>Times Literary Supplement</u>, 27 January, p. 83.

Review of Peter Costello's <u>Jules Verne: Inventor of Science Fiction</u> (D443). Verne is not a writer of science fiction at all. He "never adopts either of science fiction's two main devices: projection into the future, or introduction of alien elements into the present." His novels are set in the present and recent past, and come from a combination of known facts. His characters, in embracing science, represent a metamorphosis of the Romantic hero, their predecessors are the heroes of Dumas, and their successors lie in novels by such Soviets as Leonid Leonov or Daniil Granin.

D442   Bombard, Alain.   "Jules Verne: Seer of the Space Age." <u>UNESCO Courier</u>, 31 (March), 31-36.

Verne is one of the three most translated authors in the world, behind only Lenin and Agatha Christie. Short biographical sketch with summary of several novels. Verne was a prophet of progress, not violence, an apostle of constructive, useful science. He never produced any "politics fiction," nor, unfortunately, any "biology fiction."

D443   Costello, Peter.   <u>Jules Verne: Inventor of Science Fiction</u>. London: Hodder and Stoughton.

Verne and his writings are presented in the context
of the scientific, technical, and geographical discoveries
of his time. In this biographical study, Costello emphasizes Verne's sources and discusses their use. He
also reveals details of Verne's private life that are
not considered by earlier biographers, including Jean
Jules-Verne. His main theme is Verne's loss of faith
in the old Catholic religion and the new science. This
disillusionment makes Verne a modern figure. Verne
invented a bleak idea of the future, despite the fact
that in the nineteenth century, "Vernian" suggested the
"romantic possibilities of the future, of science, and
of exploration." There is an extensive bibliography of
Verne's works and criticism. See D441.

*D444   Miller, Walter James. The Annotated Jules Verne: From the
Earth to the Moon, Direct in Ninety-Seven Hours and
Twenty Minutes. New York: T. Y. Crowell.
Not seen. Cf. Miller's Twenty Thousand Leagues
Under the Sea (D420).

D445   Tuck, Donald Henry. The Encyclopedia of Science Fiction
and Fantasy through 1968. Vol. 2. Chicago: Advent
Press, pp. 435-437.
Bibliography of primary material, with information
about English language reprints and variant titles.

1979

D446   Angenot, Marc. "Jules Verne, the Last Happy Utopianist."
In Science Fiction: A Critical Guide, by Patrick
Parrinder. London: Longman, pp. 18-33.
Accelerated circulation is the world-view which gives
a dynamic unity to all Verne's work, not just the scientific romances. Verne's most significant characters have
ambulatory fixations, and this circulation is discussed
in relation to science and capitalism. Verne is the
"last SF writer who believes in industrialist euphoria,
even if some pessimism overshadows his last books"; he
is a "utopianist without an alternative society."

D447   _____. "New Books on Jules Verne." Science-Fiction Studies,
6 (July), 224-227.
Reviews books by Peter Costello (D443), Walter James
Miller (D420), Marc Soriano (E857, E859), and Jean-Michel
Margot (E819). Costello's work has merit, but basically
"it is simply a good classical monograph, integrating
various recently developed theses on the author." Miller's
book "renders SF criticism a major service and should open
up a new era for Verne's literary fortune in English-
speaking countries," but he erred in using Lewis Mercier's

translation as the point of departure. Soriano's works
are influenced by psychoanalytic anthropology, but it
is regrettable that such analysis "does not extend to
a more elaborate synthesis of individual experience and
the social and historical 'unconscious.'" Margot's work
"is a useful research tool of the sort that should be
made available for other major SF writers."

D448   _____. Review of Pourquoi J'ai tué Jules Verne, by Bernard
         Blanc. Science-Fiction Studies, 6 (July), 228-229.
             Blanc's polemical essay is the manifesto of a group
         of young, politically pessimistic, dystopian science
         fiction writers who have radically rejected worn out
         narrative recipes and reactionary concepts (E783).
         "Nonetheless, with its brisk, fierce and often ambiguous
         attacks, its fireworks of images, catch-phrases, insults
         and political slogans, its aggressively slangy language,
         Blanc's pamphlet illustrates in a very significant fashion
         the mixture of authentic political critique and doubtful
         political gesticulation, of instinctive rejection of an
         unbreathable society and intoxication with a counter-
         mythology, that makes this important part of contemporary
         French SF fascinating and irritating."

*D448.1 Haining, Peter, ed. The Jules Verne Companion. New York:
         Baronet.
             Not seen. Cited in SFRA Newsletter, No. 81 (May 1980),
         p. 4 among other places. Contains an abridged translation
         of Verne's essay on Poe (C5), two Verne short stories, a
         Verne poem and speech, as well as commentaries and criti-
         cal articles by such people as Erich von Daniken. (Also
         London: Souvenir Press Ltd., 1978).

NO DATE

D449 Hollow, John. "Jules Verne: Journey to the Center of the
      Earth, From the Earth to the Moon, and Twenty Thousand
      Leagues Under the Sea." Audio-tape #1303. Everett/
      Edwards, Inc. Box 1060, Deland, FL 32720.
          Thirty-five minute tape containing substantial dis-
      cussion of three novels. From the Earth to the Moon ends
      with the hope that men will come out all right. Journey
      to the Center of the Earth ends with an uncertainty about
      whether man will ever solve the riddle of the universe,
      but with an affirmation of family affection. Twenty
      Thousand Leagues Under the Sea ends with the contrasting
      figures of Aronnax and Nemo, one in love with life and
      the other choosing to die.

D450 Miller, Walter James. "Jules Verne." Audio-Cassette
        #17061. Center For Cassette Studies, 8110 Webb Ave.,
        North Hollywood, CA 91605.
            Miller interviews Mendor T. Brunetti. Both men did
        translations of Twenty Thousand Leagues Under the Sea
        in an attempt to rehabilitate Verne's reputation in
        America from damage done by incomplete and inaccurate
        translations. Miller laments the excising of Nemo's
        political motivation, and Brunetti adds the Nautilus
        and Nature to the cast of characters.

Part E: Critical Studies in French

1866

E1 Gautier, Théophile. "Les Voyages imaginaires de M. Jules
    Verne." ["Imaginary Voyages of Jules Verne"] Moniteur
    universel, No. 197 (16 July), p. 4. See E616.

1875

E2 Dubois, Lucien. "Le Roman scientifique. Jules Verne et ses
    oeuvres." ["The Scientific Novel. Jules Verne and His
    Works"] Revue de Bretagne et de Vendée, 4th series, 7
    (First Semester), 17-24.
        Some personal reminiscences of Verne, including the
    memory that he was a negligent student. Verne's reputation
    is based on his partly scientific works about which some
    reservations may be entertained similar to those that arise
    in connection with the historical novel. Verne is the French
    Walter Scott of science. Discusses Verne's Five Weeks in
    a Balloon and Adventures of Captain Hatteras. Captain
    Grant's Children is mentioned as a geographical work of
    vaster scope.

E3 I., R. "Jules Verne." L'Intermédiaire des chercheurs et des
    curieux, 25 December, p. 746.
        The Warsaw newspaper, Wiek, has published an article
    that states that Verne's real name is Olszuvic and that he
    was born in Plok, where his brother lives. The Polish
    paper Narodin Listy says the slavic word "Olse" means
    Verne, a French synonym of which is "Aune." Suggests that
    Verne is actually Polish.

*E4 Raymond, Charles. "Jules Verne." Musée des familles, 42
    (1875), 257-259.
        Not seen (cited in D137, p. 347).

1876

E5 H., A. "Jules Verne." L'Intermédiaire des chercheurs et
      des curieux, 10 January, p. 26.
          Confirms that Verne is a Frenchman, born in Nantes.

E6 Mathanasius. "Jules Verne." L'Intermédiaire des chercheurs
      et des curieux, 10 January, p. 26.
          Verne is French, born in Nantes, his father lived in
      the Rue Jean-Jacques, and he is married to the widow Morel,
      née Viane, of Amiens.

1881

E7 Topin, Marius. Romanciers contemporains. [Contemporary
      Novelists] Paris: Didier et Cⁱᵉ, pp. 375-396.
          Calls Verne the inventor of the scientific novel and
      emphasizes his treatment of the physical world. No mere
      compiler, Verne accumulated substantial scientific data
      and then exercised an artist's taste in choosing his
      materials. He created three types representing (1) an
      intelligent and directive force, (2) a material and obedient
      force, and (3) a mind casting joyous verve into the dialogue.
      Verne's English and American characters are generally people
      of initiative and energy. Normally his characters courage-
      ously conquer obstacles. He is the most popular novelist
      of his time.

1883

*E8 Audouard, Olympe. Silhouettes parisiennes. [Parisian
      Silhouettes] Paris: Marpon et Flammarion.
          Not seen (cited in D443, p. 226).

E9 Bastard, Georges. "Célébrité contemporaine: Jules Verne en
      1883." ["Contemporary Celebrity: Jules Verne in 1883"]
      Gazette illustrée, 8 September.
          See E599.

*E10 _____. Verne: auteur des "Voyages extraordinaires." [Verne:
      Author of "The Extraordinary Voyages"] Paris: Dentu.
          Not seen (cited in D443, p. 226). See also E599.

E11 Clarétie, Jules. Jules Verne. Paris: A. Quantin.
          A thirty page book, one of a collection of biographies
      of contemporary celebrities. Discusses Verne first as a
      writer of romances in verse (also quotes an early poem),
      then after treating the novels, more descriptively than
      analytically, emphasizes Verne's theatre, viewed as here-
      tofore neglected by critics. Mentions Verne's friendship
      with Dumas fils, calls Verne a "Dumas père on the phone"

and a cousin of Mayne-Reid and Fenimore Cooper. The
absence of love from his novels makes Verne something
other than a novelist properly speaking. He is the writer
of the unknown and the impossible.

1889

E12   Anon. "La Carte à payer." ["The Payment Card"] Journal
      d'Amiens, 25 June, n.p.
          See E777.

*E13 Jeanroy-Félix, Victor. Nouvelle histoire de la littérature
      française sous le second empire et la troisième république.
      [New History of French Literature Under the Second Empire
      and the Third Republic] Paris: Bloud et Barnal, pp.
      409-439.
          Not seen (cited in D137, p. 344).

E14   Saltarello, L.   Poem in La Picardie, 4 July.
          See E855.

1895

*E15 Turiello, M[ario]. "Jules Verne." In Causeries littéraires.
          Not seen (cited in D417, p. 237).

1899

E16   Brisson, Adolphe. Portraits intimes. [Intimate Portraits]
          Vol. 4. Paris: Armand Colin, pp. 111-120.
          Recounts a visit in which Verne speaks of his life and
      career. Emphasis is given to an early collaboration with
      Dumas fils (Broken Straws) and the publisher Hetzel's
      advice upon the success of Five Weeks in a Balloon that
      Verne should concentrate on this genre. Verne led a very
      regular life, devoted to work. Mentions a Thomas Cook
      advertisement as the source of Around the World in Eighty
      Days and George Sand as that of Twenty Thousand Leagues
      Under the Sea.

1903

*E17 d'Almeras, Henri. Avant La Gloire, leurs débuts: Jules
          Verne. [Before the Glory, Their Beginnings: Jules Verne]
      Paris: Société Française d'Imprimerie et de Libraire.
          Not seen (cited in D443, p. 226).

1905

*E18 Anon. "D'Anderson à Jules Verne." ["From Anderson To Jules Verne"] Le Gaulois du dimanche, 2 April.
  Not seen (cited in D137, p. 343).

E19 Blum, Léon. Article in L'Humanité, 3 April.
  See E361, E784.

*E20 Laurie, André. "Jules Verne." Le Temps, 25 March. p. 26.
  Not seen (cited in D137, p. 345).

*E21 Magasin d'éducation et de récréation, No. 248 (15 April).
  Special number on Verne. Not seen (cited in D417, p. 237).

E22 Morel, Eugène. "Jules Verne." La Nouvelle Revue, 33 (15 April), 439-449.
  Denies that Verne's readers were too young for their later life to be influenced by him. He was read everywhere and was particularly liked in England and Japan. This poet of an ungrateful time revolutionized the young "bourgeois." Tells of cool reception from Verne on meeting him, stresses Verne's desire to interest his readers, speaks of his liking for Amiens and of his practical nature, and calls him an apostle of hope.

*E23 Rauville, Hervé de. Jules Verne. Paris: Dupont.
  Not seen (cited in D443, p. 228).

*E24 Weulersse, G[eorges]. "Jules Verne éducateur." ["Jules Verne Educator"] Revue pédagogique (now L'Enseignement public), 46 (15 June), 548-553.
  Not seen (cited in D137, p. 348).

1906

E25 Bastard, Georges. "Jules Verne. Sa Vie--son oeuvre." ["Jules Verne. His Life and Works"] Revue de Bretagne 2nd series, 35 (January), 337-359.
  Details of Verne's upbringing in Nantes and his being drawn from law to theatre in Paris. Dumas fils collaborated with Verne on the play, Broken Straws. Places Verne among his friends in Paris, including the composer, Hignard, who collaborated with him on the song, Les Gabiers. Mentions Verne's marriage and two trips taken with Hignard. The last seventeen pages of the article contain comments on Verne's works. See E26.

E26 _____. "Jules Verne. Sa Vie--son oeuvre." ["Jules Verne.
His Life and Works"] <u>Revue de Bretagne</u>, 2nd series, 36
(July), 32-55.
Verne read voraciously, and among his masters were
C. Vogt, Geoffroy Saint-Hilaire, Quatrefages, Humboldt,
Herschell and the Dupetit-Thouars. Verne utilized every
kind of source, including newspapers. Force and material
laws are constantly in conflict in Verne. Plays derived
from Verne's novels are summed up. Devotes last pages
to some personal details of Verne's life. <u>See</u> E25.

*E27 Nozier. "Jules Verne et les fées." ["Jules Verne and
Fairies"] <u>Journal d'Amiens</u>, 15 October.
Not seen (cited in D299, p. 180).

E28 Toldo, Pietro. "Les Voyages merveilleux de Cyrano de
Bergerac et de Swift et leurs rapports avec l'oêuvre de
Rabelais." ["The Wondrous Voyages of Cyrano de Bergerac
and Swift and Their Relationship to the Works of Rabelais"]
<u>Revue des études Rabelaisiennes</u>, 4 (1906), 295-334.
In contrast to de Bergerac, Swift, and Rabelais, Verne
caters to the more modern reader's requirement that the
author must make what he says seem realizable.

1907

E29 Legrand, Edmée. "Anglais et Français: mot de Jules Verne."
["Englishman and Frenchman: Jules Verne's Witticism"]
<u>L'Intermédiaire des chercheurs et des curieux</u>, 10 January,
pp. 13-14.
Questions the source of the exchange in Jules Verne's
<u>Around the World in Eighty Days</u>, in which an Englishman
says that were he not English he would like to be French,
to which the Frenchman replies that were he not French
he would still like to be; suggests a seventeenth-century
writer such as Saint-Simon.

1908

E30 Lemire, Charles. <u>Jules Verne</u>. Paris: Berger-Levrault.
Treats specifically many aspects of Verne's life and
career. Covers his training, his friendships, his family
life. Portrays him as a private citizen and public
servant. Discusses Verne as a storyteller, a champion of
science, a poet, a novelist. Shows him as a member of
various learned societies. Reveals the reactions of
others to Verne both in France and abroad. Lists his
works in several categories.

*E31 Turiello, Mario. <u>Mélanges littéraires</u>. [Literary Mixtures]
Not seen (cited in D299, p. 180).

1909

E32   Barlet, H. "L'Auteur des Voyages extraordinaires." ["The
      Author of The Extraordinary Voyages"] Mémoires de La
      Société Dunquerquoise, 51 (1909), 3-48.
           Eschews listing all of Verne's works on the grounds
      they are too well known. Discusses Verne as a geographer,
      scientist, engineer, and novelist. He interests adults
      as well as children. His is a didactic and patriotic
      work.

E33   Potez, Henri. "Edgar Poe et Jules Verne." ["Edgar Poe and
      Jules Verne"] La Revue, 80 (15 May), 191-197.
           Treats Poe's influence on Verne. For example,
      Baudelaire's translation of Poe, Les Histoires extra-
      ordinaires, preceded Verne's Voyages extraordinaires.
      Poe's dirigible, "Victoria," made a fictional crossing of
      the Atlantic; Verne published Five Weeks in a Balloon.
      The denouements of "The Manuscript Found In a Bottle" and
      of "A Descent Into The Maelstrom" contributed to Verne's
      Twenty Thousand Leagues Under the Sea. "The Gold Bug"
      has resemblances to Journey to the Center of the Earth,
      and The Narrative of Arthur Gordon Pym is similar to
      Survivors of the Chancellor, Journey to the Center of the
      Earth and Adventures of Captain Hatteras. Poe's "Three
      Sundays In A Week" employs the element of time in the
      way that Verne does in Around the World in Eighty Days.

1910

*E34 Milvoy, et al. "Inauguration du monument Jules Verne."
      ["Inauguration of Jules Verne's Monument"] Bulletin
      d'Amiens Académie des Sciences, 56 (1910), 333-354.
           Not seen (cited in D137, p. 346).

1914

E35   Duquesnel, Félix. "Les Souvenirs sur Jules Verne."
      ["Reminiscences on Jules Verne"] L'Ouest Artiste, 25
      (21 March), 11-12.
           A few personal reminiscences and impressions of Verne
      by one who knew him. Describes Verne as an agreeable
      companion, a card player, a charming conversationalist.
      Going off to Paris Verne said he was either a Parisian
      from the provinces or a provincial from Paris. The day
      came when he tired of life in Paris.

E36   Tolstoï, Comte Elie. Tolstoï: souvenirs d'un de ses fils.
      [Tolstoy: Memories of One of His Sons] Paris: Calmann-
      Lévy.
           One of Tolstoy's sons mentions that his father used to
      read Jules Verne to his children.

1922

E37 R., C. "Jules Verne, Polonais." ["Jules Verne, Pole"]
L'Intermédiaire des chercheurs et des curieux, 20–30
December, pp. 958–959.
Claims a fairly long-standing legend in Poland says
that Verne's name was Olsseivicz and that he emigrated
from Poland in 1850. Verne is the French equivalent of
the Polish, Olcha. Mentions the published denials of
Verne's son and that Verne's birth certificate perished
in a fire during the Franco-Prussian War in Amiens, which,
the correspondent says, Michel Verne called his father's
birthplace. The writer asks readers for enlightenment.
See E3, E5, E6.

1923

E38 Latzarus, Marie-Thérèse. La Littérature enfantine en France.
[Children's Literature In France] Paris: P.U.F.
About ten pages of this three hundred page work are
devoted to Verne, who is listed with Louis Desnoyers,
Gustave Aimard, Assollant, and Carrey as the novelists
who drew on explorations and inventions to amuse the
young. Verne's originality is found in his unusual
treatment of the extraordinary and marvelous. Verne's
heroes are possessed of a confidence that stems from
science. Scientists discovered colored film sooner than
Verne foresaw. If toward the end of his career Verne
paints a despairing image of progress, still Verne enables
children to satisfy their imagination. However, Verne's
novels have aged because reality has outstripped his
imagination, and children no longer have the time to read
such long works.

1925

E39 Claudel, Paul. "Préface." In A La Trace de Dieu [On The
Track Of God], by Jacques Rivière. Paris: Gallimard.
Reference is made to Verne's The Mysterious Island
and the mysterious help in the form of a fire, a toolbox,
and a rope that comes to the shipwreck victims. Only the
engineer, Cyrus Smith, is curious about the source of this
aid. Jacques Rivière's attitude is similar to that of
Cyrus Smith.

1926

E40 Anon. "Michel Strogoff." La Petite Illustration cinémato-
graphique, 7 (7 August), 3–11.
An account of the film made from Verne's novel, Michel
Strogoff, directed by Tourjansky, the leading role played

by Ivan Mosjoukine. Recounts first "takes," May 14, 1925.
After many bloody scenes, Strogoff is rewarded by marriage
in Moscow to Nadia Federoff, his faithful and heroic
companion.

1927

*E41 Lepierre, Charles. Jules Verne, auteur d'une oeuvre de
      paix. [Jules Verne, Author Of a Work Of Peace] Lisbon.
      Not seen (cited in D137, p. 345).

1928

*E42 Anon. "Le Centenaire de Jules Verne." ["Centenary of Jules
      Verne"] Chronique des lettres françaises, 6 (1928),
      176-180.
      Not seen (cited in D137, p. 343).

E43   Bellesort, André. "Le Centenaire de Jules Verne, sa vie et
      son oeuvre." ["Centenary of Jules Verne, His Life and
      Works"] Journal des débats, No. 1773 (17 February), pp.
      290-292.
         As an answer to the story that Verne was a Polish Jew,
      his son published an abstract of his life on the occasion
      of his death. Bellesort recounts Verne's life and works.
      As others had vulgarized history, Verne did likewise for
      geography, seeing some of the places he described and
      reading avidly about them. Verne was didactic, but also
      a gifted storyteller. The romanesque, the geographic,
      and the scientific take turns at dominating his works.
      His heroes conquer with a Cornelian triumph of the will.

E44   Gaston-Pastre, J. L. "Jules Verne." La Revue hebdomadaire,
      25 February, pp. 483-486.
         Reviews the main trends of Verne's life, denying that
      he was a stay-at-home, pointing to the annual cruises on
      his yacht. Admires Verne's documentation, but is critical
      of his "superficial" characterization and his "elementary"
      psychology. Verne's knowing the Count of Paris did not
      alter his moderate republicanism. Explains Verne's seeming
      neglect of the French in favor of the English in terms of
      the latter's explorations and colonialism that captured
      the world's imagination. Credits Verne with influencing
      many French thinkers, including explorers and scientists.
      Concludes that despite Verne's prophesies being realized,
      reality has not always equaled his dreams.

*E45 Honoré, J. "Le Centenaire de Jules Verne." ["Centenary of
      Jules Verne"] L'Illustration, No. 86, pt. 1 (11 February),
      pp. 128-129.
         Not seen (cited in D137, p. 344).

*E46 Kessel, J[oseph]. "Jules Verne." Annales politiques et
      littéraires, 90 (1 February), 117-118.
         Not seen (cited in D137, p. 345).

E47 La Fuÿe, Marguerite Allotte de. Jules Verne, sa vie, son
     Oeuvre. [Jules Verne, His Life And Works] Paris: Simon
     Kra. Rpt. Paris: Hachette, 1953.
        Places Verne within the family circle, describing the
     writer's relationship to others within it. Emphasizes
     closeness to his brother from boyhood to the latter's
     death. Follows Verne's literary career, with attention
     paid to the role played by the publisher Hetzel. Situates
     Verne in his political ambiance and reports his opinions.
     Intimate references include those to Verne's final death-
     bed days and his confession. Pictures include one of
     the yacht, Saint-Michel.

E48 _____. "Préface." In Le Livre de Jules Verne. [The Book
     of Jules Verne] Paris: Hachette, pp. 5-16.
        Preface to a collection of tales drawn from Verne's
     novels, this provides a detailed account of the author's
     life.

E49 Lahy-Hollebeque, [M]. Les Charmeurs d'enfants. [The
     Charmers of Children] Paris: Edition Baudinière, pp.
     147-161.
        Chapters that discuss writers for the young from
     Charles Perrault to Rudyard Kipling include one on
     Verne, who, just as Walter Scott instilled a taste for
     history in the young, aroused in them a passion for
     science. Verne's originality and greatness lie in the
     constant expansion of his knowledge and his development
     as a visionary. His goal was to travel the cycle of
     human discoveries, putting them into operation and
     deducing their consequences. The discussion, broad
     rather than detailed, emphasizes that Verne was the
     precursor of inventions and instigator of explorations.
     A revolt against human nastiness and a passionate drive
     toward freedom are important aspects of Verne's
     philosophy.

E50 Morand, Hubert. "Le Centenaire de Jules Verne, son imagina-
     tion et son influence." ["The Centenary of Jules Verne,
     His Imagination And His Influence"] Journal des débats,
     No. 1773 (17 February), pp. 292-295.
        Between 1865 and 1886 Verne, a vulgarizer of geography,
     published four of his novels in the Journal des débats.
     Mathias Sandorf is an illustration of dramatic powers
     similar to those of Alexandre Dumas. Kéraban The Inflex-
     ible is an example of Verne's movement from a simple point
     of departure to events loaded with unexpected consequences.

Verne's economy of style demands the reader's concentration. Verne's psychology is defended on the grounds that he wrote for children, and that many distinguished Frenchmen have acknowledged that he instilled in his readers a feeling for research and passion for discovery. Concludes that he was a great nineteenth-century novelist and an initiator of the scientific movement of our time.

E51   Ocagne, Maurice d'. "Jules Verne." La Revue hebdomadaire, 1 September, pp. 35-54. Rpt. in his Hommes et choses de science. [Men and Things of Science] Paris: Vuibert, 1930.

    A centenary lecture, this recounts the various stages of Verne's life and career, remarking that his originality was due especially to his imagination and his regularly scheduled reading in the library of the Industrial Society. Verne kept in touch with current events by spending one week out of four in Paris even before the Franco-Prussian War. Verne, partly a romantic and partly a classicist, created a new genre and an untried combination composed of the romanesque, the geographic, and the scientific. To avoid scientific inexactitudes such as those he decried in Poe, Verne consulted experts. He foresaw the present. The article lists explorers and scientists in Verne's debt.

*E52   Praviel, Armand. "Jules Verne." Correspondant, 99 (25 January), 266-278.

    Not seen (cited in D137, p. 346).

E53   Roth, Georges. "Jules Verne et Byron." ["Jules Verne and Byron"] Revue de la littérature comparée, 8 (April), 343-345.

    Comments on an article by André Bellesort in the Journal des débats (1869), in which Verne's Captain Nemo is called Byronic. If Nemo is Byronic, it is especially through the mysterious hate that he has vowed against humanity and his love of solitude. A passage from Twenty Thousand Leagues Under the Sea is compared to one in Childe Harold.

1929

*E54   Anon. "Célébration du centenaire de Jules Verne." ["Celebration of the Centenary of Jules Verne"] La Géographie, 51 (March-April), 186-208.

    Not seen (cited in D214, p. 9).

*E55   Berge, François. "Jules Verne romancier de la navigation." ["Jules Verne Novelist of Navigation"] Revue générale, 121 (15 April), 455-468.

    Not seen (cited in D137, p. 342).

E56 Messac, Régis. Le "Detective Novel" et l'influence de la
     pensée scientifique. [The "Detective Novel" and the
     Influence of Scientific Thought] Paris: Champion.
        Four or five references to Jules Verne in this 600-
     page work on the detective novel record that Verne ex-
     plains a mystery by means of ventriloquism in César
     Cascabel and that Conan Doyle learned French by reading
     Verne, especially the captions over his illustrations.

E57 _____. "Voyages modernes au centre de la terre." ["Modern
     Voyages to the Earth's Center"] Revue de la littérature
     comparée, 9 (January-March), 74-104.
        Discusses the mixture of ancient legend and modern
     ideas in fictional trips to the Earth's center, mention-
     ing as Verne's precursors: Dante; Cyrano; the Dane, Louis
     Holberg, who published Niels Klim in Latin in 1741; Fieux
     de Mouhy; and Casanova. Speculates on Verne's possible
     debts to the past, but credits him with innovation in
     combating the theory of fire at the Earth's center. Says
     Poe was first to insist on verisimilitude in science
     fiction and places Verne within a tradition that will
     evolve with such writers as Bulwer-Lytton, J.-H. Rosny,
     Conan Doyle, Léon Groc, Edgar Rice Burroughs, and Jean
     Duval.

E58 Richet, Ch[arles]. "Jules Verne, aéronaute." ["Jules
     Verne, Aeronaut"] La Nature, No. 2803 (15 February),
     pp. 145-148.
        Verne placed his imagination and verve at the disposal
     of science. Thanks to him a vast arsenal of technical
     instruments entered the ken of young readers. He extra-
     polated the curve of phenomena beyond experience. Verne's
     Albatross, the flying machine in Clipper of the Clouds, is
     discussed in connection with subsequent developments in
     aviation.

1930

E59 Lemonnier, Léon. "Edgar Poe et le roman scientifique
     français." ["Edgar Poe and the French Scientific Novel"]
     La Grande Revue, No. 133 (August), pp. 214-223.
        Poe, introducing physics into the novel of voyages,
     modernized the genre of Defoe and created the scientific
     novel. Verne banished the marvelous and the psychology
     of the morbid from the tale of fantasy in favor of the
     positive science that Poe had introduced. Verne's An
     Antarctic Mystery differs from its model, Poe's Narrative
     of Arthur Gordon Pym, in the absence of the fantastic--
     Verne replaces Poe's marvelous with a pseudoscientific
     electrical snowstorm. A comparison of the denouements

shows Verne differing from Poe in emphasizing the reasoned
and positive sides of the adventure. Verne, owing many
themes to Poe, uses them better. Generally retaining
neither humor nor mysticism in his novel of positive
science, he achieves a more serious tone. Verne does
not totally eliminate the marvelous, the element which,
in fact, influenced his most notable successors, such as
J.-H. Rosny, the elder.

1931

E60 Charcot, [Jean]. "Quelques souvenirs des phoques de
     l'Antarctique." ["A Few Reminiscences of Antarctic Seals"]
     La Terre et la vie, July, pp. 323-329.
         The Ross seal makes a different sound than that made
     by the three other species of Antarctic seal. The others
     emit a sort of whistle and sometimes sound as if they
     were barking. The Ross seal lets out a slow and modulated
     whistle followed by a very sweet and gradually receding
     plaint. Captain Nemo on his way to the South Pole suggests
     that Homer's sirens could have been seals. When Verne
     wrote Twenty Thousand Leagues Under the Sea, the Ross
     seal was as yet unknown. See E74.

*E61 Drougard, E. Villiers de l'Isle Adam, Les trois premiers
     contes. [Villiers de L'Isle Adam, the First Three
     Stories] Paris.
         Not seen (cited in D417, p. 236).

1932

*E62 Dollfus, Charles and Henri Bouché. "Histoire de l'aéronauti-
     que." ["History of Aeronautics"] L'Illustration, No.
     182 (1932), pp. 97, 107.
         Not seen (cited in D137, p. 343).

1935

E63 Helling, Cornélis. "L'Oêuvre scientifique de Jules Verne."
     ["The Scientific Work of Jules Verne"] BSJV, 1, No. 1
     (November), 32-42.
         Names scientists and explorers whose testimony estab-
     lished Verne as a scientific prophet, but calls Verne a
     great novelist as well. He succeeded in combining science
     and fantasy. Discusses several of Verne's concrete
     scientific inventions or ideas as well as his hypotheses.
     Calls Verne the uncontested master of the didactic novel
     with a scientific base.

*E64 Kiszely, M. B. L'Image de la nation hongroise dans Jules
     Verne. [Image of the Hungarian Nation in Jules Verne]
     Debrecen, Hungary.
         Not seen (cited in D443, p. 227).

E65   Marcucci, Edmondo. "Jules Verne et les sources du Nil."
      ["Jules Verne and the Sources of the Nile"] BSJV, 1,
      No. 1 (November), 49-51.
          Since Verne's Five Weeks in a Balloon was published at
      the beginning of 1863, the author could not have known
      yet of the arrival at Khartoum of the English explorer,
      Speke, who telegraphed the news to London April 30, 1863,
      and later that year published Journal of the Discovery
      of the Sources of the Nile. Verne's reference regarding
      the Nile may have been Charles Beke's The Sources of the
      Nile, being a general survey of the basin of that river
      and of its head stream, with the history of the Nilotic
      discovery, published in London in 1860.

E66   _____. "La Nature et l'histoire dans l'oeuvre de Jules
      Verne." ["Nature and History in the Works of Jules
      Verne"] BSJV, 1, No. 1 (November), 43-48.
          Verne approached Nature not as a Romantic seeking
      answers to particular problems, but as one endowed with
      curiosity and enthusiasm. Verne, somewhat a disciple of
      Walter Scott, sometimes writes the historical novel, in
      which war inevitably plays a role. Verne's predilection
      was for wars of liberation. Distinguishes between the
      optimism of most of the Voyages extraordinaires and the
      comparative soberness of the works written in the twilight
      of Verne's life.

*E67 Ocagne, Maurice d'. "M. Georges Claude et l'énergie thermique
      des mers." ["Mr. George Claude and Thermal Energy in
      Seas"] Revue des deux mondes, 27 (15 May), 458-465.
          Not seen (cited in D137, p. 346).

E68   Roussel, Raymond. Comment J'ai écrit certains de mes livres.
      [How I Wrote Certain Books of Mine] Paris: Lemerre,
      pp. 27-28. Rpt. Paris: Jacques Pauvert, 1963.
          Contains author's tribute to Verne, crediting him with
      having attained in some of his works the peak use of
      language. See E221.

E69   Turiello, Mario. "Une Oeuvre qui ne meurt pas." ["A Work
      That Does Not Die"] BSJV, 1, No. 1 (November), 22-31.
          Refutes the view that Verne wrote books exlusively for
      children and either with a childish psychology or no
      psychology at all. Admits certain defects such as the
      abuse of the "Deus ex machina" in The Mysterious Island,
      but points out beautiful sides of Verne's work. Credits
      Verne, along with A. Laurie and M. Popp, with a beautiful
      simplicity of style, but does not go so far as S. Vinson,
      who called Verne a true stylist. Praises Verne's delicate
      intuition and fine intellectual balance. Dead thirty
      years Verne has outlived his detractors.

E70 Varmond, Jean. "Jules Verne en quelques lignes." ["Jules Verne in a Few Lines"] BSJV, 1, No. 1 (November), 12-14.
A sketch of the important events in Verne's life and career.

E71 _____. "Liminaire." ["Introduction"] BSJV, 1, No. 1 (November), 1-3.
Introduction to the Bulletin of the Jules Verne Society indicates the joys of rediscovering Verne.

1936

E72 Astier, M. "Le 'Nautilus' a-t-il eu un précurseur?" ["Did the Nautilus Have a Precusor?"] BSJV, 1, No. 2 (February), 76-80.
Refutes with he help of dates and a letter written by Verne the claim that Dr. J. Rengade (pseudonym Aristide Roger) created the precursor of Verne's submarine Nautilus in Les Aventures extraordinaires du savant Trinitus.

E73 Cocteau, Jean. Mon Premier Voyage (Tour du monde en 80 jours). [My First Trip (Around the World in Eighty Days)] Paris: Gallimard.
This is an account of a trip made by Jean Cocteau and Marcel Khill, retracing the steps of Phileas Fogg in Around the World in Eighty Days. Cocteau consequently calls Khill "Passepartout," and entitles his last chapter: "17 June.-The bet won.-Return of Phileas Fogg."

E74 Dalimier, Paul. "Une Anticipation inconnue de Jules Verne." ["An Unknown Anticipation of Jules Verne"] BSJV, 1, No. 5 (November), 221-222.
Reports on an article by Dr. Charcot (E60). Verne anticipated the sounds made by an as yet undiscovered species of seal.

E75 Fontainas, André. Confession d'un poète. [Confession of a Poet] Paris: Mercure de France.
In his youth, author was fascinated by islands. Verne held a special attraction. Mentions The Fur Country, Five Weeks in a Balloon, Adventures of Captain Hatteras, Mysterious Island, Journey to the Center of the Earth, and Twenty Thousand Leagues Under the Sea. Fontainas's youthful imagination was stimulated to embroider Verne's fiction.

E76 Garet, Maurice. "Jules Verne, Amiénois." ["Jules Verne of Amiens"] BSJV, 1, No. 3 (May), 115-135.
Paper delivered before the Société Industrielle d'Amiens, February 8, 1928. The account of Verne's life

in Amiens is quite detailed. High points include Verne's ascent in a balloon, gala balls given by the Vernes, his establishing a circus and performing other useful functions for the city, and the period in which cataracts kept him in Amiens, the recipient of many visitors.

E77   Helling, Cornélis. "Les Personnages réels dans l'oêuvre de Jules Verne." ["Real Characters in the Works of Jules Verne"] BSJV, 1, No. 2 (February), 68-75.
       An enumeration of some real-life sources of Verne's characters: Professor Fridricksson (Iceland), Nadar, Verne himself, Albert I of Monaco, Paul Verne, Phileas Fogg, Czar Alexander II, Nana Sahib, Georges Allotte de la Fuÿe, Cecil Rhodes, Aristide Briand, Badouraux, Mme Stilla, Don Pedro II of Brazil, etc.

E78   _____. "Qui pourrait nous renseigner sur M. Gabriel Annel (Jean Bellegran) auteur dramatique et secrétaire prétendu de Jules Verne?" ["Who Could Inform Us About Mr. Gabriel Annel (John Bellegran), Dramatic Author and Alleged Secretary of Jules Verne?"] BSJV, 1, No. 5 (November), 219-221.
       Evidence is presented against the claim made by Gabriel Annel in a 1935 interview for the Dutch newspaper, "De Telegraaf" to the effect that he had been Verne's secretary.

E79   _____. "Sur Une Curieuse Divergence dans les versions du conte fantastique Maître Zacharius." ["On a Curious Divergence in the Versions of the Fantastic Tale 'Master Zacharius'"] BSJV, 1, No. 5 (November), 222-223.
       In a scene in "Master Zacharius" in the Cathedral of St. Peter in Geneva, the old watchmaker is troubled and hesitant at the moment of Elevation. A comparison of the Musée des familles version with the one in the later Hetzel edition suggests that Verne may have undergone a certain religious evolution during the twenty years that separated them.

E80   _____. "Un Autre 'Nautilus' à l'Exposition universelle de 1900." ["Another 'Nautilus' at the Universal Exposition of 1900"] BSJV, 1, No. 5 (November), 217-218.
       A Nautilus was constructed in the workshops of M. de Coster at Saint-Denis under the supervision of M. Lartigues, an engineer, for the Universal Exposition of 1900. The craft, eleven meters in length, was put into the Palace of the Sea, a lake of about 1500 square meters at the Champ de Mars in Paris. Verne accepted sponsorship of the vessel.

E81 Jacobson, Alfred. "Les Prédictions de Jules Verne et les
réalisations d'aujourd'hui." ["Jules Verne's Predictions
and Today's Realizations"] Sciences. Revue de L'Association Française pour L'Avancement des Sciences, 64 (March),
1-32.
Lecture given on July 24, 1935 at the Association's
Congress in Nantes gives a sketch of Verne's life and then
treats the following topics related to him: aerial navigation, sea navigation, physics, war weapons (tanks,
cannon, poison gas), urbanism, building, and aeronautics.
The topics are discussed in terms of their appearance in
Verne's work. Poe, Cooper, and Wells did not come near
the scientific character of Verne's work.

E82 Marcucci, Edmondo. "Jules Verne et son oeuvre." ["Jules
Verne and His Works"] BSJV, 1, No. 2 (February), 81-100.
Covers Verne's life with the discussion of his work to
follow in future issues. Mentions Verne family's presence
in Switzerland following the revocation of the Edict of
Nantes and its return to France in the eighteenth century.
Details about Verne himself include the legend that he
was a Polish Jew and remarks concerning a few of his
literary relations. See E83, E84, E110.

E83 _____. "Jules Verne et son oeuvre." ["Jules Verne and His
Works"] BSJV, 1, No. 3 (May), 136-150.
Places Verne in the literary current that includes
Swift, Defoe, J. R. Wyss, Cooper, and Poe. Unlike Poe's,
Verne's imagination was disciplined by science. If it
is asked where lies the positive reality of Journey to
the Center of the Earth, it must be remembered that no
one expects a novel to supply the picture of an empirically
determined truth. Compares and contrasts Verne with
Walter Scott. Discusses the relationship between British
exploration in Africa and Verne's Five Weeks in a Balloon,
and comments on about a dozen other novels. See E82, E84,
E110.

E84 _____. "Jules Verne et son oeuvre." ["Jules Verne and His
Works"] BSJV, 1, No. 5 (November), 234-253.
Verne's sense of humor is above all a simple irony,
and several novels are discussed in connection with this
irony. Verne's characters may lack the substance to become proverbial in the sense of Manzoni's characters, but
they are sufficiently flesh and blood to interest readers.
Verne is a prudent teacher, staying on the whole within
the bounds of logic. Ends with a discussion of steam and
electricity in Verne's novels. See E82, E83, E110.

E85 Thines, Raymond. "Le Film 'Michel Strogoff.'" ["The Film
      'Michel Strogoff'"] BSJV, 1, No. 3 (May), 105-107.
          Calls the film "Michel Strogoff," which had a two-week
      run beginning March 12, 1936 in Paris, a pale and inaccu-
      rate representation of Verne's novel. Summarizes the
      action. See E92.

E86 ____. "Maître Zacharius." BSJV, 1, No. 5 (November),
      224-233.
          The two versions of "Master Zacharius" show that Verne
      did not always write in unthinking haste. Verne said
      that the theft of his watch was the point of departure
      for this story. It seems he chose Geneva as the setting
      because of that city's reputation for watchmaking. When
      Zacharius has lost his genius, customers bring back to
      him watches that don't work. Pride is at the center of
      Verne's psychological study, as seen in the Hetzel
      edition. In the Musée des familles version the old man,
      repenting, makes a passing return to religious practices.
      In the Hetzel edition pride precludes repentance. Con-
      trasted to Zacharius is the noble sacrificing nature of
      his daughter. Verne has symbolized the aberration toward
      which science can drive those whom it forces away from
      Christianity. Verne shows that Man is nothing and needs
      religion's help.

E87 ____. "Survivance." ["Survival"] BSJV, 1, No. 2 (Febru-
      ary), 53-55.
          Defends the rereading of Verne in adulthood by those
      who enjoyed him during their youth. Says that a rereading
      is a salutary renewal. We travel so far to escape, but
      we have Verne available.

E88 Tournier, Ivan. "A Propos du Tour du monde en 80 jours."
      ["Concerning Around the World in Eighty Days"] BSJV, 1,
      No. 5 (November), 218.
          It is not surprising that Phileas Fogg does not realize
      he has gained a day. Countries east of the meridian zero
      are one to twelve hours ahead of Greenwich Mean Time,
      whereas those to the west are one to twelve hours behind.
      Fogg depended on a pocket calendar and besides was
      extremely busy while in America.

E89 ____. "Comment Fixer La Date de rédaction des dernières
      oeuvres de Jules Verne." ["How to Fix the Publication
      Date of Jules Verne's Last Works"] BSJV, 1, No. 5
      (November), 219.
          Disagrees with Turiello (E90). It is more likely that
      in 1894 Verne was writing the seventy-first volume, For
      the Flag, which appeared in 1894.

E90 Turiello, Mario. "Lettres de Jules Verne à un jeune Italien."
     ["Jules Verne's Letters to a Young Italian"] BSJV, 1, No.
     4 (August), 158-161.
         Produces thirty-three letters written to him by Verne
     between June 7, 1894 and December 20, 1904, concerning
     chiefly literature in general and Verne's works in parti-
     cular. Late in the correspondence Verne accedes to his
     friendly critic's wish that he use the salutation "My
     Dear Turiello" rather than "My young friend." In a
     footnote Turiello tells of originally disagreeing with
     Verne's harsh judgment of Jean-Jacques Rousseau, only
     to come around finally to his opinion. See E89.

E91 Varmond, Jean. "Le Coin des chercheurs." ["Researchers'
     Corner"] BSJV, 1, No. 3 (May), 108.
         Les Premiers Temps de la photographie (1840-1870),
     published by Flammarion, contains photos of Nadar, the
     model for Verne's Michel Ardan. The collection includes
     a photo of Brunel at the launching of the Great Eastern.
     Why did Verne never mention that Brunel was the son of
     the French engineer who designed a tunnel under the
     Thames? L'Histoire de la marine, published by L'Illustra-
     tion, contains a print of the submarine of Villeroy,
     which must have contributed to Verne's creation of the
     Nautilus.

E92 _____. "Le Film 'Michel Strogoff.'" ["The Film 'Michel
     Strogoff'"] BSJV, 1, No. 3 (May), 107-108.
         The German version of the film "Michel Strogoff" has
     even more faults than those of the French version indicated
     by Raymond Thines (E85). The brutal scenes did not please
     the Dutch public, and in January the film was not allowed
     to be seen by the young. Mention is also made that
     L'Horizon, a Belgian newspaper, was alone in declaring
     that Verne had already recounted the story of "Mutiny on
     the Bounty" in his Voyagers of the Nineteenth Century. A
     documentary, "Twenty Thousand Leagues Under the Sea," is
     being shown in Holland.

E93 _____. "Glanes dans la presse d'aujourd'hui." ["Gleanings
     in Today's Press"] BSJV, 1, No. 5 (November), 210-211.
         A defense of Verne's writings, attacked by Pierre Bost
     in the February 26, 1936 issue of Marianne. Accuses Bost
     of peremptory and unexpected judgments. One should be
     permitted to admire the top of a giant alder without
     ceasing to love flowers. This is a play on the word
     "vergne" meaning "alder," so close to "Verne."

1937

E94   Agoëff, Dimitri W. "Michel Strogoff vu par un Russe."
     ["Michel Strogoff Seen by a Russian"] BSJV, 2, No. 6
     (March), 28-29.
       Recounts the excitement and enthusiasm evoked by the
     reading of Verne's Michel Strogoff during the writer's
     youth. Verne penetrated more deeply than has been acknowl-
     edged into the Russian psychology. He especially under-
     stood that the old Russia was Holy Russia. He showed
     awareness of Slavic resignation and fatalism. A particular
     pleasure in reading this novel was afforded by the ruses
     of war, the Cossack horsemen, and the pursuits over the
     Siberian plain.

E95   Bailly, Auguste. "Jules Verne." Candide, 11 February, n.p.
       Discusses the lists of books that people make up when
     they imagine themselves in a circumstance that exiles
     them from free circulation in the society they know. If
     he could have only one author available it would be Verne.

*E96 Beliard, O[ctave]. "Jules Verne avait prévu. . ." ["Jules
     Verne Had Foreseen. . ."] Annales politiques et lit-
     téraires, No. 109 (10 January), pp. 21-23.
     Not seen (cited in D137, p. 342).

E97   Collin, Paul-Victor. "Jules Verne et ses imitateurs."
     ["Jules Verne and His Imitators"] BSJV, 2, No. 9 (Decem-
     ber), 164-167.
       Verne was plagiarized by many mediocre imitators.
     There were also some respectable successors, among whom
     the two best in France were Louis Boussenard and Paul
     d'Ivoi.

E98   Dalimier, Paul. "Zoölogie et botanique dans la trilogie."
     ["Zoology and Botany in the Trilogy"] BSJV, 2, No. 8
     (September), 132-143.
       Zoology and botany are of a most variable interest and
     importance in what is known as Verne's trilogy. In Twenty
     Thousand Leagues Under the Sea there are numerous long
     digressions consisting of descriptions of animals; in
     Captain Grant's Children and The Mysterious Island flora
     and fauna are of a secondary interest, comprising the
     framework for the action. The examination of the novels
     shows that one must not expect any profound thought to
     emanate from the study of natural history in them. It
     is only there as a setting or to add dramatic, picturesque,
     and instructive incidents.

E99 Dollfus, Charles. "L'Origine du Nautilus." ["The Origin
of the Nautilus"] BSJV, 2, No. 7 (June), 79–85.
Verne was probably in communication with Louis Figuier,
the famous historian of applied sciences and author of
Les Merveilles de la science, L'Année scientifique, and
other publications that must have helped him. The name
that Verne gave his submarine Nautilus had already been
used by Fulton, the Coëssin brothers, and Hallet, who
with the Count de Rottermund gave the name to their
diving bell. Verne wrote at a time when the submarine
was already a reality. Mention is made of the unrealistic
size of Verne's submarine's propeller.

E100 Gehu, Edmond-P. "La Géographie polaire dans l'oeuvre de
Jules Verne." ["Polar Geography in Jules Verne's Works"]
BSJV, 2, No. 9 (December), 181–197.
A study of Verne's polar geography in Adventures of
Captain Hatteras, The Fur Country, and An Antarctic
Mystery. Verne depends on Ross, Kennedy, and the best
maps of the time to chart accurately the Forward's
course while in the then-known polar regions. Then his
imagination takes over, sometimes with an astonishingly
prescient intuition. He can not be faulted for knowing
no more than the experts of his time. As for red snow,
John Ross on his voyage with Perry found some in 1818
on the rocks of Cape York. See E128, E129.

E101 Helling, Cornélis. "A Propos du Château des Carpathes."
["Concerning the Castle of the Carpathians"] BSJV, 2,
No. 7 (June), 56–57.
In answer to a writer's inquiry, Professor Mario
Turiello has written that the composer Arconati and
the opera Orlando, attributed to him in the Castle of
the Carpathians, are figments of Verne's imagination.

E102 _____. "Description détaillée de notre couverture."
["Detailed Description of Our Cover"] BSJV, 2, No. 6
(March), 2–5.
Identifies the Verne characters depicted on the cover
of this issue. The drawing is from a colored poster
published about 1900 by Hetzel. Therefore, none of the
heroes of the seventeen novels appearing between 1900
and 1919 are depicted.

E103 _____. "A Propos d'Un Détail technique relatif au Géant
d'acier (La Maison à vapeur)." ["Concerning a Technical
Detail of the Steel Giant (The Steam House)"] BSJV, 2,
No. 6 (March), 16–18.
Corrects the impression shared by many that Verne's
"Steel Giant" traveled on feet. Passages are quoted that
prove the machine rolled on wheels. The illustrator,

Benett, carefully hid these in his representation in order to maintain aesthetic and magic effects.

E104 _____. "Jules Verne et la guerre aérienne." ["Jules Verne and Aerial Warfare"] BSJV, 2, No. 7 (June), 69-78.

Verne foresaw and was horrified by the terrors and cruelties of aerial warfare. The bombing of a Dahomey tribe from his airship Albatross has been duplicated in actual warfare. Other analogies are easily found. Verne would have been appalled to see the horrors of the Great War and those of the one threatening to break out.

E105 _____. "Jules Verne fut-il un romancier prophétique?" ["Was Jules Verne a Prophetic Novelist?"] BSJV, 2, No. 9 (December), 161-163.

A truly prophetic novelist places his action in the future. A striking feature of the Voyages extraordinaires is that Verne generally sets the action before the publication date. Lists seven novels of Verne deserving to be called prophetic because their action occurs later than the date of publication.

E106 _____. "'Sherlock Holmes' retrouvé dans les Enfants du capitaine Grant?" ["'Sherlock Holmes' Found in Captain Grant's Children?"] BSJV, 2, No. 8 (September), 109-116.

Conan Doyle read Verne as a boy. It has been assumed that Sherlock Holmes is a combination of Dr. Joseph Bell, a professor of Doyle's when the latter was studying medicine in Edinburgh, and Poe's detective, Auguste Dupin. One should add to the amalgam Verne's Australian police officer who makes a brief appearance in Captain Grant's Children, a conclusion supported by a quotation from this novel. Among other Doyle novels suggesting Verne's influence are The Lost World, The Poison Belt, and The Land of Mist.

E107 Jacobson, A[lfred] and A. Antoni. Des Anticipations de Jules Verne sur réalisations d'aujourd'hui. [From Jules Verne's Anticipations To Today's Realizations] Paris: J. de Gigord.

Discusses scientific phenomena foreseen by Verne as part of our daily life. Subjects include air and sea navigation, electricity, liquefied gasses, television, and weapons of war. See E123.

E108 Laport, George. "Jules Verne à Liège." ["Jules Verne in Liège"] BSJV, 2, No. 7 (June), 65-68.

Gives a resume of Verne's "The Rat Family" and explains why his reading of it at Liège November 25, 1887 failed

to interest listeners. The nineteenth century had inherited the antipathy toward fairy tales that the end
of the eighteenth century adopted under the influence
of Rousseau.

E109 Liefde, W. C. de. "Chimie et physique dans L'Ile mystérieuse." ["Chemistry and Physics in The Mysterious
Island"] BSJV, 2, No. 8 (September), 144-151.
Distinguishes The Mysterious Island from Verne's
other works by its seriousness. Examines especially the
solutions to chemical problems found by Verne in the
person of the engineer Cyrus Smith. Verne would seem
to have had an excellent and extensive knowledge of the
matters he treats.

E110 Marcucci, Edmondo. "Jules Verne et son oeuvre." ["Jules
Verne and His Works"] BSJV, 2, No. 6 (March), 38-52.
Discusses Verne's treatment of the conquest of the
air, his use of geography, and the ways he draws on
various sciences. The central idea of the Voyages
extraordinaires is the simple and energetic celebration
of the heroism and sacrifice that have allowed Man to
face Nature calmly. Ends with a few pages on Verne's
imitators, including the Italians E. Salgari, U. Grifoni,
and E. Novelli. See E82, E83, E84.

*E111 Ransson, R. Jules Verne que j'ai connu. [Jules Verne Whom
I Have Known] Amiens: Académie d'Amiens.
Not seen (cited in D443, p. 228).

E112 Rey, Arnold. "Guillaume le Taciturne cité par Jules Verne."
["William the Silent Cited by Jules Verne"] BSJV, 2, No.
7 (June), 57-58.
Where did Verne find what he calls the motto of William
of Orange in the seventeenth century and used on page 10
of the Hetzel edition of The Mysterious Island: "I don't
need to hope in order to undertake nor to succeed in order
to persevere"? Dutch historians find no evidence to show
that William the Silent actually said it. Furthermore,
he died in 1484. Did Verne confuse the two Williams?
Will a Verne manuscript someday unravel the mystery?

E113 Thines, Raymond. "Chronique cinématographique." ["Cinema
Chronicle"] BSJV, 2, No. 8 (September), 107.
Calls the film version of Captain Grant's Children
produced by the Russian, Vlainstock, vague and slow
moving, but credits it with scenic beauty. A new version
of Michel Strogoff is being done in Hollywood with the
Viennese actor, Adolphe Wohlbrück, and the English
actress Margot Grahame.

E114 _____. "Hatteras." BSJV, 2, No. 9 (December), 168-180.
    The hero of The Adventures of Captain Hatteras says
that there are no uncrossable obstacles, there are only
more energetic and less energetic wills. The feat of
four Soviet aviators in reaching the North Pole the
previous May and attempting to settle in for the winter
illustrates the truth of Hatteras's statement. There
are a number of parallels between the Soviet achievement
and that of Hatteras. It is wrong to suppose that the
latter is mad at the beginning of his expedition. There
is a subtle nuance between an immoderate desire to reach
the North Pole and madness. The novel's moral required
that Hatteras's mind be irremediably engulfed by an ill
that he could not overcome.

E115 _____. "L'Ecole du progrès." ["The School of Progress"]
BSJV, 2, No. 6 (March), 25-27.
    Verne well understood that to recognize the disasters
that pave the route of progress is not to deny it. His
heroes must struggle against dangers and obstacles on
every page. They are cautious pioneers who ever go
forward knowing that civilization does not retrogress.
Their efforts do not always succeed, but their self-
confidence enables them to envisage the future in a less
somber light than theretofore.

E116 _____. "Nemo." BSJV, 2, No. 7 (June), 86-104.
    This analysis of Verne's Captain Nemo is called by its
writer a voyage across a human conscience. The moral
portrait of Nemo is that of Verne himself. They share
a love of music and of the sea. Nemo sweeps those seas
that are filled with oppressors. He is neither a monster
nor a fool, and he is not devoid of humanitarian feelings.
He would dispense justice to avenge the victims of wrong-
doing, but he sees evil holding sway all about him. His
life is first like a raging storm, then like one that
subsides to a calm left with an infinite sadness and a
stoic resignation. His life thus divides into revenge
and reconciliation. It is inevitable that he would say
he is dying for having thought one could live alone. By
making Nemo a Hindu, Verne created a mysterious environment and a man enigmatic even as to race. Nemo remains
pure Hindu throughout his experiences. Reminds those who
blame Nemo for dispensing justice himself that he is also
the defender of the oppressed.

E117 Tournier, Ivan. "Communications." BSJV, 2, No. 7 (June),
62-63.
    Three subjects: (1) Verne's sources for his descrip-
tion of the region near Lake Victoria described in Five
Weeks in a Balloon could have been Speke's work, translated

into French in 1862, Voyage aux grands lacs, and an
account by the explorer Debono that appeared in Les
Nouvelles Annales des voyages (July 1862); (2) perhaps,
as Italian and Spanish translators suggest, X. Nagrien's
Prodigieuse Découverte was actually by Verne; (3) mentions
Hughes's translation of Poe's "Three Sundays in a Week"
as the source of errors at one time or another by Verne
and Nagrien regarding a day gained or lost crossing the
International Date Line from east or west.

E118   _____. "L'Oeuvre de Jules Verne est-elle 'dévaluée' par la
'faillite du progrès'?" ["Are Jules Verne's Works De-
valued by the 'Failure of Progress'?"] BSJV, 2, No. 9
(December), 157-160.
    When Verne wrote Five Weeks in a Balloon, modern
scientific and industrial civilization was only a few
decades old (Watt's steam engine, for example, was invented in 1767.) Verne bet on the continuation of the
technical revolution, but today, after one terrible war
and perhaps on the brink of another, one wonders. We
must realize we are in an aging classical period, the
end of an "Ancien Régime." We must adopt Verne's reasonable realism. In the last century or two humanity's
situation has improved. The revolution of knowledge is
also the restoration of the notion of the wondrous and
infinite.

E119   _____. "Optimisme et pessimisme dans Les Voyages extraordinaires." ["Optimism and Pessimism in The Extraordinary Voyages"] BSJV, 2, No. 6 (March), 21-24.
    Verne's work derives its unity from being essentially
an odyssey. An odyssey requires an itinerary and a
vehicle. Verne's heroes as they travel everywhere in
all sorts of means of transport make readers aware of
the progress implicit in the human odyssey. But pessi-
mists ask where it all will end. Verne seems to share
this pessimism in "Eternal Adam." Perhaps H. G. Wells
is right in saying the world will experience total death,
but if a Creator be admitted will He not be concerned
with his creation's ultimate fate? Despite Verne's most
controversial novel, nothing cancels out what his work
as a whole teaches the reader: emulation of intrepidity
and generosity, faith in the value of the human family's
progress and in the success of our obstinate search for
truth, beauty, and what is good.

E120   Turiello, Mario. "La Foi et la morale dans Les Voyages
extraordinaires." ["Faith and Ethics in The Extraordinary
Voyages"] BSJV, 2, No. 6 (March), 30-37.
    Professes to carry further an article by Brandicourt,
published in 1928 in the newspaper La Vie catholique.

Agrees that Verne was a believer, but takes exception
to Brandicourt's limited evidence. Most of Verne's
heroes are religious. There are many analogies to the
Book of Job in the Voyages extraordinaires. A moral
tone predominates throughout Verne's novels. Verne's
love of science never accepted the ideas that seduced
Renan. Despite one or two aberrations that have been
noted by critics, Verne's religiosity never disappears.

E121   Varmond, Jean. "Chronique cinématographique." ["Cinema
        Chronicle"] BSJV, 2, No. 6 (March), 14.
        A new film version of Twenty Thousand Leagues Under
        the Sea, made in the United States, the underwater
        scenes shot with the aid of John Williamson's "Underwater
        Eye," was announced by the Dutch newspaper De Haagsche
        Post, August 24, 1936. Invasion of the Sea is being
        made in the Danakil desert in Ethiopia. A new film
        version of Michel Strogoff was begun in November in
        Hollywood with Adolphe Wohlbrück and Margot Grahame.
        In the Ukraine a new film version of Around the World
        in Eighty Days is being made.

E122   ____. "Communications." BSJV, 2, No. 7 (June), 64.
        Concerns the 1937 Exposition in Paris where the
        lighting system, creating what have been called artificial
        moons, will recreate what Verne already did in Floating
        Island. The hope is expressed that a Verne stand will
        be a part of the displays in the pavilion devoted to
        literature.

E123   ____. "Des Anticipations de Jules Verne aux réalisations
        d'aujourd'hui." ["From Jules Verne's Anticipations to
        Today's Realizations"] BSJV, 2, No. 6 (March), 6-11.
        A review of a book by Jacobson and Antoni, Des Antici-
        pations de Jules Verne aux réalisations d'aujourd'hui
        (E107). Because Verne did not foresee every single
        advance that science has made, he is sometimes denied
        credit for all that he did. This book rectifies that
        attitude, but not without indicating some Verne mistakes.
        The authors have written perhaps the definitive work on
        Verne's influence on science today.

E124   ____. "Glanes dans la presse d'aujourd'hui." ["Gleanings
        From Today's Press"] BSJV, 2, No. 7 (June), 59-61.
        Lists a number of articles that touch directly or
        indirectly on Verne: Auguste Bailly in Candide, February
        11, 1937; Francis de Croisset in Gringoire, August 14,
        1936; Edmond Jaloux in Excelsior, February 9, 1937;
        Roger Launes in L'Echo d'Oran, February 7, 1937; André
        Toulemon in Courrier du centre, March 9, 1937; Robert

Kemp in Le Temps, February 14, 1937; Maurice Victor in
Les Ailes, December 3, 1936; M. L. Bertrand in Le Petit
Dauphinois, October 18, 1936; Roger Vercel in Gringoire,
February 17, 1937; and an article, "Les Naufragés du
Jonathan" ["The Survivors of the Jonathan"] in Les
Annonces d'Annecy, February 19, 1937.

E125 ____. "Trois Iles." ["Three Islands"] BSJV, 2, No. 8
(September), 117-131.
      The trilogy Captain Grant's Children, Twenty Thousand
Leagues Under the Sea, and The Mysterious Island is the
kernel of Vernian cosmology. The Mysterious Island is
the logical finale to the trilogy and elucidates the two
other novels. Notes the resemblance of Verne's island
to Tabor Island in the Pacific. The charm of The
Mysterious Island is that it concentrates on the struggle
of a group of men against Nature, which finally becomes
their ally. Questions the verisimilitude of Ayrton's
saving of the chest after the explosion at the end. See
E140, E141.

E126 ____. "Une Légende qui s'écroule." ["A Legend That is
Crumbling"] BSJV, 2, No. 6 (March), 15-16.
      A letter from Miss Thora Fridriksson, daughter of
the Icelandic philologist and professor, denies that
there was any correspondence in Latin or any other
language between her father and Verne. The latter, like
Pierre Loti, could have obtained his information from
French sailors returning from Iceland. Verne's probable
source was Charles Edmond's Voyage dans les mers du Nord
à bord de la corvette "La Reine Hortense" (1857).

1938

E127 Dalimier, Paul. "Quelques Remarques sur la flore et la
faune du Pays des fourrures." ["A Few Remarks on the
Flora and Fauna of The Fur Country"] BSJV, 3, No. 10
(March), 28-30.
      Natural history is of only relative importance in
The Fur Country, but the flora and fauna in the vicinity
of Cape Bathurst are among the factors that make Lt.
Hobson decide to establish his fort where he does.
His descriptions contain both accuracies and inaccuracies.

E128 Gehu, Edmond-P. "La Géographie polaire dans l'oeuvre de
Jules Verne." ["Polar Geography in the Works of Jules
Verne"] BSJV, 3, No. 10 (March), 31-44.
      The geographic fresco in The Fur Country is narrower
than in the The Adventures of Captain Hatteras. Verne's
treatment of geography, astronomy, and currents in The
Fur Country lacks the documentary wealth with which he

endowed <u>Hatteras</u>, and the scientific elements are less
homogeneous, but the adventure is based on a perfectly
plausible premise. <u>See</u> E100, E129.

E129 _____. "La Géographie polaire dans L'oeuvre de Jules Verne."
["Polar Geography in the Works of Jules Verne"] <u>BSJV</u>,
3, No. 11-12-13 (June, September, December), 76-1<u>84</u>.
An <u>Antarctic Mystery</u>, the conclusion to Poe's <u>Narrative</u>
<u>of Arthur Gordon Pym</u>, is rather different from Verne's
other polar stories. More fantasy is mingled with science
and more imaginary geography with real geography. From
the point of view of geography this novel is essentially
heterogeneous, although the early chapters have qualities
of detail and a richness of documentation typical of
Verne's early career. Verne had to give his imagination
full play because knowledge of the Antarctic was limited
to what had been revealed by the explorers Cook, Bellingshausen, Weddell, Biscoe, Wilkes, and Ross. For decades
explorers had been showing more interest in the South
Pole. Lauds Verne's description of icebergs and his
succinct resumé of the first Austral voyages of Cook,
Smith, Krusenstern, Bellingshausen, Weddell, Kemp, and
Balleny. Concludes that in geography the <u>Hatteras</u> is
the superior work of the trilogy. <u>See</u> E1<u>00</u>, E1<u>28</u>.

E130 Hankiss, Jean. "<u>Jules Verne</u>." <u>BSJV</u>, 3, No. 10 (March),
3-8.
Two extracts of Hankiss's <u>Jules Verne</u> translated from
the Hungarian by Mme Balasko-Moreau. Verne's first
readers were preponderantly adults, then their number
diminished while the percentage of young readers increased. How did this happen in the very period when
science and technology attained a place of honor? A
smaller number of adult readers does not prove that
Verne is out of style. Yesterday's readers of Verne are
today writing the epic of which he created the heroic
ideal. Verne's French characters, not playing an important role for a long time in his novels, become increasingly significant and are both varied and true to life.
In general Verne's sources for various aspects of the
French character are in himself and in public opinion.
Through them we manage to know the writer and his ideals
better.

E131 Helling, Cornélis. "Les Drapeaux dans les <u>Voyages extra-</u>
<u>ordinaires</u>." ["Flags in The <u>Extraordinary Voyages</u>"]
<u>BSJV</u>, 3, No. 10 (March), 12-1<u>4</u>.
Verne's novels contain a great many flags, some real,
others the product of his imagination. The author's
powers of description in this area are likened to those
of Victor Hugo.

E132   _____. "Les Illustrateurs des <u>Voyages extraordinaires</u>."
        ["Illustrators of <u>The Extraordinary Voyages</u>"] <u>BSJV</u>, 3,
        No. 11-12-13 (June, September, December), 140-146.
            Admiration for the Hetzel editions in which the il-
        lustrations are of the highest aesthetic quality.
        Illustrators discussed include Férat, Riou, de Neuville,
        Roux, and Benett. <u>See</u> E146, E188, E193, E237, E264, E686.

E133   _____. "Un Portrait oublié de Jules Verne." ["Forgotten
        Portrait of Jules Verne"] <u>BSJV</u>, 3, No. 11-12-13 (June,
        September, December), 161-163.
            Quotes a physical description of Verne on his yacht
        found in <u>Six Semaines en vacances</u> ["Six Weeks on Vaca-
        tion"] by Paul Poire (Bibliothèque des Ecoles et des
        Familles; Hachette, 11th edition, 1911).

E134   Louÿs, Pierre. <u>Broutilles</u> ["Trifles"]. Paris: G. C.
        Serrière.
            Character traits discerned in Verne's handwriting.
        <u>See</u> E154.

E135   Pavolini, A. "Les Chiens dans l'oeuvre de Jules Verne."
        ["Dogs in Jules Verne's Work"] <u>BSJV</u>, 3, No. 11-12-13
        (June, September, December), 164-168.
            An homage to four of the more important dogs in Verne's
        works: Top, Duk, Dingo, Serko. Calls them friends on
        whom one can count in any place and at any time. Likens
        them to Ulysses's Argo.

E136   Scantinburgo, Mario and Edmondo Marcucci. "L'Extraction du
        sodium de l'eau de mer par le capitaine Nemo." ["Extrac-
        tion of Sodium from Sea Water by Captain Nemo"] <u>BSJV</u>,
        3, No. 10 (March), 15-17.
            Captain Nemo's procedure for the extraction of sodium
        from sea water would not have been scientifically
        possible.

E137   Thines, Raymond. "En Compagnie de Jules Hetzel." ["In
        Jules Hetzel's Company"] <u>BSJV</u>, 3, No. 11-12-13 (June,
        September, December), 130-139.
            A tribute to the role played by the publisher Hetzel
        in the career of Verne. One wonders what might have
        happened to Verne's career without the publisher's
        sympathy and guidance.

E138   Tournier, Ivan. "Composition et publication des premiers
        <u>Voyages extraordinaires</u>." ["Composition and Publication
        of the First <u>Extraordinary Voyages</u>"] <u>BSJV</u>, 3, No. 10
        (March), 9-11.
            Direct indications: references to correspondence and
        biographical information; and indirect indications:

precise dates as to when the edition was in the bookshop (available in the Bibliographie de la France, appearing weekly since 1811), and dates of publication in the Magasin d'éducation and other periodicals are to be used in determining the chronology of the publication of Verne's works. Lists fifteen works of Verne with dates reflecting the above methods.

E139   Turiello, Mario. "La Femme dans les Voyages extraordinaires: Mistress Branican." ["Woman in The Extraordinary Voyages: Mistress Branican"] BSJV, 3, No. 11-12-13 (June, September, December), 147-160.
　　　　Many of Verne's female characters lack grace. Mary Grant is an exception. Miss Campbell in The Green Ray has good qualities. Alice Watkins in The Vanished Diamond is even better. Also nicely portrayed is Miss Anna Watson in Foundling Mick. But Verne's women are all secondary and incomplete with the exception of Mrs. Branican. The strength of Mrs. Branican's characterization is that her total devotion to one man does not prevent her from doing good for other people.

E140   Varmond, Jean. "Trois Iles." ["Three Islands"] BSJV, 3, No. 10 (March), 9-27.
　　　　An article, "Promontoire flottant," in the journal, Magasin pittoresque (1870, p. 100) may be not only the source of Rimbaud's Bateau ivre as suggested by Marc Isambard in the Mercure de France, August 15, 1935, but also the source for Verne's The Fur Country. An analysis of Verne's work shows it to be one of pure adventure. An analogy is made between this adventure and that of the Soviet icebreaker, Tcheliouskine, in 1933. Also mentioned are resemblances between Verne's Mrs. Barnett and a Dutch murder victim, Alexandrine Tinne. See E125, E141.

E141   _____. "Trois Iles." ["Three Islands"] BSJV, 3, No. 11-12-13 (June, September, December), 169-175.
　　　　Speculates on how long Verne may have contemplated writing about a moving island, Floating Island. He had already written Floating City on his return from the 1867 trip to New York. The idea is expressed both in The Fur Country and The Giant Raft. The description of the island shows that the illustrator, Benett, made two mistakes in his depiction. Three material weaknesses are noted: the island is not free of the Earth, Verne does not use morse code (Paris already had it in 1870), and freighters instead of helicopters are used to bring in fresh supplies. See E125, E140.

1939

E142 Devaux, P[ierre]. "Jules Verne a-t-il prévu la guerre
scientifique?" ["Did Jules Verne Foresee the Scientific
War?"] L'Illustration, No. 204 (1939), pp. 475-476.
Some of Verne's novels make him the prophet of war's
future horrors: giant cannons, flamethrowers, gas,
racism, submarines, and certain uses of electricity.

1941

E143 Frank, Bernard. Jules Verne et ses voyages. [Jules Verne
and His Voyages] Paris: Flammarion.
A very personally oriented book on Verne, based on
the biographical work of Allotte de la Fuÿe and documents
furnished by the heirs. Nantes during the Regency and
in 1827, Verne's family and his childhood, his friendships, the initial contacts with theater and with Dumas,
and the paris of the second Empire occupy a considerable
portion of the material. Among details of Verne's family
life are his cameraderie with his mother, quarrels with
relatives, and even the purchase of a piano. Accounts
of his voyages include the information that Le Figaro
used carrier pigeons to keep in touch with Verne on some
of his trips. His works are not so much analyzed as
discussed with regard to the circumstances of their
publication. Stress is laid upon the equivalence of the
storyteller's probity and scientific honesty.

1945

E144 Bessy, Maurice and Lo Duca. Georges Méliès mage et "Mes
Mémoirs" par Méliès. [Georges Méliès, Magician, and
"My Memoirs" by Méliès] Paris: Prisma.
An account of the career of George Méliès, magician
and filmmaker, known as the Jules Verne of the cinema.
Among Méliès's films were Twenty Thousand Leagues Under
the Sea (1901) and Trip to the Moon (1902).

1947

E145 Lemonnier, Léon. Edgar Poe et les conteurs français.
[Edgar Poe and French Storytellers] Paris: Aubier,
Editions Montaigne.
Six pages of one hundred and fifty on Poe and French
storytellers are devoted to a comparison of Verne with
Poe. Verne extracted from Poe the element of positive
science. He developed it without ever shocking common
sense with mysticism or humor, yet allowing positive
science to discover the marvels of Nature.

1949

E146 Borgeaud, Georges. "Les Illustrateurs de Jules Verne."
      ["Jules Verne's Illustrators"] Arts et lettres, 15
      (1949), 71-72.
        Pays tribute to Verne's illustrators, including Riou,
      Benett, Férat, de Ruffray, Roux, Montaut, Philippoteaux,
      de Beaurepaire, and de Neuville. Max Ernst is seen as
      having extracted the strange and cruel poetry of some of
      the illustrations, putting them to surrealistic use in
      La Femme cent têtes. In the Hetzel collection the
      legends taken from the texts and those texts complement
      each other. Only Alice in Wonderland can boast of such
      empathy between author and illustrator. See E132, E188,
      E193, E237, E264, E686.

E147 Boudet, Jacques. "Jules Verne et les mondes du XIXe siècle."
      ["Jules Verne and Nineteenth Century Worlds"] Arts et
      lettres, 15 (1949), 78-99.
        Situates Verne in his century, finding him closely in
      touch with his times and yet suffering the solitude of
      prophets. Supplying France's readers with a fresh
      universe opening to the moon in contrast to the closed
      world of Zola, Verne in a highly political century
      experienced the separation from society that is the
      natural lot of one who had affinities with Poe and
      Baudelaire. Verne foresaw the tragedy of mechanized man,
      born of the union of capitalism and the machine. Verne,
      attacking the moneyed world's scorn of the Creator, shone
      in the world of the Boulevards, where fantasy rather than
      money was the criterion of values. Living in an era of
      penury for scientists and inventors, Verne foresaw better
      days. The travelers in his books, unlike most Frenchmen
      of his time, made extraordinary voyages, not as national-
      ists and colonialists, but largely, although not exclu-
      sively, from the love of geography.

E148 Butor, Michel. "Le Point suprême ou l'âge d'or à travers
      quelques oeuvres de Jules Verne." ["The Supreme Point
      or the Golden Age Through a Few Works of Jules Verne"]
      Arts et lettres, 15 (1949), 3-31.
        Verne's work contains the seeds that would flower into
      the surrealist manner and surrealist themes. But it also
      contains mysteries of a different nature that lead one
      into the area of metaphysics. See also Essais sur les
      modernes (E206).

E149 Carrouges, Michel. "Le Mythe de Vulcain chez Jules Verne."
      ["Vulcan's Myth in Jules Verne"] Arts et lettres, 15
      (1949), 32-58.

The presence of a floating island/ship motif in
Verne's Voyages extraordinaires attests to a certain
originality, and the mystery of islands lends to the
quest by the hero of a central secret and four often
repeated themes or problems: the cryptogram, the
entrance, the passage across a field of treasures, and
the exit. Motherhood, scarce in ordinary terms in the
Voyages, is omnipresent as Mother Nature. The repeated
search of children and others for their loved ones
indicates how Verne enlarges the day-to-day experience
to cosmic proportions with some tragic implications.
Also entailing tragic implication is the role of evil
supermen whose triumphs over science threaten humanity
with annihilation. The Voyages are replete with myths,
perhaps the most striking of which is that of the descent
into Hades, of which Verne's subterranean and underwater
plunges are profane transpositions. Verne understood
the grandeur but also the dangers of Prometheanism, and
realized that the central secret of the cosmos, viewed
as the possession of a restored paradise, retreats as
Man and Science advance.

E150 Devaux, Pierre. "Jules Verne est-il encore un prophète?"
["Is Jules Verne Still a Prophet"] Arts et lettres, 15
(1949), 73-77.
    Our heritage, bequeathed us by Verne, is an optimistic
belief in science, amply exemplified by the enthusiasm
for it in America. And yet the legacy is very French;
one has only to compare Verne's work with the depressing
portrayal of gigantic forces crushing man in H. G. Wells.
Verne's novels contain many scientific predictions that
have come to pass--the performance of the submarine,
aviation, weapons of war, etc. Verne sometimes allows
his imagination to lead him astray, but this is not
always unconsciously. Verne would be amazed by twentieth-
century phenomena, but he taught that in order to think
progressively one must abandon old, intellectual concep-
tions, and he shows that great ideas in which one believes
are realizable.

E151 Fourré, Maurice. "A Propos de Cinq Semaines en ballon."
["Concerning Five Weeks in a Balloon"] Arts et lettres,
15 (1949), 59.
    Discusses the author of Five Weeks in a Balloon as a
visionary haunted by the poetry of the cosmos. The point
of departure is the reminiscence of a childhood reading
of the novel.

E152 Guigues, Louis-Paul. "Baroquisme de Jules Verne." ["Jules
Verne's Baroque"] Arts et lettres, 15 (1949), 63-70.

If the baroque man is defined as one who needs to
feel united to the Universe, Verne is baroque indeed.
His is a joyful integration with his environment. Verne
is quite different from Wells: the one speculates while
the other derives; the one keeps his sang-froid while
the other becomes upset; the one organizes, while the
other communes.

E153 Leiris, Michel. "Une Lettre de Raymond Roussel." ["Letter
of Raymond Roussel"] Arts et lettres, 15 (1949), 100-101.
Publishes a letter written in the spring or summer
of 1921 by Raymond Roussel, addressed to Eugène Leiris.
Roussel protests at being asked to lend Leiris an edition
of a work by Verne, whom he calls the greatest literary
genius of all time.

E154 Louys, Pierre. "Graphologie de Jules Verne." ["Jules
Verne's Graphology"] Arts et lettres, 15 (1949), 11.
Eight character traits discerned in Verne's hand-
writing. See E134.

E155 Peslin, Ch.-Yves. "Les Marins bretons précurseurs de
l'aviation. Jules Verne." ["Breton Sailors Precursors
of Aviation. Jules Verne"] Nouvelle Revue de Bretagne,
6 (November-December), 419-424.
Article limits itself to Verne as a child in love with
the sea, as the moving narrator of trips through the air,
and as the prophet of the helicopter. His novels fitting
this context are discussed. Also mentioned are daily
trips in May 1940 from an airfield near Brest of an aircraft named the Jules Verne that made sorties deep into
Germany.

E156 Schwab, Raymond. "Et Pourquoi Pas Michel Strogoff?" ["And
Why Not Michel Strogoff?"] Arts et lettres, 15 (1949),
60-62.
It is time to pose the question as to why Verne's
Michel Strogoff cannot be named in the same breath as
those characters traditionally recognized as truly
literary, for example Ulysses or Quasimodo.

1950

E157 Bridenne, Jean-Jacques. La Littérature française d'imagination scientifique. [French Literature of the Scientific
Imagination] Paris: Dassonville.
Differentiates between Poe and Verne, noting that the
latter abandons the irrational and the morbid. Poe is
a materialist, while Verne remains a Christian although
also a man of the nineteenth century. Finds that although Verne's style deteriorates from initial alertness

and vigor, it always spurs interest and even attains
grandeur. Calls Verne the father of the scientific
novel and discusses his literary posterity. Two of
the book's thirteen chapters directly concern Verne.

1951

E158   Castex, Pierre-Georges. Le Conte fantastique en France de
       Nodier à Maupassant. [The Fantastic Tale in France from
       Nodier to Maupassant] Paris: José Corti.
           Contains two brief references to Jules Verne. Tales
       of scientific extrapolation like those in Verne's
       Voyages extraordinaires are said not really to belong
       to the genre of strict fantasy. The hero of Verne's
       "Master Zacharius" is described as succumbing to an
       all-powerful fever that drives him to compete with God.

*E159 Nattiez, J. Un Modèle de Jules Verne: l'acteur Paul
       Saverna. [Model of Jules Verne: The Actor Paul Saverna]
           Not seen (cited in D299, p. 180).

1952

*E160 Arts, No. 341 (January).
           Special number on Verne. Not seen (cited in D417,
       p. 237).

E161   Baleine, Philippe de. "Jules Verne." Paris-Match, 2
       February.
           Credits Verne with foreseeing the future application
       of such things as the underwater chamber, the atomic
       bomb, TV, the V2 rocket, speleology, electric motor
       power, the rarefied gas lamp, the liquid air bomb, the
       utilization of the sea's thermal energy, the microphone
       and loudspeakers, the assault tank, the skyscraper, the
       technique of advertising by playing lights on clouds,
       space exploration, helicopters, remote-control bombers,
       etc.

1953

E162   Bridenne, Jean-Jacques. "Pérennité de Jules Verne."
       ["Topical Jules Verne"] L'Information littéraire, 5
       (May-June), 85-90.
           Verne's success as an anticipator goes far to explain
       the interest now being shown in him by adults. And yet
       should he be called a prophet? Certainly his success
       cannot be explained by his being prophetic. The pre-
       dominant characteristic of his books is that he offers
       an exact and moving reflection of the forces of the
       universe and integrates them through a novelist's

artistry. The reader is afforded an epic participation.
Author criticizes the absence of the moral world or its
conventionality when it is present. Notes Verne's dis-
approval of Poe's materialism. Verne never evinced a
euphoric confidence in human possibilities or mechanical
progress.

E163   Butor, Michel. "La Crise de croissance de la Science-
Fiction," ["Growth Crisis of Science Fiction"]. Essai
sur les modernes. [Essay on the Moderns] Paris:
Editions de Minuit, pp. 222-237.
Verne and H. G. Wells represent two stages in the
development of science fiction. The Wells stage is less
convincing than that of Verne, who carefully inventoried
the geographic lacunae of his time, filling them with the
extension of known facts and achieving a synthesis,
which, although naive, surpasses in amplitude and harmony
anything done by his successors. See D307.

E164   Parménie, A. and C. Bonnier de la Chappelle. Histoire d'un
éditeur et des ses auteurs P.-J. Hetzel. [The Story of
a Publisher and His Authors] Paris: Albin Michel.
Account of the career of the publisher, P. J. Hetzel.
Describes the latter's role in the publication of many
leading writers of the nineteenth century, including
Verne. Narrative and correspondence reveal Hetzel's
vigorous criticism of Verne's writing and support of
his career with an historical backdrop including French
politics and the Franco-Prussian War. Publishing details
show the Russian ambassador to Paris instrumental in
choosing the name Michel Strogoff (Verne first called
that novel Le Courrier du Tzar), and Verne winning as
the defendant in a suit for plagiarism.

*E165 Poignant, R. "Jules Verne: écrivain et précurseur."
["Jules Verne: Writer and Precursor"] Documents
Rassemblés.
Not seen (cited in D299, p. 180).

1954

E166   Bornecque, Jacques-Henry. "Le Sous-Marin ivre de Rimbaud."
["Rimbaud's Drunken Submarine"] Revue des sciences
humaines, new series, 73 (January-March), 57-66.
Acknowledges other critics who have found resemblances
between Rimbaud's Bateau ivre and Verne's Nautilus.
Compares several passages to show how Verne might be
considered a source for some parts of Rimbaud's poem.

1955

E167 Abraham, Pierre. "Jules Verne?" Europe, 33, No. 112-113
      (April-May), 3-10.
         Discusses scientific confirmation of some of Verne's
      fantasies and calls Mathias Sandorf a novel of national
      liberation. Children are not aware of the subtleties of
      Verne until they reread him on growing up.

E168 Alphanderie, Fernande. "Jules Verne, conseiller municipal."
      ["Jules Verne, Municipal Councilor"] Europe, 33, No.
      112-113 (April-May), 106-110.
         Tells of Verne's keen desire to become a municipal
      councilor in Amiens and his zealous attention to urban
      affairs after his election in 1888. A major triumph
      was his being instrumental in the building of an edifice
      containing 4000 seats to hold circuses.

E169 Andreev, Cyrille. "Préface aux oeuvres complètes." ["Pre-
      face to the Complete Works"] Europe, 33, No. 112-113
      (April-May), 22-48.
         François Hirsch translates Cyril Andreev's preface
      to the Russian edition of Verne's Complete Works. The
      political events during Verne's life are reviewed with
      mention that some of Verne's reactions may be in as yet
      unpublished documents. The preface speaks of Verne's
      dream of freeing humanity from its chains through science
      and technology and of Verne's friendship with Félix
      Tournachon, who shared the Saint-Simonian ideas of
      Charles de Lesseps. In the 1860s Verne made friends with
      future leaders of the Paris Commune. Freedom was the
      key word of Utopian Socialism in the Voyages extra-
      ordinaires. Verne's later works are social or historical,
      or sociohistorical, reflecting the author's new belief
      that technology alone will not produce solutions. These
      must await a better climate, free of such obstacles as
      imperialism. Verne's later descriptions of America
      denounce it, as he hated capitalism. Verne's success
      stems from his writing the novel of scientific anticipa-
      tion with scientifically based fantasy. Criticism has
      not fully recognized Verne's creation of a new type of
      hero. In Verne humanity supercedes technology.

E170 Anon. "Témoignage de Mlle S. G. (11 ans)." ["Evidence of
      Miss S. G. (11 years old)"] Europe, 33, No. 112-113
      (April-May), 60-61.
         Reaction of an eleven-year-old girl to Verne's writings,
      followed by those of a thirteen-year-old boy (p. 61) and
      a fifteen-year-old girl (pp. 62-63). Style reflects the
      children's supposed age--the eleven-year-old is guilty
      of the orthographical and grammatical errors made by a
      young pupil.

E171 Bauchère, Jacques. "Il y a Cinquante Ans mourait Jules
      Verne." ["Death of Jules Verne 50 years Ago"] Cahiers
      français d'information, No. 272 (March), pp. 4-6.
         A short sketch of a few of the events in Verne's life
      and career starting with his running away and boarding
      ship when a boy. Tells of Poe's influence on him, his
      meeting with the publisher, Hetzel, and his worldwide
      success. Calls him a prophet of his time and a poet.
      All the novels that we now call science fiction are but
      an extension of Verne's work.

E172 Bouissounouse, Janine. "Jules Verne. . .à Toulon."
      ["Jules Verne in Toulon"] Europe, 33, No. 112-113
      (April-May), 103-106.
         Recounts an interview with Jules Verne's grandson,
      President of the Civil Court of Toulon, where are to be
      found all of Verne's manuscripts except for Five Weeks
      in a Balloon and Twenty Thousand Leagues Under the Sea.
      Verne's grandson discusses the merits of his grand-
      father's works.

E173 Duhamel, Georges. "Le Souvenir de Jules Verne." ["The
      Memory of Jules Verne"] Livres de France, 6 (May-June),
      3.
         Verne belongs to the ranks of writers with a gifted
      imagination, among whom the English have been particularly
      distinguished: Swift, Defoe, Stevenson, Butler, and
      Wells. Did Verne realize that science might bring an
      end to the species and to the planet itself?

E174 Escaich, René. Voyage au monde de Jules Verne. [Trip
      Through the World of Jules Verne] Paris: Editions
      Plantin.
         Lists all Verne's works, discussing the author's gifts
      of observation and calling erudition and imagination the
      main sources of inspiration. The Voyages extraordinaires
      are classfied geographically and also according to genre.
      Analyzes and synthesizes such subjects as Verne's themes,
      characters, and nationalities. Evaluates the novels from
      the worst group to the best. Praises Verne as a serious
      thinker. Appeared originally in 1951, published by La
      Boétie in Brussels, under the title Voyage à travers le
      monde Vernien.

E175 Fournier, Georges. "Le Capitaine Nemo est toujours vivant."
      ["Captain Nemo Is Still Alive"] Europe, 33, No. 112-113
      (April-May), 111-114.
         An imaginary encounter with Jules Verne's Captain
      Nemo and the submarine, Nautilus. Nemo is pictured as
      convinced of human solidarity and hope and as continuing
      the struggle for justice.

E176 Frank, Bernard. "Comment Naquirent Les Voyages extraordinaires." ["How The Extraordinary Voyages were Born"]
Livres de France, 6 (May-June), 7-8.
Corrects the legend that names Amiens as Verne's
birthplace and the belief that Verne never traveled.
Recounts Verne's early life in Nantes and Paris, his
marriage and friendships, for example with Nadar and
Hetzel, and the beginning of his literary career. Verne
inspired young readers who later forged an empire.

E177 Gamarra, Pierre. "Jules Verne ou le printemps." ["Jules
Verne or Spring"] Europe, 33, No. 112-113 (April-May),
49-54.
Neglected by literary historians and critics, Verne
commands a respectable readership. His success is expli-
cable in terms of his taste for reality and his portrayal
of Man's triumph over Nature. Also important is his
championing of good against evil. Verne's work is to be
differentiated from modern science fiction because of his
documentary seriousness, its peaceful and fraternal side,
and the wholesome laughter that runs through it.

E178 Ganne, Gilbert. "Jules Verne, rêveur ou prophète?" ["Jules
Verne, Dreamer or Prophet?"] Les Nouvelles littéraires
artistiques et scientifiques, No. 1438 (24 March), pp.
1, 5.
On the fiftieth anniversary of Verne's death, answers
to the question: "Do you consider Verne a precursor of
modern applied science?" The Duc de Broglie answers that
in ideas Verne was a precursor, but that given his inability to show how they would be implemented, he was no
scientist. Louis Leprince-Ringuet of the Academy of
Sciences says Verne is a precursor not only of modern
applied science, but also of the science fiction novel.
Albert Coquet, a collaborator of Ganne, agrees essentially
with de Broglie. André George, editor of the collection
"Sciences Today" (publisher Albin Michel) says that
given the absence of any precise application stemming
from Verne, he can not be considered a precursor; but as
one who in a largely literary culture enlarged horizons
and created a technical spirit he was a precursor. The
geologist Haroun Tazieff replies negatively to the question. P. Willm, the engineer and coholder of the world
record for diving, replies that the reading of Verne
was influential on him, but took place a long time ago.

E179 Guermonprez, Jean H. "Une Oeuvre inconnue de Jules Verne."
["An Unknown Work of Jules Verne"] Livres de France, 6
(May-June), 9-10.
The publisher Hetzel rejected Verne's beginning of a
weak novel, L'Oncle Robinson, probably written about 1861.
Verne used parts of it in novels accepted by Hetzel. A
few passages are quoted.

E180   La Fu̇ye, Marguerite Allotte de. "Les Coffres des grands
       armateurs." ["The Coffers of the Great Shipfitters"]
       Livres de France, 6 (May-June), 5-6.
           Verne's boyhood days on the Isle of Feydeau with
       its shipping and import-export activity must have had
       some influence on his writing career. This is an
       extract from Mme Allotte de la Fu̇ye's book, Jules Verne,
       sa vie, son oeuvre. See E47.

E181   La Fu̇ye, Roger de. "Le Paysage dans l'oeuvre de Jules
       Verne." ["Landscape in Jules Verne's Works"] Europe,
       33, No. 112-113 (April-May), 64-90.
           Many quotations from Verne's works are used to show
       that his landscapes are those of a great painter in
       prose. Verne's seven voyages join a vivid imagination
       to create some remarkable scenes, written by a writer
       who was Chateaubriand and Poe combined. Particular
       stress is placed on Verne's descriptive powers when
       depicting the sea. The article ends with the scene at
       Verne's deathbed.

*E182 Les Lettres françaises (Paris), No. 561, 24-31 March.
           Special number on Verne. Not seen (cited in D417, p.
       237).

E183   Leveau, H. P. "Manifestation Jules Verne." Annales de
       Nantes, No. 101 (July), pp. 6-10.
           An exposition in honor of the fiftieth anniversary of
       the death of Verne was organized in Nantes from April 4
       to May 8. These are statements written in a "Golden
       Book" by many of the visitors, including members of the
       Verne and Hetzel families.

E184   Psichari, Henriette. "Que Pensent les jeunes lecteurs?"
       ["What Do the Young Readers Think?"] Europe, 33, No.
       112-113 (April-May), 55-59.
           Four points of view regarding the novels of Verne,
       supposedly representing the reactions of children: those
       of boys of ten and fourteen or fifteen years of age and
       girls thirteen and fifteen years old.

E185   Sadoul, Georges. "Notes sur Jules Verne et le cinéma."
       ["Notes on Jules Verne and the Cinema"] Europe, 33, No.
       112-113 (April-May) 99-103.
           An account of adaptation of Jules Verne's work in the
       film industry from Georges Méliès's Voyage to the Moon
       (1902) to Walt Disney's Twenty Thousand Leagues Under the
       Sea. Verne and H. G. Wells are credited with a decisive
       role in the development of cinematographic art.

E186   Salenave, Général. "A Propos de Jules Verne." ["Concerning
       Jules Verne"] Livres de France, 6 (May-June), 11.
           Laudatory statements about Verne. Dumas-fils says
       Verne's characters are like his father's, but carrying
       revolvers rather than rapiers. The engineer, Georges
       Claude, attributes to Verne his taste for science.
       Charcot, the explorer, writes that his daughters were
       brought up on Verne. A message of condolence from the
       Prussian Emperor William II on the occasion of Verne's
       death.

E187   Sexer, Alfred. "Jules Verne Yachtsman." Le Yacht, 78
       (26 March), 5-6.
           Verne learned about the sea and ships as a boy in
       Nantes. Some of his pals belonged to seafaring families.
       He sailed more than is generally supposed. He describes
       details of sailboat navigation in Dick Sands, the Boy
       Captain. Author recounts Verne's ownership of the modest
       boat, Saint-Michel I, and its two successors. Emphasized
       are the voyages on the Saint-Michel III, the largest of
       the three.

E188   Sichel, Pierre. "Les Illustrateurs de Jules Verne."
       ["Jules Verne's Illustrators"] Europe, 33, No. 112-113
       (April-May), 90-99.
           Verne was so drawn to the visual by early environment
       and by nature, his notes were so filled with drawings,
       that one imagines he would have liked to have been his
       own illustrator. It is all the stranger that there is
       no history of collaboration between him and the most
       noted illustrators. One obstacle was that Verne was
       ahead of his time. Nevertheless a Verne-Robida collabor-
       ation would seem logical, although Verne was a dreamer,
       Robida a satirist. Hetzel did obtain as illustrators for
       Verne's work Benett, Roux, Bayard, de Montaut, Férat,
       Alphonse de Neuville, and Riou. The best of these in
       order of suitability for Verne's work were Riou, de
       Neuville, and Férat. See E132, E146, E193, E237, E264,
       E686.

E189   Tenand, Suzanne. "Les Enfants du Capitaine Grant."
       ["Captain Grant's Children"] Europe, 33, No. 112-113
       (April-May), 114-121.
           Verne is the Lord Glenarvan of Captain Grant's Children.
       The work, Verne's only tender novel, was written when
       Verne's son was seven years old. If the book makes
       children cry, it also leads the childhood imagination
       toward a modern and scientific appreciation of the world.
       It has been said that this novel decided many a seafaring
       career. One of these was surely that of Verne's own son.

E190 Tersen, Emile. "Un Personnage de Jules Verne." ["A
       Character of Jules Verne"] Europe, 33, No. 112-113
       (April-May), 121-122.
           The character Tersen in Verne's novel, Floating Island,
       is identified as Gustave Tersen by his grandnephew.
       Gustave had traveled widely while serving in the medical
       corps. Another example of a Verne character being named
       after an acquaintance is that of Briand in Two Years'
       Vacation.

E191 Vazsonyi, Endre. "Jules Verne en Hongrie." ["Jules Verne
       in Hungary"] Europe, 33, No. 112-113 (April-May),
       122-125.
           Until the last war only mutilated editions of Verne
       were published in Hungary. Social and moral censorship
       forbade anything more. Verne sided with champions of
       literature, and he opposed injustice as in The Secret
       of Wilhelm Storitz, where he writes of unequal distribu-
       tion of land in Hungary. Since the last war Hungarians
       have had available the unabridged editions that allow
       a complete picture of Verne.

E192 Ziegler, Gilette. "Jules Verne (1828-1905), professeur
       d'énergie, amuseur et prophète." ["Jules Verne (1828-
       1905), Professor of Energy, Entertainer and Prophet"]
       Europe, 33, No. 112-113 (April-May), 11-21.
           A quite detailed account of Verne's life and career.

1956

E193 Marcucci, Edmondo. Les Illustrations des "Voyages extra-
       ordinaires" de Jules Verne. [The Illustrations of "The
       Extraordinary Voyages" of Jules Verne] Bordeaux: Société
       Jules Verne.
           Since critics called Verne's work unartistic, there
       was no collaboration between Verne and the illustrator
       Gustave Doré. Verne's weaknesses (artistic defects,
       scientific errors, excessive patriotism, and racism)
       are outweighed by his merits. Lists and discusses the
       illustrators of Verne's first essays in the Musée des
       familles followed by the illustrators of Voyages extra-
       ordinaires. The illustrators of the Hetzel editions
       catch the spirit of Verne's work and times better than
       their successors. About thirty pages of text precede
       thirty more of reproductions, including two drawings by
       Leo Tolstoy. See E132, E146, E188, E237, E264, E686.

E194 Rivemale, Alexandre. Nemo. Paris: Flammarion.
           This play, inspired by Verne's famous Captain Nemo,
       was directed by Simone Volterra, with music by Louis
       Bessières, and played at the Théâtre Marigny. The author,

explaining his play in the program notes, likens Verne's
hero to Don Quixote and calls him proud, grandiloquent,
a misanthrope, and a megalomaniac living in his submarine,
Nautilus. He becomes tired of producing income for Verne
and the publisher Hetzel and decides to strike out on
his own in real life where earning a living, loving and
being loved, and managing to put up with happiness are
not easy things to achieve. He understands a little too
late that one must be destined at birth to being simply
a man.

1957

E195 Barthes, Roland. Mythologies. Paris: Editions du Seuil.
The chapter "The Nautilus and 'The Drunken Boat,'"
shows that Verne's overriding existential principle is
the ceaseless action of secluding oneself. The ship in
Verne is both symbol of departure and emblem of closure.
Most ships in legend or fiction are like the Nautilus,
the theme of cherished seclusion. Rimbaud's "Drunken
Boat," proceeding toward a genuine poetics of exploration,
is the opposite of Verne's Nautilus. See D363.

*E196 Cluzel, Etienne. "Jules Verne et le préhistoire." ["Jules
Verne and Prehistory"] Bulletin du Bibliophile et de
Bibliothécaire, No. 1, pp. 27-44.
Not seen (cited in D299, p. 179).

E197 Cressard, Pierre. Les Maisons inspirées. [The Inspired
Houses] Rennes: Plihon.
A short chapter in this book says it took Mme Allotte
de la Fuÿe's Jules Verne, sa vie, son oeuvre to lay to
rest a generation after Verne's death the story that he
was a Polish Jew. Recounts Verne's life in Nantes, his
sailing experiences, and his schooldays. Records his
study of law in Paris, his losing a sweetheart to another man, the bohemian life he led in Paris, where
Dumas interested him in the theatre, and his marriage
to the widow Honorine de Viane. References are made to
his literary career. There is an illustration by X.de
Langlais.

1958

E198 Heuvelmans, Bernard. Dans Le Sillage des monstres marins.
[In the Wake of Sea Monsters] Paris: Plon.
This book on sea monsters calls H. G. Wells rather
than Verne the true father of science fiction. Verne,
inventing nothing, produced views of the future that were
only naive extrapolations, almost always unrealizable.
His Nautilus is the replica of the submarine Plongeur

conceived by naval officer Bourgeois and polytechnician
Brun, launched in 1863. The name <u>Nautilus</u> came from the
submarine built in 1800 by Fulton, the model for Captain
Nemo. Notes that Verne's scientists never find anything
they don't already know about. Verne's lack of scientific
background meant that although he read prodigiously, it
was without discrimination. His monumental ignorance
embraced at least physics, chemistry, geology, and
astronomy as well as zoology. Emphasizes his confusing
squid with octopus. Verne's misuse of A. Fredol's <u>Le
Monde de la mer</u>, a good book but with grave errors, led
even some scientists to inaccuracies.

*E199 Jeoffroy, Pierre. "Jules Verne, le voyant." ["Jules
Verne, the Seer"] <u>Paris-Match</u>, 11 October, p. 69.
Not seen (cited in D443, p. 227).

1959

E200 Baudouin, J.-F. "En 1865, Jules Verne écrivait: 'Cap
canaveral est le seul endroit d'où l'on doit lancer une
fusée vers la lune.'" ["In 1865, Jules Verne Wrote:
'Cape Canaveral Is the Only Place from which a Rocket
Must be Launched to the Moon'"] <u>Téléprogramme magazine</u>,
5 (26 April-2 May), 14-17.
   Notes that Verne's boyhood was surrounded by the
vision of ships' masts in Nantes, that artificial rain
is mentioned in <u>The Barsac Mission</u>, and the atomic bomb
is mentioned in <u>For the Flag</u>. There are a number of illustrations, one of which shows Albert Robida watching
a telephonoscope about 1880, this concept of what would
become TV predating Verne's ideas on the subject. Verne
saw in Florida the logical launching site for a space
flight.

E201 Cluzel, Etienne. "Un Livre négligé ou les incroyables
anticipations de Jules Verne." ["A Neglected Book or
Jules Verne's Incredible Anticipations"] <u>Bulletin du
Bibliophile et du Bibliothécaire</u>, No. 2, pp. 60-76.
   Concerns a story in Verne's collection of short
stories and novels, <u>Yesterday and Tomorrow</u>, published
by Hetzel in 1910: "The Day of an American Journalist
in 2889 A.D." The story first appeared in English in
the American magazine <u>The Forum</u> in February 1889. It is
analyzed in Charles Lemire's biography of Verne. Today
it is easier to demonstrate how prophetic the story was.
Among the extraordinary number of prophecies that have
come true are radio, television, calculators, etc.

E202 Day, Hem. <u>Louise Michel</u>. <u>Jules Verne</u>. Paris: Editions
      pensées et actions.
      Refutes claims that Verne in writing <u>Twenty Thousand</u>
      <u>Leagues Under the Sea</u> was merely completing a book
      begun by Louise Michel, and cites as the source of this
      "legend" Fernand Planche and Ernest Girault.

*E203 Guérard, J. "Trois Romans de Jules Verne portés à l'écran."
      [Three Novels of Jules Verne Brought to the Screen"]
      <u>Image et son</u>, 120 (March).
      Not seen (cited in D417, p. 238).

E204 La Fuÿe, Roger de. "Jules Verne inconnu mon oncle."
      ["Unknown Jules Verne, My Uncle"] <u>Connaissance du monde</u>,
      new series, 3 (February), 51-60.
      There were two branches of Verne's mother's family in
      Britain, one English and one Scottish. Only nine genera-
      tions separated the Scottish knight of the Allotte family
      and Verne's mother. Details complications arising from
      intermarriages within the de la Fuÿe family. A number
      of illustrations accompany this account of Verne's life
      and career. Considers the choice of Florida as the
      launching site of space vehicles to be Verne's most
      astounding prophecy made in 1865 during the writing of
      <u>From the Earth to the Moon</u>.

*E205 Moré, Marcel. "Jules Verne et Aristide Briand." <u>Critique</u>,
      15 (April), 319-328.
      Not seen (cited in D299, p. 180).

1960

E206 Butor, Michel. <u>Essais sur les modernes</u>. [Essays on the
      Moderns] Paris: Editions de Minuit, pp. 36-94. Also
      in <u>Répertoires</u>. Paris: Editions de Minuit, 1960, pp.
      130-162.
      Six essays, the first of which, "Les Mondes connus et
      inconnus," calls Jules Verne's <u>Voyages extraordinaires</u>
      the source of writers of modern fantasy. "Le Crypto-
      gramme" discusses Verne's easy passage from the known
      to unknown world. Verne constantly uses cryptograms to
      decipher the world. The cryptogram is among Verne's
      enigmas. Verne's enigmas of fact are essential, while
      unexplained phenomena are submitted to scientific ex-
      planation, which often explains without exhausting the
      meaning of the phenomena. "L'Elément" shows the North
      and South Poles are the usual goal of Verne's voyages.
      Humans live in an elemant peculiar to them, such as
      the cold. Captain Hatteras is a good example. "Le Point
      suprême" ["The Supreme Point"] stresses the symbolic

importance of the sea becoming free of the Earth as seen
in the multitude of birds in the sky in The Adventures
of Captain Hatteras. Man can come close to the Pole but
never quite arrive there. This accords with late nineteenth-century cosmology. Journey to the Center of the
Earth and The Adventures of Captain Hatteras illustrate
these points. "La Providence" ["Providence"] treats The
Mysterious Island as a first formulation of the general
plan of Les Voyages extraordinaires. Men must often be
saved from peril by chance, technical progress not
always sufficing. On the mysterious isle, the just are
saved only through their saving the reprobate, Ayrton.
Captain Nemo, who represented revolt and justice in
Twenty Thousand Leagues Under the Sea, symbolizes peace
and Providence in The Mysterious Island. In a way, he
is the guilty one, but he is also the figure of God,
"La Terreur." Man's path from The Mysterious Island to
"Eternal Adam" is marked by increasing pessimism and a
growing distrust of science. Man is helpless because
the world is a cosmos in which his place is determined.
See E148.

E207 Moré, Marcel. Le Très Curieux Jules Verne. [The Very
Curious Jules Verne] Paris: Gallimard.
Drawing on published documents only, shows the constant
reflection of Verne's life in his works; for example,
Captain Nemo is his publisher, Hetzel. Numbers in the
cryptograms of the novels have associations with dates
of personal importance to Verne. His favorite theme of
the two brothers stems from his love of his brother,
and some of his writing reflects the unhappy relationship with their father, including corporal punishment
inflicted by the latter. Other associations with Verne's
life and times include his character, Briant (Verne knew
Aristide Briand), and episodes deriving from two young
Belgians convicted of piracy and murder (see For the
Flag). Also discussed are the influence of Dostoyevsky
on Verne, and the latter's relations with his son, from
whom Verne is said to have been aloof until a cruise they
took in 1884. See D220.

E208 Pichois, Claude. "Avant-Propos." In "Aventures d'Arthur
Gordon Pym" par Edgar Poe, traduction de Charles Baudelaire
avec la conclusion imaginée par Jules Verne dans "Le
Sphinx des glaces." ["Foreword." In "Narratives of
Arthur Gordon Pym" by Edgar Poe, Translation by Charles
Baudelaire with the Conclusion Imagined by Jules Verne
in "An Antarctic Mystery"] Paris: Club des Librairies.

Verne's works are truly poetic. Their seed is in Poe and Baudelaire, while Arthur Rimbaud, writing his Bateau ivre, follows in the wake of Verne's Nautilus. Discusses the admiration of Baudelaire and Verne for Poe. Verne's enthusiasm was limited largely to Poe the storyteller, rather than the aesthetician of the poetic principle.

1961

*E209   Cluzel, Etienne. "Les Anticipations de Jules Verne et celles de Marcel Robida." ["Anticipations of Jules Verne and Those of Marcel Robida"] Bulletin du Bibliophile et de Bibliothécaire, No. 1, pp. 64–80.
        Not seen (cited in D299, p. 179).

E210   Gouzil, M. "Jules Verne." Bibliothèque de travail, No. 502 (10 October), pp. 1–24.
        Main events of Verne's life and career. Quotes Admiral Byrd and the Russian cosmonaut, Yuri Gagarin, both crediting Verne as a major factor in determining their careers. Includes a list of Verne's books with scientific or engineering manifestations and their realizations. The preface by Jean Crumois implicitly considers Verne a writer for the young.

E211   Wissani, André de. Dictionnaire rose et noir. [Rose and Black Dictionary] Paris: Editions du Scorpion.
        Included in this dictionary of sayings and people is the fact, unknown to Verne himself, that the real Phileas Fogg was the illegitimate son of Lord Byron and Althea, eldest daughter of Fisher King, a British major stationed on Malta. Hence Around the World in Eighty Days is a roman à clef.

1962

E212   Albérès, R. M. Histoire du roman moderne. [History of the Modern Novel] Paris: Albin Michel.
        A brief mention of Verne credits him with having explored the Earth's riches first in geography, then through inventions. The world he creates offers a delightful mixture of conformity and anarchism, such as a patriarchal society in Captain Grant's Children and Captain Nemo's revolt. Verne also shows the intrusion of the "impossible adventure" in human existence with explorations and conquest involving land, sea, air, and outer space, and even shows the acceleration of time in "Doctor Ox." The scientific Utopia of his time has become the reality of ours.

*E213 Moré, Marcel. "Hasard et providence chez Jules Verne."
        ["Chance and Providence in Jules Verne"] Critique, 18
        (May), 417-431.
            Not seen (cited in D299, p. 180).

E214 Renoux, Alfred and Robert Chotard. Le Grand Test secret
       de Jules Verne. [Jules Verne's Great Secret Test]
       Paris: Chotard.
           A numerological approach to the life and works of
       Verne. Speaks of a pact among Verne or Dad and Thomas
       Edison with the Great Dead, Sir John Franklin, the
       explorer who perished in the Arctic in 1847, and Abraham
       Lincoln. Joining the first three through a variety of
       numerological circumstances are Amundsen, Jack London,
       Sturd, Jossel, and Renoux, described as the potential
       gods of a new mythology. Human, terrestrial, and cosmic
       events combine to produce proofs that should persuade
       man to change his ways and be saved from perdition. See
       E222, E291.

*E215 Suyeux, Jean. "Jules Verne du 'Nautilus' à la sécurité
        sociale, a tout prévu, sauf la fusée." ["Jules Verne
        from the 'Nautilus' to Social Security, Foresaw Everything
        Except the Rocket"] Science et vie, 51 (February), 88-96.
            Not seen (cited in D299, p. 180).

1963

E216 Anon. "Jules Verne." Documents pour la classe, No. 178
       (14 October), pp. 13-24.
           A short summary of Verne's life followed by certain
       topics elucidated briefly through quotations from a
       number of sources: literary histories, prefaces to
       Verne's works, correspondence, and newspaper articles,
       including some by Léon Blum, who in L'Humanité discusses
       Verne's aspirations for society. Some pictures illustrate
       an account of the main events in Twenty Thousand Leagues
       Under the Sea. Composed as an aid to students.

E217 Jeune, Simon. De F. T. Graindorge à A. O. Barnabooth.
       [From F. T. Graindorge to A. O. Barnabooth.] Paris:
       Didier.
           American types in the French novel and theatre (1861-
       1917) include some of those created by Verne. Verne is
       said to have preferred the South to the North once
       slavery was ended, and to have introduced Americans into
       his works as regularly as he did the English. American
       moral qualities until Verne's later novels outweigh
       faults, although Verne creates two types of American
       hero: (1) a mixture of good and bad traits and (2) the

solely virtuous. Some are comic, some are serious, and
very few are unlikeable. About fifteen of this book's
four hundred seventy-six pages concern Verne.

E218 Métral, Maurice. Sur Les Pas de Jules Verne. [In the
      Steps of Jules Verne] Neuchâtel: Nouvelle Bibliothèque.
         Tries to dispel certain naivetés concerning Verne,
      revealing facets of his childhood, his environment, his
      reactions, his mood, and loves. Places Verne among the
      characters he created, quotes Kipling and De Amicis on
      Verne, and distinguishes between him and Dumas as writers
      of the popular novel.

E219 Moré, Marcel. Nouvelles Explorations de Jules Verne. [New
      Explorations of Jules Verne] Paris: Gallimard.
         Treats three questions: the evolution in music in the
      twentieth century foreseen by Jules Verne even before
      1880; Verne's misogamy and constant references in his
      work to marriage and widows; and a comparison of The
      Castle of the Carpathians with Villier de l'Isle-Adam's
      L'Eve future, which centers on the theme of the machine-
      woman in the Voyages extraordinaires. One chapter dis-
      cusses Verne's influence on Huysmans and Léon Bloy.

E220 Pourvoyeur, R[obert]. Anticipations de Jules Verne. [Jules
      Verne's Anticipations] Brussels: Saint-Eloi.
         A small brochure published and distributed by
      Fabrimétal with illustrations from the novels of Verne.
      Emphasizes the serious adult nature of his work.

*E221 Roussel, Raymond. Comment j'ai écrit certains des mes
      livres. [How I Wrote Certain of My Books] Paris:
      Jean-Jacques Pauvert.
         See E68.

1964

E222 Chotard, Robert and Alfred Renoux. Jules Verne le divin
      magicien. [Jules Verne, The Divine Magician] Paris:
      Chotard.
         Companion volume to Le Grand Test secret de Jules
      Verne (E214). Again the lines and works of Verne and
      his associates are approached numerologically. An
      important chapter is devoted to Roald Amundsen. Verne's
      Great Test shows Man, who feels ready to become God's
      equal, that he is merely an apprentice on Earth. Life
      is a mysterious force that animates brute matter, and the
      soul is perfected through a succession of lived experi-
      ences. The soul is immortal by nature, but in the course
      of human experience can change, fail, or even be destroyed.

The Team of the Great North, in connection with Verne's
Great Secret Test, was conceived to allow Man to better
his existence, to clarify his terrestrial position in
relation to the Universe and the Cosmos. Existence on
Earth is but a transition from a worse world to a better
one. The motives of the Great Test are all included in
Verne's works. See also E291.

E223 Diffloth, Gérard. Science-Fiction. Paris: Gamma-Presse.
      The term "science fiction" is an ambiguous one and
has incorrectly led some people back to Verne, the most
widely translated of French authors. Credits Verne with
intuitions of genius in the area of technology. An illustration shows Captain Nemo taking a bearing at sea.
Wells and Verne are fathers of the portion of science
fiction that was to develop and assume its definitive
form about 1930. There were a few isolated cases of
works of anticipation, for example Sébastien Mercier's
L'An 2440 [The Year 2440] (ca. 1780), written before
Wells and Verne, which today would be considered science
fiction. The years that marked the erection of the
Eiffel Tower and Verne's success spurred the efflores-
cence of science fiction. Albert Robida parodied
Verne's Voyages extraordinaires.

E224 Goupil, Armand. Le Personnage du savant dans l'oeuvre de
      Jules Verne. [The Character of the Scientist in the
      Works of Jules Verne] Caen: Faculté des lettres et
      sciences humaines.
      Thesis for the degree of "études supérieures."
Discusses Verne's formative years, then explores various
kinds of scientists in Verne's work and their roles.
Treats Verne's heroes as well as the responsibility of
the scientist.

E225 Schneider, Marcel. La Littérature fantastique en France.
      [Fantastic Literature in France] Paris: Fayard.
      Two brief references to Verne state that his Castle
of the Carpathians is a better "roman noir" than
Erckmann-Chatrian's Hugues-le-Loup, and that Verne joined
science to adventure in such a way that the latter becomes
fantasy in The Mysterious Island, Twenty Thousand Leagues
Under the Sea and Journey to the Center of the Earth.

1965

E226 Asselinau, Roger. "Introduction." In Nouvelles Histoires
      extraordinaires [New Extraordinary Stories], by Edgar
      Allan Poe. Paris: Garnier-Flammarion.

Poe, applying the scientific premises used by Defoe in Robinson Crusoe, created the novel of anticipation as practiced later by Verne and Wells, and more recently under the heading "science fiction".

E227 Auger, Pierre. "La Science-Fiction dans les galaxies." ["Science Fiction in the Galaxies"] Le Figaro littéraire, 25-31 March, p. 20.

Answers to an interview occasioned by the flight of Soviet cosmonaut Léonov. The public's reaction is something of a blasé one since Verne predicted a landing on the moon such a long time ago, and science fiction novels along with comic strips have accustomed the public to the idea of a moon landing.

E228 Chapelan, Maurice. "Nadar était là." ["Nadar Was There"] Le Figaro littéraire, 8-14 April, p. 22.

In connection with a Paris Exposition of Photographs, the reader is reminded of Nadar's interest in heavier-than-air machines. His ascent in the balloon "Giant" and other aeronautical interests recall his friendship with Verne, who is not, however, mentioned in the article.

E229 Dervenn, Claude. Hommes et cités de Bretagne. [Men and Cities of Brittany] Paris: Editions du Sud.

A chapter entitled "Le Prodigieux Monsieur Jules Verne" ["The Prodigious Mr. Jules Verne"] discusses a few key points in the life and career of Jules Verne. Among these are the lasting influence of the atmosphere of Nantes, Verne's childhood there, his collaboration with Hetzel, the role of a Thomas Cook travel poster in connection with Around the World in Eighty Days, and the success of d'Ennery's adaptation for the stage. Also mentioned are Verne's sense of humor during his impecunious law student days, his chance meeting with Dumas, and his moving and picturesque Captain Antifer.

E230 Guider, Charles. "Qui était Jules Verne?" ["Who Was Jules Verne?"] Atlas, 6 (February), 130-140.

Verne was retiring, eschewed interviews, and rejected the idea of a biography. This quite detailed account of his life claims that he boarded the ship, La Coralie, as a boy because his cousin, Caroline, asked him to prove his love by getting her some coral--the episode attesting to his liking for plays on words. Records his family life, friendships, and associations, integrating them where appropriate with his works.

E231 Hemmerdinger, Bertrand. "Nadar et Jules Verne." ["Nadar and Jules Verne"] Belfagor, 20 (January), 102-107.

Discusses Verne's interest in aviation and membership
in such organizations as the Heavier-than-Air Society
(reflections of which are found in <u>Clipper of the Clouds</u>).
Verne participated in discussions that foresaw the Wright
brothers, but he left no trace of them in his works.
Through Nadar Verne passed from eighteenth- to twentieth-
century aeronautics. Contrary to widely held belief,
Verne originally read Poe, whom he first mentions in
1862, in the translation of Baudelaire, an old friend
of Nadar, whom Verne met in 1861. Verne criticizes the
mechanics presented by Poe in "The Balloon Hoax," but
borrows his themes, notably from <u>The Narrative of Arthur
Gordon Pym</u>, in <u>An Antarctic Mystery</u>.

E232 Rheims, Maurice. <u>L'Art 1900 ou le style Jules Verne</u>.
      [<u>Art in 1900 or the Jules Verne Style</u>] Paris: Arts et
      Métiers Graphiques.
         Illustrated with many photographs. Gives an account
of various stylistic phenomena to be found in Europe
and America during the "Belle Epoque" or the late nineteenth and early twentieth centuries, years in which
Verne was alive. Includes a few pages on machines.

1966

E233 Auteuil, Henri. "L'Extraordinaire Jules Verne." ["The
      Extraordinary Jules Verne"] <u>Supplément à Echo de la
      mode</u>, 15 (10 April), 4.
         Lists a number of events coinciding with the latest
"Livre de Poche" edition of the <u>Voyages extraordinaires</u>:
expositions, the new Verne museum in Nantes, the revival
of the Société Jules Verne, etc.

*E234 Barjavel, R[ené]. "Sans lui, notre siècle serait stupide."
      ["Without Him Our Century Would Be Stupid"] <u>Les Nouvelles
      littéraires</u>, 44 (24 March), 1-7.
         Not seen (cited in D417, p. 237).

*E235 Bellour, Raymond and Jean J. Brochier. <u>Jules Verne</u>. Paris.
         Not seen (cited in D443, p. 226).

E236 Bellour, Raymond. "La Mosaïque." ["The Mosaic"] <u>L'Arc</u>,
      No. 29 (1966), pp. 1-4.
         Compliments Michel Butor for being the first to see
in terms of modern criticism that Verne's works may be
deciphered without yielding any of their naive enchantment. A study of Verne's texts shows that however often
disguised, similar elements within books and from book
to book combine and correspond to form an astonishing
mosaic, giving to each of the <u>Voyages extraordinaires</u>
a density and strangeness not always recognized.

E237 Borgeaud, Georges. "Jules Verne et ses illustrateurs."
["Jules Verne and His Illustrators"] L'Arc, No. 29
(1966), pp. 46-49.
Stresses Verne's expression of his opinion on the
illustrations of the Hetzel edition. The importance of
the illustrations lies in that they go beyond the mere
representation of a limited event to include everything
that surrounds it: the immensity of the sky, of the
sea, of the earth, of a room, indeed, of time. For
Verne's illustrators the context was supremely important.
They succeeded in exploiting the remarkable style of
Verne, who was a cosmic rather than a scientific writer.
See E132, E146, E188, E193, E264, E686.

E238 Brion, Marcel. "Le Voyage initiatique." ["The Initiatory
Voyage"] L'Arc, 29 (September), 26-31.
All the themes of imaginary voyages are in Verne's
Journey to the Center of the Earth. Whereas in Dante and
Goethe the Eternal Feminine is the prime mover, in Verne
women can not participate in the main action. They
remain accessory, belonging to prologue or epilogue.
Journey resembles a novel of chivalry, and Axel's initiation begins, in accord with tradition, in a grotto,
symbolic of the matrix where the birth of a new man is
prepared, similar to Theseus's Labyrinth. Verne himself
was probably not aware of the deeper implications of his
work. Yet his story can be read as a mystery of the
Ancients. Witness the journey itself with the descent
into darkness in the frozen North and the emergence in
the brilliant clarity of the sunny Mediterranean. Like
Dante, Axel and Lidenbrock come out new men. The reason
for the quest, as in all initiatory voyages, is the
search for the center, where the sought one and the
seeker face each other.

E239 Butor, Michel. "Lectures de l'enfance." ["Childhood
Readings"] L'Arc, No. 29 (1966), pp. 43-45.
The Thousand and One Nights, Gulliver's Travels, and
Robinson Crusoe, so different in many respects, have
one point in common: they are all "extraordinary
voyages," opening for children, enclosed in the world of
grownups, a window on the outside world. Verne in his
works also brings to children this other world, outside
the experience of parents.

E240 _____. "L'Image du monde au 19e siècle." ["Picture of
the World in the 19th Century"] Arts et Loisirs, No.
27 (30 March-5 April), pp. 8-10.
Places Verne's description of the world within its
time. Discusses the author's use of detail and shows
how Verne's stylistic devices are distinctly modern.

E241   Caputo, Natha. "Une Interview de P.-A. Touttain sur Jules
        Verne." ["Interview with P.-A. Touttain on Jules Verne"]
        L'Ecole et la nation, No. 152 (October), pp. 29-32.
             An interview with P.-A. Touttain, the man behind the
        publication of the complete works of Verne in the "Col-
        lection du Grand Jules Verne," published by Lidis-Gründ
        before the Livre de Poche undertaking. Considers The
        Barsac Mission to be Verne's most polished work, contain-
        ing all his themes and myths. Floating Island evokes
        the work of Jacques Cousteau. Verne recognized pan-
        Germanism in postwar (1870) Germany and even foresaw the
        concentration camps. Calls The Begum's Fortune excellent
        Dumas, Stevenson before his time, and Kafka as a counter-
        point. Calls Verne anticonformist rather than really
        socialist, but mentions some leftist friends of Verne.
        Lists ten major themes of Verne's novels.

E242   Castelot, André. "Ce Merveilleux Jules Verne." ["That
        Marvelous Jules Verne"] Miroir de l'histoire, No. 199
        (July), pp. 46-54.
             Details of Verne's life and career. These include
        his boyhood escapade of running away from home to board
        ship; his leaving Nantes after being jilted by Caroline;
        the meeting with Hetzel, his future publisher; and the
        real counterparts of the fictional Nautilus.

E243   Chesneaux, Jean. "Critique sociale et thèmes anarchistes
        chez Jules Verne." ["Social Criticism and Anarchist
        Themes in Jules Verne"] Le Movement social, No. 56
        (July-September), pp. 35-63.
             Verne's work should be understood in terms of certain
        currents of nineteenth-century minority ideas. The
        spirit of national movements of 1848, a Saint-Simonian
        faith in economic expansion, social criticism pushed to
        the extremes of anarchists and libertarians -- these are
        all present in Verne's works. Studies these manifesta-
        tions in detail in the Voyages extraordinaires. Points
        out Verne's friendship with the "Communard," Paschal
        Grousset, and his Leftist attachments during the Third
        Republic. See E295.

E244   Cluny, Claude-Michel. "Jules Verne et le feu sacré."
        ["Jules Verne and the Sacred Fire"] Lettres françaises,
        No. 124 (24-30 March), pp. 1-6.
             The elements play an important role in Verne's works.
        Among them, fire exerts its sacred nature to kill, but
        also to liberate and even bring redemption.

E245   Cordroc'h, Marie. De Balzac à Jules Verne, un grand éditeur
        du XIXe siècle, P.-J. Hetzel. [From Balzac to Jules
        Verne, a Great 19th Century Publisher, P.-J. Hetzel]
        Paris: Bibliothèque nationale.

Catalogue of an exposition held in April. Shows
specific examples of the collaboration between the
publisher Hetzel and Verne. Hetzel was a friend as
well as business associate.

*E246 Courville, Luce. "A Bas les masques." ["Down with Masks"]
Les Nouvelles littéraires, 44 (24 March), 8.
Not seen (cited in D417, p. 238).

E247 _____. Catalogue Exposition Jules Verne, Centenaire de
"De La Terre à la lune" 1865-1965. [Jules Verne
Catalogue. Centenary of "From the Earth to the Moon"]
Nantes: Bibliothèque Municipale.
Catalogue of the Exposition in Nantes marking the
hundredth anniversary of the publication of Verne's
From the Earth to the Moon. Compiled by Luce Courville
with the assistance of Antoine Bloch-Michel and Yvonne
de Baudinière, preface by Victor L. Tapié (see E280).
Contains a bibliography of Verne's works and of books
and articles concerning Verne, a chronology of his life
with a separate section on 1828-1866, a list of editions
of From the Earth to the Moon, some pages on space
research in 1966, on Verne's popularity abroad, and
finally an iconography listing portraits, photos, caricatures, etc., of the author.

E248 Dilasser, Antoinette and Jean Prinet. Nadar. Paris: Colin.
This life of Gaspard-Félix Tournachon, to be known as
Nadar, photographer and aviation pioneer, tells of the
admiration in which he was held by Verne, whose Michel
Ardan in From the Earth to the Moon resembles Nadar, a
resemblance honored by the illustrators of the Hetzel
edition. Verne in 1863 joined a society founded in
1852 and devoted to the concept of heavier-than-air
machines. The discussions in which Verne, Nadar, and
other members participated are reflected in Verne's
Clipper of the Clouds.

E249 Dorléac, B[ernard]. "Une Imagination jamais absurde."
["A Never Absurd Imagination"] Arts et Loisirs, No.
27 (30 March-5 April), pp. 8-10.
Verne's use of archetypes and his influence on later
writers.

E250 Foucault, Michel. "L'Arrière-Fable." ["After-Fable"]
L'Arc, No. 29 (1966), pp. 5-12.
Distinguishes between fable and fiction to be found
in any story. Fable is what is told, whereas fiction is
how the story is told. Verne's tales constantly show
the relationship established among narrator, discourse,
and fable to be broken up only to be reconstituted.

Behind the characters of the fable are a host of dis-
embodied voices struggling to tell the fable. These
are found variously distant from the visible forms of
the fable. The exchanges among these voices of the
"arrière-fable" determine the thread of the fiction. In
themes and fables Verne's tales are close to first novels,
but in fiction they are at the antipodes.

E251 Gheerbrant, Bernard. "Jules Verne ressuscité." ["Jules
Verne Revived"] Quinzaine Littéraire, 15 April, pp.
24-25.
Verne was for a long time relegated to the realm of
children's literature. He has also been considered
simply as a vulgarizer of science. Now criticism is
acknowledging him as a poet of nature.

E252 Guider, Charles. "Jules Verne, plus jeune que jamais."
["Jules Verne Younger Than Ever"] Lectures pour tous,
No. 150 (June), pp. 10-16.
Recounts some of Verne's disappointments and struggles.
Says the great charm of reading him is that he remains a
superb writer of the adventure novel.

E253 Huet, Marie-Hélène. "Jules Verne et la tradition celte."
["Jules Verne and the Celtic Tradition"] Annales de
Bretagne, 73 (September), 459-461.
Verne's birth place, Nantes, and his early upbringing
in that port city of Brittany make it natural that
aspects of the Celtic tradition should appear in his
works. Discusses evidence of the tradition in Verne's
characters.

E254 Kanters, Robert. "Situation de Jules Verne." ["Jules
Verne's Situation"] Le Figaro littéraire, 21 April,
pp. 16-17.
Verne's inventions bear little resemblance to what
actually exists today, but far from being a drawback,
this is an attractive quality.

E255 Kent, Georges. "Il nous avait promis la lune." ["He Had
Promised Us the Moon"] Sélection du Reader's Digest,
September, pp. 22-29.
Simon Lake, the American submarine pioneer, Auguste
Piccard, Marconi, Marshal Lyautey, and others have
credited Verne with contributions toward the progress
of science. Gives a brief account of Verne's life on
the occasion of the one hundredth anniversary of the
publication of From the Earth to the Moon.

E256   Lacassin, Francis. "Les Naufragés de la terre." ["Ship-
       wrecked of the Earth"] L'Arc, No. 29 (1966), pp. 69-80.
          There are fewer meaningful comparisons to be made
       between Verne's predecessors and Verne himself than
       between the latter and his imitators. Verne was timid
       with regard to action in space because he limited himself
       to the realizable in the light of contemporary science.
       Others to go further than Verne include Wells, Le Rouge,
       Burroughs, Rosny, and Jack London. In certain respects
       Verne is master of the genre in Twenty Thousand Leagues
       Under the Sea. Verne's major contribution to the develop-
       ment of science fiction is his premonition of the applica-
       tions of science to the means of locomotion. Verne is
       not and never could be the father of science fiction, but
       he is the chief promoter of the scientific novel. Listed
       are some Verne works underestimated by the critics.

E257   Le Clézio, Jean-Marie-Gustave. "L'Iliade des enfants
       d'aujourd'hui." ["The Iliad of Today's Children"]
       Arts et Loisirs, No. 27 (30 March-5 April), pp. 8-10.
          Each age of man and every age of human beings have
       their myths. Those of Verne have replaced the myth of
       Homer for today's children.

E258   Lecomte, Marcel. "Le Thème du grand nord." ["Theme of
       the Great North"] L'Arc, No. 29 (1966), pp. 66-67.
          Since the beginning of the second half of the nine-
       teenth century, the Great North has been a Vernian
       concept. Verne looms as a kind of seer if one looks
       at the destiny of the three nations that form the Great
       North: the U.S.S.R, the U.S.A., and Canada. A reading
       of Verne reveals the North Pole as Earth's really active
       pole. Verne has awakened readers to other zones of the
       world, especially in the Voyages extraordinaires.

E259   Martin, Charles-Noël. "Aspect scientifique dans la trilogie
       de Jules Verne." ["Scientific Aspect in Jules Verne's
       Trilogy"] In Ile mystérieuse [Mysterious Island], by
       Jules Verne. Vol. 2. Lausanne: Editions Rencontre,
       pp. 867-876.
          Discusses four of Verne's characters who represent
       scientists: Nemo, Paganel, Aronnax, and Smith. Shows
       their relationship to scientific currents, and invites
       a comparison among them.

E260   _____. "Préface." In Château des Carpathes [The Castle
       of the Carpathians] and Volcan d'or [Golden Volcano],
       by Jules Verne. Lausanne: Editions Rencontre, pp. 7-15.
          Discusses the creative process in these works and
       focuses on the correspondence of Verne with his publisher,
       Hetzel.

E261 _____. "Préface." In Cinq Cents Millions de la Bégum
[The Begum's Fortune] and Tribulations d'un chinois en
Chine] [Tribulations of a Chinaman in China], by Jules
Verne. Lausanne: Editions Rencontre, pp. 7-14.
Discusses Verne's utopian philosophy, and sees it as
related to scientific problems.

E262 _____. "Préface." In De la terre à la lune [From the
Earth to the Moon] and Autour de la lune [Around the
Moon], by Jules Verne. Lausanne: Editions Rencontre,
pp. 7-20.
Points out many areas of exploration and invention
in which Verne is to be credited with presenting something
new to his readers. On the other hand, Verne must be
charged with scientific mistakes.

E263 _____. "Préface." In Docteur Ox [Dr. Ox] and Forceurs du
blocus [Blockade Runners], by Jules Verne. Lausanne:
Editions Rencontre, pp. 7-16.
Discusses the dates on which Verne's tales were
written.

E264 _____. "Préface." In Nord contre sud [North Against the
South], by Jules Verne. Lausanne: Editions Rencontre,
pp. 5-10.
Discusses the integral role played by the illustrations in the Hetzel editions of Verne's works. Names
and compares the various illustrators. See E132, E146,
E188, E193, E236, E686.

E265 _____. "Préface." Pays des fourrures [Fur Country], by
Jules Verne. Lausanne: Editions Rencontre, pp. 5-23.
Discusses the creative process involved in writing
this work.

E266 _____. "Préface." In Robur-le-conquérant [Clipper of the
Clouds] and Maître du monde [Master of the World], by
Jules Verne. Lausanne: Editions Rencontre, pp. 7-15.
Discusses the sources of these works, and orients
the discussion toward the heavier-than-air machine.

E267 Micha, René. "Les Légendes sous les images." ["Legends
Beneath the Pictures"] L'Arc, No. 29 (1966), pp. 50-54.
The legends accompanying the illustrations to Verne's
works are descriptive, narrative, tragic, comic, sometimes deal with an insignificant fact, or may even mis-
lead the reader. But the illustrations and their legends
faithfully reflect the story and add to the work by
being a story within the story. The coincidence of
picture and word bears witness to the truth, while their
separation makes the truth all the more acute.

E268 Moré, Marcel. "Un Révolutionnaire souterrain." ["An Under-
       ground Revolutionary"] L'Arc, No. 29 (1966), pp. 33-42.
       Verne's life might appear on the surface as that of
       a member of the conservative middle class. But his life
       contained elements of revolt and dissimulation: revolt
       against his father and against his wife; dissimulation
       exemplified by his politicking in Amiens. Beneath the
       surface of his existence were such things as the mystery
       of why a nephew should shoot him. Portions of his life's
       acts and attitudes appear clearly in his works, for
       example his hostility to marriage. Pierre Louys and
       Nietzsche used the word "underground" to describe Verne.
       The latter had many affinities, and there may have been
       a literary influence in both directions. Certainly
       Nietzsche influenced Verne. Was not Verne, by treating
       the implications of the machine age in novels written
       to amuse youth rather than in philosophical writings,
       indulging in an underground and revolutionary work?

E269 Pub-Renault. "Exposition Jules Verne. Hier et demain."
       ["Jules Verne Exposition. Yesterday and Tomorrow"]
       Paris: Livre de Poche.
       Catalogue of a Verne exposition held in March and
       April. Lists his "inventions" and some of their modern
       materializations.

E270 Robichon, Jacques. Extraordinaires Histoires vraies.
       [Extraordinary True Stories] Paris: Librairie
       Académique Perrin.
       Contains chapters on World War II episodes, and what
       it calls "secret documents of the past," and has one on
       "The Secret of Jules Verne." Departing from questions
       raised by Mme Allotte de la Fuÿe and Marcel Moré, the
       author views the works of Jules Verne as a massive
       cryptogram, beneath which lies a personal tragedy.
       Certain implications arise from Verne's love for his
       brother, from the absence of female participants in his
       novels' adventures, and the attempt on his life by his
       nephew. After that attempt Verne became a recluse in
       the sense that he gave up trips to Paris, visited
       neither the Exposition of 1889 nor that of 1900, and
       never saw the Eiffel Tower. Verne is the Dmitri of
       Drama in Livonia, but the assassination attempt remains
       a family secret.

E271 Roudaut, Jean. "Le Château des Carpathes." ["The Castle
       of the Carpathians"] L'Arc, No. 29 (1966), pp. 21-25.
       Studies The Castle of the Carpathians in terms of
       structure and the grouping as well as relationships of
       characters. Time is the novel's central subject, and

the reader often asks not only what the time is, but also
where the action is occurring. Just as the novel is in
two parts, so is life seen in two parts which reflect
and duplicate each other but remain separate. Why does
the reader feel an irrational and yet real fright on
reading this novel? It is that the book does not lead
from an obscure beginning to a clear ending; rather, it
portrays an inner voyage during which the notion of the
person is split.

E272   Schneider, Marcel. "Mythes les plus anciens." ["Most
       Ancient Myths"] Arts et Loisirs, No. 27 (30 March-5
       April), pp. 8-10.
          There is a mysterious, hidden element in Verne's
       novels. Each one is a kind of magic work.

E273   Serres, Michel. "Géodésiques de la Terre et du Ciel."
       ["Geodesics of Earth and Sky"] L'Arc, No. 29 (1966),
       pp. 14-19.
          Journey to the Center of the Earth is the perfect
       work of an Empedocles complex. The novel is encyclopedic
       with its odyssey that circumscribes knowledge. It is
       "initiatory" as are the voyages of Ulysses, the Exodus
       of the Hebrews, and the journey of Dante. Verne is the
       only recent French writer to gather together and hide,
       under picturesque trappings and the contemporary taste
       for science, practically the totality of European tradi-
       tion in the subject of myths, esotericism, initiatory
       and religious rites, and mysticism. Mythology is the
       only science of which Verne may be called a past master.

E274   Sigaux, Gilbert. "Portrait de Jules Verne." ["Portrait of
       Jules Verne"] In Cinq Semaines en ballon [Five Weeks
       in a Balloon], by Jules Verne. Lausanne: Editions
       Rencontre, pp. 5-36.
          Discusses Verne's life and works.

E275   _____. "Préface." In Michel Strogoff, by Jules Verne.
       Lausanne: Editions Rencontre, pp. 5-11.
          Discusses this work's dramatic implications and studies
       its adaptation to the theatre.

E276   _____. "Préface." In Vingt Mille Lieues sous les mers
       [Twenty Thousand Leagues Under the Sea], by Jules Verne.
       Lausanne: Editions Rencontre, pp. 7-19.
          Discusses Verne's trilogy and pays particular atten-
       tion to Captain Nemo.

E277   _____. "Préface." In Voyage au centre de la terre
       [Journey to the Center of the Earth], by Jules Verne.
       Lausanne: Editions Rencontre, pp. 5-9.

Discusses a recent trend in criticism toward an initiatory interpretation of Verne's work. The initiatory reading of Verne can reach unrealistic proportions.

E278 _____. "Préface." In Voyages et aventures du capitaine Hatteras [The Adventures of Captain Hatteras], by Jules Verne. Lausanne: Editions Rencontre, pp. 5-11.

Discusses the presence of myth in Verne's works. A study of Verne leads one to the question of scholarship and recognition that Verne both preserved and created myth.

E279 Soriano, Marc. "Adapter Jules Verne." ["Adapting Jules Verne"] L'Arc, No. 29 (1966), pp. 86-91.

In the form of a debate, Marc Soriano explains for the Czech magazine, Zlaty Maj, the reasons and technique behind his adaptation of the novels of Verne for the "Bibliothèque Verte." The major points: Verne's first readers were uncritical members of the "serial" public; with Hetzel's project of the Magasin d'éducation Verne aimed at youth but was also aware of the necessity to write for a broader audience, including plays for popular consumption. Today the readership consists of adults and youth; two World Wars have changed the tastes of youth, but Soriano's project to publish Verne as an antidote to bad literature has succeeded; adaptations that cater to youthful taste are defended, but they are to be condemned when they become wholesale. Verne's chauvinism is seen as a form of anticolonialism. Verne's caricatural portrait of Isaac Hakhabut does not justify the charge of anti-Semitism against the writer, whose chief merits are seen in his humanity and in his renewal of the didactic genre.

E280 Tapié, Victor L. "Préface." Exposition Jules Verne. Centenaire de "De la terre à la lune," 1865-1965. [Exposition Jules Verne. "From the Earth to the Moon" Centenary] Nantes: Bibliothèque Municipale.

Preface to catalogue of the 1965 Exposition in Nantes, marking the centenary of the publication of Verne's From the Earth to the Moon. See E247. Verne's work presages modern space flights to a limited degree. It attests to Man's insatiable curiosity. In 1865 during a positivistic age people saw in science a panacea, while Romantic fervor was not long past. Verne found the right literary form to express the mixture of science and fiction. He helped create a state of mind by encouraging the vocation of real scientists or engendering in others an interest in discovery. Among those to acknowledge a debt to Verne were Edouard Belin, George Claude, and Charcot.

E281 Touttain, Pierre-André. "Visionnaire trop lucide." ["Too
Lucid Visionary"] <u>Nouvelles littéraires</u>, 44 (24 March),
6.
Verne would seem to be wholly devoted to progress,
and yet his attitude is a paradoxical one, since he is
keenly aware of the dangers of progress. This awareness
leads to a pessimism comparable to Nietzsche's.

E282 Versins, Pierre. "Le Sentiment de l'artifice." ["Sentiment
of Artifice"] <u>L'Arc</u>, No. 29 (1966), pp. 56-65.
Notes two movements in Verne: the structure and the
application. Quotes Hetzel to the effect that Verne's
goal was to amuse while instructing and to instruct while
amusing. With regard to plan, three eighteenth-nineteenth
century precursors were Louis-Guillaume de La Follie
(1739-1780), Félix Nogaret (1740-1831) and Népomucène
Lemercier (<u>L'Atlantaïde</u>, 1812). A schematic arrangement
in tabular form shows thirty-one works of earlier date
that contained themes used by him.

E283 _____. "Prodigieuse Découverte." ["Prodigious Discovery"]
<u>L'Arc</u>, No. 29 (1966), pp. 92-95.
Discusses the authorship of <u>Prodigieuse Découverte</u>
<u>et ses incalculables conséquences sur les destinées du</u>
<u>monde</u>, published in 1867 under the name X. Nagrien,
whose dates of birth and death are on the same day as
Verne. Points out, quoting Edmondo Marcucci, that the
work was published in Spain (1872) and Italy (1892) under
Verne's name, adding that works published abroad under
the author's name often appear under a pseudonym in
France. The work is called a curious and interesting
book, but not a good novel.

E284 Vierne, Simone. "Authenticité de quelques oeuvres de Jules
Verne." ["Authenticity of a Few of Jules Verne's Works"]
<u>Annales de Bretagne</u>, 73 (September), 445-458.
Establishes authenticity of Verne's posthumous works
through the correspondence of Verne with his publisher
Hetzel. However, two works signed X. Nagrien are not by
Verne. <u>Begum's Fortune</u> and <u>The Vanished Diamond</u> are
adaptations from André Laurie. <u>See</u> E296.

1967

E285 Bridenne, J[ean]-J[acques]. "Qui était André Laurie?"
["Who Was André Laurie?"] <u>BSJV</u>, NS No. 4 (4th Trimester),
pp. 2-4.
André Laurie may have collaborated more than is known
with Verne. He himself published a number of novels of
adventure directed toward a young readership. His real
name was Paschal Grousset.

E286   Butor, Michel. <u>Portrait de l'artiste en jeune singe</u>.
        [<u>Portrait of the Artist as a Young Monkey</u>]. Paris:
        Gallimard.
            Of some interest for those concerned with the symbolic
        implications of Verne's works, especially <u>Castle of the
        Carpathians</u>. Includes the element of cartomancy, which
        is evident in discussions of Verne, to whom this work
        makes no specific reference.

E287   Chesneaux, Jean. "Jules Verne et la tradition du socialisme
        utopique." ["Jules Verne and the Tradition of Utopian
        Socialism"]. <u>L'Homme et la société</u>, 4 (April–June),
        223–232.
            Verne's novels are in the tradition of Saint-Simon
        and Fourier with their emphasis on the systematic exploi-
        tation of the globe as humanity's essential mission. <u>The
        Mysterious Island</u>, a hymn to work, is a Saint-Simonian
        parable. Verne subscribes to Saint-Simon's vision of a
        world run by scientists. He founds societies on science
        and work in <u>The Begum's Fortune</u> (its city of France-Ville
        is utopian), in <u>Child of the Cavern</u> (its Coal City is more
        socioeconomically oriented), and in <u>Mathias Sandorf</u> (the
        isle of Antekirrta is a utopian scientific colony).
        Verne belongs in the company of those whose dreams
        contemplated establishing new societies on American
        soil. Verne's essay, "An Ideal City," delivered as a
        public address before the Academy of Amiens, December
        12, 1875, shows concern for social progress. Verne's
        colonizers, often progressive men of the military, sug-
        gest an analogy to Enfantin's "Peaceful Army of Workers."
        Although the working class is almost absent from the
        <u>Voyages extraordinaires</u>, Verne evokes an unmistakable
        echo of Saint-Simonianism and Fourierism; see his contacts
        with Lesseps, Nadar, Edouard Charton, Henri Duveyrier,
        and Félicien David. Only access to the correspondence
        will reveal Verne's relations with the later Saint-
        Simonians (1860–1870). Influences on Verne may include
        Dr. Guépin's <u>Nineteenth Century Philosopher, Encyclopedic
        Study on the World and Humanity</u>.

E288   _____. "La Pensée politique de Jules Verne." ["Political
        Thought of Jules Verne"] <u>Cahiers Rationalistes</u>, No. 249
        (September–October), pp. 274–304.
            A study of the significance of the political dimensions
        of Verne's work. It is wrong to see nothing but a con-
        formist and reassuring facade in Verne with regard to
        politics. He has strong affinities with the spirit of
        nationalism in 1848 and the struggle against slavery.
        His works contain a utopian socialism, a Saint-Simonianism.
        One may also speak of an anarchistic and libertarian

individualism in Verne. Article reviews certain
contradictions, for example nationalism vs. internationalism. As for religion, Verne when he died had not been
a practicing Catholic for a long time.

E289 _____. "Science, machine et progrès chez Jules Verne."
["Science, Machine and Progress in Jules Verne"].
Pensée, No. 133 (June), pp. 62-85.
Verne's unique contribution was his introducing science
into literature. This happens in various forms, but
especially in the shape of machines. Through machines
Man is seen to control Nature. In Verne's later works,
however, the theme of Nature's aberrations develops.

E290 _____. "Vers Une Réévaluation littéraire de Jules Verne."
["Toward a Literary Reevaluation of Jules Verne"] BSJV,
NS No. 3 (3rd Trimester), pp. 3-5.
Verne was for half a century considered exclusively
an author for the young. This is changing. Articles
by Brion, Butor, Carrouges, Foucault, Soriano, etc. and
books by Macherey and Moré show that criticism is taking
Verne seriously as a writer with secrets, signs, and
cryptograms to be deciphered.

E291 Chotard, Robert. De Jules Verne aux extra-terrestres.
[From Jules Verne to the Extraterrestrials]. Paris:
Chotard.
Verne's works are seen in terms of analogy, intuition,
and comparison, wherein mind and soul are distinguished.
Stress is laid on the symbolism of letters and words.
Dad chose Verne to demonstrate the soul's immortality
by performing after his departure from this planet a
series of rigidly determined actions, secretly controlled
by seven men of worth following a signal from the deceased
Verne. Séances recorded include one on October 27, 1964
in which the medium contacted Roald Amundsen, Jack London,
and Verne. Verne's role takes on a religious tinge as
reference is made to Moses as the first man on Earth to
receive from God's Son the universal law of fraternity
observed by the inhabitants of all planets except those
of Earth. This numerological approach to Verne's works,
with an emphasis on psychic phenomena suggests that Verne's
concern with outer space confirms religion as divine
truth. Past voyages into space, bearing God's laws,
prove that human life exists on other regions. See
E214, E222.

E292 Cluzel, Etienne. "Curiosités dans l'oeuvre de Jules Verne."
["Curiosities in the Works of Jules Verne"] BSJV, NS
No. 1 (2nd Trimester), pp. 2-10.

Discusses some errors, some deemed unintentional, others intentional, in The Field of Ice and The Adventures of Captain Hatteras. Among these: Verne's light in the latter work would not have been strong enough to be seen any distance at night; the speed attained by the sloop in The Field of Ice equals 169,000 km/hr.; and the electric power needed to propel the Nautilus in Twenty Thousand Leagues Under the Sea could not have been generated. See E293.

E293 _____. "Curiosités dans l'oeuvre de Jules Verne." ["Curiosities in the Works of Jules Verne"] BSJV, NS No. 3 (3rd Trimester), pp. 9-12.
Examines Fur Country and The Mysterious Island and finds more errors and inaccuracies. Rather than being blamable, these show what confidence Verne had in the future of science. See E292.

E294 Compère, Daniel. "Jules Verne et le cinéma." ["Jules Verne and the Cinema"] BSJV, NS No. 4 (4th Trimester), p. 13.
Film adaptation of Verne's The Chase of the Golden Meteor was a great success. Five films based on Verne are being made: Secret of Wilhelm Storitz in Czechoslovakia; Voyage to the Moon in Ireland with Bing Crosby; Two Years' Vacation in Czechoslovakia; Michel Strogoff in Hungary and Finland; and Captain Nemo in France. Radio-Television Belgium from September to July is giving a program based on An Antarctic Mystery.

E295 Day, Hem. "Autour de Louise Michel et de Jules Verne." ["Around Louise Michel and Jules Verne"] Défense de l'homme, Golfe-Juan, 219 (January), 29-32.
Opposes view that Jules Verne expressed Leftist and even anarchist attitudes as stated by Jean Chesneaux. See E243. Anarchism had no role in either Verne's life or his works.

E296 Dumas, Olivier. "S. Vierne: Authenticité de quelques oeuvres de Jules Verne." ["S. Vierne: Authenticity of a Few Works of Jules Verne"] BSJV, NS No. 4 (4th Trimester), pp. 5-6.
Reports on article by S. Vierne (E284) that argues for the authenticity of Verne's posthumous works, regrets the attribution to Verne of some of Nagrien's books, and discusses the Verne-André Laurie relationship.

E297 Dumas, O[livier], J[oseph] Laissus, and L. Le Garsmeur. "Bibliographie des oeuvres de Jules Verne I." ["Bibliography of Jules Verne's Works I"] BSJV, NS No. 1 (1st Trimester), pp. 7-12.

Stating that bibliographical data on Jules Verne is
still quite incomplete, the three authors have combined
their personal documentation and collections in a
bibliography begun in this issue and to be continued.
See E298.

E298 _____. "Bibliographie des oeuvres de Jules Verne II.
["Bibliography of Jules Verne's Works II"] BSJV, NS No.
2 (2nd Trimester), pp. 11-15.
Only two of Verne's novels clearly concern the future.
More than forty contain no scientific anticipation. So
there exists a Verne other than the precursor of modern
science. It is all the more important to have a detailed
bibliography. The Adventures of Captain Hatteras is the
first voyage to be published as part of Les Voyages
extraordinaires (1867). Discusses formats and illustrations. This continuation of the bibliography begun in
the first issue contains data sent to the bibliographers.
See E297.

E299 _____. "Bibliographie des oeuvres de Jules Verne."
["Bibliography of Jules Verne's Works"] BSJV, NS No. 3
(3rd Trimester), p. 13.
The Magasin d'éducation et récréation published most
of Verne's works for the first time, beginning with The
Adventures of Captain Hatteras, but not every volume was
published in this magazine, which ceased publication in
1906. Discusses problems of identifying a first edition,
and comments on the covers of editions.

E300 _____. "Compléments à la bibliographie. Les Volumes
polychromes 'Des Phares.'" ["Complements to the
Bibliography. The Polychrome Volumes with the 'Lighthouse Back'"] BSJV, NS No. 4 (4th Trimester), pp. 15-16.
Discusses polychrome editions of Verne. First example
of polychrome with the lighthouse depicted on the back
is Mistress Branican in 1891.

E301 Faivre, Jean-Paul. "Un Ami de Jules Verne Nadar." ["A
Friend of Jules Verne Nadar"] BSJV, NS No. 3 (3rd
Trimester), pp. 6-7.
Recounts Verne's participation in an aeronautical
society formed by Nadar.

E302 Gondolo della Riva, Piero. "Ouvrages attribués à J. Verne."
["Works Attributed to Jules Verne] BSJV, NS No. 4 (4th
Trimester), p. 14.
Attributions, some justifiable, of certain works by
Verne in France, Spain, Italy and Russia. See E335,
E336, E440.

E303 Grangier, B[ernard]. "L'Asie à la vapeur." ["Asia By
Steam"] La Vie du rail (Special Christmas issue), No.
124 (17 December), pp. 14-19.
Gives details of the Trans-Caspian Railway begun by
the Russians in 1880 and described by Napoleon Ney in a
book, En Asie centrale à la vapeur. Thinks this book
was read by Verne before he created the "Transasiatic"
railway to Peking in his novel, Claudius Bombarnac.

E304 Guth, Paul. "Jules Verne." In Histoire de la littérature
française. [History of French Literature] Vol. 2.
Paris: Fayard, pp. 538-550.
Second volume of a history of French literature.
Devotes a few pages to Verne, trying to place his life
and works within the period 1828-1905.

E305 Helling, Cornélis. "Le Roman le plus Poe-esque de Jules
Verne." ["Jules Verne's Most Poe-like Novel"] BSJV,
NS No. 3 (3rd Trimester), p. 8.
Verne's Giant Raft is his most Poe-esque work, borrow-
ing as it does from "The Murders in the Rue Morgue,"
"The Gold Bug," and "The Mystery of Marie Rogêt."

E306 Jules-Verne, Jean. "Avant-propos." ["Foreword"] In Jules
Verne et le courant scientifique de son temps. [Jules
Verne and the Scientific Current of His Time] Paris:
Ecole Technique Supérieure du Laboratoire, pp. 13-16.
Foreword to catalogue of an exposition. Verne's
grandson states that Verne was not an inventor -- he
foresaw scientific hypotheses for the future. Many of
these have become reality.

E307 Laissus, Joseph. "Introduction." In Jules Verne et le
courant scientifique de son temps. [Jules Verne and the
Scientific Current of His Time] Paris: Ecole Technique
Supérieure du Laboratoire, pp. 17-24.
Introduction to catalogue of an exposition. Verne is
described as more than a writer of scientific anticipation. Shows how the writer, also an artist, used science
as an integral part of his creative process.

E308 _____. "Jules Verne, l'extraordinaire voyageur." ["Jules
Verne, the Extraordinary Voyager"] In Comptes rendus du
91e Congrès National des Sociétés Savantes. [Proceedings
of the 91st National Congress of Learned Societies]
Paris: Gauthier-Villars and Bibliothèque nationale.
Details of Verne's life, some of which are said to
emanate from unpublished documents.

E309 _____. "Vente du Saint Michel III." ["Sale of the
Saint Michel III"] BSJV, NS, No. 1 (1st Trimester),
pp. 5-6.

Uses the date of the bill of sale, February 15, 1886, to prove that contrary to what others have suggested, Verne sold his last yacht, <u>Michel III</u>, three weeks before he was shot by his nephew and a year to the day before his mother's death. There is a photo of the last page of the bill of sale on the last page of the issue.

E310   Martin, Charles-Noël. "Préface." In <u>Capitaine de quinze ans</u> [<u>Dick Sands, the Boy Captain</u>], by Jules Verne. Lausanne: Editions Rencontre, pp. 5-10.
    Verne has often been dismissed as a mere writer of children's stories. This preface in the midst of a continuing debate emphasizes the importance and influence of childhood readings.

E311   _____. "Préface." In <u>Deux Ans de vacances</u> [<u>Two Years' Vacation</u>], by Jules Verne. Lausanne: Editions Rencontre, pp. 5-11.
    Discusses the analogies between Verne's devices and those seen in <u>Robinson Crusoe</u>.

E312   _____. "Préface." In <u>Etoile du sud</u> [<u>Vanished Diamond</u>] and <u>Epave du Cynthia</u> [<u>Salvage of the Cynthia</u>], by Jules Verne. Lausanne: Editions Rencontre, pp. 7-15.
    Discusses the creative process involved in the writing of both works and takes into account the sources in André Laurie's scenarios.

E313   _____. "Préface." In <u>Hector Servadac</u>, by Jules Verne. Lausanne: Editions Rencontre, pp. 5-15.
    Discusses the imaginative devices that result in an environment of fantasty in <u>Hector Servadac</u>. Notes technological mistakes made by Verne, and records some national attitudes.

E314   _____. "Préface." In <u>Indes noires</u> [<u>Child of the Cavern</u>] and <u>Rayon vert</u> [<u>Green Ray</u>], by Jules Verne. Lausanne: Editions Rencontre, pp. 13-23.
    Discusses the literary and scientific sources of these two works.

E315   _____. "Préface." In <u>Jangada</u> [<u>Giant Raft</u>], by Jules Verne. Lausanne: Editions Rencontre, pp. 5-17.
    Verne's themes contain the element of the secret. A cryptographic approach is often needed to unravel them.

E316   _____. "Préface." In <u>Kéraban-le-têtu</u> [<u>Kéraban the Inflexible</u>], by Jules Verne. Lausanne: Editions Rencontre. pp. 5-12.

Explores one of the reasons for the popularity of Verne: his sense of humor. Also treats his attitude toward women and the often discussed question of his misogyny.

E317 _____. "Préface." In Mathias Sandorf, by Jules Verne. Lausanne: Editions Rencontre, pp. 5-10.
Mathias Sandorf has both a literary and a biographical source. Dumas père's Monte Cristo is the former, and a Mediterranean trip taken by Verne is the latter.

E318 Moré, Marcel. Les Noces chimiques du capitaine Némo et de Salomé. [The Chemical Marriage of Captain Nemo and Salome] Paris: Gallimard.
Called by its author an opera-ballet without music in two acts, this work contains a dramatic-philosophic conception of musical art that poses for Verne's Captain Nemo a question he can't answer. Among composers mentioned are Bach, Beethoven, Rameau, Mendelssohn, and Chopin, but the musical world indirectly evoked is chiefly that of the first third of the twentieth century, the period also of the first surrealist manifesto (1924) and the first talking movies. In act I, the Paris Opera House, adrift in the ocean, is almost run into by Captain Nemo in the submarine Nautilus. He enters the Opera, sees Verne, and meets Salome. In act II he takes her to his submarine, where through the use of a magic screen he fails to entertain her with a succession of grand operas, operettas, ballets, and talking films. She leaves him, saying in a note that the kiss of his intelligence could not extinguish the kisses in her past. See E324.

E319 Ricardou, Jean. Problèmes du nouveau roman. [Problems of the New Novel] Paris: Seuil.
In this study of the new novel, the author states that Verne apparently thought that his An Antarctic Mystery was an ending for Poe's Narrative of Arthur Gordon Pym. Thus Verne failed to understand that Poe's work is a voyage ". . .to the end of the page."

E320 Robichon, Jacques. "Le Secret de Jules Verne." ["Jules Verne's Secret"] A La Page, 38 (August), 1216-1227.
In contrast to the jolly host at the costume ball at Amiens in 1877, Verne held within him some secret tragedy. Marcel Moré has divined this in his psychoanalytical detective approach to Verne's works. Moré seizes on some capital events in Verne's life, his being jilted by Caroline, the death of his brother Paul, the attempt on his life, to make of Verne's works a giant cryptogram containing personal secrets.

E321 Vierne, S[imone]. "A Propos des Erreurs relevées par M.
      Cluzel dans Le Pays des fourrures." ["Concerning Errors
      Detected by M. Cluzel in Fur Country"] BSJV, NS No. 4
      (4th Trimester), p. 12.
            The errors made by Verne in his Fur Country, pointed
      out by Cluzel, may be explained by the possibility Verne
      could have used a manuscript written before the appearance
      of his Voyages extraordinaires, in which appear the novel
      Twenty Thousand Leagues Under the Sea, published before
      the Fur Country and without errors. Political and family
      crises were distracting Verne.

E322 _____. "A Propos des Oeuvres de X. Nagrien." ["Concerning
      the Works of X. Nagrien"] BSJV, NS No. 4 (4th Trimester),
      pp. 7-11.
            Rejects the claim that Verne was the author of two of
      Nagrien's novels. Quotes a letter to prove that Verne
      read Nagrien's Prodigieuse Découverte and Incalculables
      Conséquences sur les destinées du monde. Hetzel sometimes
      used Verne as a consulting reader. Furthermore, the
      publisher knew the handwriting of Verne and his copyists
      too well to be fooled by any manuscript.

1968

E323 Albors, Enrique Garcia. "Le Coup de Théâtre Final du Tours
      du monde en 80 Jours." ["The Final Surprise of Around
      the World in Eighty Days"] BSJV, NS No. 6 (2nd Trimester),
      pp. 10-12.
            Translated from the Spanish. The point of departure
      for Verne's Around the World in Eighty Days was probably
      not a Cook's Agency poster as thought by Mme de la Fuÿe
      and Bernard Frank, but more likely an article appearing in
      the Magasin pittoresque in 1870 celebrating the opening
      of the Suez Canal, as Pierre Escaich has shown. Verne
      is partial to the unexpected conclusion in his novels.
      In this case the probable source for the day gained-day
      lost element that heightens suspense was probably Poe's
      "The Week of Three Sundays."

E324 Anon. "Les Noces chimiques du capitaine Nemo" par Marcel
      Moré." ["The Chemical Marriage of Captain Nemo" by Marcel
      Moré"] La Métropole Anvers, 11 February, n.p.
            Review of Marcel Moré's opera--ballet without music,
      published by Gallimard. Detects influence of surrealism
      and the evocation of the great artistic and musical
      events of the first third of the twentieth century.
      Recounts the plot involving Verne's Nautilus and Captain
      Nemo. Calls it brilliant. See E318.

E325 Brandis, Eugène. "Jules Verne en Russie et en Union
soviétique." ["Jules Verne in Russia and in the Soviet
Union"] BSJV, NS No. 5 (1st Trimester), pp. 2-16.
In the mid 1860s Verne's work suffered from censorship
in Czarist Russia, to the vast annoyance of progressivists.
Things improved for them as the century progressed. Marko
Vovtchok, like many democratic Russians of the '60s, was
interested in natural history, and her translations of
Verne, however inexact, were important. Verne also interested Tolstoy and Turgenev. By the end of the century
almost all of Verne's writings had been translated. The
most widely distributed edition before the Revolution
was P. P. Soikine's eighty-eight volume collection. By
1905 Verne was accepted somewhat reluctantly by Czarist
censors as a conformist. The public was enthusiastic.
Since the Revolution Verne has been seen as a writer of
children's classics. His works were not republished
before 1927, since the regime looked askance at foreign
works. Between 1920-1930 children's literature was out
of official favor despite protests by Tolstoy, Gorki,
and Tchoukovsky among others. A government measure in
1933 finally called for publication of the best children's
literature, specifically naming Defoe, Swift, and Verne.
In the period 1918-1961 nearly seventeen million copies
of Verne have been printed in U.S.S.R. Only Hugo and
London are ahead of him. Successful film adaptations
have included Captain Grant's Children, The Mysterious
Island (1941) and Dick Sands, the Boy Captain (1946).

E326 Bridenne, J[ean]-J[acques]. "G. de la Landelle, Probable
Inspirateur de Jules Verne." ["G. de la Landelle,
Probable Inspirer of Jules Verne"] BSJV, NS No. 6 (2nd
Trimester), pp. 7-9.
Gabriel Guillaume Joseph de la Landelle, who wrote
many books about the sea, probably influenced Verne. His
literary output was of uneven quality. Like Nadar he
was an enthusiast of the heavier-then-air machine.

E327 Chapier, Georges. "L'Ile mystérieuse de Jules Verne."
["The Mysterious Island by Jules Verne"] Rhône-Presse
Lyon, n.p.
A very favorable review of the Editions Rencontre
edition of Verne's The Mysterious Island. Notes that
this novel serves as an epilogue to Twenty Thousand
Leagues Under the Sea and Captain Grant's Children.

E328 Cluny, Claude-Michel. "Hier et demain." ["Yesterday and
Tomorrow"] Lettres françaises, No. 122 (6-12 March),
pp. 1-4.

Discusses "The Day of an American Journalist in 2889
A.D.," one of Verne's stories in the collection published
in the Livre de Poche series by Hachette. Verne's twenty-
ninth century is more idyllic than our own. Progress
in it is absolute and as unrealistic as most of his
inventions. Many of today's material comforts and
services are depicted. This Livre de Poche series is
faithful to the original editions even as to the illustrations, which have remained the best even when
poor, as they sometimes are.

E329 Compère, Daniel. "Jules Verne et le cinéma." ["Jules Verne
and the Cinema"] BSJV, NS No. 5 (1st Trimester), p. 20.
In Senegal, Nicolas Hayer, an English producer, is
going to make an adaptation of The Vanished Diamond with
Mireille Darc and Bruno Cremer. See E347.

E330 Damois, Maurice. "Le Sous-Marin peut-il être autre chose
qu'un engin de guerre?" ["Can the Submarine Be Anything
But a War Device?"] Le Réveil des combattants, March,
n.p.
Wishes the submarine would be put to peaceful uses.
Notes that the idea of the submarine antedates Verne by
far, for example Leonardo da Vinci's. James I of England
ordered one from a Dutch builder at the beginning of the
seventeenth century. The American Bushnell built the
Tortoise in 1775 for use against the British, and Fulton
in 1800 presented Napoleon I with the plan of the first
Nautilus. Article written after the catastrophe that
befell the submarine Minerve.

E331 Devaux, Pierre. "Jules Verne champion de l'insolite."
["Jules Verne, Champion of the Unusual"] Historama,
Saint-Ouen, No. 203 (September), pp. 122-129.
Calls "Master Zacharius" and "Dr. Ox" two of Verne's
less well known works.

E332 Evans, I. O. "Jules Verne et le lecteur anglais." ["Jules
Verne and the English Reader"] BSJV, NS No. 6 (2nd
Trimester), pp. 3-6.
Translated from English by C. Laurent. Verne in
England has been considered a writer of children's literature. He has suffered from bad translations and from
his tendency to put in too much geographic detail. By
1897 almost all of Verne's works had been translated.
There have been only four more since then. Evans defends
his having translated only portions of Verne's works,
indicating that to have done otherwise would have risked
an unfavorable reception by the modern reading public.

E333 Faivre, J[ean]-P[aul]. "A Propos des Tribulations d'un
      Chinois en Chine et de la chronologie Vernienne."
      ["Concerning Tribulations of a Chinaman In China and
      Vernian Chronology"] BSJV, NS No. 6 (2nd Trimester),
      pp. 14-16.
          Following on Terrasse's article (E346), this writer
      shows that Verne misses some important details of Chinese
      history in this novel. Terrasse's work points in a new
      direction: anachronism in Verne.

E334 _____. "Les Voyages extraordinaires de Jules Verne en
      Australie." ["Jules Verne's Extraordinary Voyages
      in Australia"] Australian Journal of French Studies,
      5 (May-August), 205-221.
          Domeny de Rienzi's Océanie ou cinquième partie du
      monde (1837), by listing the Terre de Grant, land named
      for its discoverer, became the source of the title of
      Verne's novel, Captain Grant's Children. The character,
      Paganel, is said to represent the principles of 1848
      espoused by the author. The voyage in the book is divided
      into three parts. Australians and natives are presented
      in a good light, but Verne would seem to prefer the
      colonials. Only the "bushrangers," convicts, oppose the
      expedition. Their leader, Ben Joyce, i.e. Ayrton, exem-
      plifies the difficulty Verne had in making outlaws al-
      together unlikeable. Verne was perhaps the first to
      raise Australia to the status of heroine, hence his
      popularity Down Under.

E335 Gondolo della Riva, Piero. "Oeuvres attribuées à Jules
      Verne en Italie." ["Works Attributed to Jules Verne in
      Italy"] BSJV, NS No. 6 (2nd Trimester), pp. 17-20.
          Shows that three works published in Italian -- Viaggio
      straordinario: 48 ore di soggiorno, I Principati
      danubiani, and I Pirati cinesi -- have been incorrectly
      attributed to Verne even though the name of each author
      was visible. Blames the format or catalogue description
      for the mistakes. See E302, E336, E440.

E336 _____. "Oeuvres attribuées à Jules Verne en Italie."
      ["Works Attributed to Jules Verne in Italy"] BSJV, NS
      No. 7-8 (3rd & 4th Trimesters), pp. 31-37.
          A list of apocryphal works that appeared in Italy
      under the name of Verne. Sometimes two titles were
      given together, the first of which was really a Verne,
      whereas the second one, which one might consider anonymous,
      was implicitly attributed to Verne. It remains to identify
      the real authors. See E302, E335, E440.

E337 Helling, Cornélis. "Jules Verne aux Pays-Bas." ["Jules
      Verne in the Low Countries"] <u>BSJV</u>, NS No. 7-8 (3rd &
      4th Trimesters), pp. 4-7.
          Verne has always been extremely popular in the
      Netherlands; novels, plays, and films attest to that.
      Verne visited the Netherlands twice, in 1881 and 1887.

E338 Jules-Verne, Jean. "Mon Grande-Père Jules Verne." ["My
      Grandfather Jules Verne"] <u>Lectures pour tous</u>, No. 173
      (May), p. 6.
          The author calls upon his own memory of contact with
      his grandfather, Jules Verne, and on family memories
      to write a rather intimate account of the famous author's
      life at home.

E339 Laissus, J[oseph]. "Qui Était Le Capitaine Boyton?" ["Who
      was Captain Boyton?"] <u>BSJV</u>, NS No. 7-8 (3rd & 4th
      Trimesters), pp. 22-25.
          A paper delivered before the General Assembly of the
      Jules Verne Society, February 10, 1968. Captain Boyton
      of <u>Tribulations of a Chinaman in China</u> is based on a real
      figure, an American of the same name, who in 1875 crossed
      from Dover to Boulogne in a kind of body-length life-
      saving suit consisting of air-filled cushions. <u>See also</u>
      <u>L'Univers illustré</u>, Paris: Michel Lévy, 18, No. 1048
      (April 24, 1875). This document is in the exposition
      "Jules Verne et le courant scientifique de son temps,"
      22nd <u>Semaine du laboratoire</u>, Paris 1967. There is a
      picture of Boyton in his suit on the last page of the
      <u>Bulletin</u>.

E340 Martin, Charles-Noël. "Préface." In <u>Ecole des Robinsons</u>
      [<u>School for Crusoes</u>], by Jules Verne. Lausanne: Editions
      Rencontre, pp. 5-11.
          Analyzes the central significance of the island theme
      in Verne's work.

E341 _____. "Préface." In <u>Maison à vapeur</u> [<u>Steam House</u>], by
      Jules Verne. Lausanne: Editions Rencontre, pp. 5-10.
          Discusses the source of the novel and its themes.

E342 _____. "Préface." In <u>Secret de Wilhelm Storitz</u> [<u>Secret</u>
      <u>of Wilhelm Storitz</u>] and <u>Hier et demain</u> [<u>Yesterday and</u>
      <u>Tomorrow</u>], by Jules Verne. Lausanne: Editions Rencontre,
      pp. 7-17.
          Discusses the authenticity of some of the posthumous
      works of Verne.

E343 Sainfeld, A. "Jules Verne et Alexandre Dumas (Père et Fils)." ["Jules Verne and Alexander Dumas, Father and Son"] BSJV, NS No. 7-8 (3rd & 4th Trimesters), pp. 14-17.
   Discusses Verne's friendship with both Dumas, father and son: the father becoming Verne's mentor and interesting him in the theater and leaving such a mark that Verne's style has often been likened to that of the elder Dumas. The younger Dumas supported Verne's candidacy to the French Academy.

E344 Serres, Michel. Hermès ou la communication [Hermes Or Communication] Paris: Éd. de Minuit, pp. 207-213.
   Contains a few pages on Verne under the heading "Loxodromies des Voyages extraordinaires." Discusses Verne's work in terms of the navigational rhumb line.

E345 Soriano, Marc. Contes de Perrault. [Tales of Perrault] Paris: Gallimard, p. 127.
   A note points out a partial analogy between the Sleeping Beauty of fairy tales and Verne's Mistress Branican.

E346 Terrasse, Pierre. "En Quelle Année se passent les romans de Jules Verne?" [In What Year Do Jules Verne's Novels Take Place?"] BSJV, NS No. 5 (1st Trimester), pp. 17-20.
   Most of the action in Verne's novels occurs in the second half of the nineteenth century. In two the action takes place in the eighteenth century and in six in the twentieth. He goes beyond that in two others. Gives a list of forty-six novels in which the date of action can be determined. See E333, E681.

E347 _____. "Jules Verne et le cinéma." ["Jules Verne and the Cinema"] BSJV, NS No. 7-8 (3rd & 4th Trimesters), p. 38.
   The film adaptation of Vanished Diamond, announced earlier, has changed stars from Mireille Darc and Bruno Cremer to Ursula Andress, Orson Welles, and George Segal. Sounds quite far removed from the novel. See E329.

E348 _____. "Un Voyage à reculons." ["Backward Voyage"] BSJV NS No. 6 (2nd Trimester), p. 13.
   Verne frequently hesitated in choosing the title of a novel. In 1889 it was announced that Un Voyage à reculons would appear in 1890. A passage in César Casacabel proves that this was the work in preparation. The trip involved is not actually a trip backward.

E349 _____. "Une Boutade de Jules Verne: Dix Heures en chasse."
["Jules Verne's Witticism: 'A Ten Hour Hunt'"] BSJV, NS
No. 7-8 (3rd & 4th Trimesters), pp. 26-30.
Paper delivered before the General Assembly of the
Jules Verne Society, February 10, 1968. "A Ten Hour
Hunt" is a spoof in which Verne writes of contravening
certain hunting laws and giving a friend's name when
apprehended, thus requiring the friend to pay a fine.
The text of 1882 drops some points of the 1881 edition.
Probably the publisher Hetzel thought it wise to delete
these points that showed an unorthodox attitude toward
the law.

E350 Vierne, S[imone]. "Vers une Reévaluation littéraire à
propos de Jules Verne." ["Toward a Literary Reevaluation
of Jules Verne"] BSJV, NS No. 6 (2nd Trimester), p. 14.
Articles in a recent issue of L'Arc take some new
approaches to Verne. Prior articles by Michel Butor and
Michel Carrouges must be mentioned. Also notes an
article in the Swiss journal, Action et Pensée. No.
37 (3 September), 1961 and M. Cellier's article in
Cahiers internationaux du symbolisme, No. 4, 1964, pp.
31+.

1969

E351 A., F. "Jules Verne parmi les cent livres des hommes."
["Jules Verne Among Men's Hundred Books"] Liberté, 6
December, n.p.
Verne would have to be in any "hundred books" list.
Claude Santelli and Françoise Verny have chosen The
Mysterious Island for such a group, since it is one of
Verne's most characteristic works. And it is there that
we finally learn the identity of the mysterious Captain
Nemo.

E352 Anon. "Aventure spéléologique dans les anciennes mines de
cuivre du Hochwald." ["Speleological Adventure in the
Ancient Copper Mines of the Hochwald"] Le Républicain
Lorrain, 13 August, n.p.
Verne has had extraordinary resurgence as world events
make him ever more topical -- for instance, the exploits
of American astronauts have made some people think of
his From the Earth to the Moon. The resurgence may also
be spurring speleological and subterranean explorations.

E353 Anon. "Des Prédictions de Jules Verne à la réalité d'Apollo."
["From Jules Verne's Predictions to the Reality of Apollo"]
Nord-Littoral, 13 September, n.p.

Comments on similarities between Verne's predictions and modern space flights. Points out that some of the illustrations in Verne editions could apply to today's explorations.

E354 Anon. "Essais du 'Redoutable' aux cents ans du 'Nautilus.'" ["Tests of the 'Formidable' a Hundred Years After the 'Nautilus'"] Eclair, 7 April, n.p.

In connection with an Exposition celebrating the hundredth anniversary of the publication of Twenty Thousand Leagues Under the Sea, this article suggests that Verne's Nautilus may have been inspired by the successful submarine experiments in the Bay of Bourgneuf in 1832 by Villeroi, Verne's math and drawing teacher. Refers to article by Genevois in Cahiers des Salorges, No. 15, which notes early submarine experiments by French, English, American, and Spanish inventors. The Americans built the "Villeroi Submarine Boat" in 1861 at Philadelphia.

E355 Anon. "Jules Verne déjà. . . ." ["Already Jules Verne. . . ."] Le Parisien, 25 September, p. 19.

In a page discussing the transporting of oil through polar regions, reference is made to Verne's Adventures of Captain Hatteras as a novel in which Verne foresaw the problems awaiting future conquerors of the Arctic. Two illustrations and a quotation from the novel accompany the short article.

E356 Anon. "Médecine insulaire à la Jules Verne." ["Insular Medicine according to Jules Verne"] Télémédecine, 7 December, pp. 29-34.

There are not many doctors in Verne despite the Balzacian scope of his work. Nevertheless, there are references to various cures offered by plants, herbs, and trees, such as the eucalyptus. There are some old therapeutic measures in Verne's novels that fortunately succeed. In The Mysterious Island, malaria is one of the diseases encountered. Certain aspects of medicine are indicated, including the question of nutrition.

E357 Anon. "Vigie." ["Lookout"] Le Lotus bleu, December, pp. 305-306.

It is remarkable that Verne should have foreseen so many realities of lunar explorations. His space travelers, launched from a cannon, were propelled, as are today's, by just enough force, neither too much nor too little. He estimated correctly that it would require a speed of 25,000 miles an hour to become free of gravity. His vehicle's descent resembled those of today. Verne was

a man of science, but his prescience shows that future
events, made inevitable by already established facts
and tendencies, can be projected on a sensitive
imagination.

E358   Berg, Serge. "De Jules Verne à Neil Armstrong." ["From
       Jules Verne to Neil Armstrong"] Journal de Téhéran
       (Iran), 20 July, n.p.
           Makes comparisons between the lunar flights of Verne's
       Around the Moon and that of Apollo 11. Verne said
       Americans were the world's best mechanics or engineers,
       just as Italians are musicians and Germans metaphysicians.

E359   Berthe, P.-V. "Attention procès." ["Attention Lawsuit"]
       République du centre, Orléans, 8 December, n.p.
           Regrets the present litigious age in which authors
       are so liable to be sued for plagiarism. Verne's
       Mathias Sandorf was admittedly a transposition of The
       Count of Monte Cristo by Alexandre Dumas. Mathias
       Sandorf was dedicated to Dumas's son, the father having
       died, and Verne presented it as the Monte Cristo of the
       Voyages extraordinaires. Aristide Briand did not become
       annoyed at being the Briant of Verne's Two Years'
       Vacation.

E360   Birnie, William. "Jules Verne." Sélection Reader's Digest,
       December, pp. 216-220.
           Some comparisons between Verne's lunar trip and that
       of Apollo 11 show striking resemblances -- Verne's ship
       has an initial speed of 11,000 meters per second, Apollo
       11 reached 10,830 meters per second after the lighting
       of the third stage. The times spent on the Earth-Moon
       trip are not dissimilar: in Verne 97 hours, with Apollo
       103 hours. Both vehicles went around the moon at the
       same altitude. Both crews suffered weightlessness.

E361   Blum, Léon. "Jules Verne." Coopérateur de France, No. 480
       (24 May), n.p.
           This article was originally published in L'Humanité
       on April 3, 1905. See E784.

E362   Boch, Charles. "Entre Phileas Fogg et Passepartout. Pour
       un véritable code de l'informatique." ["Between Phileas
       and Passpartout. For a True Communication System Code"]
       Le Monde, 4 November, n.p.
           The exploit of Phileas Fogg in Around the World in
       Eighty Days is made possible by the spirit of logic and
       method, by a sense of organization, precision, and
       punctuality, as well as by sang-froid, courage, endurance,
       honor, and loyalty. And yet Fogg could not have succeeded
       without the Frenchman, Passepartout, with his sense of

improvisation, his imagination, devotion, intelligence, and human warmth. The Frenchman sometimes extricates the Englishman from situations of which the latter could become victim for not being able to handle the unexpected. In the flight of Apollo 11 Armstrong is Fogg, minus Passepartout but plus a computer.

E363   Bory, Jean-Louis. "Voyage intérieur." ["Inner Voyage"] Nouvelles littéraires, 47 (24 July), 1-6.
It is a mistake to consider Verne's works as belonging solely to the realm of scientific anticipation. They should rather be viewed as a meditation of epic proportions upon Nature.

E364   Bussière, François. "A Propos du Vol d'Apollo." ["Concerning Apollo's Flight"] Europe, 47, No. 482 (June), 225-240.
Compares the space flight of Apollo 8 with that imagined by Verne in the trilogy From the Earth to the Moon, Around the Moon, and Purchase of the North Pole. Shows that Verne already suggested the U.S.A., Florida, and the Pacific as launching and recovery sites. Lists similarities and differences between the reality of 1968 and Verne's fantasy, stressing the author's concern for verisimilitude. Verne wrote both of science's potential and its limitations, and in the moral realm saw technical progress matched by Man's approach to disaster. Ultimately and paradoxically, anticipatory truth is less evident in the technological setting than in the novel's substance.

E365   C., J.-M. "L'Homme qui vivra deux siècles." ["The Man Who Will Live Two Centuries"] Antar, No. 126 (September), pp. 8-11.
Calls Verne a convinced liberal but authentic bourgeois of his time, a deist with a taste for scientific vigor, a homebody but lover of travel, the best known and most astonishing of writers who have imagined the conquest of the moon. His scientific realism often smacked of prophecy.

E366   Chapier, Georges. "La Lune dans l'oeuvre de Jules Verne." ["The Moon in Jules Verne's Works"] La Métropole, Lyon, 6 (December), pp. 41-44.
Of all the works of anticipation by Verne the double novel, From the Earth to the Moon and Around the Moon, seemed the least likely to materialize. Verne with his practical sense did not go so far as to make the moon habitable. However, his fantasy has been realized, and there are several coincidences that emerge from a comparison of his imagined flights with those of today. Article discusses these coincidences.

E367 Chaussier, Raymond. "La Columbiad de Jules Verne et son
wagon-projectile." ["Jules Verne's Columbiad and His
Projectile Wagon"] La Libre belgique, 14 July, p. 5.
A detailed account of and commentary on the moon
trip made by Verne's Impey Barbicane, Captain Nicholl,
and Michel Ardan. Comparisons are made to the 1968
flight of Borman, Lovell, and Anders. The difference
in preparation (there is almost none in Verne) is
emphasized. Places Verne's two moon novels, despite
the lack of practicality in some respects, in the
category of a pretechnological preplan to Operation
Apollo 11.

E368 Chotard, Robert. Comment Jules Verne vient de tracer dans
l'espace et le temps le destin de l'homme avec Apollo
8 et les Soyouz 4 et 5 (1968-1969)). [How Jules Verne
Has Just Traced in Space and Time Man's Destiny With
Apollo 8 And Soyuz 4 and 5 (1968-1969)] Paris: Chotard.
This brings up to date the numerological study of
Jules Verne's life and works begun by Chotard in E214,
and E222. The author now establishes a symbolic link
between Verne's birthdate, August 2, and the exploit
of Apollo 8, which he sees as the denunciation of the
childishness of the gigantic struggle that is destroying
the two great Powers. The linking of Soyuz 4 with Soyuz
5 is taken as a demonstration that the saving of man in
perdition in space has become a possibility. Addressing
the students who committed violence during the days of
May (1968), Chotard claims that Verne's symbolic message
is that knowledge and wisdom come only through sacrifice.

E369 Cluny, Claude-Michel. "Robut-le-Conquérant, De La Terre à
la lune. [Clipper of the Clouds, From the Earth to the
Moon] Magazine littéraire, No. 31 (August), pp. 10-12.
Verne's enthusiasm emanates from the realm of the
potential. However, Verne possesses the gifts of a
visionary, and these stem from the unusual.

E370 Cluzel, Etienne. "Trente Mille Lieues dans les airs."
["Thirty Thousand Leagues in the Air"] BSJV, NS No. 9
(1st Trimester), pp. 6-9.
Finds striking analogies of theme and composition in
Twenty Thousand Leagues Under the Sea and Clipper of the
Clouds. The analogies include the Albatross – the
Nautilus, Robur – Captain Nemo, "prisoners" of Robur –
"prisoners" of Nemo. See E371.

E371 _____. "Trente Mille Lieues dans les airs." ["Thirty
Thousand Leagues in the Air'] BSJV, NS No. 10 (2nd
Trimester), pp. 29-32.

In both the Clipper of the Clouds and Twenty Thousand
Leagues Under the Sea, Verne has to be something of a
prestidigitator to extract himself from a corner into
which the impossible lack of power for his vehicles puts
him. One must remember that as a novelist Verne was
also a poet. Today's developments prove that the
visionary often saw clearly into the future. See E370.

E372 Compère, Daniel. "Filmographie des oeuvres de Jules Verne."
["Filmography of Jules Verne's Works"] BSJV, NS No. 12
(4th Trimester), pp. 82-84.
Detailed list of film adaptations of Verne's works,
though Compère does not claim to be exhaustive. See
E428, E522.

E373 _____. "Le Rôle de la femme selon Jules Verne." ["Woman's
Role According to Jules Verne"] BSJV, NS No. 12 (4th
Trimester), pp. 67-68.
Paper delivered before the General Assembly of the
Jules Verne Society, February 8, 1969. A speech that
Verne grudgingly gave at a prize-giving ceremony in an
Amiens high school for girls shows him discouraging
them from careers outside the home.

E374 _____. "Renversants, ces débutants." ["Upsetting, These
Beginners"] BSJV, NS No. 10 (2nd Trimester), p. 40.
When Verne asked François Buloz, founder of the Revue
des deux mondes, how much he was going to pay him for
the article Buloz had just accepted for publication, the
answer was "nothing," and Verne took it back. Hetzel,
on the contrary, offered Verne a contract with the
stipulation that the article be rewritten. It appeared
as the novel, Five Weeks in a Balloon.

E375 Courville, Luce. "Jules Verne et le Rat goutteux." ["Jules
Verne and the Gouty Rat"] Nantes réalité, p. 42.
Verne's "Adventures of the Rat Family" appeared in
1891 and was eventually collected as the first story in
Yesterday and Tomorrow. One wonders whether it is not a
look back at the past. Is it perhaps the story created
by a sad man who conveys human foibles by means of a
fairy tale inhabited by rats? Why does he make a sage
of one of the rats? A sign showing a rat on crutches
hung outside a shop in Nantes; Verne very likely knew
it in his childhood. He could not make this rat a nasty
one like all the others.

E376 _____. "Pour Ou Contre L'Esclavage." ["For or Against
Slavery"] Nantes réalité, 30 (November-December), 57.

North Against South contains a number of discussions
on the subject of slavery. The main source of these
may be the debates among the shipfitters of Nantes.

E377 Diesbach, Ghislain de. Le Tour de Jules Verne en quatre-
vingts livres. [Around Jules Verne in Eighty Books]
Paris: Julliard.
      Verne, essentially a nineteenth-century poet, would
have disclaimed attributions to him of certain twentieth-
century phenomena that would have disappointed him.
Discusses Verne as a voice for England and the old
Europe. Colonialism made the English something less
than angels in Verne's eyes. He was repulsed by the
Germans, whom he considered malevolent fools, drawn to
Americans, and tolerant of the French whom he placed
somewhere between the Anglo-Saxons and the inferior
Latin races. A liking for the Russians prevented him
from being pro-Polish, although the Poles fascinated him.
Other Verne attitudes: The aristocracy is doomed (perhaps
the influence of 1848 on Verne), a preference for the
North in the American Civil War, a skeptical faith in
science, a belief that engineers are the masters in the
sciences, whereas astronomers, etc., are the servants.
Verne's works are moral without being Christian. Notes
strong role of revenge for Verne, who is seen as complex
and paradoxical.

E378 Dumas, Olivier. "Joseph Laissus (1900-1969)." BSJV, NS
No. 10 (2nd Trimester), pp. 21-23.
      A tribute to the deceased President of the Jules
Verne Society. Mentions activities and publications,
e.g. Comptes rendus du 91e congrès des sociétés savantes
(Rennes, 1966), Jules Verne, Extraordinary Voyager, 1828-
1905 (Paris: Gauthier-Villars and Bibliothèque Nationale,
1967, t.I, pp. 191-212), and an article in Bulletin No.
1 (January 1967). Laissus left other articles that will
be published.

E379 _____. "Le Tour de Jules Verne en quatre-vingts livres de
M. Ghislain de Diesbach." ["Around Jules Verne in Eighty
Books" by Ghislain de Diesbach"] BSJV, NS No. 11 (3rd
Trimester), pp. 51-54.
      Calls de Diesbach's book an excellent one with an
analysis that exhibits finesse with depth and a sense of
humor. Objects to the author's challenging the authenticity of the noble origins of the family of Verne's mother.
De Diesbach risks being misunderstood in emphasizing
Verne's middle-class prejudices. To criticize Verne's
social ideas one must place them in his time. For
instance, Verne is far ahead of contemporaries in his

views on blacks. For commercial reasons Verne and his
publisher, Hetzel, had to respect the prevailing attitudes. Unfortunately, de Diesbach's book has been
misunderstood by those who do not know Verne's works;
those who do understand have appreciated the discipline
in the study, its seriousness, and the author's knowledge of Verne. Regrets the author's unfamiliarity with
the Bulletin (new series).

E380 Evans, I. O. "Le Cryptogramme de La Jangada." ["The
Cryptogram of The Giant Raft"] BSJV, NS No. 9 (1st
Trimester), pp. 10-12.
In an article, "Edgar Poe and His Works," written
for the Musée des familles in 1864, Verne acknowledges
his interest in Poe's "The Gold Bug." He uses the type
of cryptogram, simple substitution, found in Poe's work
when he writes Journey to the Center of the Earth. This
system seemed too simple to Verne, so in future works such
as Mathias Sandorf and The Giant Raft, he devised something more complicated. Gives a key to The Giant Raft.

E381 _____. "Les Impressions de Jules Verne sur l'Islande."
["Impressions of Jules Verne on Iceland"] BSJV, NS No.
10 (2nd Trimester), pp. 27-28.
Present-day Reykjavik and Icelanders are very different
from the descriptions in Verne's Journey to the Center of
the Earth. Ascribes Iceland's deterioration to the
constant and increasingly tyrannical occupation of their
country. There has been steady improvement since June
17, 1944, when Iceland was declared a republic, free of
Denmark.

E382 Faivre, Jean-Paul. "Les Voyages extraordinaires de Jules
Verne en Australie." ["Extraordinary Voyages of Jules
Verne in Australia"] Australian Journal of French
Studies, 6 (No. 1), 9-25.
Reviews possible identities of Verne's Mistress
Branican and notes Verne's evocation of the legend of
the sea behind John Branican. Verne had been haunted
for years by the disappearance at sea of the Prussian
explorer, Ludwig Leichhardt. Godfrey's quest of his
father may parallel Verne's feeling that beside his
natural father, he had a "sublime father" in Hetzel.
The story becomes a family drama, the choice of Australia
reflects French interest in that country, and the desert
is a part of the Nature that is conquered by Man -- a
major theme of the Voyages. Verne salutes a new, modern
Australia, in which the desert plays the role of a
character.

E383 Galey, Matthieu. "Double Visage de Jules Verne." ["Jules
      Verne's Double Face"] Express, No. 945 (18-24 August),
      pp. 57-58.
         An account of de Diesbach's book (E377). Verne was
      a man of his time, and yet he surprisingly failed to see
      many things. He seemed blind to many social concepts.

E384 Garrigues, M. "Une Humanité insatisfaite." ["Unsatisfied
      Humanity"] Le Rouergat, Rodez, 28 November, n.p.
         On a page devoted to "the fabulous world" of science
      fiction it is mentioned that when Jonathan Swift wrote
      of Gulliver's adventures he was writing science fiction,
      notwithstanding the satirical attack on society. Cyrano
      de Bergerac also mounted an attack on a reasonable and
      fixed society. Verne, writing as a novelist, produced
      his literature during an age of belief in the unlimited
      potential of science, still in its infancy. Voltaire's
      Micromégas also places him in the company of those who
      wrote science fiction.

E385 Gondolo della Riva, Piero. "Jules Verne et L'Italie."
      ["Jules Verne and Italy"] BSJV, NS No. 7-8 (3rd & 4th
      Trimesters), pp. 9-13.
         It was only after 1870 that Verne was translated in
      Italy. Success was immediate, and some of novels were
      published by the Tipografia Editrice Lombarda almost
      concurrently with their appearances in France. Some
      Italian editions of the Voyages extraordinaires suffered
      from poor translation. Verne himself suffered from the
      rumor either that he was Italian or didn't exist at all.
      Italian scholars have interested themselves in Verne.
      Among these: Pizzi, Turiello, Ricca, and Marcucci, by
      whom Verne is no longer considered merely a writer of
      children's stories.

E386 Grégoire, Maurice. "Connaissez-vous l'été écossais?" ["Do
      You Know the Scottish Summer?"] Plein-Feu, 2nd Trimester,
      pp. 118-136.
         Contains what seem like contemporary quotations that
      are, however, identified in a footnote as coming from
      Verne's Child of the Cavern (1877) and The Green Ray
      (1882). Mentions Verne's unpublished Trip to England
      and Scotland, an account of his first trip to Scotland
      (1859), which furnished him with material for the new
      novels. In 1880 Verne again visited Scotland on his
      yacht.

E387 Hauttecoeur, J.-P. "Pour Les Poètes et les romanciers la
      lune est à la portée de la main." ["For Poets and
      Novelists the Moon is Within Reach"] La Croix-Dimanche
      du Nord, Lille, 26 July, n.p.

Goes back to Lucian to give a summation of moon trips
in literature and the appeal of the moon to writers
throughout the ages. Puts Verne in the debt of Poe
with regard to his two moon novels. Published also in
Le Semeur, a weekly of Clermont-Ferrand, July 25, 1969.

E388 Helling, Cornélis. "Jules Verne et l'esperanto." ["Jules
Verne and Esperanto"] BSJV, NS No. 12 (4th Trimester),
pp. 69-71.
Verne was honorary President of an Esperanto club in
Amiens. He created some macaronic language in his works;
for example, Captain Nemo and his companions spoke a
fabricated tongue.

E389 Hermans, Dr. Georges. "De La Terre à la lune de Jules
Verne." ["From the Earth to the Moon by Jules Verne"]
Le Livre et l'estampe, No. 59-60 (1969), pp. 3-15.
The American landing on the moon has made Verne
topical and subject to reevaluation. Lists dates of
publication of Verne's From the Earth to the Moon and
finishes with a short bibliography. See E446.

E390 Jan, Isabelle. Essai sur la littérature enfantine. [Essay
on Children's Literature] Paris. Editions ouvrières.
About ten of the one hundred and eighty pages of this
book on children's literature are devoted to Verne, who
is given sole credit for writing children's adventure
stories that enable one to say something in favor of
them. Verne is compared unfavorably to Stevenson as an
artist and to Dumas as a reconstructor of history, the
world, and society. Despite the boredom of Verne's
scientific descriptions with their number-figures and
code-figures, Verne turns science into poetry, giving
a new dimension to the Robinson Crusoe theme. Most of
Verne's works, which lead the reader to the borders of
fantasy only to dispel the mirage either with practical
details or a mocking humor, are suitable for the fifteen-
year-old. In a way Mme de Ségur, Hans Andersen, Verne,
and Lewis Carroll were all anomalies. A point is made
about the difficulty of defining "children's stories."
See D382.

E391 Laissus, J[oseph]. "La Publication de quelques oeuvres de
Jules Verne par E. Girard et A. Boitte." ["Publication
of a Few Jules Verne Works by E. Girard and A. Boitte"]
BSJV, NS No. 10 (2nd Trimester), pp. 37-39.
Paper delivered before the General Assembly of the
Jules Verne Society, February 10, 1968. The publishers
Girard and Boitte published some of Verne's works about
1886. Masters of prospectus writing and other forms of
publicity, their editions were basically the Hetzel ones,
but inferior in one way or another.

E392 _____. "Le Voyage à travers l'impossible." ["Voyage Across the Impossible"] BSJV, NS No. 12 (4th Trimester), pp. 79-81.

Gives a resumé of this play, written by Verne and A. d'Ennery, which had its premiere in Paris at the Porte Saint-Martin Theatre, November 25, 1882. Its scenario does not appear to have been published. Was not one of the collaborators' better works. Nothing would be known of the play except that the Théâtre moderne illustré in an undated issue gives the resume. See E838.

E393 de Lassée, [Marie-Thérèse]. "L'Origine des Allotte de la Fuÿe." ["Origin of the Allottes de la Fuÿe"] BSJV, NS No. 11 (3rd Trimester), pp. 55-56.

After having read de Diesbach's book on Verne, Mme Lassée (née Allotte de la Fuÿe) traces her family back to the arrival of a Scot in France in 1462, a member of Louis XI's Scottish guard, and brings it forward to the present.

E394 Martin, Charles-Noël. "Il y a cent ans le Nautilus et le Capitaine Nemo faisaient le tour du monde." ["A Hundred Years Ago the Nautilus and Captain Nemo Circled the World"] Science et Vie, 116 (November), 76-83.

The history of the submarine demonstrates a truly valid realization of Verne's Nautilus as the model. The latter has movements and possibilities that have been realized only through atomic power. Verne knew practically nothing of submarines in 1869. Recounts the history of experiments in the seventeenth and eighteenth centuries. Credits the Coessin brothers with creating the first true submersible vehicle (1819), although it couldn't be steered once it had dived. Among the probable sources of inspiration for Verne's Nautilus are the submergible of his Nantes math teacher, Villeroi, with a successful experiment in 1832; the Villeroi submarine boat built by the American, Commodore Samuel Francis Dupont, in Philadelphia (1861); and Verne's trip on the ship, Great Eastern, to New York (1867). Verne was wrong in thinking electricity would power submarines, but in other respects there are startling resemblances between his vessel and the nuclear sub. Verne feared the destructive uses to which submarines would be put, but of course could not foresee the extent of the horrors of modern warfare.

E395 _____. "Neuf Erreurs de Jules Verne ou les jeux de la mécanique céleste." ["Nine Errors of Jules Verne or the Games of Heavenly Mechanics"] Science et Vie, 115 (March), 54-59, 154.

Verne is guilty of mistakes in his novels concerning
the moon. However, they compensate by allowing the
reader to dream.

E396 _____. "Préface." In Archipel en feu [Archipelago on
Fire] and Sans dessus dessous [Purchase of the North
Pole], by Jules Verne. Lausanne: Editions Rencontre,
pp. 5-12.
Describes the struggle of the Greek people. Focuses
on the scientific value of Purchase of the North Pole.

E397 _____. "Préface." In César Cascabel, by Jules Verne.
Lausanne: Editions Rencontre, pp. 5-12.
Verne was intent on serving Amiens when he was elected
as a Municipal Councillor. The post gave scope to his
genuine interest in urban problems. Verne concentrated
on Amiens's theatre and circus.

E398 _____. "Préface." In Chancellor, Martin Paz and Billet de
Loterie [Lottery Ticket], by Jules Verne. Lausanne:
Editions Rencontre, pp. 7-15.
Discusses the creative process involved in the compos-
ition of these three works. Also takes up the shipwreck
motif.

E399 _____. "Préface." In Mistress Branican, by Jules Verne.
Lausanne: Editions Rencontre, pp. 7-13.
Shows that the idea of the lack of importance of
women in Verne's life and works has been overdone.

E400 Michaelis, Dr. Anthony R. "Sur Les Pas de Jules Verne."
["In Jules Verne's Footsteps"] BSJV, NS No. 11 (3rd
Trimester), pp. 48-50.
This article appeared in English in the Daily Telegraph.
The writer visited Florida in an attempt to find Stone's
Hill, the launching point for the "Columbiad's" journey
into space in From Earth to the Moon. He was unsuccess-
ful due among other things to the different system now
employed to plot longitude and latitude based on Greenwich.
He decided that Lake Harbor came the nearest to Verne's
launching point. Dr. Michaelis has arranged with the
State of Florida for the erection of a Verne statue at
Lake Harbor.

E401 Raymond, François. "A Propos du Vol d'Apollo. Jules Verne,
ou la vérité du roman." ["Concerning the Flight of
Apollo. Jules Verne, or the Truth of the Novel"]
Europe, 47, No. 482 (June), 225-240.

Verne's celebration of science's potential is not
infinite. He shows that science has definite limitations.
Particularly in his moon novels does fantasy point to the
inadequacies of the real.

E402   Raymond, F[rançois]. "Jules Verne et le collège de Pata-
physique." ["Jules Verne and the College of Pataphysics"]
BSJV, NS No. 9 (1st Trimester), pp. 13-19.
        History of Pataphysics from Alfred Jarry to the
establishment of a "College of Pataphysics," a journal
devoted to its interest, and the concern of Pataphysicians with Verne. No. 16 of the above-mentioned journal,
Dossiers, is a special number on Verne's Pole. The
Pataphysicians have spurred a different reading of Verne
in keeping with one of the definitions of Pataphysics:
"A universe that one can see and perhaps one should see
in place of the traditional one." Verne can now be read
as a writer for whom science and politics are pretexts
that enable him to be a novelist.

E403   Raymond, François. "Jules Verne ou le mouvement perpetuel
(essai de patanalyse appliquée)." ["Jules Verne or
Perpetual Movement (Essay of Applied Patanalysis)"]
Subsidia pataphysica, No. 8, 22 sable 97, pp. 20-52.
        Verne's works illustrate his views on the universe.
Time and space recur at certain intervals. There is a
relationship between psychological and physical phenomena.
Verne represents many theories without espousing any.

E404   _____. "Un Grand Historien de la littérature: Jean-Jacques
Bridenne." ["A Great Literary Historian: Jean-Jacques
Bridenne"] BSJV, NS No. 12 (4th Trimester), pp. 63-66.
        Homage to J-J. Bridenne, who died April 9, 1969.
Compliments him for having combatted the snobbism of
critics who ostracized writers like Verne. Mentions
Bridenne's La Littérature française d'imagination
scientifique and his articles, especially in Fiction,
Numbers 6, 7, 8, 20, and 21.

E405   Renau, Jean-Pierre. "Pour Tous, un même inspirateur: Jules
Verne." ["For All, the Same Inspirer: Jules Verne"]
Le Cri du monde, September, p. 7.
        Some quotations acknowledging debts to Verne by
Tsiolkovski, Goddard, and Oberth.

E406   Serres, Michel. "Un Voyage au bout de la nuit." ["Voyage
to the End of the Night"] Critique, 25 (April), 291-303.
        Associates the abandoned coal mine of Verne's Child
of the Cavern with Plato's myth of the cave, seen as
replacing Homer and the Hell of mythology. Finds that
Verne's "voyage" is characteristically in three stages:

one in ordinary or even extraordinary space, another
that is intellectual or encyclopedic, and the third an
initiatory, religious, mythical pilgrimage. Verne's
caves confirm Nietzche's view that behind every cave
there is a deeper, vaster, stranger one. The ascent of
Verne's characters into solar space is a complex one.
The writer agrees with Bachelard that Verne's imagination is a material one.

E407 Simon, Jules-Marie. "A Propos des sous-marins ce n'est
pas Jules Verne qui les a inventés." ["As For Sub-
marines, It's Not Jules Verne Who Invented Them"] La
Drome, Valence-sur-Rhône, 22 November, n.p.
   Shows that contrary to a fairly widespread suggestion,
Verne did not invent the submarine. Says there is no
mention of underwater craft before the fifteenth century.
Lists among those who have worked on the idea: the
German Sturm, the Dutchman van Drebbel, the Americans
Bushnell and Fulton, the German Klinger, Hognan in
England, and Coessin and others in France. Verne brought
to the attention of the modern navy a weapon that had
been forgotten. Fulton furnished the model for Verne's
Nautilus.

E408 Taussat, R[obert]. "Autour de la lune de la 'Columbiad'
à Apollo VIII." ["Around the 'Columbiad's Moon to
Apollo 8"] BSJV, NS No. 11 (3rd Trimester), pp. 43-47.
   Paper delivered before the General Assembly of the
Jules Verne Society, February 8, 1969. Verne probably
didn't take very seriously the imagined sending of the
"Columbiad" into space. Considers the inadequate preparation (three days), the physical incapacity of the
participants, and the total lack of comprehension of
costs. And yet there are many amazing coincidences in
the flights of the "Columbiad" and Apollo 8.

E409 _____. "Jules Verne fut-il un précurseur?" ["Was Jules
Verne a Precursor?"] BSJV, NS No. 11 (3rd Trimester),
pp. 57-60.
   Paper delivered before the General Assembly of the
Jules Verne Society, February 8, 1969. Takes exception
to the views of Matthieu Galey, critic of L'Express, for
considering that Verne, far from being a visionary, was
a short-sighted man of his time. Wonders if Galey read
de Diesbach's book too rapidly. Agrees that Verne's
society is that of the nineteenth century and not ours.
However, Verne was perfectly aware of what horrors the
future might bring.

E410   Terrasse, P[ierre]. "Autour De La Lune 1968." ["Around
       the Moon 1968"] BSJV, NS No. 9 (1st Trimester), pp.
       4-5.
           James Lovell, who with William Anders and Frank Borman
       circled the moon ten times in December 1968, revealed in
       a statement published in France-Soir that he had read
       Verne's From the Earth to the Moon and Around the Moon
       before making the flight. The press has noted a number
       of coincidences in the three: same point of departure,
       Florida; and same splashdown area, the Pacific.

E411   _____. "Jules Verne à la télévision." ["Jules Verne on
       Television"] BSJV, NS No. 9 (1st Trimester), p. 20.
           Verne's only Christmas story, "Mr. Ray Sharp and Miss
       Me Flat," was shown on television December 24, 1968.
       Congratulates those responsible, including Claude
       Santelli and Jacques Trébouta. Complains that Verne's
       names were changed and the story situated in Germany
       instead of Switzerland, where William Tell figures in
       the plot.

E412   Terrasse, Pierre. "Jules Verne et les grandes écoles
       scientifiques." ["Jules Verne and the Great Scientific
       Schools"] BSJV, NS No. 12 (4th Trimester), pp. 72-78.
           Paper delivered before the General Assembly of the
       Jules Verne Society, February 8, 1969. Not until 1879
       in The Begum's Fortune does Verne create an engineer who
       is a Frenchman, Marcel Bruckmann. The latter represents
       the Ecole Centrale des Arts et Manufactures. Lists a
       few Verne characters who are products of the Ecole
       Polytechnique and others who are graduates of unspecified
       institutions. Discusses some of Verne's personal rela-
       tions with engineers.

E413   Vierne, S[imone]. "Deux Admirateurs et un détracteur
       célèbres de Jules Verne." ["Two Famous Admirers and a
       Famous Detractor of Jules Verne"] BSJV, NS No. 10 (2nd
       Trimester), pp. 33-36.
           The importance of the reading of Verne by poets and
       novelists from the last quarter of the nineteenth century
       to the present is too often minimized or forgotten.
       Discusses Verne's welcome influence on the poet, Blaise
       Cendrars, and the novelist, Saint-Exupéry. Mentions in
       contrast Jean Giono's disliking Verne for having, so
       Giono felt, transformed Robinson Crusoe from an eclogue
       into a terrifying picture of modern industrial society.

E414   _____. Hommage à G. Sand. [Homage to G. Sand] Grenoble:
       Le Cellier, pp. 101-114.
           A comparison of G. Sand's Laura with Verne's Journey
       to the Center of the Earth shows how an intellectual

relationship can be established on the basis of an en-
counter of two fertile imaginations without any reciprocal influence being possible. Makes geological
comparisons between the geodes, a hollow mineral within
crystals, and terrestrial depths.

1970

E415 Abeck, A. "Quelques Réflexions sur l'apesanteur." ["A Few
Reflections on Weightlessness"] Travail et maîtrise,
February, p. 8.
   An article on weightlessness suffered during space-
flights is accompanied by an illustration from Verne
showing his characters, plus the dog and two chickens,
floating in space as they reach the "neutral point" when
the attractions from the Earth and the Moon are equal.

E416 Albert, Pierre. "Il y a cent ans Jules Verne publiait
Vingt Mille Lieues sous les mers." ["A Hundred Years
Ago Jules Verne Published Twenty Thousand Leagues Under
the Sea"] La Revue du Liban, 23 May, p. 40.
   In commemoration of the hundredth anniversary of the
publication of Twenty Thousand Leagues Under the Sea
some salient facts of Verne's life are evoked. Records
his friendships with scientists and travelers. Mentions
the disputed story that Louise Michel was the source for
this novel, and presents as a firmer supposition the
collection of facts by Verne in conversations with
officers and crew of the Great Eastern on his New York
trip. Debts to Verne in practical accomplishments are
enormous. In his genre only Wells perhaps equaled his
ability.

E417 Anon. "Jules Verne à la télévision." ["Jules Verne on
Television"] BSJV, NS-No. 14 (2nd Trimester), p. 132.
   Alexandre Rivemale's Nemo, produced by Jean Bacqué,
was shown on TV March 21, 1970. This is the play put
on at the Théâtre Marigny by the Grenier-Hussenot
Company, October 3, 1956 and published the same year by
Flammarion. On May 18, 1970 Claude Santelli's production of Child of the Cavern, first seen at Christmas
1964, appeared. It is the best because it is the most
faithful film adaptation of a Verne novel. The adaptation is by Marcel Moussy, the director is Marcel Bluwal.
George Poujouly plays Harry Ford and Paloma Matta plays
Nell.

E418 Anon. "Mathias Sandorf. Le Célèbre Jules Verne."
["Mathias Sandorf. The Famous Jules Verne"] L'Yonne
républicaine, 30 May, n.p.

During an unfavorable mention of a French film adaptation (1963) of Verne's <u>Mathias Sandorf</u>, shown on channel
1 of French TV, three points are made about Verne.
First, it is not true that he had a host of ghostwriters
to enable him to live up to the contract that called for
two novels a year. His brother, Paul, was his only
helper. Second, one must not see in Verne an author
going from success to success. His total production
includes a large number of forgotten works. Third,
the legend that pictures Verne as a stay-at-home is
quite untrue.

E419 Anon. "Un Rapport de visite à sec en 1861." ["Report on
a Dry Dock Inspection in 1861"] <u>Bulletin technique du</u>
<u>bureau veritas</u>, pp. 194-197.
Discusses Verne's knowledge of seafaring matters as
shown in <u>Twenty Thousand Leagues Under the Sea</u>. Starts
with an "engineer's report" on damage done to the ship,
<u>Scotia</u>, by the spur projecting from the hull of the
<u>Nautilus</u>. Verne classifies nationalities as (1) of a
frivolous disposition and (2) of a serious disposition.
His classification is oriented to reactions to the loss
of ships. Does not specify the frivolous countries,
but England, America, and Germany are serious ones.
Challenges Verne's figures on annual ship loss and some
details of the structure of the <u>Scotia</u>.

*E420 Bachelard, Gaston. <u>Le Droit de rêver</u>. [The Right to Dream]
Paris: Presses Universitaires de France.
Not seen (cited in D443, p. 226).

E421 Barthes, Roland. "Par Où Commencer?" ["Where to Begin?"]
<u>Poétique</u>, 1 (February), 3-9.
A structuralist approach to Verne's <u>The Mysterious</u>
<u>Island</u>. The work is discussed in terms of four basic
foundations or themes: the garden of Eden, colonializ-
ation, Nature transformed, and the secret of the island.

E422 Bellemin-Noël, Jean. "Analectures de Jules Verne."
["'Non-readings' of Selection from Jules Verne"] <u>Critique</u>,
26 (August), 692-704.
Point of departure is a short story by Jules Verne,
"Mr. Ray Sharp and Miss Me Flat," published in the
<u>Figaro illustré</u> of December 1893. The transformation of
animals from aquatic to aereal state, for example, rats
becoming oysters then fish and then rats again, is said
to represent prenatal and postnatal existence. Article
then develops the subject of the unconscious in the
figure of the Sphinx and discusses the text as an in-
voluntary illustration of psychic organization. Recognizes
the presence of the Oedipus theme as well as that of homosexuality in the collection of Verne's stories, <u>Yesterday</u>
<u>and Tomorrow</u>.

E423 Berger, Jean-Daniel. "Les Traces du Viennois Joseph Martin en Sibérie." ["Tracks of the Viennese, Joseph Martin, in Siberia"] Le Dauphiné libéré, Grenoble, 22 February, n.p.

    Report of Berger's lecture on Joseph Martin, the explorer (born in Vienna in 1848, died in Turkestan in 1892). He was well known in Eastern Siberia and Central Asia: a lake, a mountain range, a glacier, and a peak are named for him. He was in contact with Verne, to whom he furnished documentation for Michel Strogoff. The lecturer sums up Berger's activities.

E424 Bergier, Jacques. Admirations. Paris: Christian Bourgois.

    Book on ten authors described as writers of magic, including John Buchan, Arthur Machen, Ivan Efremov, J. R. R. Tolkien, and C. S. Lewis. Author reveals that he read Verne in Russian at the age of three. Machen was less in tune with his era than were Verne and Wells and had less success. The stories of Efremov could have been written by Verne or Conan Doyle to whom comparison is made in terms of themes, characters, and atmosphere.

E425 Bougaran, Yves. "La France dans la course au pétrole sous-marin." ["France in the Undersea Oil Race"] Moniteur du commerce international, 12 November, pp. 4695-4699.

    Describes the Agyronaut, an underwater craft designed to participate in the search for offshore oil. It could have been called the "Nautilus," for it corresponds exactly to the description given by Verne. The Russians and Americans are interested in the French submergible especially for Arctic underwater exploration.

E426 Chesneaux, Jean. "Jules Verne et le Canada français." ["Jules Verne and French Canada"] In Famille-sans-nom [Family Without a Name], by Jules Verne. Montreal: Maison édition Québec Inc., pp. vii-xviii.

    Verne's Family Without a Name illustrates the author's admiration of the revolutionary trends of 1848, including the right of national self-determination. Verne also evinces a sympathy for the Breton cause. The novel has romantic elements.

E427 _____. "Or et l'argent chez Jules Verne." ["Gold and Money in Jules Verne"] Lettres nouvelles, March-April, pp. 83-105.

    Among middle-class values, gold and silver are at first artificial and conventional in Verne. His early characters remain financially independent. Then beginning in the 1890s science develops a strong dependence on money.

E428 Compère, Daniel. "Compléments à la filmographie des oeuvres de Jules Verne." ["Complements to the Filmography of Jules Verne's Works"] BSJV, NS No. 16 (4th Trimester), p. 177.
   Complementary information to the "filmographie" in BSJV, No. 12. See E312, E522.

E429 _____. "Les Suites dans les Voyages extraordinaires." ["Sequences in The Extraordinary Voyages"] BSJV, NS No. 14 (2nd Trimester), pp. 122-128.
   Paper given before the General Assembly of the Jules Verne Society, February 7, 1970. A number of Verne's novels have been considered the continuation of others. An insistence on this approach raises a number of technical problems, mostly small ones but detrimental to the premise. Verne considered the evolution of his characters more important than material details. Actually, the so-called continuations are false ones. Each of his novels must be considered a separate part of a homogeneous whole.

E430 Courville, Luce and Francoise Decré. Hommage à Jules Verne à l'occasion du centenaire de "Vingt Mille Lieues sous les mers" 1870-1970. [Homage to Jules Verne on the Occasion of the Centenary of "Twenty Thousand Leagues Under the Sea"] Nantes: Société des amis de la bibliothéque municipale de Nantes.
   Catalogue of the Exposition in Nantes of 1970 in honor of the centenary of the publication of Verne's Twenty Thousand Leagues Under the Sea. See E466. Beginning with the Villeroi Submarine, successfully tested in Philadelphia harbor by Verne's math teacher, Villeroi, the Exposition uses official documents, Verne's correspondence, critical works (books and articles), etc., to illuminate the subject of the Exposition. The first portion ends with Nantes in the twentieth century and the modern submarine. Other portions of the Exposition treat the theme of the mysterious isle and "Robinson" books, the romantic hero and the man of science in Verne's works, and a linking of Verne to da Vinci and Cousteau. See E466.

E431 Dessaucy, Jacques. "La Prospective est-elle une science exacte?" ["Is Foresightedness an Exact Science?"] Le Cri du monde, February, pp. 44-46.
   Discussing the book of the American, C. Furnas, The Next Hundred Years: The Unfinished Work of Science, distinguishes between autodestructive and autoconstructive approaches to the future. Cites Verne as an example of the latter. Verne predicted that Man would reach

the Moon, and he has. Verne described a chimerical plan and others have made it materialize. He is not a neutral witness: his foresight is an integral part of the creative process.

E432 Dumas, O[livier]. "A Propos du Colonel Charras." ["Concerning Colonel Charras"] BSJV, NS No. 16 (4th Trimester), p. 176.
Proves that the Colonel Charras discussed by R. Taussat (E471) was mentioned anonymously by Hetzel in the preface to the first edition of Verne's La Géographie de la France (1867). In the preface to the second edition (1876), after the fall of the Empire, Hetzel felt free to identify Charras by name.

E433 Faivre, J[ean]-P[aul]. "Jules Verne et l'Australie: Mistress Branican." ["Jules Verne and Australia: Mistress Branican"] BSJV, NS No. 15 (3rd Trimester), pp. 152-155.
The main points of an article previously published (E382) and given as a paper at the last meeting of the General Assembly of the Jules Verne Society. Mrs. Branican was probably based on Lady Franklin, widow of the late explorer, Sir John Franklin. Verne was haunted by the disappearance of the Prussian explorer, Ludwig Leichhardt, who disappeared the same year as Franklin (1848). The Godfrey of the novel may reincarnate a Robert Godefroy of Amiens, but nine years before a Godfrey in search of a fiancée, not a father, appeared in School For Crusoes. To the quest of a father is added a somber family melodrama in Mistress Branican. The Australia of this novel is vaster than the one in Captain Grant's Children. Its desert is one of the book's characters. Dolly in the search for her husband followed the paths of the last great explorers: Colonel Warburton (1873) and David Lindsay (1877-1888).

E434 Faivre, Jean-Paul. "L'Australie et Les Enfants du Capitaine Grant." ["Australia and Captain Grant's Children"] BSJV, NS No. 13 (1st Trimester), pp. 100-104.
Covers the main points of the author's previously published article (E382). These points: the reason why Verne chose Australia in his Captain Grant's Children (it was a kind of phantom land); the personality of Jacques Paganel; the itinerary, with an examination of squatters and diggers; Paganel as a savior opposed to the demoniac Ayrton; and Verne's success in Australia.

E435   Favre, Marie-Françoise. "Musique, surdité et rêverie."
       ["Music, Deafness, and Dream"] Revue de l'ouïe, April,
       pp. 51-59.
          Review of film adaptation of Verne's "M. Ré-Dièze et
       Mlle. Mi-Bémol" ["Mr. Ray Sharp and Miss Me Flat"]
       published in the Figaro littéraire in 1893. A deaf
       organist dies when he learns that the organ on which
       he was playing on Christmas Eve gave out in the middle
       of the program. A wanderer arrives and replaces the
       organ with a fantastic one that enables the church to
       have Christmas music after all.

E436   Gaudin, E[dmond]. "Jules Verne et la Philatélie."
       ["Jules Verne and Philately"] BSJV, NS No. 15 (3rd
       Trimester), pp. 136-137.
          Of foreign countries only Monaco has issued a series
       of stamps illustrating Verne's Voyages extraordinaires.
       This series commemorated the fiftieth anniversary of the
       author's death. France also had an issue in 1955, and
       in 1966 there was a special cancellation on the thirty-
       centime stamps. A footnote states that Hungary, Mali,
       and Panama have recently issued Verne stamps. There is
       a picture of the Monaco stamps on the last page of the
       issue. See E493.

E437   Genevois, Alain. "Le Premier bateau-poisson." ["The First
       Fish Boat"] Nantes Réalité, January, pp. 42-43.
          An eyewitness account of the dive made August 12,
       1832, by Villeroi in the submarine he had constructed.
       Villeroi, who was Verne's math teacher, could not get
       French government support despite his successful dive.
       He went to America where the Philadelphia police seized
       a submarine of his, thinking it was a Confederate product.
       The Yankee Admiral duPont entrusted Villeroi with building
       a war submarine that was navigating in Philadelphia harbor
       in 1861. It sank during a storm in Virginia in 1863. It
       is likely that Verne was inspired by Villeroi's craft.

E438   Gondolo della Riva, Piero. "A Propos des chansons de Jules
       Verne." ["About Jules Verne's Songs"] BSJV, NS No. 13
       (1st Trimester), pp. 88-91.
          Gives titles and references to fifteen Verne songs.

E439   ____. "La Troisième Série du Magasin d'éducation et de
       récréation." ["Third Series of the Magazine of Education
       and Recreation"] BSJV, NS No. 13 (1st Trimester), pp.
       98-99.
          Paper delivered before the General Assembly of the
       Jules Verne Society, February 10, 1968. Until now two
       series of the Magasin d'éducation et de récréation have

been known. Almost all of Verne's <u>Voyages extraordinaires</u> first appeared here. The first series ran from March 20, 1864 to 1894; the second from 1895 to 1906. A third series, quite different in nature, appeared every three months on the twenty-fifth, beginning in January. Hetzel may have used it to publish less salable work of Verne. No pre-original editions are in the series.

E440 ____. "Oeuvres attribuées à Jules Verne en Italie." ["Works Attributed to Jules Verne in Italy"] <u>BSJV</u>, NS No. 14 (2nd Trimester), p. 131.

Continues previous study and lists texts about which there is no certainty. They may have been attributed to Verne through the mistakes of biographers, and they may not even exist. <u>See</u> E302, E335, E336.

E441 Guermonprez, Jean H. "Jules Verne inspirateur d'Arthur Rimbaud. Le 'Nautilus' est-il le 'bateau ivre'?" ["Jules Verne Inspirer of Arthur Rimbaud. Is the 'Nautilus' the 'Drunken Boat'?"] <u>BSJV</u>, NS No. 13 (1st Trimester), pp. 91-95.

Extract from <u>Journal de Genève</u>, January 13, 1951. Gilbert Mellano at the age of twenty was the first to bring actual proof to the thesis that Rimbaud's <u>Bateau ivre</u> was inspired by Verne's <u>Nautilus</u>. Passages from Rimbaud's poem and Verne's <u>Twenty Thousand Leagues Under the Sea</u> are juxtaposed to prove the point. <u>See</u> E470.

E442 Guillon, Yves. "Généalogie des Guillon-Verne." ["Genealogy of the Guillon-Vernes"] Photocopy. Nantes: Municipal Library (Verne Catalogue #1994).

Contains genealogy of Verne's branch of his family tree.

E443 Hautefeuille, Jean. "Le Capitaine Nemo et la ville sous-marine." ["Captain Nemo and the Underwater City"] <u>Voix du Nord</u>, 17 June, n.p.

A favorable review of the production in Panavision metrocolor by Bertram Ostrer and Steven Pallos, <u>Le Capitaine Nemo et la ville sous-marine</u> (Metro-Goldwyn-Mayer). Robert Ryan is an excellent Captain Nemo.

E444 Helling, Cornélis. "Jules Verne et les timbres-poste." ["Jules Verne and Stamps"] <u>BSJV</u>, NS No. 16 (4th Trimester), pp. 164-165.

Verne loved stamps. On December 18, 1849, he writes his mother that he keeps having a struggle with his father over them (letter in "Livres de France" vol. 6, No. 5, May-June 1955, Hachette). Another letter, written to Helling by Mme Georges Lefebvre, Verne's stepdaughter, on May 8, 1931, says she has Verne's stamp collection and would like to sell it. Two more letters in the same correspondence (March 30, 1931 and April 26, 1931) speak of Mme Lefebvre's desire to sell some of Verne's furniture and of Verne's sweet, musical voice. Mme Lefebvre knows nothing of André Laurie's collaboration with Verne.

E445 ____. "Une Nouvelle Médaille à l'effigie de Jules Verne." ["A New Medal in Jules Verne's Likeness"] BSJV, NS No. 16 (4th Trimester), p. 159.

To commemorate the flight of Apollo 12, the manufacturer of medals, Numint, of The Hague and Amsterdam, has struck a medal showing John F. Kennedy on one side and Verne on the other.

E446 Hermans, Dr. Georges. "De La Terre à la lune de Jules Verne." ["Jules Verne's From the Earth to the Moon"] Le Livre et L'Estampe, No. 61-62 (1970), pp. 3-9.

Publishes corrections, omissions, etc. indicated by readers of the previous article on the publishing dates of the novel. See E389.

E447 Klein, Gérard. "Pour Lire Verne (1)." ["To Read Verne"] Fiction, 18 (May), 137-143.

First part of what might be called a review article on Ghislain de Diesbach's "Le Tour du monde" de Jules Verne. Discusses Verne's place in the social structure, especially in relation to the bourgeoisie. Verne's presumed class based its values on the individual. The ambivalence of Verne's attitude toward the Anglo-Saxon world is made clear. The role of the proletariat in Verne is almost always that of a servant. As for religion, the role of Providence seems to weaken as Verne gets older. De Diesbach's thesis leaves unexplained many characteristics of Verne's work. See E448.

E448 ____. "Pour Lire Verne(2)." ["To Read Verne"] Fiction, 18 (June), 143-152.

Questions whether it suffices to see in Verne's work simply the reflection of the collective conscience of a social class. Verne's heroes exercise their talents outside of society. For Verne, society, not power, corrupts. His heroes give him revenge for his own "rejection" by society. Michel Strogoff takes place in a country of medieval aristocratic values. Verne may be closer to Zola with respect to the recognition of oppression and violence in society than has been thought. His last work, Barsac Mission, shows bourgeois society and science both threatened by the phenomenon of monopolies. Verne's work may go beyond de Diesbach's collective conscience. See E447.

E449 Laissus, Joseph. "Jules Verne dans l'imagerie publicitaire."
      ["Jules Verne in Publicity Pictures"] BSJV, NS No. 16
      (4th Trimester), pp. 166-167.
         Mentions a number of instances in which Verne's like-
      ness has been used for advertising purposes. Describes
      in particular a polychrome picture of Verne that the
      department store, Les Galeries Lafayette, distributed
      in the years before the first World War, showing Verne
      at a table in a setting of fantasy and flanked by two
      of his novels.

E450 _____. "Jules Verne et la petite bibliothèque blanche
      illustrée." ["Jules Verne and the Little Illustrated
      White Library"] BSJV, NS No. 14 (2nd Trimester), pp.
      111-112.
         Chiefly about Hetzel and a new series he published in
      1879, "La Petite Bibliothèque blanche illustrée," and
      the appearance in it of the adventures of Tom Thumb.
      These included a page of drawings evoking the works of
      Verne.

E451 _____. "Paris au Rhin." ["Paris on the Rhine"] BSJV, NS
      No. 14 (2nd Trimester), pp. 129-130.
         Describes Verne's Paris au Rhin published by Hetzel
      in 1870 on the occasion of the Franco-Prussian war.
      This is actually an extract from Géographie illustrée
      de la France et de ses colonies, written by Verne and
      Théophile Lavallée, published by Hetzel in 1868. The
      Paris au Rhin is a 176-page brochure, and concerns the
      twenty départements or regions involved in the war.

E452 Mariage, Pierre. "Robert Esnault Pelterie." Forces
      aériennes françaises, January, pp. 55-61.
         Tribute to Robert Pelterie, who is credited with
      being the real precursor of modern space flights.
      Mention is made of the frequent references to Verne,
      master of works of imagination and pioneer of science
      fiction. His From the Earth to the Moon and Around the
      Moon have rendered such references inevitable. Verne
      must be credited with having given the impetus to several
      distinguished careers. Criticizes Verne's use of a
      cannon as a launching apparatus, saying that the would-be
      voyagers would have been instantly crushed.

E453 Martin, Charles-Noël. "Préface." In Agence Thompson and
      Co. et Révoltes de la "Bounty" [Thompson Travel Agency
      and Co. and Mutineers of "The Bounty"] by Jules Verne.
      Lausanne: Editions Rencontre, pp. 7-15.
         Discusses tales written by Verne at the time he was
      also writing the Voyages extraordinaires.

E454 _____. "Préface." In <u>Aventures de trois Russes et de trois</u>
<u>Anglais</u> et <u>Invasion de la mer</u> [<u>Meridiana</u> and <u>Invasion</u>
<u>of the Sea</u>], by Jules Verne. Lausanne: Editions Ren-
contre, pp. 7-13.
Discusses the creative process exercised by Verne in
writing these two novels.

E455 _____. "Préface." In <u>Claudius Bombarnac</u> et <u>Pilote de</u>
<u>Danube</u> [<u>The Danube Pilot</u>], by Jules Verne. Lausanne:
Editions Rencontre, pp. 7-15.
Discusses the creative process involved in Verne's
writing of these two novels.

E456 _____. "Préface." In <u>Clovis Dardentor</u> and <u>Frères Kip</u>
[<u>Kip Brothers</u>], by Jules Verne. Lausanne: Editions
Rencontre, pp. 7-13.
Shows that Verne draws on two areas in writing both
these novels -- biographies and reality.

E457 _____. "Préface." In <u>Naufragés du "Jonathan"</u> [<u>Survivors</u>
<u>of "The Jonathan"</u>], by Jules Verne. Lausanne: Editions
Rencontre, pp. 7-13.
Examines two aspects of this novel. The first concerns its authenticity, the work being posthumous. The
second treats the creative process of its composition.

E458 _____. "Préface." In <u>Sphinx des Glaces</u> et "Edgar Poe et
ses oeuvres." [<u>An Antarctic Mystery</u> and "Edgar Poe and
His Works"], by Jules Verne. Lausanne: Editions Rencontre, pp. 13-21.
Discusses Poe's influence on Verne.

E459 Michel. "La Peur à table. <u>Autour de la lune</u>." ["Fear at
the Table. <u>Around the Moon</u>"] <u>Montrueil</u>, February, p. 4.
In <u>Around the Moon</u> Verne offers the outrageously
impossible spectacle of a spaceship's porthole being
opened without consequences in order to throw out a
dead dog. Barbicane also got rid of some debris that
way. This is nonsense, but we should remember the
present-day concern with the escape of microbes from a
craft that has completed its space journey.

E460 Pascal, Edith. "Jules Verne n'a pas inventé les voyages
sous-marins." ["Jules Verne Did Not Invent Submarine
Voyages"] <u>Télé Magazine</u>, 21 March, pp. 38-40.
Underwater exploration would seem to have existed
before Christ. Medieval accounts tell of it in 325
B.C. and claim that Alexander remained submerged for
seven hours. In 1470 the Venetian Roberto Valturio wrote
almost perfect descriptions of modern submarines. There

is evidence of underwater craft or chambers in the six-
teenth century in Portugal and in the Ukraine. Records
seventeenth-century examples in England and the first
operational submarines during the American Revolution.
First submarines to take an active role in war were in
the American Civil War. Verne, rather than being a
visionary of genius, was simply a novelist who kept up
with science.

E461 Pia, Pascal. "Sur Un Poème érotique de Jules Verne." ["On
      an Erotic Poem of Jules Verne"] Magazine littéraire,
      No. 43 (August), p. 35.
         A poem entitled "Lamentations d'un poil de cul de
      femme" ["Lamentations of a Hair from a Woman's Arse"]
      is attributed to Verne. He is said to have written it
      when a youth.

E462 Raymond, F[rançois]. "L'Homme et l'horloge chez Jules
      Verne." ["Man and the Clock in Jules Verne"] BSJV, NS
      No. 16 (4th Trimester), pp. 169-175.
         Paper delivered before the General Assembly of the
      Jules Verne Society, February 7, 1970. Uses several
      methods to examine the man-time relationship in Verne's
      works. "Master Zacharius" well represents the usurpation
      by Verne's characters of God's functions in space and
      time. Titans may be merely marionettes. J. T. Maston
      in From Earth to the Moon is a good example. Marcel
      Moré thinks that clocks symbolized to Verne the unimagin-
      ative strictness of his father. A corollary of that
      deduction is that Verne, the writer, frees himself of an
      oppressive father by caricaturing him and creating his
      double in grotesque rivals, while surrounding him with
      young, joyful companions. See E511.

E463 Robert, Frédéric. "1875 voyage dans la lune avec Jacques
      Offenbach." ["Voyage to the Moon with Jacques Offenbach"]
      Journal musical français, April, pp. 31-33.
         Aurélien Scholl, the only journalist to rally to the
      new ideas of the post-Franco-German war era of the 1870s,
      also defended the pseudoscientific novels of Verne, which
      interested and informed the masses. The Voyages extra-
      ordinaires lent to theatrical adaptations. La Presse
      of October 29, 1875 announced that Verne was working on
      a new play for the Porte-Saint-Martin theatre: Captain
      Grant's Children. The great attraction would be a walrus
      hunt in the ice according to Biard's painting. Jacques
      Offenbach at the insistence of Scholl and of his creditors
      undertook the opera Voyage dans la lune, libretto by
      Leterier, Vanloo, and Mortier. He borrowed from Verne
      only the means of locomotion.

E464 Roy, Claude. "Hommage à Jules Verne." ["Homage to Jules Verne"] In Poésies. Paris: Gallimard.

In an homage to Jules Verne, the poet evokes names of characters and places in Verne's works as he pictures his memories having traveled twenty thousand leagues under the seas.

E465 Sainfeld, A. "Jules Verne et la publicité commerciale au début du siècle." ["Jules Verne and Commercial Publicity at the Turn of the Century"] BSJV, NS No. 13 (1st Trimester), pp. 96-97.

Paper delivered before the General Assembly of the Jules Verne Society, February 8, 1969. About 1900 Verne seems to have been a more or less willing victim of commercial advertising. In a little brochure extracted from the Mariani Albums, entitled Quelques Figures contemporaines [Some of Today's Figures], Verne, shown beneath the now classic picture of him by Nadar, seems to be extolling the virtues of Mariani wine. Mention of his works is incomplete and inaccurate.

E466 Santelli, Claude. "Préface." In "Hommage à Jules Verne à l'occasion du centenaire de "Vingt Mille Lieues sous les mers: 1870-1970. [Homage to Jules Verne For the Centenary of the Publication of "Twenty Thousand Leagues Under the Sea"], by Luce Courville and Françoise Decré. Nantes: Société des amis de la bibliothèque municipale de Nantes, p. 5.

Preface to the catalogue of the Exposition in Nantes, honoring the centenary of the publication of Verne's Twenty Thousand Leagues Under the Sea. Children love Verne because he builds personal and extravagant shelters. Often the shelter is a grotto. In this novel it is the submarine, Nautilus. Nemo is exiling himself from injustice. The prophecies of Verne show him to be a scientific genius. He is the greatest French writer of the fantastic tale. Twenty Thousand Leagues Under the Sea is the nineteenth-century Odyssey. See E430.

E467 Serres, Michel. "Oedipe-Messager." ["Oedipus-Messenger"] Critique, 26 (January) 3-24.

Verne's Michel Strogoff is studied as a recomposition of the Oedipus legend. Strogoff is Oedipus, but the concept here is circular so that Oedipus is Strogoff. The latter is the Oedipus of the complex rather than of the legend. Michel's voyage is first a family one: the words father, mother, brother, sister, daughter, and son recur constantly. Michel is in some respects the union of Oedipus and Cocles. The author refers the reader both to Georges Dumézil and Freud. Notes that Verne's novel achieves a religious tone.

E468 Taussat, R[obert]. "Le Malheureaux Destin du 'Great
Eastern.'" ["The Unfortunate Destiny of the 'Great
Eastern'"] BSJV, NS No. 15 (3rd Trimester), pp. 138-141.
Paper delivered before the General Assembly of the
Jules Verne Society, February 7, 1970. Recounts the
many misfortunes of the ship, Great Eastern, on which
Verne crossed the Atlantic. The vessel seemed jinxed
from the start. Its construction began May 1, 1855
when it was called the Leviathan. It was not built to
be a cable-layer despite performing that function. There
is a photo of the Great Eastern at the front of the issue.

E469 Taussat, Robert. "Mise au point (A Propos Du Sous-Marin
ivre de Rimbaud)." ["Focus. (Concerning Rimbaud's
Drunken Submarine)"] BSJV, NS No. 16 (4th Trimester),
p. 168.
Quotes letter from Jean-H. Guermonprez that shows
that the latter and J.-H. Bornecque worked unknown to
each other on Rimbaud's Bateau ivre and the Nautilus.
Hence there is no question of the originality of
Bornecque's work.

E470 _____. No title. BSJV, NS No. 13 (1st Trimester), p. 91.
Invites attention to Jean-H. Guermonprez's study,
the first exhaustive one of Verne, that appeared in the
Journal de Genève in 1951. It can no longer be found,
but is listed in the Laffont-Bompiani Dictionary. See
E441 for extract from the Journal de Genève.

E471 _____. "Qui servit de modèle au Capitaine Nemo?" ["Who
Served as the Model for Captain Nemo?"] BSJV, NS No. 14
(2nd Trimester), pp. 113-115.
Verne's Captain Nemo was based on a certain Colonel
Charras, mentioned by Verne in a letter to Hetzel.
Charras seems to have been unafraid to be counted among
the opposition to Napoleon III. See E432.

E472 _____. "Rêverie sur un vieil almanach." ["Revery on an
Old Almanack"] BSJV, NS No. 16 (4th Trimester), pp.
160-163.
A report on names found in Almanach du commerce de
Nantes et du département de la Loire-Inférieure, année
bissextile 1828. [Business Almanac of Nantes and the
Department of Loire-Inférieure, Leap Year 1828]. This
almanac, of course, can not include the name of Verne,
who was born in the year it was published, but a reading
of the names of important people in many walks of life
in Nantes or elsewhere recalls many of those found in
biographies of Verne and raises enigmatic questions
about some of them. Three pages of the almanac are
depicted on the last page of this issue.

E473 Terrasse, Pierre. "Jules Verne et les chemins de fer."
      ["Jules Verne and Railways"] <u>BSJV</u>, NS No. 14 (2nd Tri-
      mester), pp. 116-121.
           Paper delivered before the General Assembly of the
      Jules Verne Society, February 7, 1970. Verne was practi-
      cally born with the railroads, since the first line,
      Saint-Etienne to Andrézieux, was opened a year before
      his birth. Article treats the importance of trains in
      three Verne works: <u>Around the World in Eighty Days</u>, <u>The
      Will of an Eccentric</u>, and <u>Claudius Bombarnac</u>. <u>See</u> E650.

E474 Terrasse, P[ierre]. "Jules Verne et le cinéma." ["Jules
      Verne and the Cinema"] <u>BSJV</u>, NS No. 16 (4th Trimester),
      p. 178.
           An Italian film with Kirk Douglas, Virna Lisi, James
      Mason, and Alan Bates, based on <u>Lighthouse at the End
      of the World</u>, is to be produced in Spain. <u>See</u> E482. A
      <u>Michel Strogoff</u> has been produced by Eriprando Visconti
      in Italy and Bulgaria.

E475 Touttain, Pierre-André. "Lord Glenarvon et Alcide Jolivet."
      ["Lord Glenarvon and Alcide Jolivet"] <u>BSJV</u>, NS No. 13
      (1st Trimester), pp. 105-106.
           Alexandre Dumas may be the source of two names given
      by Verne to characters. Dumas has a Jolivet in his
      <u>Impressions de voyage en Suisse</u>, hence Verne's Jolivet
      in <u>Michel Strogoff</u>. One of Dumas's collaborators,
      Félicien Mallefille, put on a play in 1835 called
      <u>Glenarvon</u>. The Glenarvan of Verne's <u>Captain Grant's
      Children</u> is also a Scot.

E476 Van Herp, Jacques. "Le Mystère ne plane plus." ["The
      Mystery No Longer Soars"] <u>Désiré</u>, No. 26 (February),
      pp. 757-766.
           Verne's <u>Barsac Mission</u> was known to Georges Montignac
      before its publication. It is clear that the latter
      borrowed from it in writing <u>Le Mystère plane</u>. This
      answers any questions as to the composition of Verne's
      novel.

E477 Vierne, Simone. "Critiques et lecteurs de Jules Verne en
      France." ["Critics and Readers of Jules Verne in France"]
      <u>Studi francesi</u>, 14, No. 42 (September), 490-495.
           Far from being merely a writer of children's stories,
      Verne has had an impact on French literature in general.
      The technique of novel writing has been influenced by
      him. Also, he bequeathed a heritage of poetic dreams
      and myth.

E478 Vierne, S[imone]. "Mais où sont les lunes d'antan?" ["But
Where Are the Moons of Yesteryear?"] BSJV, NS No. 15
(3rd Trimester), pp. 142-151.
   The moon described by Verne in From the Earth to the
Moon and Around the Moon is neither the moon of the
scientists nor that of the cosmonauts. It is a mythical
and poetic moon. Quotes some of Verne's descriptions
of the moon.

E479 Vierne, Simone. "Les Refuges dans les romans de Jules
Verne." ["Refuges in Jules Verne's Novels"] Circe
(Cahier du Centre de Recherche sur l'imaginaire), No.
2, pp. 53-106.
   Examines various kinds of refuges in Verne, starting
from the premise that a novel of adventure is an escape
from some refuge or other, such as the home or parental
control. There are natural refuges, such as trees and
ones that are built by man, such as cities. Refuges
may be classified according to the degree of security
and happiness they afford. By their nature natural
refuges are in violent conflict, the constructed ones
in less violent opposition. The refuge conforms to the
initiatory aspect of Verne's novels. The image of the
refuge in these works is shown to raise at several levels
the question of Man's relationship to the world. Many
pictures from the novels accompany this study.

1971

E480 Anon. "Jules Verne à la télévision." ["Jules Verne on
Television"] BSJV, NS No. 17 (1st Trimester), p. 27.
   Critical of Byron Haskins's 1958 American film version
of From the Earth to the Moon, shown on French television
on March 7, 1971. Says the producers should have opted
for nineteenth-century scientific possibilities as Verne
saw them, or for contemporary accomplishments. The film
does neither.

E481 Anon. "Jules Verne au cinéma, à la radio et à la télévision."
["Jules Verne in the Cinema, on Radio, and on Television"]
BSJV, NS No. 19 (2nd Trimester), p. 76.
   J. A. Bardem, it was announced in July, will co-produce
with France a project of Edouardo Manzanos, Mysterious
Island, based on Verne's novel. The Hungarian member of
the Jules Verne Society, Zoltan Péter, is planning a TV
show for 1973 to celebrate the one hundredth anniversary
of the publication of Around the World in Eighty Days.

E482   Anon. "Jules Verne et le cinéma." ["Jules Verne and the
         Cinema"] BSJV, NS No. 20 (4th Trimester), p. 100.
              The film, Lighthouse at the End of the World (mentioned
         in E474), came out in November 1971. This Spanish film
         made by Kevin Billington and starring Kirk Douglas and
         Yul Brynner is a waste of Douglas's talents and one more
         film to add to those of recent years in which there is
         little relationship to the novel.

E483   Baudin, Henri. La Science Fiction. Paris: Bordas.
              A history and analysis of science fiction. Contains
         some referenes to Verne, who is recognized as an ancestor
         of science fiction, which is called an American genre.
         The term "anticipation" has been linked since Verne and
         Wells to the type of novel that led to science fiction.
         Verne's From the Earth to the Moon contains interesting
         calculations, but also lacks verisimilitude. Verne has
         suffered from the fact that the realization of an anti-
         cipation destroys the wondrous. Fortunately Verne pos-
         sessed other literary resources. The development of
         science requires a distinction between the fantasies of
         science fiction and those of the novels of anticipation
         that it has replaced. Verne's explanations are sometimes
         unscientific. Science fiction unites Verne's anticipa-
         tions with Wells's emphasis on the possible consequences
         of scientific development.

E484   Bottin, André. Jules Verne sa vie son oeuvre son temps
         (1828-1905). [Jules Verne -- His Life and Works and
         His Times (1828-1905)] Nice: Galerie des Ponchettes.
              Catalogue of the Jules Verne Exposition, held in
         Nice from June 8 to July 4, 1971, and organized by André
         Bottin. The catalogue lists books, autographs, drawings,
         and various documents and items on exhibit. In the pre-
         face Bottin calls Verne a great writer and genial vi-
         sionary and regrets that despite all Verne's readers,
         young and old, he is not understood by a vast majority.

E485   Chambers, Ross. L'Ange et l'automate. Variations sur le
         mythe de l'actrice de Nerval à Proust. [Angel and Auto-
         maton. Variations on the Myth of the Actress from Nerval
         to Proust] Paris: Lettres modernes, pp. 36-40.
              Verne's Castle of the Carpathians integrates two
         themes: Satanism and Science.

E486   Chesneaux, Jean. Une Lecture politique de Jules Verne.
         [A Political Reading of Jules Verne] Paris: Maspero.
              Shows that Verne's early works do not equate scienti-
         fic anticipations with sociopolitical ones, as will his
         later novels, in which his attitude toward science,

machines, and progress evolves toward pessimism.
Describes Verne's Fourierism and Saint-Simonianism,
while noting in Verne's novels such concepts as nationalism, revolution, libertarianism, racism, the good and
bad savage, utopianism, militarism, romanticism, and
deism or pantheism. Recognizes that the Voyages extraordinaires contain myths common to all eras, but stresses
nineteenth-century phenomena: sensitivity to popular
movements, the Saint-Simonian ideal of the domination of
Nature, praise of unsubmissiveness, faith in science,
and a keen feeling for the absurdity of many social
conventions. See D366, D389.

E487   Compère, Daniel. "A Propos de La Science fiction de Jean
       Gattegno." ["Concerning Science Fiction by Jean
       Gattegno"] BSJV, NS No. 20 (4th Trimester), pp. 84-86.
       Very unfavorable review of Gattegno's treatment of
       Verne in his book, La Science fiction. Aside from
       errors, even in the spelling of Verne's books and
       characters, and inaccuracies in statements about the
       texts, the review disagrees with the premise that Verne
       is a writer of science fiction.

E488   _____. "Conseil." BSJV, NS No. 19 (3rd Trimester), pp.
       67-68.
       Verne knew Jacques-François Conseil, who experimented
       with the submarine but could never get financial support.
       Verne may have wanted to console him by making him one
       of the main characters of Twenty Thousand Leagues Under
       the Sea. And, of course, Conseil may have given Verne
       some technical tips. The last page of the issue has a
       sketch of a Conseil craft.

E489   _____. "Explorateur de l'impossible: Jules Verne."
       ["Explorer of the Impossible: Jules Verne"] Picardie
       information, No. 2 (April), pp. 36-39.
       Purports to offer new details of the life of Verne
       in Amiens.

E490   _____. Jules Verne à Amiens. [Jules Verne at Amiens]
       Amiens: Musée de Berny.
       Catalogue for an Exposition held in Amiens and featur-
       ing the life of Verne in that city.

E491   _____. "Le Château des Carpathes de Jules Verne et E.T.A.
       Hoffman." ["The Castle of the Carpathians by Jules
       Verne and E.T.A. Hoffman"] Revue de la littérature
       comparée, 45 (No. 4), 594-600.
       Indicates that Jules Barbier's opera, The Tales of
       Hoffmann, gave Verne the idea of writing The Castle of
       the Carpathians, and shows his debt to E.T.A. Hoffmann's
       three stories that are also the source of the opera.

E492   Fichet, Jean. "Nemo. . .ou l'anti-Dakkar." ["Nemo. . .or
        the Anti-Dakkar"] BSJV, NS No. 19 (3rd Trimester), pp.
        62-66.
            It is difficult to reconcile the concept of Captain
        Nemo with that of a Hindu, Prince Dakkar. If as Dakkar
        Verne's hero can have the bodies of civilians thrown
        down a well, then as Nemo he can logically sink English
        ships to ensure there will be no survivors. The indif-
        ference to human life paradoxically gives Nemo an affin-
        ity to Hinduism. However, a host of Nemo's reactions
        are western -- for example, his democratic principles
        are incompatible with the caste system.

E493   Gaudin, E[dmond]. "Jules Verne et la philatélie." ["Jules
        Verne and Philately"] BSJV, NS No. 19 (3rd Trimester),
        pp. 69-73.
            American and Russian space flights have increased
        awareness of Verne's works. One expression of this has
        been in the issuing of special stamps honoring space
        flights, or Verne in particular. The following countries
        have such issues: Central African Republic, Gabon, Mali,
        Guinea, Bhutan, Hungary, Panama, Czechoslovakia, and
        Yemen. See E436.

E494   Helling, Cornélis. "Le Capitaine Nemo, ce grand inconnu!"
        ["Captain Nemo, That Great Unknown One"] BSJV, NS No.
        19 (3rd Trimester), pp. 59-61.
            Paper delivered before the General Assembly of the
        Jules Verne Society, February 6, 1971. Verne does not
        identify Captain Nemo in Twenty Thousand Leagues Under
        the Sea. However, in The Mysterious Island Nemo is
        identified as the Indian Prince Dakkar, the embodiment
        of Indian hatred for the English. However, several dates
        in the two works are irreconcilable, and in Twenty
        Thousand Leagues Under the Sea the English are portrayed
        in a favorable light. The crew of the Nautilus was
        probably multinational, not solely Indian. Very likely,
        Verne wanted to keep Nemo's nationality a mystery -- a
        Poe technique.

E495   _____. "Quelques Nouvelles Identifications dans l'oeuvre
        de Jules Verne." ["A Few New Identifications in Jules
        Verne's Works"] BSJV, NS No. 19 (3rd Trimester), pp.
        74-75.
            Finds an analogy between the commander of Verne's
        Abraham Lincoln and Admiral Farragut in command of the
        Tecumseh, both rather rash officers. Also points out in
        connection with the corvette Susquehanna in Around the
        Moon that there was actually an American frigate by
        that name.

E496 Hermans, Georges. "Bibliographie des romans lunaires de
Jules Verne." ["Bibliography of Jules Verne's Lunar
Novels"] BSJV, NS No. 17 (1st Trimester), pp. 23-26.
Gives publication dates of original editions of Verne's
first seven novels. Also provides some descriptive in-
formation on editions of Verne's works.

E497 Macherey, Pierre. Pour Une Théorie de la production littéraire. [For a Theory of Literary Production] Paris:
François Maspero.
Part three of Pierre Macherey's book on literary
theory concerns the works of Verne. Calls Verne's
essential theme the conquest of Nature by Industry, but
distinguishes between the ideological plan of a literary
work and real, individualized themes, which are symbolic
figures. Names voyages, scientific inventions, and
colonization as elements seen in time and space in
Verne's work that constitute the articulation of Nature
on Industry, and vice versa. Notes a special role
played by trains. An essential phenomenon of the
voyages is that anticipation is expressed as retrospec-
tion. The discussion of Verne closes naming Robinson
Crusoe as the thematic ancestor of Verne's island motif.

E498 Malestroit, Jean de. "Jules Verne parmi nous." ["Jules
Verne Among Us"] In Saint-Stanislas. Nantes: St.
Stanislas School, pp. 21-22.
Speaks of Verne's school days at the Saint Stanislas
School. Notes that Verne was not much of a student, and
yet his imagination was already active. One of his pals
once heard him describe a steam elephant bus, an outline
of which he then drew on the blackboard. Borrows from
Mme Allotte de la Fuÿe's biography for one or two details
of Verne's boyhood.

E499 Martin, Charles-Noël. Jules Verne, sa vie et son oeuvre.
[Jules Verne. His Life and Works] Lausanne: Editions
Rencontre.
Fourteen of the eighteen chapters of this book concern
the life and career of Verne. Two other chapters list
Verne's novels, stories, and other writings, and a third
discusses the debates that have surrounded Verne's treatment of science. References are made to contributions
of Michel Verne, Robida, and Wells to the work of Verne,
who is called a scientific writer rather than a precursor
of science fiction. The concluding chapter, a personal
reminiscence, appeared as an article in the Gazette des
hopitaux, February 28, 1971. Some of Verne's business
arrangements are revealed in appendices, and a few pages
are devoted to discounting the claim that Verne was a
Polish Jew.

E500 _____ . "Préface." In Bourse de voyage [Travel Bag] and
Chasse au météore [Chase of the Golden Meteor], by
Jules Verne. Lausanne: Editions Rencontre, pp. 7-15.
Discusses problems of chronology in these two works.
Verne looks at two old manuscripts toward the end of
his life.

E501 _____ . "Préface." In Chemin de France [Flight to France]
and Famille-sans-nom [Family Without a Name], by Jules
Verne. Lausanne: Editions Rencontre, pp. 7-13.
Discusses these works as patriotic novels and in terms
of their sources.

E502 _____ . "Préface." In Etonnante Aventure de la mission
Barsac [Barsac Mission] and "Comte de Chantelaine"
["Count of Chantelaine"], by Jules Verne. Lausanne:
Editions Rencontre, pp. 7-15.
Discusses Verne's participation in the editing of the
final novel published after his death.

E503 _____ . "Préface." In Face au drapeau [For the Flag] and
Superbe Orénoque [Superb Orenoco], by Jules Verne.
Lausanne: Editions Rencontre, pp. 7-13.
Treats these works thematically and discusses their
sources.

E504 _____ . "Préface." In Ile à l'hélice [Floating Island]
and Village aérien [Village in the Tree Tops], by Jules
Verne. Lausanne: Editions Rencontre, pp. 7-15.
Examines the two novels from several points of view.
The theme of isolation is important. The relationship
to Darwinism helps place these works in their century.
Also treated are the areas of music and language.

E505 _____ . "Préface." In Mirifiques Aventures de Maître
Antifer [Captain Antifer] and Phare du bout du monde
[Lighthouse at the End of the World], by Jules Verne.
Lausanne: Editions Rencontre, pp. 7-13.
The publication dates of these two novels do not in
themselves explain the creative process of their composi-
tion, for they were composed at essentially the same time.

E506 _____ . "Préface." In P'tit Bonhomme [Foundling Mick] and
Histoires de Jean-Marie Cabidoulin [Stories of Jean-Marie
Cabidoulin], Lausanne: Editions Rencontre, pp. 7-17.
Discusses the creative process of these two works and
shows the importance of tales of navigation.

E507 _____ . "Préface." In Seconde Patrie [Second Country] and
Drame en Livonie [Drama in Livonia], by Jules Verne.
Lausanne: Editions Rencontre, pp. 7-15.

These Verne works have affinities with the detective story. Discusses Verne's liking for that genre as well as his collaboration with his son, Michel.

E508 _____. "Préface." In Testament d'un excentrique [The Will of an Eccentric] and Drame au Méxique [Drama in Mexico], by Jules Verne. Lausanne: Editions Rencontre, pp. 7-13.
Discusses the background of Verne's Will of an Eccentric, and studies the genesis of its composition. Also treats Verne's collaboration with the Musée des familles.

E509 Olivier-Martin, Yves. "Jules Verne et sa postérité." ["Jules Verne and His Posterity"] BSJV, NS No. 18 (2nd Trimester), pp. 45-51.
More than eighty titles of novels of the scientific imagination inspired by Verne are classified according to theme, such as: the individual against society, the city (sometimes underground or in a ship), the balloon, the plane, vanished civilizations, the all-powerful will, human and animal mutations, etc. See E612, E630, E672.

E510 Pourvoyeur, R[obert]. "Verne et Offenbach." ["Verne and Offenbach"] BSJV, NS No. 20 (4th Trimester), pp. 87-99.
Verne influenced Offenbach; Offenbach influenced Verne; and there was a reciprocal influence. The first type is illustrated by Offenbach's operetta, The Trip to the Moon (1875); the second by Verne's novel, Castle of the Carpathians (1892); and the third by the "opéra-bouffe" Dr. Ox (1877). See E544.

E511 Raymond, François. "L'Homme et l'horloge chez Jules Verne." ["Man and the Clock in Jules Verne"] BSJV, NS No. 17 (1st Trimester), pp. 7-14.
Verne is ambivalent. The clock-man, Fogg, would seem to become humanized. Verne's love of trains seems to waver in the face of more fluid transport. His cities are destroyed or appear as caricatures and marvelous parodies. Verne is the master of time, his time being one of poetry. See E462.

E512 Simon, Christiane. "Mythes verniens: genèse et progrès." ["Vernian Myths: Genesis and Progress"] Cahiers du Cercle inter-facultaire de littérature de l'Université de Liège, No. 1, pp. 45-46.
Verne's The Mysterious Island is a symbolic work. Within it are described all the paths ever traversed by humanity.

E513 Taussat, Robert. "L'Epave du Cynthia." ["Salvage of the
      Cynthia"] BSJV, NS No. 17 (1st Trimester), pp. 15-22.
      This work would seem to be the only novel published
      by Verne with an official collaborator. It is not
      possible to tell how much and what was done by Verne or
      by André Laurie. However, a review of its themes
      certainly shows it to be a synthesis of the Voyages
      extraordinaires. Verne's role in writing the work must
      be considered essential.

E514 Terrasse, P[ierre]. "Le Centenaire de Vingt Mille Lieues
      sous les mers à l'Académie de Marine." ["Centenary of
      Twenty Thousand Leagues Under the Sea at the Naval
      Academy"] BSJV, NS No. 20 (4th Trimester), pp. 81-83.
      Dr. Dumas's speech at the French Naval Academy
      emphasizes Verne's love of the sea and the fact that
      French naval vessels have been christened the Nautilus
      and the Jules Verne.

1972

E515 Anon. "Congrès Jules Verne à Nantes." ["Jules Verne
      Congress in Nantes"] Nantes-Saint-Nazaire Réalité, No.
      43 (February-March), pp. 18-19.
      Mentions the revival of the Jules Verne Society. The
      writer has been prompted to recall the Nantais roots to
      be found in certain novels written by Verne.

E516 Anon. "Glanes et notules." ["Gleanings and Notes"] BSJV,
      NS No. 22 (2nd Trimester), p. 140.
      In the The Adventures of Captain Hatteras, Clawbunny
      compares the snow house that has been built in the novel
      to a house built of ice on the order of Empress Anne in
      1740. He quotes a book by an author named George Kraft.
      Thiéri Foulc has discovered, so reports François Raymond,
      that Kraft's book of thirty-two pages has been found,
      translated from the German by P. L. Leroy, and printed
      by the Academy of Sciences in St. Petersburg in 1741.

E517 Anon. "Jules Verne au cinéma et à la télévision." ["Jules
      Verne in Cinema and on Television"] BSJV, NS No. 22
      (2nd Trimester), p. 148.
      The Le Figaro August 1-2, 1972, announces that Jess
      Franco has begun in Portugal to make a film, Un Capitaine
      de quinze ans, after Verne.

E518 Bya, Joseph. "Parcours de Jules Verne." ["Running Through
      Jules Verne"] Manteia, 4 (January-June), 91-115.
      Discusses the abundance of enumerations and also of
      the use of synonyms in Verne's works.

E519 Caradec, François. <u>Vie de Raymond Roussel</u>. [<u>Life of</u>
<u>Raymond Roussel</u>] Paris: Jean-Jacques Pauvert.
　　Mentions Verne on six pages of this 380-page work
on Raymond Roussel. Recorded are Roussel's meeting in
1898 with Verne, whose works he had read and admired,
and some of whose writing technique he had adopted.
There is a quotation from Marcel Moré's <u>Jules Verne</u>.
Another quotation calls Roussel's <u>Impressions d'Afrique</u>
an amalgam in which d'Ennery and Verne might have collaborated with Shakespeare. Finally, Roussel's auto-
camper is seen as inspired by Verne's <u>Steam House</u>.

E520 Chapelot. Pierre and Jacques Sternberg. <u>Le Tour du monde</u>
<u>en 300 gravures</u>. [<u>Around the World in Three Hundred</u>
<u>Drawings</u>] Paris: Editions planète.
　　Collection of prints inspired by explorations of the
period 1837-1900 and appearing in the publication <u>Le</u>
<u>Tour du monde</u>, founded in 1860. Contains many prints
by the main illustrators of Verne's works.

E521 Chesneaux, Jean. "L'Invention linguistique chez Jules
Verne." ["Linguistic Invention in Jules Verne"]
<u>Langues et Techniques</u>. <u>Nature et Société</u>. Offprint.
Paris: Klincksieck, pp. 345-351.
　　Throughout his works Verne evinces a taste for verbal
invention, which allows him to emphasize the atmosphere
of fantasy. Sometimes there are hidden meanings in his
names. Verne has some characters speak a language in
which syllables are exchanged with a resulting confusion.
Article evokes the problems of an artificial language
and notes Verne's interest in Esperanto. Verne demonstrates an interest in anthropological implications of
the early uses of language during the transitional period
between monkey and man.

E522 Compère, Daniel. "Compléments à la filmographie." ["Complements to the Filmography"] <u>BSJV</u>, NS No. 21 (1st Trimester), p. 123.
　　Adds other film adaptations of Verne's works to
previous lists. <u>See</u> E372, E428.

E523 ____. <u>Hommages à Jules Verne</u>. [<u>In Homage to Jules Verne</u>]
Amiens: Centre de Documentation Jules Verne.
　　Catalogue of a Verne Exposition held in Amiens from
November 1972 to March 1973. Various expressions of
praise for the novelist from other novelists, poets,
travelers, artists, etc.

E524 _____. "Jules Verne et les bandes dessinées." ["Jules Verne and Comic Strips"] BSJV, NS No. 22 (2nd Trimester), pp. 137-139.
   The beginning of a bibliography of comic strips based on Verne.

E525 _____. "J. Verne, hors de la science-fiction." ["Jules Verne Outside Science Fiction"] Mal d'aurore, No. 7 (Summer), pp. 14-18.
   Science fiction has had many definitions, some of them conflicting. One must arrive at one definition if Verne is to be placed in the genre. Verne's scientific explanations are sometimes deemed inadequate by his readers.

E526 _____. "La Dé-production littéraire ou: Le Cas Jules Verne." ["Literary Deproduction or the Jules Verne Case"] Europe, 50, No. 523-524 (November-December), 252-258.
   Shows parallels between father-son relationships in Verne's Drama in Livonia and those of Gaston Verne with his father and his uncle Jules, on whose life he made an attempt. Refutes Marcel Moré's suggestions of a homosexual relationship between Gaston and his uncle. Another novel, The Castle of the Carpathians, may unravel the mystery of Verne's love life. The name, Maria Koltz, corresponds with Castle Koltz in Romania. The novel's schoolmaster, Homorod, recalls the village by the same name. The real schoolmaster's daughter married a Frenchman and went to France where she had an affair with Verne (1882-1885) and died, quite possibly explaining why Verne's demonstrated interest in Central Europe began at that time. They may have had a son. There are parallel events in the novel. Verne possibly had another affair as early as 1874 with an actress.

E527 _____. "La Quinzaine Jules Verne d'Amiens" ["Two Jules Verne Weeks at Amiens"] BSJV, NS No. 21 (1st Trimester), pp. 106-107.
   Report on Verne festivities at Amiens in January 1972 includes mention of Karel Zeman's film Aventures fantastiques based on Verne's For the Flag. The Bazilier company put on a show, Pierre Gamarra's adaptation of Twenty Thousand Leagues Under the Sea.

E528 _____. "Lecteurs de Jules Verne." ["Readers of Jules Verne"] Supplement to Mobile, No. 9 (December), pp. 31-33.
   Verne's readership was not a fixed, unchanging one. One can study this phenomenon best by considering it in connection with the history of the publication of his works.

E529 Courville, Luce. <u>Jules Verne de Nantes</u>. [<u>Jules Verne of</u>
<u>Nantes</u>] Nantes: Centre d'Etudes Verniennes.
Catalogue of the Exposition held in Nantes in February
commemorating the role played by Nantes as the inspiration
of some of Verne's novels.

E530 Dumas, Dr. Olivier. "Jules Verne et la mer." ["Jules
Verne and the Sea"] <u>Cols bleus</u>, No. 1255 (18 November),
pp. 6-12.
Extracts of a lecture given by Dr. Dumas, President
of the Jules Verne Society, to the French Naval Academy.
Verne's love of the sea was a heritage from his mother's
side of the family. His yacht <u>Saint-Michel III</u> had a
captain and a crew of nine. It is fitting that the
Naval Academy should choose the centenary of <u>Twenty</u>
<u>Thousand Leagues Under the Sea</u> to honor its author,
since the sea is the main character of this novel.
Describes technical details of Verne's <u>Nautilus</u> and
shows its relationship to the history of real submarines.

E531 Escaich, René. "Il y a cent ans: <u>Le Tour du monde en 80</u>
<u>jours</u>." ["A Hundred Years Ago: <u>Around the World in 80</u>
<u>Days</u>"] <u>Histoire pour tous</u>, No. 150 (October), pp. 82-85.
Discusses sources of the novel, <u>Magasin pittoresque</u>,
and Edgar Allan Poe.

E532 Gaudin, Edmond. "Les <u>Voyages extraordinaires</u> en disques."
["<u>The Extraordinary Voyages</u> on Records"] <u>BSJV</u>, NS No.
22 (2nd Trimester), pp. 131-136.
Thinks that Verne with Molière may be the most often
recorded French author. Long list of recordings.

E533 Gondolo della Riva, Piero. "La Pensée politique et l'utopie
chez Jules Verne." ["Political Thought and Utopia in
Jules Verne"] Thesis, University of Torino.
This thesis on Verne's political thinking was defended
before the Law Faculty of the University of Torino June
6, 1972.

E534 Helling, Cornélis. "Jules Verne et Napoleon." ["Jules
Verne and Napoleon"] <u>BSJV</u>, NS No. 22 (2nd Trimester),
pp. 141-142.
Verne was highly critical of Napoleon's "detestable
passion" for war in <u>Exploration of the World</u>. Two quotations from his fiction present a more sympathetic reaction
to the Emperor (in <u>Clipper of the Clouds</u> and <u>César</u>
<u>Cascabel</u>).

E535 Jarry, Alfred. Gestes et opinions du docteur Faustroll
      pataphysicien. [Gestures and Opinions of Dr. Faustroll,
      Pataphysician] In Oeuvres complètes. Vol. 6. Paris:
      Gallimard.
          This work, described on the title page as a neo-
      scientific novel, first published in its entirety in
      1911, is an example of symbolic sign structuration
      containing a number of disparate elements. One of these,
      a garnishment on property for default of payment, in-
      cludes in the seized property a volume of Verne's
      Journey to the Center of the Earth. Book III, entitled
      "From Paris to Paris by Sea or the Belgian Robinson,"
      is suggestive of Verne and the latter's island motif.

E536 Lebois, André. "Poétique secrète de Jules Verne." ["Secret
      Poetics of Jules Verne"] Annales de l'Université de
      Toulouse, 8 (No. 2), 131-151.
          Calls Verne an analytical genius, but also a poetic
      philosopher. A study of some of the works may suggest
      incorrectly Verne's denial of freedom, but not if one
      accepts the idea that an individual's freedom ends where
      another's (in this case God's) begins. Though Verne
      announced the infinite potentials of science, he warned
      of the terrible consequences, and yet he should not be
      considered a pessimist. He managed to make the unreal
      plausible and to create scientifically the wondrous.

E537 Malherbe, Gaston. "Dossier-Magazine" sur Cinq Semaines en
      ballon. ["Magazine File" on Five Weeks in a Balloon]
      Lausanne: Eiselé.
          The text of Verne's Five Weeks in a Balloon with a
      number of illustrations. Also some texts on Africa and
      on Verne.

E538 _____. "Dossier-Magazine" sur Tour du monde en 80 jours.
      ["Magazine File" on Around the World in Eighty Days]
      Lausanne: Eiselé.
          The text of Verne's Around the World in Eighty Days.
      There are a number of illustrations and also texts on
      nineteenth-century voyages and on Verne.

E539 Pavlovic, Mihailo. "Jules Verne et les Yougoslaves."
      ["Jules Verne and the Yugoslavs"] Revue des sciences
      humaines, No. 147 (July-September), pp. 407-413.
          Discusses sources of some scenes in Verne's Mathias
      Sandorf. Refers to Charles Yriarte's Bords de l'Adri-
      atique et le Monténégro.

E540 Pividal, Rafaël. Le Capitaine Nemo et la science. [Captain
      Nemo and Science] Paris: Grasset.

Describes the present era as mutilated, castrated, and unsexed by the cult of rigor and the superstition of technology. A scientist's life is boring, predictable, and uneventful. Without great ideas scientific rigor is merely another prejudice. Scientific writing is a sacred language whose symbolic cipher tries to preserve the mystery of discovery. Technology would suppress every obstacle to the satisfaction of desire. The constant satisfaction of desires in Verne's The Mysterious Island accounts for the pleasure in its reading. The Nautilus gives uninterrupted pleasure. The submarine reconciles body and mind. A host of Verne machines cater to our need for satisfaction. Space in Verne enables one to replace psychology with a topology. Traveling material- izes science, brings knowledge to fruition, and concret- izes dreams. Today science and technology have been de-eroticized and unsexed. Verne gives an example of eroticized technology in that the Nautilus is a desirable object. Contemporary science and technology are not really useful, addressing themselves to Man, mutilated and bereft of appetites.

E541   Poncey, Jean-Pierre. "Jules Verne, autopsie d'un échec."
       ["Jules Verne, Autopsy of a Failure"] Horizons du
       fantastique, No. 21 (30 September), pp. 25-29.
          Verne's works have been said to symbolize middle-class
       progress. Actually, they portray a middle class that is
       ill and in its dotage.

E542   Pons, Dr. Henri. "Jules Verne, la médecine et les médecins."
       ["Jules Verne, Medicine and Doctors"] BSJV, NS No. 23
       (3rd Trimester), pp. 157-175.
          Lists thirty-one doctors in Verne's works. Distin-
       guishes among them to indicate their relative importance.
       Their patients exhibit exotic diseases such as scorbut
       and tropical fevers. Only five medicines are mentioned
       by Verne, who evinces a skepticism regarding all other
       therapeutics. A "Post-Scriptum" adds the name of Dr.
       Trifulgas, brought to Pons's attention by Terrasse and
       Saltet. The notation adds to Verne's credit a very
       modern medical concept. See E564.

E543   Pourvoyeur, R[obert]. "L'Influence de Jules Verne sur la
       zarzuela." ["Jules Verne's Influence on the Zarzuela"]
       BSJV, NS No. 24 (4th Trimester), 188-193.
          Paper delivered before the General Assembly of the
       Jules Verne Society, February 5, 1972. Gives brief
       history of the zarzuela genre. beginning with El Golfo
       de la sirenas (1657) by Calderon, and its nineteenth-
       century role in opposition to the Italian influence in
       music. Discusses several Verne works that were the

source for zarzuelas in Spain, e.g. Around the World in Eighty Days (an example of the "travel zarzuela") and Captain Grant's Children. See E709.

E544 _____. "Verne et Offenbach." ["Verne and Offenbach"] BSJV, NS No. 21 (1st Trimester), pp. 112-122.
Further discussion of Dr. Ox. It was not a success. Another musical adaptation of Dr. Ox was mounted by Annibale Bizzelli at the Teatro reale dell'Opera in Rome in 1935-36 under the direction of Tullio Serafin. The score was published in 1936 by Ricordi. A conjecture suggests that Verne may have been influenced by the Tales of Hoffmann when he wrote The Castle of the Carpathians (1892). This is not to deny the possible influence of Villiers de L'Isle Adam's L'Eve future (1886). See E510.

E545 Raymond, François. "Trois Réincarnations de Jules Verne." ["Three Reincarnations of Jules Verne"] BSJV, NS No. 21 (1st Trimester), pp. 108-111.
Three evocations of Verne: (1) a painting by Paul Delvaux of Verne's hero, Otto Lidenbrock, shown at the Grand Palais; (2) Boulgakov's satirical play L'Ile pourpre drawn from Verne; (3) Verne himself figures in at least one of many comic strips inspired by the Voyages extraordinaires.

E546 Santraud, J. M. "Dans Le Sillage de la baleinière d'Arthur Gordon Pym: Le Sphynx des glaces, Dan Yack." ["In the Wake of Arthur Gordon Pym's Whaler: Antarctic Mystery, Dan Yack"] Etudes anglaises, 25 (July-September), 353-366.
Studies the analogies among Poe's Narrative of Arthur Gordon Pym, Verne's Antarctic Mystery and Blaise Cendrars' Dan Yack. Poe, Verne, and Cendrars all felt the need to break monotony and normal rules. All three in an unusual, extraordinary, and possible universe met the Sphinx. But Verne brought the enigma back to an intel-ligible proposition. On the contrary, Poe and Cendrars dared the cataclysm that denounces the wide open door of Knowledge, the gigantic symbol of Reality behind Appearance.

E547 Sternberg, J[acques] and P[ierre] Chapelot. "Le Tour du monde en trois cents gravures." ["Around the World in 300 Prints"] Paris: Planète.
The best illustrations in Verne's Around the World in Eighty Days from 1860 to 1890. Illustrators include E. Bayard, A. de Neuville, and Riou.

E548 Taussat, Robert. "Anarchisme divin: de l'Ile Lincoln à
l'Ile Hoste." ["Divine Anarchism: From Lincoln Island
to Hoste Island"] Annales de l'Université de Toulouse,
8 (No. 2), 111-129.
Verne's heroes seem to find a place beyond society.
Their anarchist outlooks give them a divine air.

E549 ____. "J. Verne, ingénieur ou Poète." ["J. Verne,
Engineer or Poet?"] Mal d'aurore, No. 7 (June), pp.
3-6.
The technical vocabulary of Verne is huge. Its
confines are not always wholly realistic, as the writer
allows his romantic flair full rein.

E550 ____. "Machines magiques." ["Magic Machines"] BSJV, NS
No. 24 (4th Trimester), pp. 194-198.
Paper delivered before the General Assembly of the
Jules Verne Society, February 5, 1972. Verne's machines
really don't have in themselves an invincible strength.
One may remember the Nautilus breaking its projecting
prong on a small steamer. There is something cumbersome
and impractical about the Albatross or the Steel Giant.
However, we are dealing with a world of poetry. These
machines succeed as long as men remain convinced of their
magic powers.

E551 Terrasse, Pierre. "George Sand et Vingt Mille Lieues sous
les mers." ["George Sand and Twenty Thousand Leagues
Under the Sea"] BSJV, NS No. 22 (2nd Trimester), pp.
143-147.
Paper delivered before the General Assembly of the
Jules Verne Society, February 5, 1972. Through dates
of letters written by George Sand, it is proven that
Charles Lemire was probably wrong in suggesting that Sand
gave Verne the idea for Twenty Thousand Leagues Under the
Sea. However, there is little doubt that Sand did have
an influence on this novel. See E555, E627.

E552 Van Herp, Jacques. "Survie des héroes de J. Verne."
["Survival of J. Verne's Heroes"] Mal d'aurore, No. 7
(June), pp. 12-13.
Verne has lived on through other authors. The latter
have borrowed both his characters and his scripts.

E553 Versins, Pierre. Encyclopédie de l'Utopie, des voyages
extraordinaires et de la science fiction. [Encyclopedia
of Utopia, Extraordinary Voyages, and Science Fiction]
Lausanne: Editions l'Age d'Homme, pp. 929-932.
This illustrated encyclopedia of about 1000 pages on
conjectural literature includes an article on Verne.
Verne's works are listed, and the point is made that

Verne's readership blossomed when he began to be appreciated by the crypto-Marxist-Leninist generation.
He is credited with putting the second literary artificial satellite into space, after the Swiss, Toepffer,
but before the American, Edward E. Hale (both of whom
may be looked up in this Encyclopedia). Verne's value
is seen less in originality than in descriptive powers.
A schema accompanying the article on H. G. Wells lists
the works and dates of "The Four Great": Verne, Robida,
J.-H. Rosny, Sr. and Wells.

E554   Vierne, S[imone]. "A Propos d'Aberfoyle." ["Concerning
       Aberfoyle"] BSJV, NS No. 23 (3rd Trimester), pp. 154-156.
          One should be prudent about assuming that Aberfoyle
       is a name resulting from a sort of game played by Verne.
       An Aberfoyle exists in Scotland and figures in the works
       of Walter Scott and Charles Nodier. Probably literary
       memories and Verne's trip to Scotland explain his choice
       of name.

E555   _____. "George Sand, Jules Verne et le Nautilus." ["George
       Sand, Jules Verne and the Nautilus"] BSJV, NS No. 24
       (4th Trimester), pp. 184-185.
          The idea that Verne was given the concept for his
       Twenty Thousand Leagues Under the Sea by George Sand
       should be abandoned. Letters written in 1865 by Verne
       do not allow for the thesis that Sand was Verne's source.
       See E551, E627.

1973

E556   Anon. "Actualités de Jules Verne." ["News of Jules Verne"]
       BSJV, NS No. 28 (4th Trimester), p. 74.
          Mame published in December Verne's The Mysterious
       Island as a comic strip (a bound album, ninety-two colored
       pictures).

E557   Anon. "Jules Verne à la télévision." ["Jules Verne on
       Television"] BSJV, NS No. 28 (4th Trimester), pp. 95-96.
          French television showed six episodes from The Myster-
       ious Island from December 17 to December 22. This was
       derived from the film of J. A. Bardem and H. Colpi. On
       the whole poor, not to be compared to Santelli's.

E558   Anon. "Jules Verne au cinéma et à la télévision." ["Jules
       Verne in the Cinema and on Television"] BSJV, NS No.
       26-27 (2nd & 3rd Trimesters), pp. 71-72.
          The film, Marcel Brian's Maître Zaccharius, produced
       by Pierre Bureau, shown on French television on September
       11, was interesting, but fell short of Verne's "Master

Zacharius." Mysterious Island, a Franco-Italian-Spanish
film came out September 26. Strays rather far from
Verne's novel partly to accommodate the presence of Omar
Sharif in the cast.

E559 Anon. "Livres de Jules Verne, l'évolution de l'édition. . .
et celle des lecteurs." ["Jules Verne's Books, the
Evolution of Publication and of the Readers"] Courrier
picard, No. 9081 (12 December), n.p.
      An exposition on Jules Verne's books was held in Amiens
by the Jules Verne Documentation Center in November and
December. Emphasized the change in Verne's readership.

E560 Caillois, Roger. La Pieuvre essai sur la logique et
l'imaginaire. [The Octopus Essay on Logic and the
Imaginary] Paris: La table ronde.
      In this history of the octopus in literature, chapter
4 considers it "according to the Romantic Bible" and
discusses reactions to the octopus by Michelet, Hugo,
and Lautréamont before Verne's. De Neuville's illustrations in the Hetzel edition of Twenty Thousand Leagues
Under the Sea always show the octopus in the same place,
the lower right hand corner of the drawing. Verne
doesn't use the word pieuvre just employed by Hugo, but
prefers the traditional term poulpe. Verne confuses
poulpe with calmar (squid) as he makes his creature the
larger species, whereas it is the smaller.

E561 Compère, Cécile. "Maroussia, soeur de Michel Strogoff?"
["Maroussia, Sister of Michel Strogoff?"] BSJV, NS No.
26-27 (2nd & 3rd Trimesters), pp. 52-61.
      Paper delivered before the General Assembly of the
Jules Verne Society, February 3, 1973. Lists several
resemblances between the novel, Maroussia (1883), by
Stahl (i.e. Hetzel, Verne's publisher) and Verne's
Michel Strogoff (1886) -- similarities of plot, moral
outlook, physical appearance, and technical details.
Evidence does not permit one to assume that Verne
borrowed from Hetzel, but that the latter was influenced
by reading Verne's manuscript is likely.

E562 _____. "Toponymie Vernienne." ["Vernian Toponomy"] BSJV,
NS No. 26-27 (2nd & 3rd Trimesters), pp. 34-35.
      A list of localities particularly in Northern France,
but also in the Netherlands, England, and the United
States (a New York restaurant) that have honored Verne
by naming streets, etc., for him. See E598, E661.

E563 Compère, Danile. "Portugais et Brésiliens dans l'oeuvre de
Jules Verne." ["Portuguese and Brazilians in the Works
of Jules Verne"] In La Bretagne, Le Portugal, Le Brésil.
Echanges et rapports. Rennes: Université de Haute
Bretagne, pp. 395-415.

Some of Verne's characters are Portuguese or Brazilians. These include travelers, adventurers, and liberators.

E564 Compère, Daniel and Cornélis Helling. "Jules Verne, la médécine et les médecins." ["Jules Verne, Medicine and Doctors"] BSJV, NS No. 25 (1st Semester), pp. 8-9.
Compère would add to Dr. Pons's list of doctors in Verne's works (see E542) one in a humorous story, "An Ideal City." That doctor suggests a kind of social security in which patients pay the doctor only when they are well. Verne himself had unsatisfactory experiences with doctors. Helling writes that Clipper of the Clouds should have been included by Dr. Pons in his list of novels that have madmen.

E565 Cortazar, Julio. "Préface." In Histoires extraordinaires [Extraordinary Stories], by Edgar Poe. Paris: Gallimard.
In the preface to Poe's Extraordinary Stories, the Baudelaire translation, it is stated that Poe is the source of Verne and of a goodly portion of H. G. Wells. The preface is translated from Spanish by Laure Guille-Bataillon.

E566 Dulmet, Florica. "Voici cent ans: Le Tour du monde en 80 jours." ["A Hundred Years Ago: Around the World in Eighty Days"] Ecrits de Paris, No. 325 (May), pp. 97-104.
On the hundredth anniversary of Verne's Around the World in Eighty Days, the novel is discussed with respect to theme as well as its antecedents and sources. It is placed in the literary current.

E567 Escaich, René. "A Propos des Aventures du Capitaine Hatteras." ["Concerning The Adventures of Captain Hatteras"] BSJV, NS No. 28 (4th Trimester), pp. 87-89.
Emile de Bray, who had served on one of the ships searching for the lost explorer, Franklin, wrote on his return to France a journal giving an account of the Antarctic. He knew Verne, who, according to Admiral Cornuault, borrowed extensively from the journal in the writing of Adventures of Captain Hatteras. Verne seems not to have asked himself the real reasons for the catastrophe that befell Franklin's expedition.

E568 Ezine, Jean-Louis. "Jules Verne, ou le sens de la perpendiculaire -- entretien avec Jean Jules-Verne." ["Jules Verne, or the Sense of the Perpendicular: Conversation with Jean Jules-Verne."] Nouvelles littéraires, 51 (1-6 May), 9.
In a way, Verne's works comprise a multi-stylistic effort. The universally recognized roles of fantasy

and imagination are accompanied by strong strains of realism. These are often manifested in a satirical vein. These variations are discussed in an interview with Verne's grandson, Jean Jules-Verne.

E569 Gondolo della Riva, Piero. "Jules Verne à Malte." ["Jules Verne in Malta"] BSJV, NS No. 25 (1st Trimester), pp. 5-7.

Finds an analogy between the ship Ferrato in Mathias Sandorf and Verne's Saint-Michel. Both vessels put in for repairs at Samuel Grech and Co. at Valetta in Malta. The company still exists and has a copy of a letter of gratitude written by Verne. His writings are very popular in Malta.

E570 Hamon, Philippe. "Discours contraint." ["Constrained Language"] Poétique, No. 16 (October-December), pp. 411-445.

A stylistic examination of Verne shows that the language of realism follows particular patterns. In Verne it is important to consider his vocabulary.

E571 Helling, Cornélis. "Une Autre Origine du 'Nautilus'?" ["Another Source for the 'Nautilus'?"] BSJV, NS No. 26-27 (2nd & 3rd Trimesters), pp. 46-47.

Evidence suggesting that a kind of submarine, called the Nautilus, built by an American, Hallet, and recently (reference made in 1854) tested in the Seine, may be the source of Verne's famous submarine.

E572 _____. "Une Singulière Erreur dans Le Pilote du Danube." ["Odd Mistake in Danube Pilot"] BSJV, NS No. 26-27 (2nd & 3rd Trimesters), p. 51.

Explains why the investigating magistrate in Danube Pilot is called Izar Rona in chapter 13, but Franz Richter on p. 176 of the original Hetzel edition. The novel is a posthumous work. It is likely that Verne called the judge Richter. His son, going over the manuscript, realized the Hungarian had been given a German name and changed it. The change was overlooked by Michel Verne and the proofreaders on p. 176.

E573 Huet, Marie-Hélène. L'Histoire des Voyages extraordinaires. [History of The Extraordinary Voyages] Paris: Minard.

Jules Verne is read not because his inventions are still timely, but because they are out of date. His work addresses adults as well as children, and he links history to scientific inventions. The inventions, far from serving history, rewrite it. Emphasizes the concept of nationality and the phenomenon of insurrection.

Verne's earlier heroes are not so much individuals as types who travel on behalf of nations, which become the primary heroes. Distance made it easier for Verne to create the English or American type than the French type. The Voyages extraordinaires is not a purely political work, but Verne's landscapes and inventions change as his political conscience is modified. Verne's originality lies not in his having imagined the twentieth century, but in his having depicted the nineteenth century's deeds and intentions, describing the accomplished triumphs and the realizable exploits.

E574 Jules-Verne, Jean. "En marge de la fantaisie et du fantastique." ["On the Edge of Fantasy and the Fantastic"] Nouvelles littéraires, 51 (1-6 May), 10-11.
  The creative process in the composition of Twenty Thousand Leagues Under the Sea. This is from Jules-Verne's Jules Verne (E575).

E575 ____. Jules Verne. Paris: Hachette.
  An intimate portrait based on family documents and correspondence. No solitary misanthrope could ever have written literature so full of the ideal of freedom and love of humanity. This biography, almost four hundred pages, discusses the life and works of Verne in detail, the latter being given ample individual treatment. See D417.

E576 Lucien. "Quelque Notes de lecture touchant Jules Verne." ["A Few Reading Notes Touching on Jules Verne"] BSJV, NS No. 26-27 (2nd & 3rd Trimesters), pp. 69-70.
  Departing from a moment in Verne's Green Ray when Aristobulus Ursiclos breaks off a piece of granite on the Isle of Iona, Lucien shows that there are no longer any happy islands of the Robinson Crusoe tradition. To support this contention he cites Golding's Lord of the Flies (1954), Marcel Tinel's Ile mélanésienne (1961), and Jean Reverzy's Le Passage (1954). As for Verne, his novels date 1874-1888, the beginning of the "Great Depression." Perhaps in spite of it Verne and his public were happy.

E577 Margot, Jean-Michel. "Verne et Agassiz." ["Verne and Agassiz"] BSJV, NS No. 26-27 (2nd & 3rd Trimesters), pp. 62-65.
  Sketches the career of Jean-Louis-Rodolphe Agassiz. Tells of his Brazilian expedition, lists four editions, including the three in French, of A Journey in Brazil by Agassiz and his wife (published Boston: Ticknor and Fields, 1868). Thinks Verne borrowed for his novel, The Giant Raft (1881), from the first French edition.

E578 Martin, Charles-Noel. "George Sand et el 'Nautilus.'"
["George Sand and the 'Nautilus'"] BSJV, NS No. 26-27
(2nd & 3rd Trimesters), pp. 36-45.
Through references to correspondence, a new chronology
is arrived at for Verne's first nine novels and his
Geography of France. The point of departure is a letter
written by G. Sand and mentioned in Charles Lemire's
book, Jules Verne, 1828-1905. Corrects an impression
that Adolphe Brisson visited Verne in 1898; the visit
was in 1897. Discussion bears on whether Sand had any
part in inspiring Twenty Thousand Leagues Under the Sea.

E579 _____. "Les Amours de jeunesse de Jules Verne." ["Loves
of Jules Verne's Youth"] BSJV, NS No. 28 (4th Trimester),
pp. 79-86.
By dating certain events with the help of correspondence, one arrives at a rejection of the story, first
told by Marguerite Allotte de la Fuÿe and copied by
succeeding biographers, that years after being jilted
by Caroline Tronson, Verne was still deeply saddened.
Part of the cause of mistakes regarding this part of
Verne's life is in garbled versions of his correspondence
in which portions of different letters are made to seem
to fit together. Also, Mme Allotte de la Fuÿe is charged
with inaccuracies. Verne was more saddened at the time
of Caroline's marriage by her husband's being nineteen
years older than she than by being jilted. See E628.

E580 Montaland, Gilles. "De peur d'être ridicule." ["For Fear
of Being Ridiculous"] Flash, No. 13, p. 17.
Much has been written about Verne's readership. Seen
by some as the writer of children's stories, Verne has
also been recognized as an author of books for grownups.
Today's young people would comprise a very reasonable
readership.

E581 Pons, Henri. "Jules Verne en Norvège." ["Jules Verne in
Norway"] BSJV, NS No. 28 (4th Trimester), pp. 75-78.
In Jules Leclerq's Voyage dans le Nord de l'Europe
there is mention of Verne's signature in a visitor's
book at Dal, in Norway, dated 1861. Verne would use
his notes and memories twenty-four years later in
Lottery Ticket, in which the action takes place in Dal.
Leclerq's itinerary was Verne's, because it was the only
possible one. The city of Rjukan has replaced Dal on
the map now. Verne's geography was precise. He did
allow himself the license of making the inn at Dal in
his novel much larger and better maintained than the
real one. See E734.

E582 Pourvoyeur, Robert. "A Propos de 'M. de Chimpanzé.'"
      ["About 'Mr. Chimpanzee'"] BSJV, NS No. 26-27 (2nd &
      3rd Trimesters), pp. 48-49.
      Refers to speculations of others about the date of
      Verne's M. de Chimpanzé, a comic opera. Agrees with
      Albert de Lasalle, who wrote in Histoire des Bouffes-
      Parisiens that the work was first played on February 17,
      1858. The choice of 1860 made by many seems wrong.

E583 _____. "De L'Invention des mots chez Jules Verne." ["About
      the Invention of Words in Jules Verne"] BSJV, NS No.
      25 (1st Trimester), pp. 19-24.
      Groups the new words used by Verne into three divisions
      to show (1) the cryptic writer; (2) the ragamuffin
      writer; and (3) the serious or scientific writer. Under
      number one are found fantastic names, some of them
      cryptic, and sounds that become important -- for instance,
      Verne is very partial to the "k" sound. Under number two
      one finds the punster, (e.g., T. Artelett or Ox and Ygène),
      and under number three one wonders about Verne's onomas-
      tics, seeing the English and German names he creates.

E584 Robida, Fred. "Jules Verne et Albert Robida." ["Jules
      Verne and Albert Robida"] Vieux Papier, 74 (January),
      27-29.
      Confirms observations of others to the effect that
      Robida would have been a very appropriate illustrator
      of Verne's works. The two men were similarly inspired
      and showed other similarities.

E585 Robin, Christian. "Livre et Musée." ["Books and Museum"]
      BSJV, NS No. 26-27 (2nd & 3rd Trimesters), p. 32.
      The editorial committee of BSJV sums up a paper given
      by Christian Robin at the 97th Congress of Learned
      Societies, held in March 1972. Verne's works in a way
      contain a whole museum inviting readers to read more in
      many fields.

E586 Sadoul, Jacques. Histoire de la science-fiction moderne.
      [History of Modern Science Fiction] Paris: Michel.
      Poe, Verne, and Wells are named as founders of science
      fiction. Also shown is the relationship of other writers
      of the genre to Verne, described as a nationalist of a
      sort and anti-Semitic. Wells and Rosny are differentiated
      from the author of the Voyages extraordinaires. Among
      Verne's contributions to science fiction are: the pos-
      sibility of life inside the Earth and under the sea,
      invisibility and television, and finally the cataclysmic
      destruction of our civilization. European science fiction
      was at its height between 1870 and 1930. Edgar Rice
      Burroughs's originality is in his having broken away from

Verne and Wells. An important date in the history of
science fiction was April 1926, when Hugo Gernsback
published the first issue of the magazine, Amazing Stories,
with the names of Wells, Verne, and Poe on the cover.
Among writers showing a Vernian confidence in the poten-
tials of science is Stanton A. Coblentz (The Making of
Misty Isle). Verne's optimism is distinguished from the
pessimism of Wells. With the launching of Sputnik in
1957, Verne's shadow recedes as science fiction becomes
a critique of the present rather than a prediction of
the future.

E587   Sainfeld, A. "Jules Verne et la Bourse." ["Jules Verne
       and the Stock Exchange"] BSJV, NS No. 25 (1st Trimester),
       pp. 10-18.
          Verne worked in the Stock Exchange for almost six
       years without developing any enthusiasm for it. The
       experience seems not to have influenced his writings,
       since only in the posthumous Chase of the Golden Meteor
       does the Exchange figure importantly. This novel may
       have been the product of the influence or even collabora-
       tion of Michel Verne. Points out that G. de Diesbach and
       Jean Chesneaux take opposing views in the question of
       Verne's attitude toward money.

E588   Soriano, Marc. "Verne (Jules) 1828-1905." Encyclopaedia
       universalis. Vol. 16. Paris: Encyclopaedia universalis,
       pp. 706-708.
          Under the entry for Verne in this encyclopedia, a
       sketch is given of the characteristic features of his
       writing.

E589   Taussat, R[obert]. "Sur Le Secret de Wilhelm Storitz."
       ["About The Secret of Wilhelm Storitz"] BSJV, NS No.
       26-27 (2nd & 3rd Trimesters), p. 50.
          Verne and Wells (The Invisible Man) are the only
       writers to have created a character able to make himself
       invisible using not magic, but physics and chemistry.
       However, neither writer seems to have realized that an
       invisible man would be blind for three verifiable
       reasons.

E590   Terrasse, Pierre. "Jules Verne et Séraphine de Victorien
       Sardou." ["Jules Verne and Victorien Sardou's Séraphine"]
       BSJV, NS No. 28 (4th Trimester), pp. 90-94.
          The history of Victorien Sardou's play, Séraphine,
       first called La Dévote, first played in 1868, is followed
       by the suggestion that Sardou may have been indebted for
       one small detail to Verne's Captain Grant's Children.
       There are a few lines on Verne's opinion of contemporary
       theatre in 1890, and the question is raised as to whether
       Sardou and Verne (with Charles Wallut) collaborated on
       Eleven Days' Siege.

E591 _____. "Les Variantes dans deux romans de Jules Verne."
["Variants in Two of Jules Verne's Novels"] BSJV, NS No.
26-27 (2nd & 3rd Trimesters), pp. 66-68.
Verne was something of a stickler about his style.
In César Cascabel, a comparison of variants shows Verne
substituting a romantic adventure for a more prosaic one,
and by so doing adding to verisimilitude. A comparison
of variants in Captain Antifer suggests that in the first
version Verne must have thought he risked giving away
too soon the key to the enigma, so he made two appropriate
changes.

E592 Van Herp, Jacques. Panorama de la science-fiction.
[Panorama of Science Fiction] Verviers: Gérard, pp.
290-291.
Takes up the debate as to whether Verne wrote science
fiction or merely children's stories. Verne all but made
French science fiction a literature for children.

E593 Vierne, Simone. Ile mystérieuse de Jules Verne. [Mysterious
Island of Jules Verne] Paris: Hachette.
Offers a broad discussion of Verne's novels followed
by a thematic and technical examination of The Mysterious
Island. Finally, discusses various readings of this
novel.

E594 _____. Jules Verne et le roman initiatique. [Jules Verne
and the Initiatory Novel] Paris: Sirac.
An exhaustive seven hundred and fifty-page study of
the novels of Verne, following the recognition in the
introduction of previous critics including Moré, Chesneaux,
Butor, Carrouges, Cellier, Corboz, Machery, Serres, and
Barthes. Calls initiatory myth the novels' common denom-
inator, whether the approach be thematic or structural.
Discusses the Quest in terms of preparation, the voyage
to the Beyond, and the new birth. The novels have a
spiritual and sacred meaning that broadens the realm of
the imaginary beyond scientific inventions. Classifies
the novels under three headings: the voyage of exploration, the fight against the monster, and the colonization
of the island. See E596.

E595 Vierne, S[imone]. "Le Réel et l'imaginaire dans les Indes-
noires de Jules Verne." ["The Real and the Imaginary in
Jules Verne's Child of the Cavern"] BSJV, NS No. 26-27
(2nd & 3rd Trimesters), pp. 31-32.
The editorial committee of BSJV sums up a paper given
by Simone Vierne at the 98th National Congress of Learned
Societies, held April 13-17, 1973. There is a Scottish
mine in this novel that owes as much to Verne's imagination as to his technical information.

271

E596 Vierne, Simone. <u>Rite, roman, initiation</u>. [Rite, Novel, Initiation] Grenoble: Presses Universitaires de Grenoble.

This work on initiatory literature notes the presence of the initiatory schema in Verne, where it is said to form invention and give it its meaning. A modern pessimism is seen leading Verne to doubt the ability of initiation to achieve a positive revelation of the contemporary context. The author refers the reader to her <u>Jules Verne et le roman initiatique</u> (E594).

1974

E597 Anon. "Jules Verne à la radio et à la télévision." [Jules Verne on Radio and Television"] <u>BSJV</u>, NS No. 31-32 (3rd & 4th Trimesters), pp. 189-190.

France-culture on July 1 broadcast <u>Pandemoium</u>, an opera of Georges Aphergis after Verne's <u>Castle of the Carpathians</u>. July 10 to 15 Channel 1 broadcast the six episodes of <u>Two Years' Vacation</u>, adaptation and dialogue by Claude Desailly, produced by Gilles Grangier. Has little to do with Verne's original. On July 22, Channel 2, on the program <u>Cabaret de l'histoire</u> of Guy Breton (Alexander Tarta, producer), presented Verne's song, "Notre Etoile." The Franco-Spanish film, <u>Un Capitaine de quinze ans</u>, directed by Jess Franco, appeared in March and was a disappointment.

E598 Anon. "Toponymie Vernienne." ["Vernian Toponomy"] <u>BSJV</u>, NS No. 29-30 (1st & 2nd Trimesters), pp. 133-134.

Adds other places in France where the name of Jules Verne has been honored by designating a street, etc. <u>See</u> E562, E661.

E599 Bastard, Georges. "Célébrité contemporaine: Jules Verne en 1883." ["Contemporary Celebrity: Jules Verne in 1883"] In <u>Jules Verne</u>, ed. P.-A. Touttain. Paris: Editions de L'Herne, pp. 88-92.

Starting with the purchase of a yacht by Verne, this article describes the vessel and its owner. Mentions Verne's inaccessibility whenever he was in Paris and his preference for Amiens. The article appeared in the <u>Gazette illustrée</u>, September 8, 1883.

E600 Baudou, Jacques. "Jules Verne et la cryptographie." ["Jules Verne and Cryptography"] In <u>Jules Verne</u>, ed. P.-A. Touttain. Paris: Editions de <u>L'Herne, pp</u>. 324-329.

Discusses the use of cryptograms by Poe and Verne, and describes the various types found in the latter's works.

E601   Borderie, Roger. "Une Leçon d'abîme." ["Lesson of the
        Abyss"] In Jules Verne, ed. P.-A. Touttain. Paris:
        Editions de L'Herne, pp. 172-179.
            Having been neglected so much by the critics, one
        may ask whether Verne may be read today for amusement.
        A positive reply is to be explained by Verne's use of
        the imagination, even in one of his poorer works,
        Survivors of the Chancellor, where death, horror, and
        despair abound. Verne's themes provide a catalyst for
        the totality of his literary production, e.g., the theme
        of the cave. Verne has created a myth for our time.

E602   Bradbury, Ray. "Que de merveilles et de miracles!
        Transmettez!" ["Marvels and Miracles! Pass It On!"]
        In Jules Verne, ed. P.-A. Touttain. Paris: Editions de
        L'Herne, pp. 93-98.
            Imaginary dialogue with Verne published in the New
        York Times Magazine, March 20, 1955, is translated by
        Jean Richer. Verne says that he never predicted the
        future, but did foresee some machines. Were he to
        rewrite his novels, they would not be fundamentally
        different, as his basic cause has always been humanity.
        Verne wrote novels in order to help man overcome chaos.
        Man's curiosity, his sense of beauty, and the marvelous
        can be transmitted from generation to generation. See
        D148.

E603   Buisine, Alain. "Cas limite de la description: l'énuméra-
        tion. L'exemple de Vingt Mille Lieues sous les mers."
        ["Borderline of Description: Enumeration. The Example
        of Twenty Thousand Leagues Under the Sea"] In La Descrip-
        tion. Lille: Université de Lille, pp. 81, 102.
            Description in Twenty Thousand Leagues Under the Sea
        is objective and didactic. It is a process of copying
        and transcribing. Nemo's library is an encyclopedic
        concentration of human knowledge, containing an accurate
        cataloguing of scientific facts. The method has stylistic
        consequences. Past tenses are novelistic; the present
        tense is scientifically objective. Nature, viewed through
        the porthole of the Nautilus, becomes a setting integrated
        with the interior of the submarine. Scientific names are
        hieroglyphs, and there is poetry in the names of plants
        and fish. Words are used simultaneously in two different
        descriptive codes, and scientific precision sometimes
        short-circuits metaphor. Verne's writing encloses,
        inventories, catalogues, and classifies the world in
        order better to submit it to appropriation.

E604 Chesneaux, Jean. "Jules Verne et le Québec libre." ["Verne and a Free Quebec"] In Jules Verne, ed. P.-A. Touttain. Paris: Editions de L'Herne, pp. 256-263.

Slightly reworked text of the author's preface to the 1970 Canadian edition of Jules Verne's Family Without a Name. The novel is more than a sample of Verne's Anglophobia, as it has been described by critics. It is about the militants in the anti-English national movement of 1837, but it thereby expresses Verne's sympathy with the rights of nationalities that were voiced in Europe's uprisings of 1848. In Verne's novel the leaders are peasants. Three points that reflect Verne's fundamental political views apparent in his other novels are: American democracy's prestige, the positive role of the Indians, and the relationship of the Canadians to the Celtic race. There are elements of romanticism in the manner of Hugo and Chateaubriand.

E605 Compère, Daniel. "La Part du réel dans L'Etoile du sud de Jules Verne." ["Share of the Real in Jules Verne's Vanished Diamond"] BSJV, NS No. 29-30. (1st & 2nd Trimesters), pp. 125-132.

A reworked version of a paper delivered before the General Assembly of the Jules Verne Society, February 3, 1973. Shows how Verne transformed whatever it was he got from André Laurie when he wrote this novel. Studies the factual aspects of the work: geographical, historic, the name of the diamond (an editorial note indicates there was a diamond called "Southern Star"), analogies to and parallels with real people, etc. Emphasizes Verne's procedure whereby the novel tells itself through an allegory. The novel is the central element in the guise of a diamond.

E606 Compère, D[aniel]. "L'Auberge du Tour du monde." ["The Inn of Around the World"] BSJV, NS No. 31-32 (3rd & 4th Trimesters), p. 153.

Contents of article that appeared in the Journal d'Amiens March 9-10, 1885, p. 2. Concerns second costume ball given by the Vernes March 8, 1885.

E607 Compère, Daniel. "M. Jules Verne conseiller municipal." ["Municipal Councilor Jules Verne"] In Jules Verne, ed. P.-A. Touttain. Paris: Editions de L'Herne, pp. 127-140.

An earlier version of this article was read by Daniel Compère to the General Assembly of the Société Jules Verne, February 6, 1971 in Paris. Compares political facts with political ideas in Verne's writings starting with 1888, the date of the first of Verne's four

consecutive elections to the Municipal Council of Amiens.
Verne's basic interest was not a political one, but
rather to serve his city as an administrator. He was
especially concerned with scholarships for the School
of Medicine and with urban problems. His political
concerns were oriented toward colonialism and a kind of
anarchism, which in his case might better be described
as nihilism. Verne's service as a member of the Council
finds some echo in his writings.

E608 Compère, D[aniel]. "Un Hivernage à Dunkerque." ["Winter
Stay in Dunkirk"] BSJV, NS No. 31-32 (3rd & 4th Trimesters), pp. 154-156.
Verne's short story, "A Winter Amid the Ice," is not
connected to a trip made to Dunkirk in 1851. A few months
before that trip he wrote in a letter of a plan to write
a work entitled Les Fiancés bretons. After his visit
to Dunkirk the projected betrothed Bretons became resi-
dents of that city. Why? More than any other French
port, this one opening on the North Sea looks toward the
Pole.

E609 Courville, Luce. "Le Mystérieux Passager de la cabine
numéro six." ["Mysterious Passenger of Cabin Number Six"]
In Jules Verne, ed. P.-A. Touttain. Paris: Editions de
L'Herne, pp. 109-111.
Imaginary situation in which the publisher Camille
Paganel and Jacques Paganel are being asked to identify
themselves. Jacques Paganel is the absent-minded geogra-
pher who boards the wrong ship in Verne's Captain Grant's
Children. The point is made that having been created by
Verne is a better assurance of immortality than having
published books.

E610 Coutrix [-Gouaux], Mireille. "Verne et Shakespeare."
["Verne and Shakespeare"] In Jules Verne, ed. P.-A.
Touttain. Paris: Editions de L'Herne, pp. 229-241.
Verne's trilogy, Captain Grant's Children, Twenty
Thousand Leagues Under the Sea, and The Mysterious Island
seem to go back to Greek mythology, but there is strong
evidence of affinities with Shakespeare's The Tempest.
In the works mentioned may be found the theme of Man's
struggles with Nature and psychological analogies among
the characters. This article concerns itself particularly
with the question of social and political organization and
with the problem of human personality. Verne's Nemo is
a descendant of Caliban, the anti-Prospero. Verne concludes that beyond individual revolt and the urge toward
power, the man in revolt, Nemo-Caliban, must return to
the context of Prospero in order to achieve a social and

collective solution as in a harbor. This harbor in
Verne is The Mysterious Island, a second step in the
Vernian reflection of The Tempest. The governing of
oneself becomes an important issue. Verne and Shakespeare
may be seen to doubt the reality of the world with its
hallucinatory character. The Mysterious Island echoes
The Tempest esthetically in affirming the truth of the
optical illusion.

E611   Delvaux, Paul. "Lettre." ["A Letter"] In Jules Verne, ed.
       P.-A. Touttain, Paris: Editions de L'Herne, p. 108.
           Paul Delvaux writes that he owes to the character,
       Professor Lidenbrock, the creation of a "Jules Verne
       climate" to be seen in a number of Delvaux's pictures.
       Neither date nor addressee are indicated.

E612   Editorial Committee. "Jules Verne et sa postérité."
       ["Jules Verne and His Posterity"] BSJV, NS No. 31-32
       (3rd & 4th Trimesters), pp. 178-179.
           Lists reactions to article by Yves Olivier-Martin
       (E509). The writers offer names of other works that
       would appear to have been written under Verne's influence.
       See also E630, E672.

E613   Faivre, Jean-Paul. "De Jules Verne en Arsène Lupin."
       ["Jules Verne to Arsene Lupin"] In Jules Verne, ed. P.-A.
       Touttain. Paris: Editions de L'Herne, pp. 317-323.
           Establishes a link between the beach of Etretat and
       Verne's Voyages extraordinaires, saying this lends to
       the surmise that Maurice Leblanc, creator of Arsène Lupin,
       read Verne. A second link is the "Needle," where Leblanc
       placed one of his heroes' hideout castles. Faivre is
       convinced that Leblanc's L'Aiguille creuse is Back-Cup,
       the hideout of Verne's adventurer, Count d'Artigas,
       alias Ker Karradje.

E614   _____. "Le Romancier des sept mers." ["Novelist of the
       Seven Seas"] In Jules Verne, ed. P.-A. Touttain. Paris:
       Editions de L'Herne, pp. 264-283.
           Discusses Verne's love of the sea and its appearance
       in his works as an ambivalent, living being: it liberates
       but imprisons; it destroys life, but also reconstitutes
       it. The sea sometimes leads to a port, but sometimes
       to shipwreck. The sea is often a grave and islands the
       site of happy sojourns. Verne embodies the bourgeoisie
       of Nantes and Bretagne, awakened and enriched by the
       sea. Verne has taught the French to integrate the sea
       with their dream-life and also to appreciate its reality.
       Accompanying the article is a table matching seas with
       Verne's novels.

E615 Fouchet, Max-Pol. "Mon Amérique." ["My America"] In
      <u>Jules Verne</u>, ed. P.-A. Touttain. Paris: Editions de
      L'Herne, pp. 99-103.
          Likens Verne to his distant relative, Chateaubriand,
      in their love of travel and imaginative interest in
      America. Lists American qualities, defects, and traits
      found in Verne's novels. America is called a Vernian
      country.

E616 Gautier, Théophile. "Les Voyages imaginaires de M. Jules
      Verne." ["Imaginary Voyages of Jules Verne"] In <u>Jules
      Verne</u>, ed. P.-A. Touttain. Paris: Editions de L'<u>Herne</u>,
      pp. 85-87.
          Appeared in the <u>Moniteur universel</u>, No. 197, Monday,
      July 16, 1866. Recommends especially for hot-weather
      reading Verne's <u>The English at the North Pole</u> and <u>Field
      of Ice</u>. Says that unlike the works of Lucian or Swift,
      those of Verne offer the strictest scientific possibil-
      ities.

E617 Gondolo della Riva, Piero. "A Propos d'Une Nouvelle."
      ["About a News Item"] In <u>Jules Verne</u>, ed. P.-A. Touttain.
      Paris: Editions de L'Herne, pp. 284-288.
          Concerns "In the Year 2889." Mentions other editions
      and discusses problems presented by variants, including
      changes in names of newspapers and characters in the
      story that appeared over the name of Jules Verne. Con-
      cludes that the story was written in English by Verne's
      son, Michel, with perhaps his father's help. Verne
      senior reworked it for French editions, and after his
      death his son further reworked the French edition.

E618 _____. "Jules Verne et l'Italie." ["Jules Verne and Italy"]
      In <u>Jules Verne</u>, ed. P.-A. Touttain. Paris: Editions de
      L'Herne, pp. 117-120.
          Verne, not translated in Italy until after 1870,
      suffered both because his Italian name, Giulio, led some
      to think he was Italian, and more seriously because a
      widely spread rumor held that "Jules Verne" was the
      pseudonym of a collective authorship. Poor translation
      did not prevent the popularity of Verne's works. Listed
      among Italian scholars to write on Verne are Italo Pizzi,
      Mario Turiello, Fernando Ricca, Edmondo Marcucci, and
      A. F. Pavolini.

E619 Guillon, Yves. "Jules Verne et sa famille." ["Jules Verne
      and His Family"] <u>Bulletin de la Société Archéologique</u>,
      78 (1974), 121-138.
          Uses unpublished documents to discuss some private
      aspects of Verne's biography. The grandmother of the
      article's author was Verne's niece and possessed archives
      with papers bearing on her uncle's family and on some
      personal events in his life.

E620 Helling, Cornélis. "Une Interview de Jules Verne."
["Interview with Jules Verne"] BSJV, NS No. 31-32 (3rd
& 4th Trimesters), pp. 151-152.
Translation of extract of an interview with Verne in
the Pittsburgh Gazette, Sunday, July 13, 1902. Verne
says the future of the novel is bleak. The true psychology of life will be expressed in shorter forms. Verne
has a limited pride in his writings involving modern
technology, since so much of what he presented as
reality had actually been half-discovered.

E621 _____. "Sur Quelques Invraisemblances dans L'Etonnante
Aventure de la mission Barsac." ["On a Few Improbabilities in The Barsac Mission"] BSJV, NS No. 31-32 (3rd
& 4th Trimesters), pp. 174-175.
Disagrees with René Escaich who in Voyage à travers
le monde Vernien (Brussels: La Boëtie, 1951) calls
Verne's Barsac Mission a perfect work. First of all,
it is posthumous and except for fifty pages was really
written by Verne's son, Michel. Furthermore, the novel
has lapses in verisimilitude that are rare in Verne.

E622 Herp, Jacques van. "Alexandre Dumas et Le Voyage au centre
de la terre." ["Alexandre Dumas and Journey to the
Center of the Earth"] In Jules Verne, ed. P.-A. Touttain.
Paris: Editions de L'Herne, pp. 222-224.
Lists a number of analogies between Alexandre Dumas'
Isaac Laquédem and Verne's Journey to the Center of the
Earth. This is not so much a question of the amount of
Dumas's influence on Verne. Verne may be said to repre-
sent two sides of the same talent. Whatever Dumas's
contribution to this work, it may be supposed that Verne
put some of his own research into his novel.

E623 _____. "Survie des héros de Jules Verne." ["Survival of
Jules Verne's Heroes"] In Jules Verne, ed. P.-A. Touttain.
Paris: Editions de L'Herne, pp. 305-307.
Verne reacted very moderately to Robida's rather
cavalier treatment of Verne's work in the Voyages très-
extraordinaires de Saturnin Farandoul, in which some
drawings picture Verne's virtuous heroes as indefatigable
woman-chasers. Far from being angry, Verne did some
borrowing of his own from Robida. Other adaptations of
Verne are listed and called pale copies of the original.

E624 Heuvelmans, Bernard. "Le Père contesté." ["The Disputed
Father"] In Jules Verne, ed. P.-A. Touttain. Paris:
Editions de L'Herne, pp. 121-124.
Heuvelmans thinks his changing criticism of Jules
Verne over the years has not been a sign of inconsistency,
but rather an indication of the different person he himself

has been at various times. When quite young he was put
off by Verne until his curiosity was thoroughly aroused
by Twenty Thousand Leagues Under the Sea. Rereading
this work in 1955, the writer was shocked by the gap he
felt existed between the widespread praise being heaped
upon it and its author in celebration of the fiftieth
anniversary of Verne's death and the prosaic truth of
his own evaluation. And yet Verne must be credited with
writing a work of monumental oneirism and with having
shown dreamers how to create a new reality.

E625   Heuvelmans, B[ernard]. and B. F. Porchnev. L'Homme de
       Néanderthal est toujours vivant. [Neanderthal Man Is
       Still Living] Paris: Plon.
          In the introduction Heuvelmans states that three works
       played a decisive role in his youth in steering him
       toward cryptozoölogy: Verne's Twenty Thousand Leagues
       Under the Sea, and books by Esme and Conan Doyle.

E626   Jules-Verne, Jean. "Souvenirs de mon grand-père."
       ["Memories of My Grandfather"] In Jules Verne, ed.
       P.-A. Touttain. Paris: Editions de L'Herne, pp.
       112-116.
          Reminiscences by the writer of both grandparents on
       his father's side. Remembers some childish pranks and
       punishments and special outings with Verne or Mme Verne.
       Calls Verne a mixture of the reflective and spontaneous,
       of dreams and calculation, of sensitivity and humor, of
       timidity and boldness. States that Verne's play, Monna
       Lisa, probably contains a personal confidence.

E627   Lubin, Georges. "George Sand et Vingt Mille Lieues sous
       les mers." ["George Sand and Twenty Thousand Leagues
       Under the Sea"] BSJV, NS No. 29-30 (1st & 2nd Trimesters),
       pp. 141-144.
          Follows on the articles of Pierre Terrasse (E551) and
       Simone Vierne (E555) concerning the relations between
       Verne and George Sand. Lubin assumes that they were
       unaware of his article published April 8, 1966 in the
       "Nouvelle République du Centre-Ouest" (Indre-et-Loire
       edition). Corrects the date on a Sand letter discussed
       by Terrasse and Vierne, using Verne's reply to it as a
       supporting document. Agrees that the first of two works
       that Sand acknowledges receiving from Verne was Journey
       to the Center of the Earth. Terrasse thinks the second
       was Five Weeks in a Balloon. It was more likely The
       English at the North Pole.

E628 Martin, Charles-Noël. "Les Amours de jeunesse de Jules
Verne." ["Young Loves of Jules Verne"] BSJV, NS No.
29-30 (1st & 2nd Trimesters), pp. 103-120.
Among several of these young loves was Rose Herminie
Arnault Grossetière, who married, as an examination of
correspondence and official documents prove, a certain
Armand Terrien de la Haye, July 19, 1848. Love poems by
Verne are quoted mentioning her name or dedicated to her.
Similar methods of research reveal four other girls in
Verne's youth: Angèle, Laurence, Louise, and Héloïse.
See E579.

E629 Massenet, Jules. "Lettre, A Propos de Michel Strogoff."
["Letter Concerning Michel Strogoff"] In Jules Verne,
ed. P.-A. Touttain. Paris: Editions de L'Herne, pp.
337-338.
Jules Massenet, in a letter written from Italy on
September 23, 1878 to Duquesnel, director of the theatre
of the Châtelet, turns down a request to compose the
music for d'Ennery's adaptation of Verne's Michel
Strogoff.

E630 Olivier-Martin, [Yves]. "Dans Le Sillage de Jules Verne."
["In Jules Verne's Wake"] BSJV, NS No. 31-32 (3rd &
4th Trimesters), pp. 180-183.
Lists works more directly influenced by Verne than
those listed in E509. Stresses similarity of theme.
See also E612, E672.

E631 Olivier-Martin, Yves. "Jules Verne et le roman populaire."
["Jules Verne and the Popular Novel"] In Jules Verne,
ed. P.-A. Touttain. Paris: Editions de L'Herne, pp.
289-304.
Credits Verne with giving freshness and a striking
relief to the themes and questions raised by the popular
novel of the nineteenth century. Lists children as the
vehicle for adventure, mentions orphans and the search
for family in Verne's works, discusses the positive
(good) hero as opposed to the scoundrel (both of whom
appear in Verne), calls the novel's navigators symbols
of progress, finds Verne's islands are good or bad or
neutral, and recognizes the Robinson Crusoe myth but
with an ambiguous twist. Other elements listed are:
the mad scientist, the cosmic voyage, trick effects,
hostile brothers, the macabre, mysterious messages, the
mystery being, and secrets. Considers Verne's social
criticism minor but real.

E632 _____. "Jules Verne jugé par ses contemporains." ["Jules
Verne Judged by His Contemporaries"] BSJV, NS No. 29-30
(1st & 2nd Trimesters), pp. 121-123.

Results of a poll taken by the weekly L'Opinion at
Amiens, May 9, 1909. Three people, Henry Bataille, Pierre
Mille, and Maurice Maindron were negative toward Verne's
works. René Boylesve was struck by Verne's novels, but
they had no lasting influence on him. About fifteen
positive opinions are quoted.

E633 Pons, Dr. Henry. L'Ile mystérieuse. [Mysterious Island]
BSJV, NS No. 31-32 (3rd & 4th Trimesters), pp. 166-173.
Verne placed his mysterious island in a desolate part
of the Pacific, avoided by explorers. He has been crit-
icized for putting so many animals on the island, but in
reality the zoölogical poverty of the Pacific islands,
although well known, is not uniform. Only the fauna of
Australian origin in The Mysterious Island corresponds
to the direction of ecological movement in that part of
the world. Verne's most impossible animal in the novel
is the orangutang, which couldn't survive at the latitude. Besides, Verne's orangutang resembles a chimpanzee.
Discusses the struggle between Man and Nature historical-
ly, philosophically, and as it appears in the novel. An
appendix lists seventeen fauna of the novel.

E634 Pouroyeur, R[obert]. "La Pénurie une obsession Vernienne?"
["Penury a Vernian Obsession?"] BSJV, NS No. 29-30
(1st and 2nd Trimesters), pp. 135-138.
Paper delivered before the General Assembly of the
Jules Verne Society, February 2, 1974. A striking
feature of residences (grottoes, mobile houses, the
Nautilus, the Albatross, etc.) in Verne's novels is that
he crams them full with provisions. His books usually
have a hunter who brings in delicacies to a cook who
prepares them expertly. It is as if Verne were terrified
by the thought of penury. His concern with the exhaustion
of fuel (particularly coal) is a case in point and seems
to accompany a dread of the cold. A possible interpretation of all this is that Verne wanted to remind readers how
money hoarded in a sock may contribute to national wealth.

E635 _____. "Le 'Théâtre-Lyrique' au temps de Jules Verne (1852-
1855)." ["The Théâtre-Lyrique in the Time of Jules Verne
1852-1855"] BSJV, NS No. 31-32 (3rd & 4th Trimesters),
pp. 157-163.
Recounts the history of the Théâtre-Lyrique in Paris
while Verne was its secretary (1852-1855). Lists the
works put on there, including Le Colin-Maillard (Verne
and Michel Carré, music Aristide Hignard, 1854), Les
Compagnons de la Marjolaine, a one-act comic opera written
by Verne and Carré, music by Hignard, 1855. Much later
Verne was co-librettist, again with Carré, of another
one-act comic opera, L'Auberge des Ardennes (1860), music
by Hignard, put on at the Lyric. See E674.

E636 _____. "Quelle Langue parlait Hans Bjelke?" ["What
Language Did Hans Bjelke Speak?"] BSJV, NS No. 31-32
(3rd & 4th Trimesters), pp. 176-177.
The so-called Danish spoken by the guide Hans Bjelke
in Journey to the Center of the Earth is in fact Swedish.
Two words only may be considered Danish; one of these
may be a typographical error, the other exists in both
Swedish and Danish. Perhaps another example of Verne's
liking of mystification.

*E637 Ragon, Michel. "Jules Verne visionaire de l'architecture."
["Jules Verne, Visionary of Architecture"] L'Oeil, No.
227 (June), pp. 44-49.
Not seen (cited in D443, p. 228).

E638 Raymond, François. "L'Homme et l'horloge." ["Man and the
Clock"] In Jules Verne, ed. P.-A. Touttain. Paris:
Editions de L'Herne, pp. 141-151.
This article stems from a paper given by François
Raymond before the General Assembly of the Société Jules
Verne, February 7, 1970. The time-piece in Verne's works
is not only a symbol but also a character, a term of
comparison and a model or caricature. Already in "Master
Zacharius" one sees the clash between the human and the
Divine watchmaker. Zacharius is the first of the great
Vernian Titans, while Pittonacchio prefigures all of
Verne's caricatures of men-clocks. Already one can see
the structural and psychological antithesis that will
characterize many of Verne's writings. Around the World
in Eighty Days manifests the antithesis of tragedy and
comedy, while reflecting Verne's often expressed ambivalent attitude toward mechanization. Verne both resembles
and differs from his unusual models, bearing witness to
two sides of his own existence.

E639 Richer, Jean. "Lettres, à Nadar." ["Letters to Nadar"]
In Jules Verne, ed. P.-A. Touttain. Paris: Editions
de L'Herne, pp. 75-76.
Comments on letters that follow, written by Jules
Verne to his friend Nadar, photographer and astronaut,
whose real name was Félix Tournachon. The latter is said
to have understood with Verne as early as 1862-63 that
the future belonged to heavier-than-air machines. Credits
Nadar with having played a role in the conception of the
Vernian hero.

E640 _____. "Note sur la constellation du marin." ["Note on
the Sailor's Constellation"] In Jules Verne, ed. P.-A.
Touttain. Paris: Editions de L'Herne, pp. 71-73.

This note precedes two letters by Jules Verne to his publisher Hetzel, one on September 1, 1896, the second on January 4 or 6, 1897. The note mentions Verne's Antarctic Mystery as a continuation of Poe's Narrative of Arthur Gordon Pym and discusses similarities and differences among Coleridge, Poe, and Verne. Says that Verne, who claimed to have gone further than Poe, rather did something different. Speculates as to whether B. Cendrars was so original in creating a world that he called his "own," considering what Coleridge, Poe, and Verne had done before him.

E641 Ristat, Jean. Le Lit de Nicolas Boileau et de Jules Verne. [The Bed of Nicholas Boileau and of Jules Verne] Paris: Gallimard.
       After discussing uncertainties surrounding the birth-place and birth date of Boileau, the author establishes that he himself was seven years old when he was born in 1943, for he is the fifth figure of the eternal return of Boileau: "So I am Boileau." The work, called a critical novel written in five meditations, includes some poetry and some analysis of Boileau's writings. They are viewed as a geometry of literature and Boileau's alexandrine is said to have the nature of an ellipsis. Verne figures in the work in a sort of analogical way. Thirty-one of his works appear in a "Table of Orientation."

E642 Roudaut, Jean. "L'Eternel Adam' et l'image des cycles." ["'Eternal Adam' and the Image of the Cycles"] In Jules Verne, ed. P.-A. Touttain. Paris: Editions de L'Herne, pp. 180–212.
       "Eternal Adam" is studied as a "reprise" of the themes in Verne, and this story, apparently the last written by him, is discussed in relation to his other novels. Human attitudes in the novels are seen as out of step with the scientific anticipations contained in them. Also considered are Verne's use of names, the presence of language as cryptogram, and the role of voyages making obscure messages intelligible. Various functions attributed to individuals by Verne are listed, and stress is laid on Verne's technique of building his novels on a series of parentheses.

E643 Sadoul, Jacques. "Horoscope de Jules Verne." ["Jules Verne's Horoscope"] In Jules Verne, ed. P.-A. Touttain. Paris: Editions de L'Herne, pp. 330–334.
       Curious about two divergent astral charts drawn up at the birth of Verne, one by a Frenchman, the other by an American, the writer of this article and another person independently drew up two more charts. They found these to be essentially in agreement with the American's. The article reviews certain events in Verne's life, connecting them to his horoscope.

E644 Samivel. "Les Surprises de Jules Verne." ["Jules Verne's
  Surprises"] In Jules Verne, ed. P.-A. Touttain. Paris:
  Editions de L'Herne, pp. 216-221.
    Calls Verne's Journey to the Center of the Earth the
  best of the famous series. Gives a resumé of the work
  and points out that Iceland, the novel's site, is traditionally the entrance to a subterranean world and was
  cited during the Middle Ages as proof of Hell's existence.
  Credits Verne with engaging in a curious task of demythi-
  cization, starting with the ancient legendary themes whose
  vicissitudes he renews and justifies with a kind of reverse
  alchemy. This article first appeared in Connaissance
  du monde in 1964.

E645 Serres, Michel. Jouvences sur Jules Verne. [Jules Verne's
  Youth] Paris: Editions de minuit.
    Stresses triple aspects of Verne's "Voyages": a dis-
  placement in ordinary space, oriented toward a horizontal
  or vertical plane; a scientific quest; the discovery of
  where the problem is resolved. The first two voyages
  normally form a cycle. Then comes the transfer to another
  world where occurs a religious type of voyage. Analogies
  are found in the Odyssey and Exodus, and comparison is
  made of Verne with Joyce, the latter reducing Homer while
  the former finishes it. Denies that Verne's work is
  science fiction, as it shows no violation of mechanical
  rules nor extrapolation of natural or physical or biolog-
  ical laws.

E646 _____. "Le Couteau de Jeannot." ["Johnny's Knife"] In
  Jules Verne, ed. P.-A. Touttain. Paris: Editions de
  L'Herne, pp. 213-215.
    Point of departure is Verne's "Doctor Ox" with discus-
  sion of an almost incestuous genealogical tree that is
  conjugal rather than filial. Concludes that Verne's
  Voyages, often written in the language of code, or the
  techniques of deciphering, are written on a parallel in
  the language of energy: steam, electricity, storms, and
  volcanoes.

E647 Taussat, Robert. "L'Anarchisme divin: de l'Ile Lincoln à
  l'Ile Hoste." ["Divine Anarchism: From Lincoln Island
  to Hoste Island"] In Jules Verne, ed. P.-A. Touttain.
  Paris: Editions de L'Herne, pp. 242-255.
    Develops the discussion as containing explicit or
  implicit judgments on the part of Verne and two of his
  characters, Captain Nemo and Kaw-Djer. Calls Verne's
  heroes fundamentally anti-bourgeois and even anarchist,
  but the latter in the sense of being outside and above
  society. Sees Verne's heroes as prisoners in enclosed
  spaces. The adventure occurs often in the center of an

island, as Lincoln Island, where the primordial cave
opens to them, whence they may sally forth to conquer,
as they are both masters and captives. Such an island
is both magic and action. Self-dictated discipline
enables the man of Lincoln Island to achieve absolute
freedom. Both Nemo and Kaw-Djer are gods and masters.
They differ in that one, victim of oppression, moves
toward an avenging anarchism, while the other, having
conceived the horror of power without suffering from it,
attains serenity. By different routes these two supermen
become gods and achieve perfect freedom.

E648   Terrasse, P[ierre]. "A Propos des Cinq Cents Millions de
       la Begum: Un Modèle de Jean-Jacques Langevol." ["Con-
       cerning The Begum's Fortune: A Model of Jean-Jacques
       Langevol"] BSJV, NS No. 31-32 (3rd & 4th Trimesters),
       pp. 184-188.
          The Begum Gokool in Verne's novel may have been
       inspired by a real Begum, Jeanne, whose eventful life is
       recounted. A case is also made to show that the character
       Jean-Jacques Langevol, described as a key figure although
       not a principal character of the novel, may have been
       modeled on a certain Captain Corcoran, an imaginary
       adventurer whose exploits are recounted in Aventures
       merveilleuses by Alfred Assolant (1827-1886).

E649   Terrasse, Pierre. "Glanes et notules." ["Gleanings and
       Notes"] BSJV, NS No. 31-32 (3rd & 4th Trimesters), pp.
       164-165.
          Oliver Sinclair in Verne's Green Ray certainly repre-
       sents the author when in chapter 13 he expresses regrets
       at never having followed the sea.

E650   _____. "Jules Verne et les chemins de fer." ["Jules Verne
       and the Railways"] In Jules Verne, ed. P.-A. Touttain.
       Paris: Editions de L'Herne, pp. 311-316.
          Essentially a paper given by its author before the
       General Assembly of the Jules Verne Society, February 7,
       1970. It discusses trains as Verne's heroes' favorite
       means of transportation and describes some of them. See
       E473.

E651   Touttain, Pierre-André. "Aspect du romantisme souterrain:
       les Indes Noires." ["An Aspect of Underground Romanti-
       cism: Child of the Cavern"] In Jules Verne. Paris:
       Editions de L'Herne, pp. 225-228.
          Mentions Verne's visit to Scotland in 1859 with his
       friend, Aristide Hignard, as a romantic source of this
       novel. Adds as possible literary influences on this
       romantic novel Shakespeare, Walter Scott, Nodier's

<u>Voyage en Ecosse</u>, and Mendelssohn's <u>Scottish Symphony</u>.
Cites such French influences as Dumas père and George
Sand. Possible influences are seen in Hoffman, Tieck,
and Novalis. Notes that Verne's <u>Green Ray</u> (1882) appeared
two years after the novelist had made another trip to
Scotland.

E652   ____. "Du <u>Voyage au Centre de la terre</u> aux <u>Phases de la</u>
<u>lune</u>." ["From <u>Journey to the Center of the Earth</u> to
<u>Phases of the Moon</u>"] In <u>Jules Verne</u>. Paris: Editions
de L'Herne, pp. 104-107.
    Concerns the fascination that Verne's Professor Otto
Lidenbrock, the fearless geologist, leader of the expedition in <u>Journey to the Center of the Earth</u>, held for Paul
Delvaux. Between 1939 and 1971 Lidenbrock was the subject
in at least twenty-three of Delvaux's paintings and
sketches. These are listed with an identification of
the collection to which each belongs. (Some are in
unnamed private collections.)

E653   ____. "<u>Mathias Sandorf</u> au Château de Monte-Cristo."
["<u>Mathias Sandorf</u> to The Castle of Monte-Cristo"] In
<u>Jules Verne</u>. Paris: Editions de L'Herne, pp. 308-310.
    Verne paid homage to Alexandre Dumas-père in writing
<u>Mathias Sandorf</u>, which he dedicated to Dumas fils. The
opinion is offered that Verne wanted Dumas père's Château
de Monte-Cristo to be graphically represented in the
edition of <u>Mathias Sandorf</u>. At any rate, Benett's illustration bears comparison to an old view of the château.

E654   ____. "Verne et la musique." ["Verne and Music"] In
<u>Jules Verne</u>, Paris: Editions de L'Herne, pp. 339-342.
    Gives the history of musical adaptations of Verne's
works. Notes that Verne bought a piano in 1855 and that
among his best friends were three musicians: Aristide
Hignard, Léo Delibes, and Victor Massé. Verne's favorite
composers are mentioned in his <u>Floating Island</u> (1895):
Mendelssohn, Weber, Beethoven, and Mozart.

E655   ____. "Verniana." In <u>Jules Verne</u>. Paris: Editions de
L'Herne, pp. 343-347.
    Four-and-a-half pages of statements about Verne made
by celebrities, mostly writers, but including Marshal
Lyautey and Admiral Byrd.

E656   ____, ed. <u>Jules Verne</u>. Paris: Editions de L'Herne.
    Contains some of Verne's letters to his family and
various correspondents including Louis-Jules Hetzel,
Nadar, and Paul Verne. Includes Verne's play <u>Monna Lisa</u>
and his <u>Souvenirs d'enfance et de jeunesse</u>. Over thirty

articles by authors beginning with Théophile Gautier and ending with the book's editor discuss aspects of Verne's writing. These studies are listed herein separately under each author's name. The book has a fairly extensive bibliography.

E657 Vierne, Simone. "Puissance de l'imaginaire." ["Power of Imagination"] In Jules Verne, ed. P.-A. Touttain. Paris: Editions de L'Herne, pp. 152-171.

Imagination has a poetic function in the works by Verne, who is a dream merchant. Analysis is made of the ways in which Verne obeys the impulses of imagination. He sometimes had to overcome the demands of his publisher, Hetzel, and the exigencies of his novel's logic. Verne's imagination is shown reacting in three different ways in three works. Some novels are discussed in terms of theme and are seen to be related through the presence of such basic forces as the Nile, the Earth's center and the Pole, or the moon. Water or infinite space, the cave or enclosed space, and the image of the Cycle or the figure of time are presented as basic to the mythical adventure.

1975

E658 Anon. "Jules Verne à la radio et à la télévision." ["Jules Verne on Radio and Television"] BSJV, NS No. 33-34 (1st & 2nd Trimesters), p. 48.

France-Régions, in a new program meant for young readers, ("Improvisations on a Book," by Jouhauld-Castro) featured Mistress Branican, told by the niece of the geographer Elisée Reclus mentioned by Verne in Castle of the Carpathians.

E659 Burgaud, Ph[ilippe]. "Les Annales politiques et littéraires et Jules Verne." ["Political and Literary Annals and Jules Verne"] BSJV, NS No. 33-34 (1st & 2nd Trimesters), pp. 13-14.

Verne's name appears on the same page with C. Flammarion and E. Bergerat in the Golden Book issued by the magazine Les Annales politiques et littéraires on its tenth anniversary in 1893. In a letter Verne says that Five Weeks in a Balloon was his first novel, says Africa always had interested him, and that failing to go there himself he decided to send imaginary heroes.

E660 Compère, Cécile. "Histoire d' 'A' ou les prénoms des femmes dans l'oeuvre de Jules Verne." ["The Question of 'A' or First Names of Women in the Works of Jules Verne"] BSJV, NS No. 33-34 (1st & 2nd Trimesters), pp. 28-31.

Paper delivered before the General Assembly of the
Jules Verne Society, February 2, 1974. Speculates on
reasons why Verne should have so liked names ending in
"A" for his characters. Sixty-two of his female characters have a name ending in "A." Could it be that the
letter being the first one in the word "Amour" (Love),
Verne wished to show a connection between the character
and love? Most of his heroines with a name ending in
"A" do fall in love.

E661 _____. "Toponymie Vernienne." ["Vernian Toponomy"] BSJV,
NS No. 33-34 (1st & 2nd Trimesters), p. 15.
More names are listed showing additional tributes to
Verne by various French localities (and one Dutch) naming
streets, hotels, or restaurants for Verne or one his
characters. See E562, E598.

E662 Compère, Daniel. "Claudius Bombarnac: Verne, Saverna,
Caterna." BSJV, NS No. 35-36 (3rd & 4th Trimesters), pp.
92-94.
Paul Saverna, an actor, was the model for Adolphe
Caterna in Claudius Bombarnac. Saverna was received
socially in the Verne home. Discusses reality (Verne,
Saverna) becoming the imagined (Bombarnac, Caterna).

E663 _____. "De Jules Clarétie à quelques oeuvres de Jules
Verne." ["From Jules Clarétie to a Few Works of Jules
Verne"] BSJV, NS No. 33-34 (1st & 2nd Trimesters), pp.
20-26.
Verne did not borrow from Clarétie in writing Mathias
Sandorf either the name Sandorf or the phenomenon of
hypnotism. On the other hand, Clarétie's Jean Mornas
probably influenced Verne, who gave characters in four
of his novels either the exact name or something different by a letter. Clarétie's Carlos et Cornélius was
probably influenced by two Verne works. Other aspects
of the Verne-Clarétie relationship are discussed.

E664 _____. "Jules Verne et le roman gothique." ["Jules Verne
and the Gothic Novel"] BSJV, NS No. 35-36 (3rd & 4th
Trimesters), pp. 72-78.
Paper delivered before the General Assembly of the
Jules Verne Society, March 1, 1975, identifies the gothic
elements in Verne's novels and discusses their function.
Defines "gothic" and mentions the influences of Walpole,
Reeve, Radcliffe, Lewis, the romantic "semi-gothic"
tradition, and Ossian.

E665 Compère, François. "Les Coureurs du Tour du Monde."
["Globetrotters of Around the World"] RLM, No. 456-461
(July-October), pp. 169-175.

Gives the list of globetrotters who set new records
through various means of transportation that took them
around the world to beat Verne's eighty days.

E666   Destombes, Marcel. "Le Manuscrit de Vingt Mille Lieues
       sous les mers de la Société de Géographie de Paris."
       ["Paris Geographic Society's Manuscript of Twenty Thousand
       Leagues Under the Sea"] BSJV, NS No. 35-36 (3rd & 4th
       Trimesters), pp. 59-70.
          Paper delivered before the General Assembly of the
       Jules Verne Society on March 1, 1975. The Society owns
       two Verne manuscripts: Twenty Thousand Leagues Under
       the Sea and a fragment of Five Weeks in a Balloon. A
       letter from Michel Verne allows one to suppose that Prince
       Roland Bonaparte, traveler, scientist, and President of
       the Society, may have been given the manuscript by the
       Verne family. Main part of the article compares two
       manuscripts of Twenty Thousand Leagues Under the Sea.
       Mentions some corrections revealing as to Nemo's charac-
       ter and to the close association with Hetzel.

E667   Dumas, Dr. O[livier]. "Coup de filet dans Le Musée des
       familles." ["Caught in Le Musée des familles"] BSJV,
       NS No. 35-36 (3rd & 4th Trimesters), pp. 79-82.
          Paper delivered before the General Assembly of the
       Jules Verne Society, March 1, 1975. Verne was rather
       badly treated as a young author by the Musée des familles,
       in which for at least seven years he is identified as
       Charles Verne. In some issues his name is spelled
       "Vernes," and his Amérique du Sud is called Amérique du
       Nord. Cites Verne's taste for inaccurately quoted
       proverbs and shows that George Sand was not the sole
       inspiration for Twenty Thousand Leagues Under the Sea.

E668   Editions André Barret. Album Nadar. [Nadar Album] Paris:
       Barret.
          Verne figures among fifty pictures of Nadar's contem-
       poraries. Includes an account of Verne's relations with
       Nadar.

E669   Evans, I. O. "Glanes et notules." ["Gleanings and Notes"]
       BSJV, NS No. 35-36 (3rd & 4th Trimesters), p. 70.
          Evans claims to have found the source of the battle
       between the ichtyosaurus and the pleisiosaurus, in Journey
       to the Center of the Earth (chapter 33), in Great Sea
       Dragons by Thomas Hawkins (London, 1840).

E670   Garnier, Jacques. Théodore Rancy et son temps. [Theodore
       Rancy and His Times] Paris: Garnier.

Contains an account of the inauguration June 23, 1889 of the Municipal Circus of Amiens. Includes excerpts of the speech made by Verne as a city Councilor and champion of the project.

E671 Goupil, Armand. <u>Jules Verne</u>. Paris: Larousse.
The selections from Verne in this volume of the "Textes pour aujourd'hui" series have been carefully chosen to represent the spectrum of Verne's thinking. Verne's vision will interest the twentieth-century reader who seeks the sources of contemporary thought in order to know himself or herself better. Verne, an everyday bourgeois with an anarchist's heart, did not believe in a socialism based on historical materialism, of which he offers only the caricature. The selections are drawn from the Livre de Poche edition that began in 1966.

E672 Helling, Cornélis. "Jules Verne et sa postérité." ["Jules Verne and His Posterity"] <u>BSJV</u> NS No. 33-34 (1st & 2nd Trimesters), p. 27.
Names six more authors and their works that either go back directly to Verne or continue the tradition. <u>See</u> E509, E612.

E673 Jules-Verne, Jean. "Autour de <u>Kéraban-le-Têtu</u>." ["Around <u>Kéraban-the-Inflexible</u>"] <u>BSJV</u>, NS No. 33-34 (1st & 2nd Trimesters), pp. 16-19.
Extracts of lectures during a cruise to the Black Sea that retraced the steps of <u>Kéraban-the-Inflexible</u>. Comparison is made with Homer, another writer of adventure stories. Verne created <u>Kéraban</u> in the spirit of a vaudeville entertainment.

E674 Pourvoyeur, R[obert]. "Glanes et notules." ["Gleanings and Notes"] <u>BSJV</u>, NS No. 35-36 (3rd & 4th Trimesters), p. 71.
Adds to E635 the number of performances of Verne's comic operas according to <u>L'Histoire du théâtre lyrique</u> by Albert Soubies (Paris: Fischbacher, 1899).

E675 _____. "Le Répertoire de ce bon M. Caterna." ["Repertoire of that Good Mr. Caterna"] <u>BSJV</u>, NS No. 33-34 (1st & 2nd Trimesters), pp. 32-43.
Verne published <u>Claudius Bombarnac</u> in 1892, a long time after his days at the Lyric Theater. However, he never lost his love of the theater, and the character Adolphe Caterna, the actor, who appears in the novel, helps prove it. There are twenty-six quotations in the novel that evoke the theater.

E676 _____. "Masaniello de La Maison à vapeur." ["Masaniello of The Steam House"] BSJV, NS No. 33-34 (1st & 2nd Trimesters), pp. 46-47.

    Shows that Verne in The Steam House evokes a passage from the opera Masaniello by Michel-Henri Carafa de Colobrano (1787-1872). The passage seems to support the view sometimes expressed by Carafa's critics that his lack of success was due to the words and libretto. Calls this particular opera his best.

E677 _____. "Réflexions sur l'esprit scientifique de Jules Verne." ["Reflections on Jules Verne's Scientific Mind"] BSJV, NS no. 35-36 (3rd & 4th Trimesters), pp. 83-91.

    Paper delivered before the General Assembly of the Jules Verne Society, March 1, 1975. Examines whether Verne was truly the incarnation of the scientific method with respect to its rigor. Finds errors and negligence in Verne's approach to various scientific disciplines. His meticulous documentation and intellectual curiosity are scientific, but he is only partially scientific. His work is the product of the combination of his heart's desire to write for the theater and his brain's will to fill a gap in French literature.

E678 Rache, Capitaine-Commandant, J[acques] de. "L'Officier dans l'oeuvre de Jules Verne." ["Officers in the Works of Jules Verne"] BSJV, NS No. 35-36 (3rd & 4th Trimesters), pp. 56-58.

    Excerpts from a paper delivered before the General Assembly of the Jules Verne Society, February 2, 1974. Michel Strogoff is the best example in Verne's novels of the officer dedicated to serve his country. Hector Servadac is less admirable. Verne's English officers are true to the ideal of obedience or to service involving hardships. Mentions the Picard, Natalis Delpierre, in Flight to France. Verne seems to have had a good understanding of the mission of officers.

E679 Robin, Christian. "Le Tour du monde en 80 jours." ["Around the World in Eighty Days"] Maison de la culture de Nantes informations, February, March, April, pp. 6-7.

    The many media through which Verne's Around the World in Eighty Days has achieved articulation attest to its popularity. A recent example is Monique Creteur's adaptation for marionnettes. In the novel Verne achieves the summit of art expected in a serial.

E680 Rottensteiner, Franz. La Science Fiction illustrée. Paris: Editions du Seuil.
    See D406.

E681   Sagot, R. "En Marge de la Croisière de Rotterdam à Copenhague." ["On the Fringe of the Cruise from Rotterdam to Copenhagen"] BSJV, NS No. 33-34 (1st & 2nd Trimesters), pp. 9-13.
       Tries to determine the dates of the action in twenty Verne novels not covered by Pierre Terrasse (E346). Bases investigations on astronomic phenomena and calendar references within the novels. The account of the trip De Rotterdam à Copenhague, written by Paul Verne and put in the 1881 edition of Giant Raft, mentions a comet in chapter 10, and allows one to date the action within the account. This article deals with the research that determined dates of importance regarding the genesis and publication of the works concerned.

E682   Terrasse, P[ierre]. "La Dédicace de Vingt Mille Lieues sous les mers." ["Dedication of Twenty Thousand Leagues Under the Sea"] BSJV, NS No. 35-36 (3rd & 4th Trimesters), pp. 55-56.
       It is known that Verne dedicated a few of his works to individuals. Twenty Thousand Leagues Under the Sea was dedicated to the readers of the Magasin d'éducation et de récréation. Since the dedication was not included when the work was published in a single volume, its existence is not widely known.

1976

E683   Anon. "Jules Verne à la télévision et au cinéma." ["Jules Verne on Television and in the Cinema"] BSJV, NS No. 39-40 (3rd & 4th Trimesters), p. 190.
       Cites newspaper and magazine coverage of the adaptation by Armand Lanoux of The Castle of the Carpathians.

E684   Burgaud, Philippe. "Michel Strogoff et les théâtres de Bruxelles." ["Michel Strogoff and the Brussels Theaters"] BSJV, NS No. 37-38 (1st & 2nd Trimesters), pp. 116-122.
       Paper delivered before the General Assembly of the Jules Verne Society, March 1, 1975. Recounts the showings of the play, Michel Strogoff, based on Verne's novel, and shown over two hundred times in Brussels.

E685   Central File of the Theses of Nanterre and Christian Robin. "Travaux en cours sur Jules Verne." ["Works in Progress on Jules Verne"] Archives des lettres modernes, 161, No. 1 (June), 73-76.
       Lists: (1) theses on Verne in preparation for the "Doctorat d'Etat" and "Doctorat d'Université" as well as the "Doctorat de troisième cycle," and (2) studies to appear. See E716.

E686 Chesneaux, Jean. "Illustrations des romans de Jules Verne."
["Illustrations of Jules Verne's Novels"] BSJV, NS No.
37-38 (1st & 2nd Trimesters), pp. 114-115.
    Report on an unpublished study by Pierre Pitrou, a
student of Marc Soriano. Illustrations in the Hetzel
edition of Verne's Voyages extraordinaires complement
the texts in a functional role, not merely a decorative
one. See E132, E146, E188, E193, E237, E264.

E687 _____. "Le Tour du monde en quatre-vingts jours." ["Around
the World in Eighty Days"] RLM, No. 456-461 (July-October), pp. 11-20.
    Around the World in Eighty Days is a hymn to steam-
driven machinery in boats and locomotives in the Saint-
Simonian tradition of Enfant and Michel Chevallier. The
rail is a metal ribbon that enables us to circle the
globe. The railway, superior to India's wild animals,
nevertheless becomes integrated with Nature in the Sierra
Nevada. The railway car offers social amenities in
motion, contrary to its antisocial successor, the motor-
car. Vernes's hero, Phileas Fogg, is immersed in the
concept of the machine, but he is gradually humanized,
especially through Aouda. To some extent Verne admires
British colonial policy, but not its trade in opium with
the Chinese, nor its preferential treatment of English
merchants in India. He admires American efficiency, but
not the vulgarity and monotony of American life. Criticism of American and East Indians is almost racist, although he excepts the Parsees. Fogg shows that with
money one can control the world of machines. The novel
presents a West of machinery and capitalism, proudly
proclaiming that it is European.

E688 _____. "Une Lecture extra-terrestre du Tour du monde:
The Other Log of Phileas Fogg, de P. J. Farmer." ["Extra-
terrestrial Reading of Around the World: P. J. Farmer's
The Other Log of Phileas Fogg"] RLM, No. 456-461 (July-
October), pp. 158-167.
    Discusses P. J. Farmer's The Other Log of Phileas Fogg
as a product of Around the World in Eighty Days. A
reading of Farmer's novel can elucidate Verne's. The
point of departure is in the fact that Fogg had by 1872
absorbed a lot of the elixir of Eridan, which assures
longevity. The Eridaneans, arriving on Earth light-years
ago, came into conflict with another group landing from
Capella. Destroying each other, they had to adopt Earth
dwellers to assure survival. Fogg is one of these
adoptees. See D381, E762.

E689 Compère, Daniel. "Autour du Film de Mike Todd: Le Tour du monde en quatre-vingts jours." ["Around Mike Todd's Film: Around the World in Eighty Days"] BSJV, NS No. 37-38 (1st & 2nd Trimesters), pp. 123-126.

Criticizes Mike Todd's filming of Around the World in Eighty Days. Sarcastically points out the money spent to engage various stars so that we see Fernandel's teeth, Martine Carol's breasts, Marlene Dietrich's legs, and Frank Sinatra's eyes. No sum of money assures a masterpiece.

E690 _____. "Bibliographie des études relatives au Tour du monde en quatre-vingts jours." ["Bibliography of Studies About Around the World in Eighty Days"] RLM, No. 456-461 (July-October), pp. 189-203.

Lists studies devoted to Around the World in Eighty Days, adaptations of the novel to stage and film, and emulations of Phileas Fogg's feat.

E691 _____. "Le Jour fantôme." ["Phantom Day"] RLM, No. 456-461 (July-October), pp. 31-51.

Three different times in Around the World in Eighty Days converge at the novel's dramatic end: London time on Fogg's watch, the time recorded in Fogg's notebook, and the time on Passepartout's watch. If one accepts the influence of literary sources, Verne's novel may be discussed in terms of Edouard Cador, Edmond Plauchet, Edgar Allan Poe, Alexander Dumas, Lewis Carroll, X. Nagrien, and others. Probably what is involved is not sources as such, but rather what may be called supportive publications. The debatable sources listed above would lay claims of influence chiefly, although not exclusively, on the basis of a preoccupation with the loss or gain of a day on crossing and recrossing the equator. Readers of Verne should know about John Herschel's Treatise on Astronomy, one of Poe's sources. Phileas Fogg is best seen through the optic of astronomy. He is a planet and his Other is not Aouda but rather the Sun's fire, present throughout the novel. The voyage occurs around a hidden or absent circle. Fogg, the eccentric, has written himself--by suppressing his Other, by stealing from the Sun--a day that is the novel's center, an unseizable, phantom day.

E692 Courville, Luce. "Quatre-vingts-douze." ["Ninety-Two"] BSJV, NS No. 39-40 (3rd & 4th Trimesters), pp. 174-176.

This paper was delivered before the General Assembly of the Jules Verne Society, February 28, 1976. It connects some events of Verne's novels with his life and with Nantes. The title "Ninety-Two" refers to the publication in 1892

of the novels <u>Castle of the Carpathians</u> and <u>Claudius
Bombarnac</u>. Speculates as to whether the heroines are
Carolina, the girl who jilted him, and Stilla, the
singer.

E693 Diot, Auguste. "Jules Verne et Provins." ["Jules Verne
and Provins"] <u>BSJV</u>, NS No. 37-38 (1st & 2nd Trimesters),
pp. 101-105.
This article first appeared in 1928 in the <u>Bulletin
de la Société d'Histoire et d'Archéologie de l'Arrondisse-
ment de Provins</u>. Reviews Verne's genealogy, showing that
some of his antecedents were natives of Provins.

E694 Dumas, Olivier. "Chronologies des oêuvres romanesques de
Jules Verne." ["Chronology of Jules Verne's Novelistic
Works"] <u>Archives des lettres modernes</u>, 161, No. 1 (June),
77-83.
Bibliography limited to Verne's novels, tales, and
short stories. Gives title date and number of volumes
of original edition. Mentions that Gondolo della Riva
is working on a more extensive bibliography. <u>See</u> E716.

E695 Génin, Paul. "La Poésie du point final chez Jules Verne."
["Poetry of the Final Period in Jules Verne"] <u>BSJV</u>, NS
No. 39-40 (3rd & 4th Trimesters), pp. 182-184.
The ending of a Verne novel is frequently charged
with emotion. He may end with the classical "and they
lived happily ever after," or finish with an aphorism.
He seems to want to make history last beyond the final
page. His best ending is the last ten lines of <u>Twenty
Thousand Leagues Under the Sea</u>. This paper was presented
before the General Assembly of the Jules Verne Society,
February 28, 1976.

E696 Gondolo della Riva, Piero. "Bibliographie (des éditions)
du <u>Tour du monde en quatre-vingts jours</u> (roman)."
["Bibliography (of the editions) of <u>Around the World in
Eighty Days</u> (novel)"] <u>RLM</u>, No. 456-461 (July-October),
pp. 185-187.
This extract from Gondolo della Riva's analytical
bibliography (E743) describes the early history of the
editions of <u>Around the World in Eighty Days</u>.

E697 _____. "Les Jeux et les objets inspirés du <u>Tour du monde
en quatre-vingts jours</u>." ["Games and Objects Inspired
by <u>Around the World in Eighty Days</u>"] <u>RLM</u>, No. 456-461
(July-October), pp. 177-181.
Lists some games, such as goose-chase, and objects,
such as children's miniature stages with characters, all
inspired by Verne's <u>Around the World in Eighty Days</u>. Has
a short bibliography, pp. 185-186.

E698   Hegart, Paul. "Jules Verne avait tout prévu, même la
       télévision." ["Jules Verne Had Foreseen Everything,
       Even Television"] Toptélé, 14 (15 December), 28-29.
          Watching French television's adaptation of The Castle
       of the Carpathians, produced by Christophe Averty, was
       probably the best way to do homage to Verne. All the
       words and pictures mysteriously produced by the diabolical
       Baron Gortz that frightened the hero are nothing more nor
       less than modern television. A case can be made for
       saying that Verne's only invention was steak tartare,
       which appears the first time ever in Michel Strogoff.
       But Verne's gift was to be able to start with a minor
       scientific detail and imagine the rest.

E699   Huet, Marie-Hélène. "Exploration du jeu." ["Exploration
       of the Wager"] RLM, No. 456-461 (July-October), pp.
       95-108.
          The comparison of Verne's Will of An Eccentric with
       Around the World in Eighty Days proves how the latter,
       quite different from the author's first novels, fore-
       shadows the later ones. Both novels use a wager as point
       of departure, and both protagonists devote themselves to
       the wager. Nevertheless, there are differences in the
       role of chance and in the protagonists' attitudes.
       Both, unlike explorers whose primary goal is a place to
       be investigated, consider the arrival home to be all-
       important. Both heroes win against initially heavy odds.
       Reintegrated into society, they become normal and no
       longer interesting. Around the World in Eighty Days
       announces what will be a concern in the later works,
       namely, the death of a hero.

*E700 Le Méhauté, Pierrette Aline. "Le Thème de la survivance
       dans la littérature conjecturale française du vingtième
       siècle." ["The Theme of Survival in Twentieth Century
       French Speculative Literature"] Ph.D. dissertation,
       University of California, Los Angeles (French text).
          A study of the post-catastrophe motif in twentieth
       century French speculative fiction. Verne's "Eternal
       Adam" is studied in context of works by Emile Solari,
       Noëlle Roger, Régis Messac, René Barjavel, Christophe
       Paulin, Roger Ikor, Robert Merle, and François Clement.
       Not seen (cited in Dissertation Abstracts International,
       37 (1976), 362A).

E701   Lebois, André. "Poétique secrète du Tour du monde en
       quatre-vingts jours." ["Secret Poetic of Around the World
       in Eighty Days"] RLM, No. 456-461 (July-October), pp.
       21-29.
          The four elements and a few simple myths contribute
       through the art of novelist-poet Verne to the adventures

of Phileas Fogg. Gold is indispensable to him, but
Providence sees to its effective employ. Fire and water
are attendant upon his peregrinations and intermingle
with nobility and poetry of spirit. Around the World in
Eighty Days, a novel of space and time, expresses a
reverence for Science with a capital "S," but Verne
achieves a tour de force in reconciling mathematical
exactitude and poetry. There are analogies between the
human aspects of the Fix-Fogg relationship and those of
the tie that binds Hugo's Javert and Jean Valjean. Fogg,
a sort of superman, accepts challenge as an act of faith
in Providence, a hymn of love for Science and a chivalric
oath. Poetry, love, sport, moral idealism, and a sense
of humor are the ingredients of this novel.

E702   Olivier-Martin, Yves. "Le Tour du monde et littérature
       populaire." ["Around the World and Popular Literature"]
       RLM, No. 456-461 (July-October), pp. 139-155.
           A descriptive account of precursors and successors
       of Verne's novel, with a bibliography.

E703   _____. "Tour du monde en quatre-vingts jours." ["Around
       the World in Eighty Days"] BSJV, NS No. 39-40 (3rd &
       4th Trimesters), pp. 180-181.
           This novel probably inspired the greatest number of
       authors, as it responded to the needs of the end of the
       nineteenth century, e.g., the various means of transport.
       However, a second aspect of Verne's work, a certain
       derision of science, may be seen in some imitators like
       Frédéric Mauzens and Majel Kaiet.

E704   Pioud, Jean-François. "Musicologie d'une nouvelle." ["The
       Music of a Short Story"] BSJV, NS No. 39-40 (3rd & 4th
       Trimesters), pp. 157-161.
           Discusses the musical base of "Mr. Ray Sharp and
       Miss Me Flat." Rossini's William Tell, Bach, Beethoven,
       Debussy, Clérambault, Balbastre, and Ockeghem are men-
       tioned, with references to Gregorian chant and the
       Dictionary of the Organ.

E705   Poncey, Jean-Pierre. "Misère de Jules Verne." ["Wretchedness
       of Jules Verne"] RLM, No. 456-461 (July-October), pp.
       53-65.
           In accepting an unreasonable bet, Phileas Fogg upholds
       the honor of the nineteenth century, of which Verne
       presents a deceptive picture, but Verne fails in his
       embellished portrait. The very shape of the Earth makes
       inevitable that Verne's travelers return to their point
       of departure. If there is a woman at the end of the
       journey, she is there only for the most bourgeois of

reasons, namely, to furnish creature comforts. Fogg
is merely the symbol of modern man, the Charlie Chaplin
of Modern Times. The triumph of Science yields to the
law of money.

E706 Pons, H[enri]. "André Laurie." BSJV, NS No. 39-40 (3rd &
4th Trimesters), pp. 164-166.
Facts about André Laurie (Paschal Grousset), Verne's
sole official collaborator. Anti-Empire, he became
embroiled with Prince Pierre Bonaparte. He supported the
Commune, was arrested, deported, and escaped to England,
from which a general amnesty allowed a return. Collaboration with Verne may seem strange, but the latter's politics
were complex. The article was a paper delivered before
the General Assembly of the Jules Verne Society, February
28, 1976.

E707 Pourvoyeur, R[obert]. "Pour une sémantique de la Vernologie."
["For a Semantics of Vernology"] BSJV, NS No. 39-40
(3rd & 4th Trimesters), pp. 162-163.
In this paper, delivered before the General Assembly
of the Jules Verne Society, February 28, 1976, a host of
terms based on Verne's name are coined: vernology,
vernomania, hypervernism, vernocosm, vernilinear,
vernuous, and vernorama.

E708 _____. "Un Assassiné volontaire." ["Willing Murder Victim"]
BSJV, NS No. 39-40 (3rd & 4th Trimesters), pp. 177-179.
If Verne borrowed from Vanloo the idea of a voluntary
murder victim when planning to write a fantasy along the
lines of "Dr. Ox," the borrowing was no doubt unconscious.

E709 _____. "Un Tour en Zarzuela." ["A Tour in the Zarzuela"]
BSJV, NS No. 39-40 (3rd & 4th Trimesters), pp. 182-189.
When the play based on Around the World in Eighty Days
was having its success in Paris, the zarzuela was flourish-
ing in Spain. A type of zarzuela concerned travel, and
one of the first of these was an adaptation of Around the
World in Eighty Days. Information is given about the
composers and librettist. The Spanish work is quite
different in spirit. See E543.

E710 Raymond, François. "Connaissance de Verne." ["Knowledge of
of Verne"] Archives des lettres modernes, 161, No. 1
(June), 5-40.
Verne is still not well known and is difficult to
classify. The Arts et lettres special number in 1949
started a serious interest in him. Discusses significant
critics. Verne criticism has taken two directions: (1)
"Immanent Criticism" in the Barthes sense, and (2) the
deciphering of the Voyages extraordinaires with the help
of certain keys. There is a place now for university

298

criticism. It is important to consider a triple authorship to the Voyages: Verne, his son, and Hetzel. Verne's
work is both a system of explorations and a trip through
a literary space in which the original genre, the adventure tale, sometimes gives way to other genres. See
E716.

E711 _____. "Glanes et notules." ["Gleanings and Notes"] BSJV,
NS No. 39-40 (3rd & 4th Trimesters), p. 173.
Robert Taussat's article constitutes not only a bril-
liant and new reading but a somewhat hypothetical one of
Around the World in Eighty Days. To confirm this a
letter from Hetzel to the illustrator Benett is quoted.
See E720.

E712 _____. "Guide pratique pour l'étude de Jules Verne."
["Practical Guide for the Study of Jules Verne"]
Archives des lettres modernes, 161, No. 1 (June), 85-93.
Editions, anthologies, biographies, periodicals,
essential studies, bibliographies, and information
centers. See E716.

E713 _____. "Pour Un Espace de l'exploration." ["For Exploration
Space"] RLM, No. 456-461 (July-October), pp. 5-9.
Introduction to issue of articles on Around the World
in Eighty Days. Intention of the Verne series will be to
explore the ever-widening field of Vernian writings,
proceeding from the known to the unknown, around major
themes, aspects or contexts, to test and compare the
results and methods of three types of criticism until
now excessively separated: the university, the scholarly,
especially that of the Jules Verne Society and its
"Bulletins," and finally the criticism of "marginal
research."

E714 _____. "Tours du monde et tours du texte: Procédés verniens,
procédés roussellians." ["Around the World and Around the
Text: Vernian Techniques, Roussellian Techniques"] RLM,
No. 456-461 (July-October), pp. 67-88.
Contrary to many contemporary studies, this one considers a more literal interpretation of the text. Emphasizes the circular nature of the tale and compares
Verne's style to that of Raymond Roussel. Verne wrote
largely for his own age, but also for us and for himself.

E715 Raymond, François and Daniel Compère. "Bibliographie des
études Verniennes de langue française, 1966-1973."
["Bibliography of Vernian Studies In the French Language"]
Archives des lettres modernes, 161, No. 1 (June), 41-67.

This bibliography claims to be ample, but not complete, and refers the reader to the bibliographical file of Jean-Michel Margot, which is kept up to date by a computer. See E716.

E716 _____. Le Développement des études sur Jules Verne. [Development of Studies on Jules Verne] Paris: Minard. General title given to the collection of articles E685, E694, E710, E712, E715, E717.

E717 Robin, Christian. "Enseignements et directions de recherches universitaires (1969-1976)." ["Teachings and Directions of University Research"] Archives des lettres modernes, 161, No. 1 (June), 69-71.
Thanks the Grenoble Center of Bibliographical Documentation and Research, François Raymond, and other respondents to a questionnaire. Lists thirteen authors' names with bibliographical references and refers the reader to future issues of the Jules Verne series. See E716.

E718 Rosset, Clément. "Les Eaux étroites de Julien Gracq." ["Narrow Waters by Julien Gracq"] Le Quotidien de Paris, 24 December, n.p.
One of Gracq's favorite themes relates to a situation separated from the main current, in a neutral space, like works by Poe, Gérard de Nerval, and Verne. Verne's Steam House provides a finished model of a place safely isolated from the environment, an enclosure of security that glides among the Indies without ever coming into contact with them or being threatened by them. Gracq creates a similar locale.

E719 Taussat, Robert. "Les Machines et la décrépitude." ["Machines and Decrepitude"] BSJV, NS No. 39-40 (3rd & 4th Trimesters), pp. 167-169.
It may seem strange that the novels of Verne, the propagandist for technical progress (at least early in his career), should be strewn with the debris of all sorts of means of transport and other devices. Can this not symbolize an unconscious distrust of what man manufactures? Modern technology has enslaved us. And yet Verne's heroes manage to free themselves before it is too late.

E720 _____. "Mondial-Circus." ["World Circus"] BSJV, NS No. 37-38 (1st & 2nd Trimesters), pp. 127-143.
Despite the great success of the theater adaptation of Around the World in Eighty Days by Verne in collaboration with d'Ennery, many readers of the novel must have missed its rigorous structure. The novel offered the unity of action in the bet, the unity of time in the eighty days, and that of place in the Earth's spheroid. This last phenomenon makes the novel, taking place on a

circular stage, a kind of World Circus. Indeed, the 1972 adaptation was staged as theater in the round. Discusses the impact of this setting on plot, characters, and spectators.

E721 Terrasse, Pierre. "Etudes de Jules Verne." ["Studies of Jules Verne"] BSJV, NS No. 37-38 (1st & 2nd Trimesters), pp. 106-114.

Paper delivered before the General Assembly of the Jules Verne Society on February 28, 1976. Recounts Verne's years as a student, noting that it is not always the best students who succeed in life. Constant Latin quotations reflect Verne's early liking for the language.

E722 Terrasse, Pierre and François Raymond. "Glanes et notules." ["Gleanings and Notes"] BSJV, NS No. 39-40 (3rd & 4th Trimesters), pp. 170-172.

The existence of Louis Cornaro, mentioned in Claudius Bombarnac (chap. 6), may be verified in Bouillet's Dictionnaire Universel d'Histoire et de Géographie. Cornaro's Vita sobria was included in a list of readings composed by Auguste Comte.

E723 Terrasse, Pierre. "Le Tour du Monde au Théâtre." ["Around the World in the Theatre"] RLM, No. 456-461 (July-October), pp. 109-121.

Verne had more to do with Adolphe d'Ennery's dramatic adaptation of Around the World in Eighty Days than has been supposed. A new character, Archibald Cox, an American, marries Aouda's sister in the last act, and Passepartout is enabled to marry within his class, the servant Margaret. There are two shipwrecks, one of which adds a character, Nakahira, the Queen of Charmers. The play was very successful, with 415 performances between November 7, 1874 and December 20, 1875. With some additional materials, it ran again 177 times from June 1 to November 10, 1878. Put on again in 1886 by the Théâtre du Châtelet, the play reached its 1550th performance in 1898.

E724 Vierne, Simones. "Le Poète autour du monde." ["The Poet Around the World"] RLM, No. 456-461 (July-October), pp. 89-94.

What is interesting in Jean Cocteau's account of his retracing the steps of Verne's Phileas Fogg is the rela- tionship between the carefully constructed novel and Cocteau's imagination. Around the World in Eighty Days contains a myth in modern form, for to circle the globe is to recognize the limits of man's domain. Fogg's achievement resembles the surmounting of obstacles found in chivalric literature. And yet Fogg, although rescuing his lady, is a kind of antihero through the very excess of his qualities. Fogg is his voyage and is his quest of time and space. He can satisfy the aspirations of the imaginary if we but look through the eyes of a child or of a poet like Cocteau.

1977

E725   Anon. "Jules Verne à la radio et à la télévision." ["Jules Verne On Radio and Television"] BSJV, NS No. 41 (1st Trimester), p. 32.
Journey to the Center of the Earth, an American film by Henry Levin, was shown on French television. Despite some liberties taken with the text, this is one of the less objectionable film adaptations.

E726   Anon. "Le Nouveau Souffle de Jules Verne." ["Jules Verne's Second Wind"] Dernière Heure, Lyonnaise, 20 March, n.p.
Describes some of the Verne editions apparently spurred by the walk on the moon. On the heels of Verne, science fiction has expanded in all directions.

E727   Anon. "Voyage au centre de la terre." ["Journey to the Center of the Earth"] Toptélé, 19 January, p. 9.
Favorable review of the Hollywood adaptation. Warns lovers of realism to abstain.

E728   Barlow, Michel. Une Oeuvre; La Chasse au météore, Jules Verne; Un Thème de la science-fiction à la réalité; Einstein, P. Langevin, G. Bessière. [A Work; Chase of the Golden Meteor, Jules Verne; A Theme from Science Fiction to Reality] Paris: Hatier.
Integrates extracts from Chase of the Golden Meteor with other texts and accomplishments. Einstein, Langevin, and Bessière are used as a compass bearing on Verne's ideas.

E729   Compère, Daniel. Approche de l'île chez Jules Verne. [The Island Approach to Jules Verne]. Paris: Lettres Modernes.
Speculates on best method to use in studying Verne's novels. Finds the island arrival motif to be at the heart of the action. There are many variations among over a hundred and fifty arrivals at islands. Another portion of the book takes approaches in the areas of mythology, psychoanalysis, and ideology.

E730   _____. "Ce Bon Vieux Jules." ["That Good Old Jules"] Confluent, NS 27 (January), 6.
Verne never claimed to have invented anything. Did not wish to be considered an anticipator or prophet. When he wrote about cars, submarines, and airships, they were already half-discovered. His modernity comes not from technical and scientific progress, but rather from all the problems associated with it, including literary progress.

E731 _____. "Le Dernier Tyran." ["The Last Tyrant"] BSJV, NS
No. 43 (3rd Trimester), pp. 75-79.
A paper delivered before the General Assembly of the
Jules Verne Society on March 26, 1977. Observing the
cardinal rules for a pastiche, i.e., exaggeration and
derision, Compère creates one out of some of Verne's
texts.

E732 _____. "Le Tour en trois bandes et trente-trois tours."
["Around the World In Three Strips and Thirty-Three
Turns"] BSJV, NS No. 41 (1st Trimester), pp. 16-21.
Compares three illustrated strips of Around the World.
On the whole the reaction to them is unfavorable. Espe-
cially critical of the depiction of the main characters.

E733 _____. "Les Indes noires sur blanc." ["Child of the Cavern
on White"] BSJV, NS No. 42 (2nd Trimester), pp. 60-63.
Acknowledges other studies of Child of the Cavern by
Moré, Chotard, Serres, and Touttain, saying this one will
be about how Verne says things rather than about what he
says. Indicates precise vocabulary, mini-tales, sub-units,
spoken and written words that have the value of a prediction. Mentions debt to Scott and Cooper.

E734 _____. "Un Billet de loterie." ["Lottery Ticket"] BSJV,
NS No. 44 (4th Trimester), pp. 103-106.
Recounts a visit to the part of Norway described in
Lottery Ticket. The hamlet, Dal, still exists, despite
H. Pons's statement to the contrary (E581). Verne pre-
sents Norway as a utopia. The number of the lottery
ticket is seen to contain a secret and an enigma. The
ticket is the novel.

*E735 _____. Un Voyage imaginaire de Jules Verne: Voyage au
centre de la terre. [An Imaginary Voyage of Jules Verne:
Journey to the Center of the Earth] Paris: Litt. Mod.
Minard.
Not seen (cited in 1977 Modern Language Association
International Bibliography, p. 45, #2259).

E736 Courville, Luce. "Du Nouveau sur Famille-sans-nom."
["Something New on Family Without a Name"] BSJV, NS No.
41 (1st Trimester), p. 9.
In response to a question by Martin (E501), Firmin
Roz's Vue générale de l'histoire du Canada (Paris:
Hartmann, 1934) shows there really was a ship named
La Caroline, and that it was set afire by some loyalist
volunteers.

E737 _____. "Les 32 Bonnes Adresses de Jules Verne." ["Jules Verne's Thirty-Two Good Addresses"] BSJV, NS No. 43 (3rd Trimester), pp. 71-74.

Speculates on why Verne gives specific addresses to many of his characters, most addresses being in the United States (fourteen). From 1864 on the author consistently does this. To establish a link between an address and a personality is difficult, although Fogg's indicates that this hero of movement has a very fixed point in his life; namely, 7 Saville Row. One wonders whether the reading of Balzac influenced Verne in this area.

E738 Danzas, Minnie. "Un Monstre sympathique." ["A Likeable Monster"] France-Soir, 26 January, n.p.

A favorable review of Henry Levin's film adaptation of Journey to the Center of the Earth, although the connection between novel and film is tenuous. The film captured 33 percent of the viewing audience and elicited greater satisfaction than shows on the other channels.

E739 Droin, Richard. "Les Rêves extraordinaires de Jules Verne." ["The Extraordinary Dreams of Jules Verne"] BSJV, NS No. 42 (2nd Trimester), pp. 50-53.

Resumé of a doctoral thesis. Verne's voyages have in common their beginnings and endings surrounding the central telling of the tale. The beginnings and endings are marked by a loss of consciousness or a passivity. The thesis will make a psychoanalytical reading of Verne to show him accomplishing an exclusively psychological voyage from the conscious to the unconscious. The "Other Scene" becomes for the hero the new psychic dimension of his extraordinary adventure.

E740 Dumas, Olivier. "Bibliographie des Voyages extraordinaires." ["Bibliography of the Extraordinary Voyages"] BSJV, NS No. 41 (1st Trimester), pp. 22-29.

Re-edits and brings up to date, pending the appearance of Gondolo della Riva's bibliography, the bibliography begun in the first issues of BSJV. Much descriptive factual information about publications.

E741 _____. "Hector Servadac à 100 ans." ["Hector Servadac at One Hundred Years"] BSJV, NS No. 42 (2nd Trimester), pp. 54-59.

This paper was delivered before the General Assembly of the Jules Verne Society on March 26, 1977. Discusses some differences between the Magasin d'éducation et de récréation edition of Hector Servadac and the Hetzel edition. Also explains Verne's anti-Semitism on the grounds that Verne, contrary to nineteenth century practice, scorned money and usurers and was perhaps

affected by his son's indebtedness to the latter. Shows
that this novel well illustrates Droin's points. See
E739.

E742 Goimard, Jacques. "Prologue dans le logos." ["Prologue
      In the Logos"] Europe, 55, No. 581 (August-September),
      3-13.
         Preface to a science fiction issue. France produced
      several first rate science fiction writers at a time
      when the only comparable foreign author was Wells.
      Children's literature became enormously important, with
      Verne integrating into it the theme of the extraordinary
      voyage, borrowing from the utopian and anti-utopian
      concepts carried into the area of the fantastic. A
      consequence of this was that for a long time science
      fiction was considered to consist solely of this
      Vernian current.

E743 Gondolo della Riva, Piero. Bibliographie analytique de
      toutes les oêuvres de Jules Verne. [Analytical Bibliogra-
      phy of All the Works of Jules Verne] Vol. I. Paris:
      Société Jules Verne.
         First of two volumes. Volume I contains bibliographi-
      cal data on novels, short stories, and other fictional
      works. Volume II will deal with nonfiction, unpublished
      works, plays, and correspondence. Probably will be the
      standard bibliography of primary material.

E744 _____. "L'Affaire Pilote du Danube." ["The Danube Pilot
      Case"] BSJV, NS No. 44 (4th Trimester), pp. 99-102.
         Paper delivered to the Jules Verne Colloquium in
      Amiens, November 11, 1977. Verne won a suit for defama-
      tion brought by chemist Eugène Turpin, who thought he
      recognized himself in the character Thomas Roch of For
      the Flag, and Michel Verne won one brought by Jackel Semo
      for the use of his name assigned to a bandit in Danube
      Pilot. Verne did not use the name in the original
      version; Michel remembered the name of a man he once met
      on the Danube.

E745 Goracci, Serge. "Jules Verne: un romancier populaire?"
      ["Jules Verne: A Popular Novelist?"] BSJV, NS No. 42
      (2nd Trimester), pp. 38-42.
         Opposes those who see Verne as a writer addressing
      the people and even the workers. Verne reached an
      adolescent public thanks to serial publication and stage
      adaptations as well as public libraries. Verne addressed
      comparatively homogeneous groups of adolescents belonging
      to his own class, transmitted fundamentally middle-class
      values, and we should not make of him a product of popular
      culture.

E746 _____. "Verne et Tourguéneff." ["Verne and Turgenev"]
BSJV, NS No. 41 (1st Trimester), pp. 10-12.
Hetzel asked Turgenev to read a manuscript of what
would become Michel Strogoff. Verne and Turgenev had
a similar temperment, shared a sensitivity to the
principle of nationality, a belief that man could trans-
form Nature, an admiration for Americans, and a devotion
to the idea of "the new man." Above all, they both moved
toward a vision of a tragic world.

E747 Helling, Cornélis. "Glanes et notules." ["Gleanings and
Notes"] BSJV, NS No. 42 (2nd Trimester), p. 54.
A review of a book on the Cunard Line mentions that
Cunard's last paddle-driven ship was the Scotia that
figures in Twenty Thousand Leagues Under the Sea. Even
though the collision of the Scotia and the Nautilus is
a minor episode in the novel, this shows a widespread
continuing interest in the ship.

E748 Koster, Sergé. "A Propos de Jules Verne: de quelques
apparitions de l'auteur." ["Concerning Jules Verne:
About Some of the Author's Guises"] BSJV, NS No. 42
(2nd Trimester), pp. 43-49.
Identifies Verne himself in the following characters,
among others: Dr. Dean Pitferge, Dr. Clawbunny, Van
Mitten. Verne takes delight in absenting himself from
his works only to appear in a character or perhaps
merely in a footnote.

E749 Lacarrière, Jacques. "Le Goulag du bonheur." [Gulag of
Happiness"] Nouvelles Littéraires, 6 January, n.p.
Part of the preface to a new edition of a little-known
work of Restif de la Bretonne, La Découverte australe.
Like Cyrano de Bergerac, Restif chooses the air as his
heroes' means of liberation. Verne in a way carries
this a step further in such works as Clipper of the
Clouds and Master of the World. Restif's novel might
perhaps be considered one of anticipation, as well as
a tale of utopian nature. As a dreamer, Restif in some
respects appears closer to Verne and Wells than to the
"philosophers" of his time.

E750 Laroche, Robert de. "Pour Haroun Tazieff Le Voyage au
centre de la terre est une aberration." ["For Haroun
Tazieff, Journey to the Center of the Earth is a Mistake"]
Toptélé, 19 January, p. 45.
In connection with Levin's film version, Haroun Tazieff,
an expert on volcanoes, states that Verne's fantasy is
very far from reality. He notes three sources of inspiration: historical and geographical vulgarization, serious
science fiction, and pure fiction.

E751 M., Ph. "Du Côté d'Averty." ["Toward Averty"] Espoir
      Tours, 1 January, n.p.
         Favorable review of Averty's television adaptation
      of Castle of the Carpathians. This interesting, little-
      known novel combines elements of the imaginary, surreal-
      ism, and science fiction. Verne foresaw television and
      also realized that science might be put to evil ends.
      This novel offers an example of the evil scientist.
      (For an unfavorable review, see Georges Suffert, Le
      Point, December 27, 1976).

E752 Margot, Jean-Michel. "Jules Verne: Catalogue par mot-clés
      et par auteurs." ["Jules Verne: Catalogue By Key Words
      and By Authors"] BSJV, NS No. 41 (1st Trimester), pp.
      30-31.
         Announces a catalogue, not just a list of Verne
      editions, with more than seven hundred entries to help
      those doing research on Verne.

E753 Olivier-Martin, Yves. "Autour de Jules Verne." ["Around
      Jules Verne"] BSJV, NS No. 43 (3rd Trimester), pp.
      82-83.
         One measure of the importance of Verne's work is the
      writing of many books and pieces in which Verne or his
      characters figure, often in an amusing way. Among the
      authors of these works are Tristan Bernard, Curnonski,
      Oscar de Poli, and Gilbert d'Alem.

E754 Olivier-Martin, Yves and Jacques Goimard. "Les Noms."
      ["Names"] Europe, 55, No. 581 (August-September),
      20-22.
         Discusses the problem of giving a name to works that
      one would wish to classify as science fiction. Wells
      used the expression "scientific romances." In Verne's
      time a host of works appeared centering on the theme of
      discovery. Hetzel produced the name Voyages extraordin-
      aires. Other titles of the time included Voyages excen-
      triques and Voyages fantastiques.

E755 Omoo. "Géographies." L'Alsace, Mulhouse, 18 August, n.p.
         Verne speaks of the Scottish Isle of Stoffa in his
      little-known work Green Ray, and writes elsewhere in a
      rather partisan tone of Pitcairn Island and the famous
      mutiny on the Bounty.

E756 Police, Gérard. Jules Verne au Portugal; La Bretagne, Le
      Portugal, Le Brésil; Echanges et Rapports. [Jules Verne
      In Portugal; Brittany, Portugal, Brazil; Exchanges and
      Reports] Nantes: U. de Nantes, pp. 433-441.
         Verne gives little place to Portuguese and Brazilians
      in his works. However, the translation of the Voyages

307

extraordinaires into Portuguese was immediate. Discusses anthologies and encyclopedias in which Verne appears. Brazil is more conscious than Portugal of the ties between Verne's scientific work and modern literature of anticipation.

E757 Pourvoyeur, R[obert]. "Glanes et notules: Un Prédécesseur peu connu de Hans Pfaall." ["Gleanings and Notes: A Little-Known Predecessor of Hans Pfaall"] BSJV, NS No. 44 (4th Trimester), p. 108.

Verne analyzes Poe's "The Unparalleled Adventures of One Hans Pfaall" in a Musée de familles essay in 1864, and the story is cited in From the Earth to the Moon. The Dutch writer Willem Bilderdijk (1756-1831) anticipated Poe in Brief Narration of a Remarkable Aerial Trip and the Discovery of a New Planet (1811).

E758 _____. "Kéraban au théâtre." ["Kéraban in the Theater"] BSJV, NS No. 44 (4th Trimester), pp. 111-119.

Verne's play Kéraban the Inflexible (1883) was not published. Verne thought in terms of the play when he wrote the novel on which it is based. The play was a failure, and Verne attributed this to the actors' not being comic actors. A number of negative assessments of the play are quoted.

E759 _____. "Le Page de Madame Malbrough." ["Madame Malborough's Page"] BSJV, NS No. 43 (3rd Trimester), pp. 80-81.

L. Henry Lecomte attributes to Verne a one-act operetta entitled Le Page de Madame Malbrough. It remains to be proven whether this attribution is correct. If Verne was the author, he may have chosen a pseudonym thinking the subject of the operetta didn't quite correspond to the sedateness required by his recent marriage and his connection with the Stock Exchange.

E760 _____. "Une Autre Lecture de Nord contre Sud." ["Another Reading of North Against South"] BSJV, NS No. 43 (3rd Trimester), pp. 84-88.

Verne must have felt that the best way to understand the globe was to submit it to the discipline of geometry and trigonometry. His characters are happiest when plotting a position, when figuring longitudes and latitudes. His liking for points or lines placed on a map may have sprung from his desire to see Man make his mark. Hence Hatteras and Nemo want to have direct contact with the North and South Poles respectively. In North Against South the number three and the triangle are important to the structure.

E761   Raymond, François. "De Jules Verne à Raymond Roussel."
        ["From Jules Verne to Raymond Roussel"] BSJV, NS No. 44
        (4th Trimester), pp. 109-110.
            In a television program based on the work of Raymond
        Roussel, "Impressions d'Afrique," Jean-Christophe Averty
        used illustrations from the Hetzel editions as background.

E762   _____. "Glanes et notules." ["Gleanings and Notes"] BSJV,
        NS No. 44 (4th Trimester), p. 107.
            Philip José Farmer's The Other Log of Phileas Fogg is
        in a sense a critical reading of Around the World in
        Eighty Days and Twenty Thousand Leagues Under the Sea.
        His story confirms the mythological dimension of Fogg
        and Nemo. Verne's heroes achieve their place among the
        heroes of our time. See D381, E688.

E763   Robin, Christian. "Jules Verne à l'université." ["Jules
        Verne In the Universities"] BSJV, NS No. 42 (2nd Tri-
        mester), pp. 35-37.
            A list of some theses prepared and some topics dis-
        cussed at French universities, 1965-1977, all having to
        do with Verne.

E764   _____. "Jules Verne à l'université." ["Jules Verne In the
        Universities"] BSJV, NS No. 43 (3rd Trimester), pp.
        69-70.
            Journey to the Center of the Earth, the Verne novel
        most often studied in the universities, has been included
        in the program of the "agrégation" degree, which means it
        will be read more widely than ever. This suggests that
        a reevaluation of Verne is under way. Other course
        activities are described.

E765   _____. "Livre et musée: sources et fins de l'éducation
        encyclopédique proposée aux jeunes lecteurs de Jules
        Verne." ["Book and Museum: Sources and Goals of the
        Encyclopedic Education Suggested to Young Readers of
        Jules Verne"] Actes du 97th Congrès National des
        sociétés savantes, Nantes, II, 473-486.
            In Verne's works the scientist is presented as a
        constant student, every bit of acquired knowledge lending
        itself to becoming the immediate object of instruction.
        There is an evolution in the scientists who are narrators.
        The scientists are devoted to museums as well as books.
        A reading of the Musée des familles or the Magasin
        d'éducation et de récréation shows that Verne shared
        approaches with other writers.

E766   _____. "Modernité de Jules Verne." ["Jules Verne's
        Modernity"] Europe, 55, No. 581 (August-September),
        170-175.

A quite detailed account of articles published in a small volume, Le Développement des études sur Jules Verne, in Archives des lettres modernes (E716).

E767   Terrasse, Pierre. "Glanes et notules." ["Gleanings and Notes"] BSJV, NS No. 42 (2nd Trimester), p. 64.
       A recent article in Le Figaro (April 5, 1977) brings to mind that in the last century Orélie-Antoine I, a former lawyer in Périgueux, held the throne of Araucania. Orélie I is mentioned in Captain Grant's Children, in which Paganel says it's perhaps easier for a lawyer to make a good king than vice versa.

E768   Terrasse, René. "L'Eau qui flambe." ["Water That Ignites"] BSJV, NS No. 41 (1st Trimester), pp. 13-15.
       Paper delivered to the General Assembly of the Jules Verne Society on February 28, 1976. Contemporary use of hydrogen as a source of power (it is already being used in industry) and the process of electrolysis in its conversion shows that Cyrus Smith in The Mysterious Island was prophetic in his discussion of the future necessity to replace traditional sources of power as they become exhausted.

E769   Tournier, Michel. "A Propos de Marcel Brion L'Allemagne romantique, III; Les Voyages initiatiques" (Michel Albin). ["Concerning Marcel Brion's Romantic Germany, III; Initiatory Voyages"] La Nouvelle Critique, June, pp. 106-107.
       Calls Stendahl's Le Rouge et le noir and Cervantes's Don Quixote novels of confrontation rather than of initiation because the hero in each case is not embarking on a successful tour of events that will educate him. And yet Around the World in Eighty Days is an example of a novel of confrontation that is triumphant. Fogg sets out on his journey with a head full of book learning, but unlike Quixote he has learned the practical information to enable him to achieve his goal. If Fogg had given up his bet after discovering Hindu philosophy, if Quixote had given up his dreams and become reasonable, their authors would have written novels of initiation.

E770   V., J. Volga ou Le Châtelet retrouvé. [Volga or The Little Castle Found] La Croix, 24 January, n.p.
       In a review of the operatta Volga, it is stated that much is owed by its libretto to Michel Strogoff. It contains a courier of the Czar, the cossack Colonel Boris Gorski, sent to Volga Maya to stamp out a peasant revolt, who falls in love with the beautiful leader of the insurgents to the point of espousing her cause, thus jeopardizing his honor and his life. The relationship to Potemkin seems quite distant.

E771   Van Rolleghem, John. "Jules Verne, précurseur de l'an
       2000." ["Jules Verne, Precursor of the Year 2000"]
       Touring, No. 887 (January), pp. 18-25.
           Accompanied by a number of illustrations from Verne's
       novels and three pictures connected with his life, the
       article evokes especially the Nantes, Paris, and Amiens
       in which he lived. A number of quotations are from the
       studies of Michel Serre and André Touttain.

E772   Versins, Pierre. "L'Art dans la S.F." ["Art in Science
       Fiction"] Confluent, NS 27 (January), pp. 4-5.
           Verne will remain one of the rare anticipators to
       have really spoken of a revolutionary music in Floating
       Island.

1978

E773   Anon. "Actualitiés de Jules Verne." ["News of Jules Verne"]
       BSJV, NS No. 46 (2nd Trimester), pp. 155-157.
           News of various recent activities including Verne
       fairs, expositions, and publications, including a Moscow
       book by E. Brandis.

E774   Anon. "Hommage philatélique à J. Verne au Musée de Picardie."
       ["Philatelic Homage to J. Verne In the Picardy Museum"]
       Le Courrier Picard, 6 February, n.p.
           Report on a philatelic exposition at the Picardy
       Museum in honor of the 150th anniversary of the birth of
       Verne.

E775   Anon. "Jules Verne." Bulletin des services culturels de
       L'Ambassade de France aux Etats-Unis, 13 (December),
       n.p.
           Verne is being rediscovered as one of the fathers of
       science fiction, and yet he remains something of an un-
       known behind whose facade there is a being hurt by life
       and the passions within. Verne presents masks in the
       style of "Commedia dell' Arte," portrays Americans as
       nationalists willing to share discoveries with the rest
       of the world, and, though privately conservative, opposes
       such pillars of society as police, justice, and prison
       in his works. Comments on illustrators, inventions, and
       recent critics.

E776   Anon. "Jules Verne et le Carquois." ["Jules Verne and the
       Carquois"] Picardie laïque, No. 218 (January-February),
       pp. 7-8.
           The players known as La Troupe Le Carquois in Amiens
       gave a group of plays and programs to celebrate the 150th
       anniversary of Verne's birth. The first theme was "The

Marvelous Voyages of Jules Verne," a second featured
Purchase of the North Pole. Hoped to show that Verne,
though born in Nantes, belonged to Amiens, and produced
a cosmopolitan and futuristic work.

E777   Anon. "La Carte à payer." ["The Payment Card"] In César
       Cascabel, by Jules Verne. Paris: Union Général
       d'editions, pp. 437-438.
            This anonymous article appeared June 25, 1889, in the
       "Journal d'Amiens." At the inauguration of the Amiens
       Circus (Verne's favorite entertainment), the cost was
       estimated to be high. But the circus will cost less
       than indicated; no new taxes are necessary.

E778   Anon. "Le Musée Jules Verne." ["The Jules Verne Museum"]
       Nantes votre ville, No. 4 (April), pp. 6-8.
            Comments on the new Jules Verne Museum, whose goal is
       to make Verne accessible to the public and not merely to
       a small circle of researchers.

E779   Anon. "Le Passionnant roman que Jules Verne aurait pu
       écrire: Foire expo an 78." ["The Exciting Novel That
       Jules Verne Could Have Written: Fair Expo Year 78"]
       Special: Foire-exposition de Picardie. Official News-
       paper of the Fair-Exposition of Picardie.
            For the first time in its thirty-nine year history,
       the Picardy Fair-Exposition is featuring the name of a
       famous writer, Verne. The genius of Verne presides over
       the fair: his inventiveness, his love of Amiens, his
       imagination that fed on so many localities in Picardy.

E780   Anon. "Un Jules Verne peu connu." ["A Little-Known Work by
       Jules Verne"] Presse-Océan, 2 February, p. 4.
            Discusses Verne's "Count of Chanteleine," which
       concerns the glory of the Royal and Catholic army and the
       resistance to the Revolution in lower Brittany. Verne's
       plan to publish a second edition fifteen years after the
       original was vetoed by Hetzel because he did not want
       to offend part of his clientele.

E781   Baras, Jean-Pol. "Editorial." Dossiers du cacef, No. 57
       (April), p. 1.
            Verne remains an enigma despite numerous studies.
       See E792, E833, E841, E845, E858, E863.

E782   Belloc, Marie A. "Interview de Jules Verne." ["Interview
       of Jules Verne"] RLM, No. 523-529 (April-June), pp.
       142-152.
            Originally published in 1895 in the Strand Magazine
       (D30); also published in Journal d'Amiens, November,
       26-27, 1933.

E783   Blanc, Bernard. <u>Pourquoi J'ai tué Jules Verne</u>. [<u>Why I
Killed Jules Verne</u>] Paris: Stock.
A study in which the author claims to have killed
Verne. The fantasy of the author is combined with that
of his hero.

E784   Blum, Léon. "Préface." In <u>Invasion de la mer</u> [<u>Invasion
of the Sea</u>], by Jules Verne. Paris: Union Générale
d'editions.
Appeared in <u>L'Humanité</u>, April 3, 1905, a few days
after Verne's death. Protests the neglect of Verne.
Why should those who write for the people be ignored, "a
priori?" His work will keep its educational and pedagogical value for a long time. His first works are best,
but he must be judged on the total work. The verdict
must be positive when one thinks of Verne's enormous
educational and moral influence on the young. <u>See</u> E361.

E785   Bottin, André. <u>Bibliographie des éditions illustrées des
"Voyages extraordinaires" de Jules Verne en cartonnage
d'éditeur de la collection Hetzel</u>. [<u>Bibliography of the
Illustrated Editions of Jules Verne's "Extraordinary
Voyages" In the Publisher's Bindings of the Hetzel Col-
lection</u>] Paris: Bottin.
Chronology of Verne and his times. Detailed descrip-
tions of the covers of the <u>Voyages</u> in the Hetzel collec-
tion. Bibliography of works and articles relating to
Verne.

*E786   Buisine, Alain. "Circulations en tous genres." ["Publishings
in All Genres"] <u>Europe</u>, 56, No. 595-596 (November-December),
48-56.
Not seen (will be cited in 1978 <u>Modern Language Association International Bibliography</u>, #2413).

E787   _____. "Repères, marques, gisements: à propos de la
robinsonnade vernienne." ["Landmarks, Markers, Bearings:
Concerning the Vernian Robinsonade"] <u>RLM</u>, No. 523-529
(April-June), pp. 113-139.
Defoe's Crusoe moves from an original fault to follow
a positive itinerary of development and progress. Ayrton
of <u>The Mysterious Island</u>, placed initially in the same
position, represents the opposite movement toward disintegration and regression. Variations of the motif
during the nineteenth century are discussed. In Verne
it is present collectively rather than in one person.
The "robinsonade" must be passed because it represents
the persistence of a condition that is becoming daily
more archaic.

E788　Chevrel, Yves. "Questions de méthodes et d'idéologies chez
　　　　Verne et Zola: Les Cinq Cent Millions de la Begum et
　　　　Travail." ["Questions of Methods and Ideologies in
　　　　Verne and Zola: The Begum's Fortune and Work"] RLM,
　　　　No. 523-529 (April-June), pp. 69-96.
　　　　　　Despite differences between the works of Verne and
　　　　Zola and the authors' mutual dislike, these two novels
　　　　show that there are affinities also. Both are concerned
　　　　with the victory of good over evil, but Verne's story
　　　　moves forward in a linear fashion whereas Zola's constantly
　　　　moves back to furnish explanations. In Zola money is a
　　　　force and is necessary to those who would operate in
　　　　society; in Verne money just exists, sometimes in fabulous
　　　　sums. The contrast between Verne and Zola is not one of
　　　　an optimistic anticipator opposed to a pessimistic
　　　　realist, but rather between a man turned to the past and
　　　　a man turned to the future.

E789　Compère, Cécile. "Jules Verne et la misogynie." ["Jules
　　　　Verne and Misogyny"] BSJV, NS No. 48 (4th Trimester),
　　　　pp. 248-252.
　　　　　　The charge of misogyny against Verne in his personal
　　　　life is not always well founded. As for his novels,
　　　　they contain more than one hundred and sixty women.
　　　　Without being intellectuals or scientists, some of them
　　　　undertake expeditions, and others encourage men to do so.
　　　　One must remember that woman's role both in society and
　　　　in literature was very limited in the nineteenth century.
　　　　Mme Compère's current research will make comparisons be-
　　　　tween the women in Verne's works and those in the works
　　　　of contemporaries in order better to assess the feminine
　　　　role.

E790　Compère, Daniel. "Exposition: les machines de Jules
　　　　Verne." In Année Jules Verne 1978. ["Exposition:
　　　　Machines of Jules Verne." In The Jules Verne Year 1978.]
　　　　Amiens: Office Culturel, p. 2.
　　　　　　This brochure put out by the Cultural Service of
　　　　Amiens and the Jules Verne Society lists programs honor-
　　　　ing the 150th anniversary of his birth. Verne never
　　　　claimed to have invented anything. His "machines" are
　　　　often means of transport or of communication inspired
　　　　by real inventions. And yet they remain imaginary.
　　　　Ephemeral, they disappear at the story's end. They have
　　　　scientific origins and literary functions.

E791　_____. "Le Fin Mot dans Voyages au centre de la terre."
　　　　["Tricky Word in Journey to the Center of the Earth"]
　　　　RLM, No. 523-529 (April-June), pp. 165-171.
　　　　　　Often in Verne the enigma is wrapped in a single word
　　　　that gives the hidden meaning of a thing and occurs at

the end of the novel. This key word may appear in different forms: in Giant Raft it emanates from a cryptogram, in Captain Grant's Children it is disguised by
apheresis, in The Mysterious Island it is disguised by
translation. Discusses the key word "envers" in Journey
to the Center of the Earth. Shows that the function of
the enigma is to mime the text. The quest of the secret
constitutes the secret itself.

E792 _____. "L'Ile à ellipse." ["Ellipsis Island"] Dossiers
du cacef, No. 57 (April), pp. 24-29.
Verne's use of the island theme places him in the
tradition of the novel of adventure as seen from the
Odyssey to Robinson Crusoe. However, there is more to
it than this. Verne's island themes reveal hidden
facets of the The Mysterious Island. One may speak,
then, of the island of ellipsis. The dissimulations
function in three ways: to transfer personal ideas, to
establish a distance to the adventure, to play with the
imaginary.

*E793 _____. "Jules Verne et la modernité." ["Jules Verne and
Modernity"] Europe, 56, No. 595-596 (November-December),
27-36.
Not seen (will be cited in 1978 Modern Language
Association International Bibliography #2416).

E794 _____. "Pourquoi Jules Verne?" In Année Jules Verne 1978
["Why Jules Verne?" In The Jules Verne Year 1978]
Amiens: Office Culturel, n.p.
For several years a new Verne has appeared, worthy of
figuring among great writers of the nineteenth century
like Hugo, Balzac, and Zola. Verne was a political as
well as literary figure. His less well known facets
must be brought to light.

E795 _____. La Vie amiénoise de Jules Verne. [Jules Verne's
Life In Amiens] Amiens: Annales du centre régional de
documentation pédagogique.
Admittedly not a complete biography, this work seeks
to treat aspects of Verne's life that have to do with
Amiens, using documents unavailable to others. Also
contains information on his stays in Crotoy and Tréport.
There are also a few less well known texts and some
pictures.

E796 _____. La Vie de Jules Verne [The Life of Jules Verne]
Amiens: Centre de Documentation Jules Verne.
Concentrates almost exclusively on Verne's private
life. Says his nephew shot him because he would not lend
him the money to go to England. Purchase of the North

Pole is the beginning of Verne's satirical view. Calls
the political aspect of his work bolder than the technical extrapolations.

E797 Compère, Daniel and Peter Hoy. "Bibliographie 1974." RLM,
No. 523-529 (April-June), pp. 185-197.
Continues through 1974 the bibliography of Verne
studies in French begun in E715.

E798 Courville, Luce. "Au Nom du père." ["In the Name of the
Father"] BSJV, NS No. 45 (1st Trimester), pp. 132-136.
The name Pierre, which was Verne's father's, occurs
often in Verne's works and in interesting ways: as the
name of the principal character, a character playing a
symbolic role, and as a walk-on's name. Represents
three aspects of the elder Verne's personality: the
sensitive, the strict (in moral matters), and the devout
(with Jansenist tendencies).

*E799 Coutrix-Gouaux, Mireille and Pierre Souffrin. "A Propos de
matière et énergie chez J. Verne." ["Concerning Matter
And Energy In Jules Verne"] Europe, 56, No. 595-596
(November-December), 67-72.
Not seen (will be cited in 1978 Modern Language
Association International Bibliography, #2419).

*E800 _____. "Mythologie vernienne." ["Vernian Mythology"]
Europe, 56, No. 595-596 (November-December), 10-18.
Not seen (will be cited in 1978 Modern Language
Association International Bibliography, #2420).

E801 Decré, Françoise. Catalogue du fond Jules Verne. [Catalogue
of the Jules Verne Deposit] Nantes: Bibliothèque Municipale. Centre Jules Verne.
Lists 2454 printed items in the permanent Verne collection in the municipal library of Nantes, plus 129
manuscripts.

E802 Doukan, Dr. G. "Un Auteur à succès malheureux en amour:
Jules Verne." ["Successful Author Unhappy In Love:
Jules Verne"] BSJV, NS No. 48 (4th Trimester), pp.
239-247.
Women in Verne's works have either a subaltern role
in relation to men or sometimes an almost masculine
capacity for decision and a virile courage and behavior.
Rejects previous critics' various suggestions that explain
the absence of sexual love in Verne's works on personal
disappointments before his marriage or on a latent
homosexuality. There is something close to pathological

in the absence of sexual love from the works. Verne
was an egocentric whose sole passion was writing. He
considered his wife frivolous and shallow. Her love
for him was maternal and domineering, hence his hostility
to marriage.

E803 Doye, Liliane. "Géographie -- Encyclopédies." ["Geography
-- Encyclopedias"] Dossiers du cacef, No. 57 (April),
pp. 58-59.
Favorable review of Géographie illustrée de la France
et de ses colonies. Combines clarity and modernity;
administrative, economic, and historical elements are
joined to the purely geographical description.

E804 Dumas, Dr. Olivier. "1978: Centenaire du Capitaine de
quinze ans." ["1978: Centenary of Dick Sands, the Boy
Captain] BSJV, NS No. 46 (2nd Trimester), pp. 164-168.
Paper given before the Jules Verne Society on April
8, 1978. Before writing Dick Sands, the Boy Captain,
Verne faced a number of family problems including his
son Michel's revolt. Dick Sands is a combination of
Michel and Verne. Verne also scrupulously transmitted
the facts of Lieutenant Cameron's "A Travers L'Afrique;
De Zanzibar à Benguela" (1877). The novel pleases the
young for combining fairy tale qualities with realism.

E805 Editorial Committee. "Réponses à une enquête: Jules Verne
est-il un romancier populaire?" ["Replies To An Investigation: Is Jules Verne A 'Popular' Novelist?"] BSJV,
NS No. 46 (2nd Trimester), pp. 174-181.
A number of people explain their replies to the
question whether Verne is a "popular" novelist or not.
Positive replies from Evelyne Diebolt, Marc Soriano (who
insists on distinguishing among the novels), Jean Leclerq
(after about 1890 when Verne is abandoned by the middle-
class), Yves-Olivier Martin. Jacques Goimard's reply is
from an article on the serial novel and so touches
obliquely on Verne. The replies show the difficulty of
generalizing on this question and prove the importance
of definitions.

E806 Foletier, François de Vaux de. "Les Tsiganes dans l'oeuvre
de Jules Verne." ["Gypsies in the Works of Jules Verne"]
Études Tsiganes, 24 (March), 49-54.
Discusses the presence and sources of gypsies in
Verne's works with particular reference to The Castle
of the Carpathians and Mathias Sandorf. Music was a
kind of bond between Verne and the gypsies.

E807 Gaigneron, Axelle de. "Jules Verne cet inconnu." ["Unknown
      Jules Verne"] Connaissance des arts, No. 314 (April), pp.
      88-94.
           The twentieth century has discovered Verne. Psychol-
      ogists, sociologists, and representatives of other fields
      have enlarged the study of Verne beyond literary criti-
      cism, and have thus made him the object of an interdisci-
      plinary approach. Mention is made of the new Center for
      Verne Research in Nantes.

*E808 Garavito, Julian. "Jules Verne et l'Amérique latine."
      ["Jules Verne and Latin America"] Europe, 56, No. 595-596
      (November-December), 138-145.
           Not seen (will be cited in 1978 Modern Language
      Association International Bibliography, #2422).

*E809 Gondolo della Riva, Piero. "A Propos des oeuvres posthumes
      de Jules Verne." ["About the Posthumous Works of Jules
      Verne"] Europe, 56, No. 595-596 (November-December),
      73-81.
           Not seen (will be cited in 1978 Modern Language
      Association International Bibliography, #2423).

*E810 _____. "La Chasse au météore." ["The Chase of the Golden
      Meteor"] Europe, 56, No. 595-596 (November-December),
      83-88.
           Not seen (will be cited in 1978 Modern Language
      Association International Bibliography, #2424).

E811 _____. "A Propos du Manuscrit de 'Storitz.'" ["Concerning
      the Manuscript of 'Storitz'"] BSJV, NS No. 46 (2nd Tri-
      mester), pp. 160-163.
           Paper given before the General Assembly of the Jules
      Verne Society, April 8, 1978. In a foreword to this
      article Dr. Olivier Dumas reminds us that in 1967 the
      authenticity of Verne's posthumous works seemed to have
      been established. Now Gondolo della Riva has reopened
      the whole question. The latter compares Michel Verne's
      published version of the Secret of Wilhelm Storitz to
      his father's manuscript. Differences exist in chronology,
      plot, and style.

E812 Goracci, Serge. Jules Verne éléments pour une utilisation
      pédagogique de son oeuvre. [Jules Verne -- Elements
      For a Pedagogical Utilization of His Works] Nice:
      Centre Régional du Documentation Pédagogique.
           A pedagogical tool directed at teachers of French and
      History-Geography of Cycle 1 and Cycle 2. Some of the
      Verne novels might be useful in the middle course of
      elementary teaching. A schematic arrangement of themes
      and topics emanating from Verne's works. Geography and
      the sciences are prominent.

E813 Guillon, Yves. "Jules Verne et sa famille." ["Jules Verne
      and His Family"] Bulletin Société archéologique d'Ile-
      et-Vilaine, 82 (1978), 121-138.
           Claims to be based on unpublished documents. Others
      have not emphasized sufficiently that the society of
      Nantes was a highly literary one quite likely to in-
      fluence Verne toward the career he chose. Considers his
      little-mentioned poetry sensitive and delicate.

E814 In'hui, 3 (Spring), 1-85.
           A poem to morphine, attributed to Verne, opens this
      volume containing a number of pieces parodying Verne's
      themes, inventions, plots, and language.

E815 Jacquier, Jean-François. "Dirigeables: un avenir léger."
      ["Dirigibles. A Light Future"] L'Express (Internation-
      al Edition), No. 1416 (28 August-3 September), 33.
           Finds an analogy between the transatlantic balloon
      crossing of Abbruzo, Newman, and Anderson and the
      wondrous world of Verne. Their exploit, like the ex-
      ploits of Verne's adventures, is rooted in the real and
      the imaginary, in technology, and the dream. Discusses
      future possibilities of the balloon, especially as a
      carrier of freight.

*E816 Lacassin, Francis. "Le Communard qui écrivit trois romans
      de Jules Verne." ["The 'Communard' Who Wrote Three
      Jules Verne Novels"] Europe, 56, No. 595-596 (November-
      December), 94-105.
           Not seen (will be cited in 1978 Modern Language
      Association International Bibliography, #2427.

E817 _____. "Introduction." In L'Invasion de la mer, by Jules
      Verne. [Invasion of the Sea] Paris: Union Générale
      d'éditions.
           Invasion of The Sea, written late in Verne's career,
      and "Martin Paz," written early, show the continuity of
      Verne's work. Both concern the struggle of an oppressed
      majority against a colonial power, in the latter against
      the Spaniards, in the former against the French. Verne
      shows that he prefers justice to the marvels of science
      and to frenetic growth. Here again he is an innovator.

E818 _____. "Préface." In Jules Verne, Histoires inattendues.
      [Jules Verne, Unexpected Stories] Paris: Union Générale
      d'éditions, pp. 7-14.
           The eight texts chosen for this edition serve to
      reveal a Verne somewhat different from the traditional
      view. They show how diversified were his works and also
      the forgotten antecedents of the unusual aspects of a
      work that beneath its diversity obeys an underlying and
      remarkable continuity.

E819   Margot, Jean-Michel. <u>Bibliographie documentaire sur Jules</u>
        <u>Verne</u>. [Documentary Bibliography on Jules Verne]
        Ostermundigen: Margot.
            1300 documents are cited: books, articles, prefaces,
        etc., in about 280 pages. Contents include an introduc-
        tion, the statistics on documents published annually,
        between 1864 and 1978, a catalogue by key words, an
        author catalogue, a call number catalogue, a list of
        Verne's works, and a documentary thesaurus on Verne.
        (This volume was received too late to be of help in this
        study.)

E820   Margot, J[ean]-M[ichel]. "Jules Verne et la Suisse."
        ["Jules Verne and Switzerland"] <u>BSJV</u>, NS No. 48 (4th
        Trimester), pp. 262-265.
            Verne's geography in "Master Zacharius" is quite ac-
        curate. His source might be Alexander Dumas's <u>Impres-</u>
        <u>sions de voyage-Suisse</u>. "Mr. Ray Sharp and Miss Me Flat"
        also takes place in Switzerland. Speculates why Verne
        placed his story in the Canton of Appenzell and not where
        the Tell story is supposed to have happened.

E821   Martin, Charles-Noël. <u>La Vie et l'oeuvre de Jules Verne</u>.
        [The Life and Works of Jules Verne] Paris: Michel
        de l'Ormeraie.
            Part I covers personal events as well as his first
        writings, his interests in the theatre, and orientation
        toward a literary career. Part II, starting with facts
        surrounding the publication of <u>Five Weeks in a Balloon</u>,
        integrates the publication of the <u>Voyages extraordinaires</u>
        with events of the life and times of Verne.

E822   _____. "Préface." In César Cascabel, by Jules Verne.
        Paris: Union Général d'éditions, pp. 7-13.
            This comparatively unknown novel constitutes a re-
        laxation from Verne's usual method in which imagination
        and fantasy play a leading role. Other novels after
        this also have less to do with the marvelous. After
        1866 Verne traveled less, the voyages tend to become
        less extraordinary, and he entered upon his sometimes
        misunderstood political career. César Cascabel reflects
        activities connected with his administrative functions
        in Amiens.

E823   Merchot, Daniel. "Seigneur Pittonaccio, ange déchu du
        bizarre?" ["My Lord Pittonaccio, Fallen Angel of the
        Odd?"] <u>BSJV</u>, NS No. 48 (4th Trimester), pp. 266-267.
            A comparison of passages from Poe's "Angel of the Odd"
        and Verne's "Master Zacharius" suggests that Poe's work
        may have influenced Verne's creation of the character,

Pittonaccio. It is probable that Verne knew the Poe
work long before Baudelaire translated it in 1864.

E824 Mercier, Michel. "Le Dessous de la mer: de Victor Hugo à
    Jules Verne." ["Underside of the Sea: From Victor
    Hugo to Jules Verne"] RLM, No. 523-529 (April-June),
    pp. 57-69.
    Hugo's Les Travailleurs de la mer and L'Homme qui rit
    are books of revery spurred by metaphor in which Man
    confronts Nature and society, and which certainly
    stimulated Verne to dream, in Twenty Thousand Leagues
    Under the Sea for example. The convergence of Nature's
    work and Man's is not found in Hugo, but there is a kind
    of reconciliation in the immediacy of danger and shared
    pain in the fight against the octopi. Verne does not
    share Hugo's hypothesis of a sea that is the vehicle of
    a prodigious existence, finding its opposite in a
    monstrous existence.

E825 Méssadié, Gérald. "Visionnaire bien documenté." ["Well-
    Documented Visionary"] Réalités, No. 387 (May), pp.
    64-69.
    Credits Verne with the vision to imagine the eventual
    use to which scientific inventions would be put. Names
    inventions antedating Verne. Comments on the precision
    of Verne's calculations, but also lists his mistakes.
    Verne's gift is to be able to grasp an invention still
    in the schematic stage and give it a lyrical development,
    as with the movies. Verne is a combination of an un-
    bridled, even macabre romanticism with a scientific and
    technical precision that reflects the best scientific
    vulgarization of the twentieth century.

E826 Miannay, Régis. "L'Humour dans Voyage au centre de la
    terre." ["Humor In Journey to the Center of the Earth"]
    RLM, No. 523-529 (April-June), pp. 97-112.
    Verne's sense of humor is not just a convention of
    novels meant for children. It may be seen at the level
    of the scientific and initiatory aspect of the novels.
    Studies the comic elements in the novel, in which the
    comic emanates from Lidenbrock and Axel comprising a
    sort of Don Quixote-Sancho Panza combination. The
    fantastic, the burlesque, and farce are part of the
    novel's comedy. Words and mythological references are
    used to evoke comic reactions. Verne's Captain Hatteras
    goes mad for lack of a sense of humor; Axel and Liden-
    brock are saved by it.

E827　Michel, Frédéric.　Une Oeuvre: De La Terre a la lune, Jules
　　　　Verne: Un Thème: La Conquête de l'espace.　[A Work:
　　　　From the Earth to the Moon, Jules Verne; A Theme:　The
　　　　Conquest of Space]　Paris:　Hatier.
　　　　　　Integrates extracts from From the Earth to the Moon
　　　　with other texts and accomplishments, successors in
　　　　various ways to Verne's heroes.　Assembled for pedagogical
　　　　purposes.　Cyrano de Bergerac, Gagarin, Arthur C. Clarke,
　　　　and others represent Verne's theme.

E828　Mitton, Marcel.　"Jules Verne précurseur."　["Jules Verne
　　　　Precursor"]　BSJV, NS No. 48 (4th Trimester), pp. 257-260.
　　　　　　Credits Verne with having furnished a precursory
　　　　dynamism to many fields of endeavor including aviation
　　　　and space exploration.　Quotes a reference to Verne in
　　　　Histoire de l'astronautique by F. I. Ordway and Wernher
　　　　von Braun, who is reported to have read Verne.　Listed
　　　　as indebted to Verne are the Russian, Tsiolkoski, the
　　　　Frenchman, Esnault-Pelterie, the American, Goddard, and
　　　　the German, Oberth.　Two "annexes" contain documentary
　　　　evidence of Verne's interest in heavier-than-air machines.

E829　Mustière, Philippe.　"Jules Verne et le roman-catastrophe."
　　　　["Jules Verne and the Catastrophe Novel"]　BSJV, NS No.
　　　　47 (3rd Trimester), pp. 204-208.
　　　　　　Paper given before the General Assembly of the Jules
　　　　Verne Society, April 8, 1978.　Verne's works abound in
　　　　disasters, natural, accidental, and criminal.　The re-
　　　　surgence of Verne today may be partly due to his recogniz-
　　　　ing already that civilizations are mortal.　Verne belongs
　　　　to a period characterized chiefly by "mal du siècle,"
　　　　whether expressed by Zola, Huysmans, or himself.　As an
　　　　antidote to disaster, the symptom of alarm, Verne creates
　　　　strong heroes, whose consciousness of doom is not shared
　　　　by the other characters or by the reader.　The latter
　　　　plays the role of a child experiencing the pleasure of
　　　　fear.　Verne's heroes control their destiny through
　　　　individual initiative.

*E830　Neushäfer, Hans-Jorg.　"L'Oeuvre de Jules Verne."　["Jules
　　　　Verne's Works"]　Oeuvres & critiques, 2 (No. 2), 51-63.
　　　　　　Not seen (will be cited in the 1978 Modern Language
　　　　Association International Bibliography, #2434).

E831　Picot, J.-P.　"Jeu subversif et souriant de Kéraban-le-Têtu"
　　　　["The Subversive and Smiling Game of Kéraban-the-Inflex-
　　　　ible"]　BSJV, NS No. 46 (2nd Trimester), pp. 185-191.
　　　　　　There are reciprocal implications of time and space
　　　　in Verne's Kéraban-the-Inflexible.　Kéraban's trip from
　　　　West to East is a flight from an alienating and revolu-
　　　　tionary present to a reassuring Asia, fixed in tradition.

Van Mitten's trip, more than reactionary, is regressive. Kéraban, a classicist, spurns modern means of travel in favor of a sedan chair. Liberation and escape are impossible in a closed world that is circular and cyclic. The present defeats the past. Both Kéraban and Van Mitten return to their point of departure, and only chance will permit Kéraban to triumph. See E832.

E832   . "Jeu subversif et souriant de Kéraban-le-Têtu." ["Subversive and Smiling Game of Kéraban the Inflexible"] BSJV, NS No. 47 (3rd Trimester), pp. 216-230.

The obstinacy of Verne's Kéraban is the jealous protection of his personal freedom and is evident in the refusal to obey anyone's law but his own, as well as in his attitude regarding marriage. Unlike other Verne heroes, Kéraban dislikes the sea, which is for him a female and subversive element. Besides, scoundrels travel by sea; good masculine types stick to land. Actually Kéraban, a novel of the law of opposites, is inseparable from the two novels that follow it, Archipelago On Fire and Mathias Sandorf. All three are novels of liberation for peoples as well as for individuals. But Kéraban is different from the other two in not being overtly a novel of liberation. See E831.

E833   Pierpont, Jacques de. "Jules Verne cet inconnu." ["Unknown Jules Verne"] Dossiers du cacef, No. 57 (April), pp. 3-6.

Blames pictures and labels for having led to a superficial reading of Verne, with the result that he remains something of an unknown. A television program, "Jules Verne insolite," explores Verne's relation to the writers and literature of his time, his topicality, the island theme, his music and theater, and his mystifying meaning.

E834   . "Jules Verne 'père' de la Science-fiction?" ["Jules Verne -- 'Father' of Science Fiction?"] Dossiers du cacef, No. 57 (April), pp. 38-43.

Vernian specialists have grave reservations or even deny that Verne belonged to the world of science fiction, whereas its historians consider him to be one of its founders. Describes science fiction, but plays down Verne's role as an anticipator, preferring to call him a precursor of science fiction. Verne's influence was obvious in succeeding generations in America, France, and even the Soviet Union, so certainly he is a spiritual father of a sort.

E835 _____. "Les Cités de perdition. entretien inédit avec
     Jean Chesneaux." ["Cities of Perdition. Unpublished
     Conversation With Jean Chesneaux"] Dossiers du cacef,
     No. 57 (April), pp. 44-48.
         Interview given by Jean Chesneaux to Jacques de
     Pierpont. Verne's ideological plan of the Voyages extra-
     ordinaires is really expressed only in the first period
     of the author's literary career, which ended in the period
     1880-90. The novels of the second period, less known and
     often considered of inferior quality to their predecessors,
     are pointed in an entirely opposite direction. Disagrees
     with those who call the novels of the second period in-
     ferior. Verne's move toward pessimism is fundamental.
     Verne's cities, reduced to perdition, symbolize the state
     that threatens the world. What characterizes them is
     political power based on scientific knowledge that is
     translated into the control of space. The mastery of
     technology confers political power -- a thoroughly modern
     concept. The more technology has evolved, the more
     society has become policed. The spaces imagined by Verne
     are filled with prohibitions.

*E836 Pillorget, René. "Optimisme ou pessimisme de Jules Verne."
     ["The Optimism or Pessimism of Jules Verne"] Europe,
     56, No. 595-596 (November-December), 19-27.
         Not seen (will be cited in the 1978 Modern Language
     Association International Bibliography, #2435).

E837 Pourvoyeur, Robert. "Autre Lecture de Famille-sans-nom."
     ["Another Reading of Family Without A Name"] BSJV, NS
     No. 47 (3rd Trimester), pp. 209-215.
         Paper presented before the General Assembly of the
     Jules Verne Society on April 8, 1978. Family Without A
     Name contains the favorite Verne themes: brotherly love,
     patriotism, the struggle of the national minorities,
     Anglophobia, the father-son relationship, courage, and
     tenacity. The catalyst within the work is a steady
     progress toward the West and the source of the river.
     This work, one of expiation, is Verne's most Wagnerian
     novel, illustrating the opera's central theme: redemption
     through another's sacrifice. Its denouement is the sole
     integrally tragic one of the Voyages extraordinaires.
     Analogies are suggested to Verne's life: his father,
     brother, and his girl friend, Caroline. Something of
     Verne's father is seen in the notary, Nick. The novel
     may also owe something to Offenbach's Song of Fortunio
     (1861).

E838 Pourvoyeur, R[obert]. "Du Nouveau sur "L'Impossible'!"
     ["Something New On 'The Impossible'!"] BSJV, NS No. 45
     (1st Trimester), pp. 137-151.

This exhaustive study of contemporary critical reaction to the play by Verne and d'Ennery, Voyage Across the Impossible (1882), shows that Laissus was not accurate in stating that little was known about it (E392). Reaction to the play seems to have been negative both as to form and content. The authentic text is missing, but it is hard to avoid the conclusion that an anti-scientific current may have existed in Verne much sooner than is generally supposed.

E839 ____. "Glanes et notules." ["Gleanings and Notes"] BSJV, NS No. 48 (4th Trimester), pp. 269-270.
Speculates as to whether Dr. Ox's distillation of air shows that Verne knew something about homeopathic medicine. The distillation suggests that air can by itself bring on a state of inebriation.

E840 ____. "Jules Verne et le Kitsch." ["Jules Verne and Kitsch"] BSJV, NS No. 45 (1st Trimester), p. 152.
Connects Verne to the concept of kitsch, a word well known in German and connected with the art of happiness as shown by Abraham Moles in a book, Psychologie du Kitsch. -- l'art du bonheur (1971). Kitsch is at its zenith when the bourgeoisie and then the affluent classes are in the ascendant. Such a civilization, sure of itself, seeks expansion, exploration. Verne's romantic myths of extraordinary worlds cater to this spirit.

E841 Pourvoyeur, Robert. "Théâtre et musique dans l'oeuvre de Jules Verne." ["Theater and Music In The Works of Jules Verne"] Dossiers du cacef, No. 57 (April), pp. 17-23.
The influence of music in forming Verne's taste is important. The composers to mention here are Adam and Gautier; less often Gevaert, Poise, and Clapisson; occasionally Rossini, Donizetti, Thomas, Grétry, Reyer, Weber, Halévy, Auber, and Hérold. In general Verne heard pleasant comic operas. Forty-nine operas were put on by the Théâtre lyrique while he was its secretary (1852-55). Verne's works reflect his attachment to theater and music.

E842 Pourvoyeur, Robert and Piero Gondolo della Riva. "Verne et la féerie Le Voyage dans la lune." ["Verne and Fairyland Voyage to the Moon"] BSJV, NS No. 46 (2nd Trimester), pp. 182-184.
There is no question as to Offenbach's debt to Verne in composing the operetta, Dr. Ox. However, such is not the case with Voyage to the Moon. This work dates long after Verne's, exhibits the atmosphere of a baroque love story, and follows the line of utopian voyages. A letter from Verne, now in the Bibliothèque Nationale, is quoted in connection with the subject.

*E843 Prouteau, Gilbert. Le Grand Roman de Jules Verne: sa vie.
[The Great Novel of Jules Verne: His Life] Paris:
Stock.
Not seen (will be cited in 1978 Modern Language
Association International Bibliography, #2436).

E844 Raymond, François. "Confrontations." RLM, No. 523-529
(April-June), pp. 5-10.
The previous Verne volume of studies concentrated on
theme-structure. In this volume authors will stress
Verne's composition or writing. The approach will be
one of comparison of methods, contexts, and results.
The question of influences will be discussed as will
the idea of divergence and convergence of results
emanating from a diversified criticism.

E845 _____. "Le Mystifiant Jules Verne." ["The Mystifying
Jules Verne"] Dossiers du cacef, No. 57 (April), pp.
30-37.
Verne may have sung the praises of science, but he
also was capable of considerable disrespect toward it.
He inherited from Poe not only a fascination for the Pole
and the maelstrom, but also the taste for mystification.
He takes some strange liberties with science in Purchase
of the North Pole, portrays an amusing physic in Around
the Moon, and practically destroys astronomy in Chase of
the Golden Meteor. His scientists are less builders
than disturbers. Other examples outside the scientific
area suggest that Verne is his procedure of mystification
is challenging the reader to find the author. Verne
himself is never the dupe of his own creation.

E846 _____. "Où En Sont Les Etudes sur Jules Verne et le roman
populaire?" ["Where Are the Studies on Jules Verne and
the Popular Novel?"] BSJV, NS No. 46 (2nd Trimester),
pp. 162-173.
Verne's Voyages extraordinaires exhibit traits of the
"popular novel." These include the search for the sensa-
tional, for horror, pity for victims, mystery, and an
ambivalence in the character of the hero, especially of
the hero who dispenses justice. Other similarities to
note are the narrative structure and the tendency to
move from a problem (perhaps a cryptogram) to the solution, thus emphasizing the element of enigma.

E847 _____. "Voyages à travers Le Voyage." ["Voyages Through
The Voyage"] BSJV, NS No. 45 (1st Trimester), pp. 130-131.
Lists some recent publications on the subject of Verne's
Journey to the Center of the Earth, suggesting that they
were to be expected after the novel was made a part of
the 1978 university program for the "agrégation."

E848 Rivière, François. Jules Verne images d'un mythe. [Jules
Verne: Pictures of a Myth] Paris: Editions Henri
Veyrier.
This illustrated album contains pictures of places,
people, and things connected with Verne's life. Some
of the pictures are accompanied by quotations from
authors who have written about Verne.

*E849 _____. "L'un commence, L'autre continue." ["One Begins,
the Other Continues"] Europe, 56 No. 595-596 (November-
December), 37-42.
Not seen (will be cited in 1978 Modern Language
Association International Bibliography, #2438).

E850 Robin, Christian. "Jules Verne à l'université." ["Jules
Verne in the Universities"] RLM, No. 523-529 (April-
June), pp. 11-15.
The proliferation of studies in journals and elsewhere
on Verne since 1970 has resulted in an increase of courses
and lectures on him in the universities.

*E851 _____. "Le Jeu dans Robur le conquérant." ["The Game in
Clipper of the Clouds"] Europe, 56, No. 595-596 (Novem-
ber-December), 106-116.
Not seen (will be cited in 1978 Modern Language
Association International Bibliography, #2440).

E852 _____. "Le Récit sauvé des eaux: du Voyage au centre de
la terre au Sphinx des glaces." ["The Tale Saved From
the Waters: From Journey to the Center of the Earth to
Antarctic Mystery"] RLM, No. 523-529 (April-June), pp.
33-55.
A stylistic approach to Verne's art from Journey to
the Center of the Earth to Antarctic Mystery. Concerns
itself particularly with the problem of verisimilitude
and use of the first person. Verne is more a writer of
his time than has been thought. The Voyages extraordinaires recount the adventures of writing.

E853 _____. Un Monde connu et inconnu. [A Known And Unknown
World] Nantes: Centre universitaire de recherches
verniennes de Nantes.
A book with quotations from Verne's works and many
illustrations, with preface by Luce Courville. She
credits the author with giving the most important and
complete chronology of Verne's life up to date. The
reader is enabled to absorb an event in its temporal
reality, in its circumstantial function vis-à-vis Verne,
and in its novelistic implications.

E854   Roethel, Michel. "Les Cartonnages Hetzel." ["Hetzel Covers"] <u>Connaissance des arts</u>, No. 319 (April), pp. 1–5.

      Many color reproductions of covers on Hetzel editions of Verne, with explanatory text.

E855   Saltarello, L. "L'Homme du jour m'sieur Jules Verne." ["Man of the Day, Mr. Jules Verne"] In <u>César Cascabel</u>, by Jules Verne. Paris: Union Général d'éditions, pp. 433–435.

      This poem was printed July 4, 1889 in <u>La Picardie</u>. It accuses Verne of political inconsistencies caused by his ambition. To become a member of the Municipal Court, Verne put his flag in his pocket, forgetting his recent enthusiasm for the King. He must have found it difficult in his circus inauguration speech to praise the architect, Emile Ricquier.

*E856 Soriano, Marc. "Chronologie vernienne." ["Verne Chronology"] <u>Europe</u>, 56, No. 595–596 (November–December), 146–163.

      Not seen (will be cited in the 1978 <u>Modern Language Association International Bibliography</u>, #2443).

E857   _____. <u>Jules Verne</u>. Paris: Julliard.

      This biography investigates the life of Verne particularly in terms of history, psychoanalysis, and the artist's language; an appendix has an index of Verne's puns. Verne is seen as a masked, coded figure, needing decoding and bearing secrets that are perhaps also the reader's. He is described as a good father, son, and husband, but sometimes inconsistent. The novelist of science, inventor of machines, and supporter of national liberation movements, Verne was also a racist and anti-feminist.

E858   _____. "Jules Verne. Ecrivain pour enfants ou pour adultes?" ["Jules Verne. Writer For Children or Adults?"] <u>Dossiers du cacef</u>, No. 57 (April), pp. 12–16.

      Certainly Verne oriented his work toward youth, but one should also remember that he published in magazines whose readers were adults. <u>From the Earth to the Moon</u> appeared in the very serious <u>Journal des Débats</u>. Verne wrote at a time when there was not yet a clear distinction between the popular public and the juvenile. Verne's novels are marked by the presence of science, the reduced role of women, and a conservative politics, including some anti-Semitism. His contradictions were those of his era.

*E859 _____. Portrait de l'artiste jeune, suivi des quartre premiers textes publiés de Jules Verne. [Portrait of the Young Artist, along with the First Four Published Works of Jules Verne] Paris: Gallimard.
Not seen (reviewed in D447). Studies "Drama in the Air," "Castles in California," "Martin Paz," and "The First Ships of the Mexican Navy" to deduce a paradigm for Verne's entire work.

*E860 _____. "Une Lettre de Jean Jules-Verne." ["A Letter from Jean Jules-Verne"] Europe, 56, No. 595-596 (November-December), 89-93.
Not seen (will be cited in 1978 Modern Language Association International Bibliography, #2445).

E861 Taussat, Robert. "Jules Verne et Hoffmann." ["Jules Verne and Hoffmann"] BSJV, NS No. 48 (4th Trimester), p. 268.
Verne was in error when he attributed to Hoffmann the creation of the character who sells his shadow. That character is in Adalbert von Chamisso's Peter Schlemihl's wundersame Geschichte.

E862 Taussat, R[obert]. "Revanche de Michel Strogoff." ["Revenge of Michel Strogoff"] BSJV, NS No. 48 (4th Trimester), p. 261.
Quotes a hostile critique of Verne written by Emile Zola in Etudes sur la France contemporaine (1878), then a letter from Zola asking for tickets to the play, Michel Strogoff, is quoted as an inconsistency.

E863 Touttain, Pierre-André. "M. Jules Verne Officier de la Légion d'honneur." ["Mr. Jules Verne Officer of the Legion of Honor"] Dossiers du cacef, No. 57 (April), pp. 7-11.
An account of Verne's life and career emphasizing his contacts, often friendships with composers and literary figures, such as Offenbach, Massé, Délibes, and Dumas. Shows Verne's intellectual curiosity going far beyond geography and science. A list of writers of our time demonstrates the interest of the twentieth century in Verne, e.g., Apollinaire, Kipling, Proust, Mauriac, and Saint-Exupéry.

E864 _____. "Une Cruelle Fantaisie: Le Docteur Ox." ["Cruel Fantasy: 'Dr. Ox'"] RLM, No. 523-529 (April-June), pp. 155-163.
Verne's "Dr. Ox" contains perhaps more to note than critics have revealed. The work abounds in puns and other onomastic variations, the esprit gaulois, and a taste for farce. The story is one of black humor.

Discusses history of its publication and recounts the
plot. Verne unleashes cruel barbs against the unthinking
segment of the bourgeoisie of his time. Likens Verne to
Villiers de L'Isle-Adam, especially in terms of the
latter's Les Brigands.

E865 _____. Vingt Mille ronds de fumée. [Twenty Thousand Smoke
Rings] Paris: Sélé.
Shows that most of Verne's characters seem to make it
a point of honor to smoke. The book contains many pictures
of well-known scenes in the novels in which characters are
smoking. Information from the family has it that Verne
himself smoked moderately.

E866 Vautrin, Paul. "Un Picard d'adoption. Jules Verne." ["A
Picard By Adoption"] Picardie laïque, No. 218 (January-
February), pp. 5-6.
Résumé of Verne's life and career written for the
150th anniversary of his birth. He found at home a taste
for literature, a critical sense sharpened by judiciary
practice, and a fantastic imagination. Mentions his
essay on Mexico and its ships, noting in it geographical
and botanical notions that are very real. Was frightened
by the results of industrial progress and by the uncon-
trollable power given Man by science.

E867 Vierne, Simone. "Kaléidoscope de L'Ile mystérieuse."
["Kaleidoscope of Mysterious Island"] RLM, No. 523-529
(April-June), pp. 19-32.
A study of Verne's The Mysterious Island, chosen
because it has been the subject of the most diverse
forms of literary criticism. The analysis aims at
showing how the elements of the texts combine with those
afforded by a knowledge of the author, of his life and
period, etc. There is an interweaving of a network of
correspondences and homologies among the various features
of the critical landscape. There is a systematic play
of various plans occurring around the novel's fundamental
enigmas, mystery, and hidden sense.

*E868 _____. "Paroles gelées, paroles de feu, ou le double signe
de l'écriture de la folie chez Jules Verne." ["Frozen
Words, Words of Fire, or the Double Sign of the Writing
of Madness in Jules Verne"] Europe, 56, No. 595-596
(November-December), 57-66.
Not seen (will be cited in 1978 Modern Language
Association International Bibliography, #2448).

*E869 Wagner, Nicolas. "Le Soliloque utopiste des Cinq Cents
millions de la Bégum." ["The Utopian Soliloquy in Bégum's
Fortune"] Europe, 56, No. 595-596 (November-December),
117-126.

Not seen (will be cited in 1978 <u>Modern Language Association International Bibliography</u>, #2449).

<u>1979</u>

E869.1　"Actualités de Jules Verne." ["News of Jules Verne"] <u>BSJV</u>, NS No. 50 (2nd Trimester), pp. 45-49.

As usual, this section of the <u>Bulletin</u> contains bibliographical references to Verne among which are: Michel Butor, <u>Boomerang</u> (Gallimard 1978); Jean Bellemin-Noël's <u>Vers L'Inconscient du texte; L'Année 1978-1979 de la Science-Fiction et du fantastique</u>, edited by Jacques Goimard, containing under the title "Jules Verne, revisité par François Raymond" a panorama of Vernian studies as well as Vernian texts connected with science fiction or the fantastic; and <u>Visions nouvelles sur Jules Verne</u>, a volume of one hundred fourteen pages published by the Centre de Documentation Jules Verne in Amiens, containing articles treating Verne's life in Amiens, with contributions by, among others, Elisabeth Léger de Viane, and Daniel and Cécile Compère. Contains the republication of a report on the theatre written by Verne as well as some unpublished letters.

E869.2　Auriol, J. "De La Réalité à la fiction dans <u>Deux Ans de vacances</u>." ["From Reality to Fiction in <u>Two Years' Vacation</u>"] <u>BSJV</u>, NS No. 50 (2nd Trimester), pp. 75-77.

Points out anomalies and improbabilities in Verne's <u>Two Years' Vacation</u>, especially in the areas of the characters' ages, their adaptation to circumstances, the strength of Jacques, the island's shapes, the close proximity of neighboring lands, the climate, and vegetation. Concludes that every writer has the right to make up things.

E869.3　Compère, Cécile. "Jules Verne tel qu'on en parle." ["Jules Verne As He Is Talked About"] <u>BSJV</u>, NS No. 50 (2nd Trimester), pp. 50-53.

Paper given before the General Assembly of the Jules Verne Society on March 1, 1975. A fantasy biography of Jules Verne, a spoof of nonsensical things that have been said and written about him. Included are such things as: Verne commanded a ship in the Franco-Prussian War; he was engaged six times and married twice; he had two illegitimate children; he visited outer space on a flying saucer; he was buried alive and gnawed himself to the bone.

E869.4　Compère, Daniel. "Poétique de la carte." ["Poetics of the Map"] <u>BSJV</u>, NS No. 50 (2nd Trimester), pp. 69-74.

Defines poetics as everything that tends toward the creation of literary works. Describes Verne's use of real maps, his modifications, and his imaginary maps. Shows how Verne's cartography may become topography.

E870   Courville, Luce. "Jules Verne et La Femme de trente ans." ["Jules Verne and The Woman of Thirty"] BSJV, NS No. 49 (1st Trimester), pp. 18-20.

Fleeting comparisons between Balzac's Le Femme de trente ans and Verne's Twenty Thousand Leagues Under The Sea allow for a possible reminiscence on the part of Verne, whose father used to read Balzac. However, it is risky to suggest that a personal reading of Balzac inspired Verne, who never mentions him in the Voyages extraordinaires. Balzac perhaps joins other Romantic authors, especially with regard to the hero in revolt, whose vogue may well have influenced Verne.

E870.1   Goracci, Serge. "De Quelques Rapports entre les romans verniens et le roman populaire." ["Concerning a Few Connections Between Vernian Novels and the Popular Novel"] BSJV, NS No. 50 (2nd Trimester), pp. 60-68.

Acknowledges work of Yves Olivier-Martin in the study of the relationship between Verne's works and the popular novel, but suggests that further work is indicated. Discusses affinities between Verne's novels and the black novel (roman noir), Verne's hero and the Promethean hero, Verne's victims of judicial error and those of popular literature, Verne's orphans or illegitimate children and counterparts elsewhere. Does not claim a definitive case for making of Verne an author of the popular novel, but suggests a method for further study. See E631.

E870.2   Halstrom, Karen-Margrethe. "Jules Verne au 'petit théâtre' danois." ["Jules Verne in the Danish 'Little Theatre'"] BSJV, NS No. 50 (2nd Trimester), pp. 54-59.

Alfred Jacobson of Copenhagen began publishing in 1880 a cardboard theatre: stage, scenery, and characters are printed on paper before being glued to cardboard and then cut out. The characters are fixed on a tin foot and are moved from the wings by a steel wire soldered to the foot. Captain Grant's Children, Around the World in Eighty Days and Michel Strogoff were adapted. The latter's Jacobson edition enables one to reconstruct the premiere at the Théâtre du Châtelet on November 17, 1880.

E871   Koppen, E. "Séminaire Jules Verne à l'université de Mayence." ["Seminar on Jules Verne at University of Mayence"] BSJV, NS No. 49 (1st Trimester), pp. 8-10.

Reports on Verne seminar held during the winter semester, 1973-74. The central theme was the so-called "triviality" in literature in the light of three aspects:

(1) literary theory; (2) literary sociology; (3) and
cultural history. An important factor in Verne's work
is the literary presentation of the natural sciences
and of technology tied to the question of the inter-
mingling of reality and of fantasy. In the seminar the
problem of the trivial was explored through the comparison of passages in Maupassant, Balzac, Flaubert, and
Verne treating the same subject.

E872 Margot, J[ean]-M[ichel]. "Jules Verne et la Suisse: La
      Suisse dans l'oeuvre de Jules Verne." ["Jules Verne and
      Switzerland: Switzerland in Jules Verne's Works"] BSJV,
      NS No. 49 (1st Trimester), pp. 12-17.
          Finishes subject begun in a previous issue. Covers
      references to Switzerland in Verne's works. The natu-
      ralist, Agassiz, and the novelist, Hans-Rudolf Wyss (not
      Rudolf Wyss, as Verne mistakenly thought), writer of
      Robinson suisse, were sources for Verne. Discusses Swiss
      characters in Verne. Verne's references to Switzerland
      are commonplace, and none of his novels takes place in
      that country. His two short stories with a Swiss setting
      reflect a vogue.

E872.1 Pourvoyeur, R[obert]. "Cologne rajeunit Le Docteur Ox."
      ["Cologne Rejuvenates Dr. Ox] BSJV, NS No. 50 (2nd Tri-
      mester), pp. 78-79.
          For the first time in Germany, Offenbach's Dr. Ox was
      mounted in Cologne, Sept. 29, 1978. In order to give the
      maximum effectiveness to the libretto and to enable the
      text to be understood by all the spectators, roles were
      given to actors with a voice rather than to singers with
      some knowledge of acting. Despite some vocal weaknesses,
      the production was a magisterial renewal worthy of
      applause.

E873 _____. "Premier Musicien du Tour et de Grant." ["First
      Musician of Around and of Grant"] BSJV, NS No. 49 (1st
      Trimester), pp. 37-38.
          Appended to an article by P. Terrasse on the stage
      adaptation of Verne's Captain Grant's Children, recounts
      the life of Jean-Jacques Debillemont, composer of the
      music for that novel and for Around the World In Eighty
      Days. Calls the music uninspired. See E874.

E874 Terrasse, P[ierre]. "Centenaire: Les Enfants du capitaine
      Grant au théâtre." ["Centenary of Captain Grant's
      Children for the Theatre"] BSJV, NS No. 49 (1st Tri-
      mester), pp. 21-37.

An account based on six letters (five from and one to
Verne) of the genesis and development of the stage adaptation of <u>Captain Grant's Children</u>. The adaptation was
thought of as early as November 1874. Verne sent his
collaborator, d'Ennery, a rough draft in 1876. The text
underwent endless revisions. Lists modifications in the
original work for the adaptation. Efforts were made to
compensate for dramatic weaknesses with the esthetics
of the setting. Discusses the cast, the problem of
placing live bears on the stage, and the inclusion of
ballet. The play did not attain the expected success.
<u>See</u> E873.

Index to Verne's Works

["Army Clarions"], see "Clairons
   de l'armée"
Around the Moon, see Autour De La
   Lune
Around the World in Eighty Days,
   see Tour du monde en quatre-
   vingts jours
Around the World in Eighty Days
   (play), see Tour du monde en
   quatre-vingts jours (play)
"Ascension du Météore," C8
["Ascent of the Meteor"], see
   "Ascension du Météore"
Astonishing Adventure of the
   Barsac Mission, see Etonnante
   Aventure de la mission Barsac
   (sometimes referred to under
   this title)
At the North Pole, see Voyages et
   aventures du Capitaine
   Hatteras (Part 1)
Auberge des Ardennes, B8, E635
"Au bord du Lac," B17
"Au printemps," B10
Australia, see Enfants du Capi-
   taine Grant (Part 2)
Australie, see Enfants du Capi-
   taine Grant (Part 2)
Autour De La Lune, A21, A22, D38,
   D104, D119, D186, D191, D193,
   D194, D215, D222, D238, D271,
   D295, D329, D334, D335, D342,
   D345, D356, D403, D428, D429,
   E262, E358, E364, E366, E367.
   E408, E410, E452, E459, E478,
   E495, E845
"Au XXIXe Siècle: La Journée
   d'un journaliste américain en
   2889," see "In the Year 2889"
"Aventures de la Famille Raton,"
   A71, E108, E375
Aventures de trois Russes et de
   trois Anglais dans l'Afrique
   australe, A26, A28, D268,
   E454
Aventures du Capitaine Hatteras,
   see Voyages et aventures du
   Capitaine Hatteras

Baltimore Gun Club, see De La
   Terre à la lune
Barsac Mission, see Etonnante
   Aventure de la mission Barsac
Begum's Fortune, see Cinq Cents
   Millions de la Begum
"Berceuse," B17
Billet de loterie, A60, E398,
   E581, E734
Black Diamonds, see Indes noires
Black Indies, see Indes noires
[Blindman's Buff], see Colin-
   Maillard
"Blockade Runners," see "Forceurs
   de blocus"
Bourses de voyage, A89, E500
"Bras d'une mère," B21
[Broken Straws], see Pailles
   rompues
[Brothers Kip], see Frères Kip
Burbank the Northerner, see Nord
   contre sud (Part 1)
["By the Lake"], see "Au bord du
   Lac"

California Mystery, see École des
   Robinsons
Capitaine de quinze ans, A44,
   E187, E310, E804; film of,
   E325, E517, E597
Captain Antifer, see Mirifiques
   Aventures de Maître Antifer
Captain Grant's Children, see
   Enfants du Capitaine Grant
Captain Grant's Children (play),
   see Enfants du Capitaine
   Grant (play)
Captain of the Guidara, see
   Kéraban-le-Têtu (Part 1)
Carpathian Castle, see Château
   des Carpathes
Cascabel, the Conjurer, see César
   Cascabel
Castaways, see Enfants du Capi-
   taine Grant
Castaways of the Flag, see
   Seconde Patrie (Part 2)
Castle of the Carpathians, see
   Château des Carpathes

Index to Critical Studies